HUMAN TERRAIN TEAMS: AN ORGANIZATIONAL INNOVATION FOR SOCIOCULTURAL KNOWLEDGE IN IRREGULAR WARFARE

Human Terrain Teams:

An Organizational Innovation for Sociocultural Knowledge in Irregular Warfare

Christopher J. Lamb

James Douglas Orton

Michael C. Davies

Theodore T. Pikulsky

The Institute of World Politics Press

Washington

Published in the United States of America by The Institute of World Politics Press,
1521 16th Street NW, Washington DC 20036, USA

ISBN: 0988864207
ISBN-13: 978-0988864207

The views represented in this book are those of the authors alone, and are not
those of The Institute of World Politics, the United States Government, or any
other entity.

DEDICATION

This book is dedicated to United States military leaders—past, present and future—who develop and use sociocultural knowledge to improve security for our nation and allies, our armed forces, and the people they protect.

CONTENTS

	Acknowledgments	ix
	Foreword	xi
	Preface	xiii
1	Introduction	1
2	HTTs, Their Mission & Performance Standards	6
3	Historical Overview of HTS and HTTs	25
4	Analysis of Variables Explaining Performance	107
5	Performance Assessment	169
6	Observations	200
7	Conclusion	212
	Epilogue	216
	Appendix One	221
	Appendix Two	238
	Appendix Three	246
	Appendix Four	250
	Selected Bibliography	253
	Index	278
	About the Authors	290

.

ACKNOWLEDGMENTS

Initially our interest in the U.S. Army's Human Terrain Teams was stimulated by a summer intern* who had been following their progress through public sources. The small civil-military teams seemed like perfect candidates for investigation using the methodology we were developing to study other cross-functional teams in the national security system. Once we began applying the methodology (explained in Appendix Two) and discovered how controversial and complex the teams were, we realized a more concentrated research effort would be necessary, one that would demand additional resources. Those resources were provided by the Office of the Secretary of Defense, the U.S. Special Operations Command's Program on Irregular Warfare and Special Operations, and the leadership at the Institute for National Strategic Studies. We are grateful to Dr. Nick Rostow and Dr. Joseph Tonon for their support in particular.

It will also be apparent to readers that our research was critically dependent upon the willingness of commanders, members of the Human Terrain Teams, and managers in the Human Terrain System program to share their insights with us. We are thankful that the vast majority of those contacted were willing to give us their time and testimonies, not only at length but often repeatedly. We made every effort to honor their trust in us by producing a quality product.

We would also like to thank Leo Michel and Lieutenant Colonel Joel Rayburn, U.S. Army, our colleagues at the Institute for National Strategic Studies who reviewed our work and made many valuable suggestions for improvements, and Rei Tang who created the book's index. Finally, we want to express our deep appreciation to Lieutenant General Michael Flynn for his foreword to this book, and to The Institute of World Politics, and particularly Juliana Geran Pilon, J. Michael Waller, and Charles Van Someren for diligently working to bring the project to fruition. While we could not have conducted our research without the support of our sponsors, contacts and editors, any limitations or errors in the resultant description and analysis are our responsibility alone.

Note

*   Jill Page subsequently completed a thesis on the topic: Julia Page, *Human Terrain Teams*, Masters Thesis, Virginia Tech University, February 23, 2012.

FOREWORD

The post-Afghanistan security environment will present a wide range of challenges to the United States military and Defense Intelligence. The world is growing increasingly unpredictable and complex with the emergence of new centers of influence and the proliferation of non-state actors. In the Middle East, the Arab Uprising has ushered in new opportunities for states to transition to more democratic forms of governance, but has also served notice that technologically-enabled social movements carry inherent risks. The fragility of states in North Africa is expected to persist, challenging us to better understand and respond to the precursors for instability. And, in East Asia, conventional military threats continue to require vigilance on our part to maintain peace and prosperity in the region. In this fluid security environment, conventional military advantages alone will not ensure our strategic success. Our security will also require a holistic, comprehensive understanding of the human aspects of our operating environments.

The need for improved sociocultural information and analysis were highlighted in the Chairman of the Joint Chief's "Enduring Lessons from the Past Decade of Operations" (Volume I, dtd. June 15, 2012). Lesson One stated there was "a failure to recognize, acknowledge, and accurately define the operational environment," in part because of "a focus on traditional adversaries and a neglect of information concerning the host-nation population." Successfully integrating this type of information into defense analysis, planning, and operations will necessitate change. We need to systematically weave sociocultural information into defense intelligence analysis for diverse missions, customers, and topics. We must also renew our attention to training, tradecraft and region-specific knowledge, the fundamentals of the defense intelligence profession.

As we continue to record our lessons learned in Iraq and Afghanistan, we should be mindful of the unique opportunity we have to assess the utility of different approaches to understanding the human aspects of our environment. The Human Terrain System is one such innovation that was created in a compressed period of time under uncertain conditions. While the program's rapid growth rate created management challenges, it was able to fill a void in sociocultural understanding for the general purpose forces and successfully establish the value of that understanding on the battlefield. The task now falls to us to leverage their lessons learned to make evolutionary progress toward the systematic inclusion of sociocultural information in all-source analysis to support peacetime engagement as well as combat operations. The authors of this book make an important contribution to that effort by examining the causes of variation in Human Terrain Team performance. They do so with a multidisciplinary methodology that includes a rich historical analysis of how external forces and management decisions affected the performance of Human Terrain Teams in the field. It is an important read for those who seek to participate in the evolution and maturation of sociocultural capabilities that will continue to be to the key to our success across all phases of operations.

Lieutenant General Michael T. Flynn
United States Army
Director, Defense Intelligence Agency

PREFACE

We wrote this book in hopes of making a contribution to those who oversee and manage one of the U.S. military's most important programs: the Human Terrain System. The U.S. Army's Human Terrain System develops and deploys Human Terrain Teams, small cross-functional teams of sociocultural experts who explain the attitudes and behaviors of indigenous populace to assist field commanders making decisions during military operations. Those who go in harm's way for our collective security deserve the best support possible, including the sociocultural knowledge required to do their work well. We believe an in-depth explanation for Human Terrain Team operations over the past decade can be used to help improve their performance in the future. In this regard we wrote the book primarily for those involved in the human terrain enterprise. As the work progressed, however, we realized that the Human Terrain Team experience also teaches a lot about the difficulty of innovating during war, and the tension between U.S. military culture and requirements for success in irregular war. For this reason we believe the book will appeal to readers interested in military operations more generally.

The teams and their activities were controversial and complex, raising ethical, operational and academic debates. Many performed well and earned the approval of the commanders they served, but some failed completely. Performance concerns dogged the program, provoking a number of internal and external reviews and investigations. As a result, there is an amazing amount of colorful secondary literature on Human Terrain Teams, but very little rigorous scholarship on the topic. It was difficult isolating the factors that best explain their performance on the whole. We did not intend to spend almost two years researching and writing this book, but that is how long it took to produce what we consider a compelling explanation for the performance of Human Terrain Teams.

The subject matter more than justifies the resources devoted to the research. U.S. forces could not defeat their adversaries in Iraq and Afghanistan without the kind of insights Human Terrain Teams were supposed to provide. The argument for this assertion is straightforward. In these conflicts the United States ultimately adopted a population-centric counterinsurgency strategy. The strategy required U.S. forces to understand popular sentiments well enough to interact with the indigenous populace in ways that would incline them to support rather than resist U.S. objectives. Diverse capabilities can contribute to such understanding, but the Human Terrain Teams were the principal means deployed to assist field commanders trying to fathom popular attitudes. If Human Terrain Teams did their job well they could advise commanders on behaviors that would help them isolate insurgents from popular support. If not, it was far more likely that U.S. operations would alienate the population and make success unattainable. The performance of Human Terrain Teams was therefore intrinsically important.

Human Terrain Teams are also an interesting case of organizational adaptation during war. They had to be created, deployed and adjusted after U.S. forces were heavily involved in combat operations. Much has been written about the U.S. military's doctrinal adaptation to counterinsurgency and rightly so. The U.S. military could not succeed in Iraq and Afghanistan without first coming to grips with the requirements for counterinsurgency success. Yet multiple organizational elements had to adapt in order to deliver those requirements. Mine-resistant, ambush-protected vehicles that safeguarded soldiers traveling from one point to another and drones and high-value targeting teams that killed or captured enemy leadership are examples of organizational adaptations. So too were the Human Terrain Teams, which arguably were the most difficult adaptation the U.S. military undertook if for no other reason than that they were the most alien to military culture. The U.S. military routinely trains and employs small cross-functional teams capable of reliably high performance. However, the use of civilian social scientists in close proximity with combat forces made the Human Terrain Teams far more heterogeneous than typical military small groups, and the tasks associated with delivering operationally-relevant sociocultural knowledge were more ambiguous, complex and challenging than most military small team tasks.

For these reasons it is strange that the U.S. Army has not demonstrated more interest in rigorous analysis of Human Terrain Team performance. The few serious studies available were initiated by sources outside the Army and did not receive support from the Army Command that oversees the Human Terrain Teams. No doubt this was due in part to the intense controversy the teams generated. The teams were inherently controversial experiments in social science and military cooperation that galvanized the attention of journalists and Congress. Apparently those responsible for the program decided a lower profile was necessary. While understandable, this posture unfortunately also was extended to scholarly efforts, which made it difficult to learn from team experience.

National security experts, including the Army's leaders, almost universally forecast a future security environment that will continue to require in-depth sociocultural knowledge of indigenous populations. Sociocultural knowledge is not just a key requirement for success in irregular warfare, but an important advantage in all types of military operations. The way sociocultural knowledge is generated is therefore not a matter of passing interest, but an enduring requirement that must be mastered. It is a topic that challenged the Army in multiple ways; as a key capability in counterinsurgency, as an organizational adaptation during a time of war, and as a high-profile test of civil-military relations in the field. For these reasons understanding why Human Terrain Teams were difficult to develop and employ was a matter of great interest to us, and should be a matter of great import for the U.S. Army and the Department of Defense.

After a brief introduction to the general importance of sociocultural knowledge in current military operations, Chapter Two introduces readers to the teams and the program that deployed and managed them, puts the program and teams in historical context, and explains our criteria for evaluating their performance. Readers interested in how the teams were started, developed and actually deployed will be most interested in Chapter Three, which provides an historical overview of the program. Those already familiar with the teams and program may want to skip to Chapter Four, which analyzes Human Terrain Team performance through the lenses of ten performance variables borrowed from literature on cross-functional teams. Chapter Five offers a net explanation for Human Terrain Team performance that accounts for program management challenges, commander assessments and internal team dynamics. In the next two chapters on observations and conclusions we close out the book by putting the entire Human Terrain experience in historical context and suggesting how the U.S. military should capitalize on it in the future.

Finally, we note that the opinions, conclusions, and recommendations expressed or implied in this book are solely those of the authors and do not necessarily represent the views of the Department of Defense or any other agency of the Federal Government.

1 INTRODUCTION

"The human terrain is the decisive terrain."
General David Petraeus

During his confirmation hearing before taking command of U.S. and NATO forces in Afghanistan in June 2010, General David Petraeus told Congress that the decisive terrain in counterinsurgency was "the human terrain."[1] This single observation captures the essence of his profound impact on the way the United States fought in both Iraq and Afghanistan. Petraeus's population-centric approach to counterinsurgency requires protecting and eliciting cooperation from the population—the human terrain—which, in turn, requires a deep understanding of the population's social and cultural characteristics. The principal instruments for delivering this understanding to Petraeus's military forces in the field were Human Terrain Teams.[2] Establishing the program that produced the teams—the Human Terrain System—was a difficult and problematic undertaking. The teams that deployed were widely appreciated by commanders, but their performance was variable, and they did not ameliorate—much less reverse—growing cross-cultural tensions between U.S. forces and Afghans. To date, there has been no in-depth study of the teams that explains why their performance varied, and was not able to make a larger impact. This book fills this gap by explaining Human Terrain Team performance variation and impact, and providing insights to help defense leaders improve future performance in this area.

It is important to note that Petraeus's population-centric approach to counterinsurgency was not novel; indeed he insisted that his forces follow "basic" counterinsurgency principles.[3] However, basic counterinsurgency was not something the U.S. military practiced, and the rudiments had to be relearned, including what it meant to operate well in an environment where the physical terrain was less important than the human terrain. The human terrain concept encompasses the "human population and society in the operational environment as defined and characterized by sociocultural, anthropologic, and ethnographic data and other non-geophysical information about the human population and society."[4] Armed with such knowledge, U.S. forces could avoid antagonizing the population unnecessarily and increase the likelihood that the populace would resist insurgent forces and support the local government and U.S. forces.

In 2006, the same year General Petraeus's landmark counterinsurgency doctrine was published,[5] the Pentagon began funding the Human Terrain System (HTS), a program that would field Human Terrain Teams (HTTs) and other mechanisms to provide operationally relevant sociocultural knowledge to U.S. military forces. The HTTs were cross-functional, combining the skill sets of U.S. military personnel and civilian social scientists in a small team environment. Typically they were appended to a brigade-sized unit and were supposed to provide the unit with the knowledge, analysis and advice necessary to understand the human terrain in the unit's area of operations.

The first team deployed to Khost, Afghanistan in early 2007 where it advised the 4th Brigade, 82nd Airborne Division. The commanding officer, Colonel Martin Schweitzer, gave the team a glowing endorsement, testifying to Congress in April 2008 that the team reduced kinetic activity in his area of operations by 60-70 percent.[6] Schweitzer's testimony contributed greatly to the program's momentum, which was expanding rapidly. It soon became apparent, however, that the HTTs were receiving mixed reviews. Less than a year after Schweitzer's testimony, a brigade commander in Afghanistan ordered the program's in-country representative to get an HTT team leader "off my base or you and all of HTS will be out of here tomorrow."[7] The sharp contrast between the two commanders' assessments of their HTTs is emblematic of the inconsistent HTT performance. Interestingly, HTT performance variation is perceived differently by commanders and others familiar with the teams. Most commanders who have been asked say their HTTs were quite useful. As we will demonstrate, HTT members themselves, those who have studied them, and those charged with their oversight are more likely to observe that HTT performance was inconsistent.

Although previous studies of HTTs[8] note the variance in HTT performance, it has never been satisfactorily explained. HTT program leaders, as well as senior officials in the Pentagon, are candid about how difficult it is to explain HTT performance. In 2010, the Office of the Undersecretary of Defense for Intelligence told Congress that:

maximizing team performance requires an assessment process that provides a clear understanding of the relationship between program inputs (manpower, training, etc.) and outputs (improves unit operational performance) as a guide to continuous program improvement. Such an assessment process does not exist today.[9]

The Pentagon was essentially paraphrasing the venerable management adage that you can't manage what you can't measure. Thus it should have been a high priority for HTS program managers to establish desired HTT output and the factors that generate it. Only then could they manage the HTT effort to better effect, stimulating those factors that facilitate good performance and curtailing or eliminating those that impede it.

This book is the first in-depth study of HTT performance that explains the origins of the performance variation, why commanders overwhelming testify to the usefulness of HTTs, why those most familiar with HTTs emphasize their inconsistency, and also why the HTTs collectively were unable to make a major contribution to the counterinsurgency effort. It also explains the tremendous challenges the HTS program faced in starting and rapidly expanding a non-traditional military program, and why some challenges were met successfully while others were not. The purpose is to generate insights for Army leadership that will make it possible to better manage sociocultural capabilities in the future.

The book explains performance in three basic steps. First, a historical analysis explains how external forces and management decisions affected HTT performance. An organizational analysis then explains the variations in team performance by examining the teams themselves in greater detail with variables substantiated by previous studies of small cross-functional teams. We conducted more than one hundred interviews to assess the factors that best explain variations in team performance, primarily with HTT members and former staff members of the HTS program. Finally, all available commander observations on HTT performance are examined to determine the reasons commanders were satisfied or dissatisfied with HTT performance. Then the insights from the historical, organizational and commander assessments are integrated to produce the most compelling explanation for HTT performance variation.

It is important to understand HTT performance because sociocultural knowledge of an adversary is an enduring military requirement. In the past, this insight has not been embraced by the U.S. military. Now, however, some senior military leaders are insisting the importance of sociocultural knowledge is a key lesson from recent conflicts. For example, General Ray Odierno, the Chief of Staff of the Army, believes the chief lesson he learned after three combat tours in Iraq was that the best-equipped army in the world can still lose a war if it doesn't understand the people it's fighting.[10] If there is agreement that the U.S. military must understand and retain the means to generate sociocultural knowledge of human terrain, the issue is how to do it well. We argue the place to begin is by understanding what happened with HTTs. By learning from this experience, we increase the chances that the U.S. military will be able to readily and reliably provide knowledge of human terrain to U.S. forces in the future.

Toward this end the rest of the book is organized as follows. In the next section we briefly explain what is meant by sociocultural knowledge, put the U.S. military's quest for it in historical context, and explain why it is useful in irregular warfare. We also identify a standard for assessing HTT performance and explain why it is problematic but necessary. We then present a condensed history of the human terrain concept and program to establish how external forces and management decisions affected HTT performance. Having established how the program evolved, we then examine HTTs in the 2009-2010 timeframe to determine the factors that best explain whether HTTs functioned well or poorly. After explaining performance variation among the teams, we make some observations about why the program needs to pay much more attention to small-team performance factors and its proper place in a broader U.S. military sociocultural knowledge architecture.

Notes

[1] Leo Shane III and Kevin Baron, "Petraeus Confirmation Hearing, Live," *Stars and Stripes*, June 29, 2010.

[2] The term 'human terrain team' quickly became ubiquitous, permeating the general population's lexicon. In response to this, the American Dialect Society declared the term the 'Most Euphemistic' word of 2007.

[3] General David Petraeus, in Christopher J. Lamb and Martin Cinnamond, *Unity of Effort: Key to Success In Afghanistan*, Strategic Forum no. 248 (Washington, DC: NDU Press, October 2009), 2.

[4] Jacob Kipp, Lester Grau, Karl Prinslow, and Captain Don Smith, "The Human Terrain System: A CORDS for the 21st Century," *Military Review* vol. 85, no. 5 (September-October 2006), 14, footnote 2.

[5] Field Manual 3-24/Marine Corps Warfighting Publication 3-33.5, *Counterinsurgency* (Washington, DC: Department of the Army, December 2006). Hereafter FM3-24. On May 8-11, 2012, a Revision Conference was hosted at Ft. Leavenworth, Kansas, to begin the process of revising the doctrine.

[6] Colonel Martin P. Schweitzer, Commander, 4th BCT/82 Airborne, United States Army, Before the House Armed Services Committee, Terrorism & Unconventional Threats Sub-Committee and the Research & Education Sub-Committee of the Science & Technology Committee, *110th Congress*, 2nd Session Hearings on the Role of the Social and Behavioral

Sciences in National Security, *United States House of Representatives, April 24, 2008.*

[7] Program Manager Forward, Afghanistan, interviewed December 7, 2011.

[8] Yvette Clinton, Virginia Foran-Cain Julia Voelker McQuaid, Catherine E. Norman, and William H. Sims, with Sara M. Russell, *Congressionally Directed Assessment of the Human Terrain System*, CNA Analysis & Solutions, November 2010; Jack A. Jackson, S.K. Numrich, P.M. Picucci, CAPT Charles Chase, Christophe L. McCray, Dominick Wright, Mary Hawkins Conrad, Anthony Johson, Maj Kerri Uhlmeyeyer, *Contingency Capabilities: Analysis of Human Terrain Teams in Afghanistan*, Draft Final Report, The Institute for Defense Analyses, December 2011, IDA paper P-4-4809; Log: H11-001954/1. The study was commissioned under the primary sponsorship of the Joint Staff Director for Joint Force Development (J-7) in 2009.

[9] Office of the Under Secretary of Defense for Intelligence, Response to the July 15, 2010 Draft of the CNA Report, September 2010.

[10] Doyle McManus, "McManus: A smaller, smarter military: The best-equipped army in the world can still lose a war if it doesn't understand the people it's fighting," *The Los Angeles Times*, April 22, 2012.

2 HUMAN TERRAIN TEAMS, THEIR MISSION AND PERFORMANCE STANDARDS

"I asked my Brigade Commanders what was the number one thing they would like to have had more of, and they all said cultural knowledge."[1]
Lieutenant General Peter Chiarelli

Now that U.S. forces have largely withdrawn from Iraq, HTTs operate primarily in Afghanistan. These small groups of civil-military expertise are called Human Terrain Teams because the military appreciates the importance of terrain. Labeling the new teams accordingly increased the likelihood that the teams would be accepted by other military personnel. While human terrain[2] is a relatively new term, it is essentially a synonym for sociocultural knowledge, which also is hard to define (see shadow box, "Defining Sociocultural Knowledge in the U.S. Military") but nonetheless a subject of long-standing interest to the U.S. military.

Arguably, sociocultural knowledge of an adversary is an enduring military requirement. Sun Tzu's counsel, "if you know your enemies and know yourself, you will not be imperiled in a hundred battles,"[3] suggests the importance of a deep appreciation for adversary proclivities. Yet the value of sociocultural knowledge while combating or using irregular forces is even more evident. General Petraeus's population-centric approach, which he noted reflected "basic" counterinsurgency principles (i.e. time-honored lessons), presupposes adequate sociocultural knowledge. American military forces have discovered this truth repeatedly since the founding of the Republic, and even before. A brief historical survey demonstrates the U.S. military's familiarity with sociocultural knowledge and its even greater reluctance to institutionalize the capability. It also provides historical context for explaining the HTT mission and for evaluating the Army's effort to field HTTs.

Defining Sociocultural Knowledge in the U.S. Military

Sociocultural knowledge is an ill-defined sub-category of social science knowledge. Social science is generally understood to involve the study of human relationships within society, but the diverse disciplines within social science offer different definitions of "society" and "culture," and they tend to evolve. Hence it is not surprising that over time the American military also has promulgated different explanations for sociocultural knowledge. For example, the Marine Corps' 1940 *Small Wars Manual* categorizes knowledge of indigenous peoples as "psychology," or "national psychology."[4] Under this rubric the manual advises on the importance of respecting fundamental social and religious customs, and understanding revolutionary politics as well as the psychology of local individuals.

Today the preferred term is sociocultural knowledge, but it is still difficult to define.[5] For example, the HTS definition of sociocultural understanding is "knowledge pertaining to society and culture that has been synthesized and had judgment applied to a specific situation to comprehend the situation's inner relationship."[6] The definition is somewhat circular and even bureaucratic, implying the need for HTS adding value in the form of situation-specific judgments. However, it is possible to break down sociocultural knowledge into some discernible and practical sub-components. For example, the Army-Marine Counterinsurgency Field Manual emphasizes the importance of understanding "the society and its culture, to include its history, tribal/family/social structure, values, religions, customs, and needs."[7]

More generally the defense intelligence community agrees that sociocultural dynamics includes information about "the social, cultural, and behavioral factors *characterizing the relationships* and activities of the population of a specific region or operational environment (emphasis added)."[8] The focus on relationships means that cultural knowledge typically includes the mapping of social networks, a mixture of interpersonal, organizational and economic information that delineates networks of trust, dependency, and empowerment, which could include tribal connections, community institutions and types of government. Collecting and analyzing this type of sociocultural data requires a multidisciplinary scientific approach.[9] The data are gathered through short-term localized research informed by the perspective, theory, and methods derived from the social and/or behavioral sciences.[10] This information is useful but it cannot be properly assessed without long-term, in-depth expertise gained at the broad (usually regional) geographic level, where the nuances and weight given to the data are determined.[11]

Given the difficulty of defining sociocultural knowledge, the Defense Science Board has recommended that "rather than focusing on defining culture per se," it would be better for the Department of Defense to ask "what is it about culture that the soldier needs to know to improve performance at the tactical, operational, and/or strategic level?" It goes on to argue that "at each level, different aspects of culture are mission critical."

For example, at the tactical level understanding gender and family roles and how these are manifested in the way people dress, may save lives. At the strategic level, the key issue may be the dominant beliefs and attitudes that prevail and how well agreed upon they are in the population. From this perspective, the critical issue is not defining culture but identifying which manifestations need to be tracked to support mission objectives.[12]

We agree, and will argue later in this book that an intelligence architecture that incorporates sociocultural analysis must distinguish between such levels of analysis. In this respect we find useful the distinction one source has made in defining levels of cultural knowledge:

- **Cultural Awareness**: basic familiarity with language and religion and an understanding and observance of local norms and boundaries.
- **Cultural Understanding**: the "why" of behavior embodied in perceptions, mindsets, attitudes, and customs.
- **Cultural Intelligence**: the implications of these behaviors and their drivers, including ways in which culture can shape decision-making.[13]

These three levels do not perfectly align with tactical, operational and strategic levels as understood by the military, but for reasons we will review in the concluding section of the book, distinguishing between these levels of sociocultural knowledge is useful for human terrain analysis in a theater intelligence architecture.

Sociocultural Knowledge in U.S. Military Operations

Americans have a long, if uneven, history of exploiting sociocultural knowledge to gain an advantage in war. The British colonists learned the value of sociocultural knowledge in the new world by fighting with and against Native Americans who employed irregular tactics. Sometimes they suffered disastrous defeats, like the battle of Monongahela where General Braddock and 1,400 regulars were defeated by a mixed force of just 900 French and Indian guerillas.[14] Out of these defeats some British colonists—like Major Robert Rodgers—came to appreciate and eventually emulate the enemy's war-fighting culture and the tactics it informed. In 1757 Rodgers devised his "Rules of Ranging" that relied heavily on Indian tactics and culture. Rigorous selection and intense training ensured that the rules were well followed and Rodgers' Rangers became a lethal and effective light infantry force capable of meeting the Native Americans on their own terms.

More generally, Americans living along the frontier on the Eastern seaboard had a great deal to learn concerning the language, culture, and tactics of hostile tribes, and doing so often was a matter of life and death for these colonists. Later when Americans were fighting for independence they emulated Native American irregular warfare. For instance, Lieutenant Colonel Francis Marion—the famed "Swamp Fox" of South Carolina—applied what he had learned from his experience in the French and Indian wars to resist the British occupation of South Carolina. The Swamp Fox made excellent use of the human terrain, exploiting patriot sympathizers to gather intelligence for his forces and the continental army and denying support and supplies to the British by ambushing British and Tory forces.[15] This type of warfare required intimate knowledge of the local terrain, people and their social relations.

Later, irregular warfare was also a major but underappreciated dimension of the Civil War. For the many Americans involved in irregular operations, success—not to mention survival—required sociocultural knowledge so detailed it could distinguish where individual members of a family stood on the issue of secession. It is not widely known that in some areas in northern Georgia, Alabama, western Tennessee and North Carolina the majority of residents were opposed to secession.[16] Loyalty in those divided counties was determined by family lineage, geographical origin, and often class.[17] Fighting among pro-Unionist and Secessionists was so personal one had to know which towns, families, and individuals were leading the various paramilitary and military groups. This sociocultural knowledge found its outlet in blood feuds, night raids, and attacks against entire communities known to be on the other side of the civil war.

As the frontier expanded westward before and after the Civil War, Americans again discovered the utter necessity of deep sociocultural knowledge and the Army had to relearn lessons it had forgotten. Between 1865 and 1890, conflicts with Native American tribes west of the Mississippi were a major challenge. Arrayed against a fast-moving and hard-to-find enemy the Army had only 27,000 men in 255 military posts spread out across the entire continental United States.[18] Success depended on mobility, superior technology, and above all, intelligence. That intelligence came from the native scouts who could reliably find the enemy. Knowing the adversary's location wasn't enough, however; the most successful commanders came to respect Native American martial abilities and the culture that produced them. General George Crook, also known as Nantan Lupan (Grey Wolf) is one such example.

Crook had a profound respect for his Apache adversaries, calling them, "the tiger of the human species."[19] Understanding his forces' limitations and Apache strengths allowed him to identify military requirements for success. Crook admired the Apaches' warrior constitution, and their fierce independence, and believed that when "operating against them the only hope of success lies in using their own methods," which required that "a portion of the tribe must be arrayed against the other."[20] By managing Native American scouts well and using tactics appropriate to his adversary, Crook's efforts were overwhelmingly successful. However, he advised that the ultimate weapon against the nomadic Native Americans was cultural. By enticing them into a pastoral and monetary economy that diminished their poverty it was also possible to destroy their ability to sustain decentralized and autonomous operations indefinitely. Crook, however, remained a controversial figure in the Army, and his accomplishments were not widely appreciated.[21] The same is true of other Army generals who were effective in operations against Native Americans.

Following the pacification of the American West, the U.S. Army and Marines again found it necessary to develop cross-cultural knowledge. Again, the U.S. military initially operated without the advantage of in-depth social-cultural knowledge and suffered accordingly. Eventually, however, leaders arose who understood the value of knowing their adversary well and how to obtain this knowledge. One favored means of bridging the culture gap was to enlist the assistance of locals, either as native advisors or scouts, or as entire fighting units. During the 1920s the Marines employed Miskito Indians to increase the effectiveness of their force in Nicaragua.[22] Around the same time, in Haiti, a Marine officer, Second Lieutenant Herman Hanneken, was able to use his knowledge of Haitian language and culture to kill a rebel leader, thereby breaking the back of the rebellion.[23] Similarly, the U.S. Army quelled a nationalist insurgency in the Philippines. After Congress authorized a body of native troops in February 1901, the Army recruited and organized Filipino natives in 100-man companies commanded by American officers. One such American officer, Frederick Funston, posed as a prisoner with his band of his scouts, who pretended to be rebels. Under this ruse they penetrated the inner sanctum of the Filipino resistance and captured the resistance leader.[24] As General Crook had noted earlier, one key requirement for this type of cultural learning through incorporation of indigenous forces was finding U.S. commanders who appreciated their value and the utter necessity of cross-cultural learning for victory.[25]

During the Cold War, U.S. military forces fought irregular forces supported by the Soviet Union and other hostile powers, and also supported irregular forces resisting Soviet-supported governments. Army Special Forces were created specifically for these purposes. Special Forces doctrine required that they "recognize political considerations, personal antagonism, religious beliefs and ethnic differences [and to] know and respect local traditions, customs and courtesies." Similarly, the doctrine argues that when advising local forces on foreign internal defense, their success "depends more on effective cross-cultural communications and close personal relationship than on formal agreements."[26] Special Forces performed well in Vietnam, the major military contest of the Cold War, but the larger Army operated without sociocultural insights on the nature of its foe and the sociocultural context of the fight. "The massive U.S. and [South Vietnamese] intelligence empires focused mostly on that with which they were most familiar, the size and location of enemy main-force units, to the neglect of such other vital targets as the opponent's politico-military control structure."[27] By the time proper emphasis was placed on understanding and working with the local population the opportunity for victory had passed. As a recent study on sociocultural knowledge notes, in Vietnam the U.S. military "came to the cultural game late and then, when the conflict was over, turned its back on the subject as part of a conscious effort to put behind an unpleasant experience."[28]

Since the end of the Cold War, U.S. military forces have engaged a wide range of irregular forces in diverse operations, ranging from peace keeping and enforcement, to stabilization operations, to counterinsurgencies and counterterrorism operations. U.S. interventions in Haiti, Somalia, and the Balkans, among others, underscored the value of sociocultural knowledge. A common finding from the lessons-learned efforts following these operations was that the U.S. military needed better sociocultural knowledge.[29] Frequently those making the recommendations for better sociocultural knowledge were skeptical that their advice would be acted upon. For example, the authors of one Army study observed that Army leaders were not taking irregular missions seriously. Instead Army leaders commonly believed "the well-prepared soldier can do just about anything given good leadership and a little tailored training."[30] This sentiment is a common, persistent and resilient one across the U.S. military and most professional armies, which explains why appreciation for sociocultural knowledge is just the opposite: uncommon, fleeting and typically forced upon the institutional military by near-defeat or other untoward circumstances.

In summary, while history teaches the value of sociocultural knowledge, the U.S. military is widely understood to resist investing much in this area of expertise. The organizational and cultural reasons for this trend are complex, but can generally be explained by the understandable focus on and higher priority accorded to readiness for conventional warfare. Conventional wars, where large regular unit force-on-force engagements dominate and ultimately determine who the victor is, do not require the same attention to sociocultural knowledge. It can be argued that sociocultural knowledge of an adversary is useful in any type of military contest, but American strategic culture is typically understood to downplay the importance of such insights in favor of focus on other factors such as technology, small unit combat skills and large-scale military maneuver training.[31]

The marked tendency of the U.S. military to ignore sociocultural knowledge of foreign forces and populations explains one major reason it is generally unprepared for irregular conflicts. This proved to be the case following the terrorist attacks on 9/11 and the subsequent counterinsurgency operations in Iraq and Afghanistan. As counterinsurgency operations in these countries seemed to be failing, an increasing number of national security experts began arguing for greater attention to sociocultural knowledge. They worried that mainstream military officers insufficiently appreciated the importance of such information, and suggested ways to obtain it. When, after several years of fruitless counterinsurgency operations, the U.S. military realized it needed to update and reconfirm its counterinsurgency doctrine, it did so with due appreciation for the role of sociocultural knowledge.

Field Manual 3-24, *Counterinsurgency*, was written and published in 2006. The new doctrine emphasized a "population-centric" counterinsurgency model that made protecting the people against the insurgents the key requirement for success. In the words of one contributing author of the doctrine, a counterinsurgent must "know the people, the topography, economy, history, religion, and culture," and to "neglect this knowledge" is to ensure defeat.[32] While "understanding and working within the social fabric of a local area is initially the most influential factor in the conduct of counterinsurgency operations," it also is, "unfortunately…the factor most neglected by US forces."[33] Accordingly, the doctrine argued "social network analysis and sociocultural factors analysis" were critically important. It acknowledged that such analysis "requires an unusually large investment of time compared to conventional [intelligence]" but insisted it was "essential that commanders designate a group of analysts to perform" these tasks and that they "be insulated from the short-term demands of current operations and day-to-day intelligence demands." Done properly, "this knowledge allows predictive analysis of enemy actions [and] contributes to the ability to develop effective information operations and civil-military operations."[34]

As this brief historical survey demonstrates, the United States should have conducted its interventions in Afghanistan and Iraq with a deep appreciation of the importance of sociocultural knowledge if not a well-established capability for providing it. Instead it had to relearn the lesson after the fact, with help from unconventional thinkers both inside and outside the Pentagon. As it did so, proposals for new organizations to acquire the requisite sociocultural knowledge proliferated quickly. One such proposal, the Human Terrain System, managed to secure funding and was preparing to field its first team just as the Army's final draft of its new counterinsurgency doctrine was being published and about to be tested in Iraq.

The Organization of HTS and HTTs

Fielding a critically-needed human terrain program after irregular combat operations are well under way is difficult. Before examining the history of the Army's effort to do so and explaining the criteria for evaluating how successful it was, it helps to provide a brief description of the program. The U.S. Army's Training and Doctrine Command (TRADOC), manages

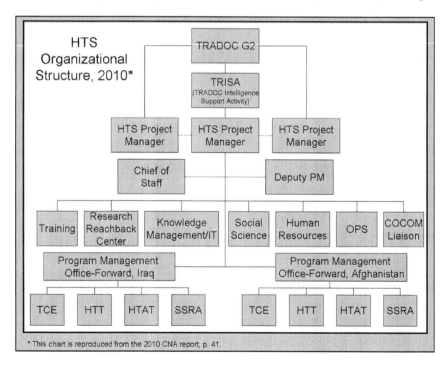

HTS from its current headquarters at Newport News, Virginia. HTS reports directly to TRADOC's Intelligence Support Activity under its intelligence staff element (see chart on previous page). The purpose of HTS is "to support operational decision-making, enhance operational effectiveness, and preserve and share sociocultural institutional knowledge."[35] To accomplish this purpose, HTS performs several key tasks. HTTs are the focus of the first task, which is to "recruit, train, deploy, and support an embedded, operationally focused sociocultural capability." The teams are trained at Fort Leavenworth, Kansas and other Army installations. Other HTS tasks include "conduct operationally relevant, sociocultural research and analysis" and "develop and maintain a sociocultural knowledge base."[36] These tasks are largely handled by HTS management and in particular by the two HTS Reachback Research Centers: one at Newport News and the other at Fort Leavenworth.

Currently, there are no HTTs in Iraq. The last one left in the summer of 2011 along with the other major U.S. forces departing the country. At the time this was written HTS had thirty-one teams in Afghanistan, but the number was expected to decline. Twenty-three of these teams were HTTs, which typically report to brigade-sized units and are commanded by colonels.[37] A typical HTT is comprised of a team leader, a social scientist, a research manager and two human terrain analysts (see chart at right, and shadowbox on HTTs as Cross-Functional Teams on p. 16). Seven Human Terrain Analysis Teams[38] (HTATs) serve the seven regional command headquarters across Afghanistan, acting as conduits of information from the HTTs to the regional commands as well as conducting their own research. They are typically comprised of one team leader, two social scientists, two to three research managers, two to three human terrain analysts and one information technology specialist. The total number of team members fluctuates as personnel frequently rotate in and out of the teams, so a team rarely matches these descriptions precisely.

The last HTS group in Afghanistan is the Theater Coordination Element in Kabul. Together with its logistical and personnel support office, the Theater Support Office, they oversee and support the other thirty teams in Afghanistan, providing coordination and quality control.[39] The Theater Coordination Element acts as an in-theater program management cell, "directly representing the HTS Program Director while providing guidance to HTS teams located throughout Afghanistan."[40] It coordinates personnel decisions, offers extra training for the teams, and provides them with administrative and logistical support through its Theater Support Office, to include sharing "guidelines for professional practice; social science research design methodologies; field work techniques for research in non-

Human Terrain Team

This is the prototypical Human Terrain Team as envisioned by HTS in 2009. Each team, aside from the 5 standard slots have up to four additional slots for more Human Terrain Analysts and Research Managers. There is a clear differentiation in roles played by the two social scientists. The first is supposed to have an anthropology/sociology background, while the second is expected to have regional expertise.

Human Terrain Team Leader
Duties: Commander's Human Terrain Advisor, Integration of human terrain with MDMP, Represent population at unit planning.

Human Terrain Social Scientist
Duties: Advise HTT and unit staff, conduct/manage ethnographic/social science research and analysis.

Human Terrain Social Scientist
Duties: Fluency in area language. Provide local area interpretation of human terrain information and run focus groups with locals.

Human Terrain Analyst
Duties: Primary human terrain researcher for Coalition elements (SOF, patrols, NGOs GOs etc)

Human Terrain Research Manager
Duties: Integrate research plan with unit intelligence collection plan. Secondary researcher.

Human Terrain Analyst
Duties: Primary human terrain researcher for Coalition elements (SOF, patrols, NGOs GOs etc)

Human Terrain Research Manager
Duties: Integrate research plan with unit intelligence collection plan. Secondary researcher.

Source: Daniel Dail, Human Terrain System Information Briefing for the 58th Annual Conference of the Civil Affairs Association Seminar on Intra-DoD Irregular Warfare Capabilities, October 30, 2009."

permissive environments," etc.[41] It also assists with integrating the HTT efforts into a theater-level Consolidated Stability Operations Center that is responsible for "an aggregate human terrain picture,"[42] conducts research for the theater command, and on occasion has briefed the theater commander directly.[43]   Finally, the Theater Coordination Element manages the Social Science Research and Analysis capability, which uses indigenous contractors (currently CGI Federal, but formerly Glevum Associates) to conduct theater-wide public opinion surveys through the use of polling.[44]

Team leaders (and sometimes other members as well) often have direct, personal contact with the brigade commanders, or his deputy commander or executive officer. They are often assigned to a specific section on the commander's staff, which the brigade commander determines. Few commanders attach their team to their intelligence section because HTT members are not trained or intended to participate in the "red layer," or kinetic targeting of enemy forces, but are instead designed to focus on the "green layer" or knowledge of the local population.[45] Most commanders place their HTTs in a planning cell under the operations section, or under the civil affairs section of their staff. Wherever they officially reside on the staff, team members often interact closely with many of the brigade staff sections. They also often cooperate with other support elements like Provincial Reconstruction Teams, Embedded Training Teams and Female Engagement Teams, just to name a few.

HTTs as Cross Functional Teams

HTTs (and HTATs) operated on the premise that they would be cross-functional teams. In other words, they were supposed to combine the talents of different functional experts. Most notably, they were intended to combine military and social science expert knowledge. As one team leader noted, HTTs were much more heterogeneous cross-functional teams than the typical military small unit or crew:

It's not like an infantry squad. I've got a new SAW [squad automatic weapon] gunner; I've got a new SAW gunner. It's an intellectual job and that will be affected by personality, background, qualifications much more than the other [military occupational specialties] and jobs. All the teams were very, very different.[46]

Beyond that, their composition included other functional capabilities such as regional and language expertise and research database management skills. Cross-functional teams have varying levels of heterogeneity, and over the course of the HTS program there was much debate over the degree of functional differentiation on the HTTs. HTS management repeatedly considered and reassessed the general qualifications for HTT members, the member qualifications that were position-specific, and the extent to which HTT members should be cross-trained on one another's job responsibilities.

Cross-functional teams are particularly appropriate for solving complex, multi-functional problems. Their members view problems differently and bring different bodies of expertise to bear on the problem-solving process, which is often a requirement for solving multi-functional problems like analysis of sociocultural trends. In theory, the performance requirements for cross-functional teams are different than those for more homogenous teams or other small groups.[47] As cross-functional groups, HTTs needed to be managed and led differently than homogenous small groups. For example, it should be expected that HTT members would frame and evaluate problems differently. Thus some degree of conflict is to be expected on cross-functional teams, and is not deleterious if managed productively. Similarly, the optimum structure for the HTTs—and thus their degree of cross-functionality—depends on their purpose, or employment concept. It makes a difference whether the team would be used primarily for data collection in the villages or for analysis at Brigade headquarters, tasks that emphasize different skill sets and knowledge levels. In the later chapters of the book we examine the cross-functional nature of the HTTs in greater depth.

Before deploying, team members receive extensive training. The current training program differs significantly from its original iteration (see Appendix One). The current training regime is separated into three distinct phases of learning. Foundation Skills and Research Operations constitute common training, or training in general aspects of HTT activity. All potential HTT members receive the same training in this regard. It is designed to provide the background that all team members will need. The next phase is individual training, which was designed to provide specialized training to trainees in the functions of the specific role they will fill. Once the trainees have received the foundations and specialized training, they move on to the third phase, collective training. Bringing the team members together in the final phase allows them to combine their specialized training in order to complete tasks similar to ones they would experience in the field. The intended result is trainees who understand how to work with their teammates on a cross-functional HTT.

Throughout the 50-day period, trainees receive 40 hours of cultural and language training. They are then given 5 days for "pre-mobilization" activities before spending 9 weeks at Fort Polk, Louisiana where they are trained in basic combat techniques, life on a Forward Operating Base and Combat Outpost, and other necessities for living and operating in a war zone. The trainees are then assigned to a team by HTS operations personnel, and deployed to Afghanistan. Assignments are ostensibly based on individual preferences and expertise, operational needs, and a trainee's personality. In some cases where a team will be going to a new location not previously assigned an HTT, some portion of the team or the entire team may be organized during training and then deploy together. In the vast majority of cases, however, HTT members deploy individually to locations where an HTT is already at work.

Teams cannot advise brigade commanders well unless the human terrain in the brigade's area of operations has been "mapped." Mapping requires data collection about the local population and is achieved by walking into a village and profiling it through interviews with the individuals who live there. Mapping also describes key leaders and important personages, and their relationship to others within and beyond the village social structure. Once they are integrated, such human terrain maps create a composite picture of the areas of tribal and key leader influence and describe the social networks operating within the area. Such activity, in the words of one social scientist deployed to Afghanistan, is "routine, nothing fancy."[48] However, such mapping must be completed and routinely updated for teams to advise brigade commanders well on specific courses of action and likely consequences.

Teams are attached to the brigades, and become a subordinate element of the unit. Thus they operate at the behest of commanders, so the products they create cover a variety of operational needs. Products required by commanders often fall within ten broad topics:

(1) Afghan Security Forces   (6) Information Operations
(2) Corruption & Economics   (7) Reintegration
(3) Education   (8) Village Stability Program
(4) Gap Analysis   (9) Water Management, and
(5) Governance   (10) Local Area Networks.[49]

These topics can be seen in a variety in HTT products and experiences. For example, one HTT helped a brigade understand its impact on the local economy. Afghans in one valley believed American forces were intentionally trying to starve them by raising local food prices. The unit was purchasing goods in foreign currency, driving up prices, and thus crowding out local Afghans. In studying the local climate, the HTT identified the problem, which was immediately addressed.[50] In a similar experience, military forces were unintentionally affecting local water allocation in a negative way, which made recruiting by the Taliban easier. The HTT discovered some locals made their livelihood by managing the region's water supply through the use of ditches created and destroyed on a daily basis. The system was "so complex and intricate," it defied description,[51] but the HTT convinced the U.S. commander to stop meddling with it and the villagers' hostility declined.

Teams also provide a wide range of ad hoc advice to the commander and his subordinates. The advice can be as mundane as warning soldiers not to yell gratuitously at villagers from moving vehicles,[52] but may have profound implications. For example, in Iraq, one team advised against the arrest of a village elder suspected of being a propagandist for the insurgency. The man possessed a weapon with a scope and suspicious literature in Arabic. However, the team determined that the weapon was a bb-gun used to ward off pests, and that the written material was just innocuous works on "Islamic history, Arab literature, and elementary reading and writing exercise books."[53] The man was released along with his possessions and profuse apologies for the error, which paid off. The village began to inform the U.S. military on the location of insurgent weapons stockpiles.[54]

Evaluating Human Terrain Teams

Although anecdotes about human terrain teams and their effects—both good and ill—abound, systematic assessment of their performance is necessary. The criteria and method for evaluating HTT performance must be clear up front so that the organization of the rest of the book and the methodology used for assessing performance in Chapter Five make sense. There is a consensus with respect to the proper criteria for assessment. HTT researchers agree that the criterion for evaluating their performance is how well they fulfill their mission objective of providing sociocultural knowledge to improve a commander's decision-making and enhance operational effectiveness. The actual assessment is difficult, however, primarily for two reasons. First, it is difficult to reliably assess local attitudes. Indigenous populations have manifold reasons to disguise their true sentiments, which may be diverse and evolve over time. For that matter, those reporting on local sympathies may not be free from prejudice either. Attitudinal data reliability is a common problem in counterinsurgency environments,[55] but it is not an impossible task. Mike Costello, a former Green Beret and a HTT member in Kandahar suggests the following measures of effectiveness are helpful for evaluating local sympathies:

- How many conversations patrols initiate with villagers
- How many times patrols are invited for tea
- How many times patrols initiate or are invited to shuras

- How many photos are taken with associated names
- How many improvised explosive devices are revealed by villagers
- How many bad guys are identified by villagers
- How many times patrols are invited to dinner by the Afghans[56]

While such metrics may not be completely reliable, along with supporting indicators they can help military leaders evaluate whether they are making progress in securing local support. Certainly they are better than no attempt to evaluate local attitudes.[57]

The second problem involves parsing out the impact of HTTs on local attitudes. HTTs are but one of many entities affecting local attitudes and counterinsurgency progress. Other non-lethal enablers such as Civil Affairs, Provincial Reconstruction Teams, and military information support activities affect local attitudes, as do combat operations, enemy operations, and the inadvertent civilian casualties they can generate on occasion. There are no reliable quantitative measures of these various influences other than polling data, which typically addresses only the impact of combat operations. Thus an assessment of HTT impact must be made qualitatively.

The military commander the HTT reports to is in the best position to make an assessment of the HTT's contribution. The best studies to date on HTTs agree on this point. The United States Military Academy at West Point,[58] Dr. Paul Joseph of Tufts University,[59] CNA Analysis & Solutions,[60] and the Institute for Defense Analyses[61] all use this approach to HTT evaluation. This study also relies upon commander assessments to establish HTT performance levels, but like the Institute for Defense Analyses study, also compares commander assessments with other sources in a position to evaluate HTT performance, including the HTT members themselves.

It has been argued that even though it is difficult to assess HTT effects, the Army should continue to support HTTs as a matter of principle;[62] because sociocultural knowledge is, in theory, important to successful counterinsurgency: "Army culture must change to embrace process more than outcome in some cases, and steer clear of using measures of effectiveness that are solely outcome-based...."[63] There are research alternatives with greater empirical merits, however. One option would be to explore commanders and staff observations about team performance in greater depth in an attempt to determine whether certain types of team behaviors are correlated with high or low quality team performance. This option is difficult because it requires a lot of time and attention from commanders who are fully occupied fighting the insurgency and who must contend with and evaluate a wide range of counterinsurgency factors. An alternative or complementary option would be to systematically assess all human terrain team output (products and advice) in hopes of finding correlations between the types and quality of output from teams and commander assessments of their productivity. Even then confidence in the resultant associations would be low absent expert opinion about the operational relevance of the specific products when they were delivered. In addition, such an approach would not be possible without access to all team output, and to date HTS program leaders have declined to support external studies in that manner.

Yet another option is to examine human terrain team performance in detail by interviewing team members to determine the factors that best explain team success and failure. This study took such an approach. We charted all known human terrain teams and their members, concentrating on the recent 2009-2010 period in Afghanistan. Using all available sources, including our own interviews with commanders, we identified the teams with reputations for high and low performance. We then conducted more than one hundred interviews with HTT and HTAT members and former HTS managers to assess the factors that best explain variations in team performance. The interviews were based on ten performance variables extracted from organizational literature on small cross-functional teams.[64] (See Appendix Two on research methodology for further information.)

To summarize, the methodological approach used in this study is similar to other studies in that it relies upon commander assessments to identify high and low team performance. It differs from previous studies in attempting to explain the variations in team performance by examining the teams themselves in greater detail with variables substantiated by previous studies of small cross-functional teams. Before looking at the teams it will help to first provide an historical overview of the HTS program and its evolution. Doing so will establish some program parameters relevant for understanding HTT performance variations.

Notes

[1] Lieutenant General Peter Chiarelli, Commanding General, MNC-1, Mapping the Human Terrain (MAP-HT) J/ACTD, FY 07 J/ACTD Candidate, PowerPoint, undated.

[2] We use human terrain for purposes of convenience since that is the label attached to the teams we are studying, but the expression "human domain" is currently preferred by Army leadership. According to Colonel Robert Simpson of the Army's Capabilities Integration Center, human domain better communicates "that the purpose of any military operations is to affect human behavior." Sydney J. Freedberg Jr., "Army Makes Case for Funding Culture Skills Beyond COIN" *AOL Defense*, July 2, 2012.

[3] Sun Tzu, *The Illustrated Art of War*, trans. Thomas Cleary (Boston, MA: Shambhala, 1998), 109.

[4] United States Government, *Small Wars Manual*, U.S. Marine Corps, 1940 (Washington, DC:

U.S. G.P.O., 1940), 18.

5 For a good treatment of this subject, see Appendix A of *Report of the Defense Science Board Task Force on Understanding Human Dynamics.*

6 The Human Terrain System (HTS), *HTS Core: Operational Planning Team (OPT)*, PowerPoint, undated.

7 FM3-24, *Counterinsurgency*, 4-3.

8 *Report of the Defense Science Board Task Force on Understanding Human Dynamics*, 73.

9 Ibid., 74.

10 Lee Ellen Friedland, Gary W. Shaeff, Jessica Glicken Turnley, "Sociocultural Perspectives: A New Intelligence Paradigm," Report on the conference at The MITRE Corporation McLean, VA, September 12, 2006, June 2007, Document Number 07-1220/MITRE Technical Report MTR070244.

11 For a deeper discussion, see Barack A. Salmoni and Dr. Paula Holmes-Eber, *Operational Culture for the Warfighter: Principles and Applications* (Quantico, VA: Marine Corps University, 2008), 44.

12 *Report of the Defense Science Board Task Force on Understanding Human Dynamics*, 37.

13 Arthur Speyer and Job Henning, MCIA's Cultural Intelligence Methodology and Lessons Learned, cited in Lee Ellen Friedland, Gary W. Shaeff, Jessica Glicken Turnley, "Sociocultural Perspectives: A New Intelligence Paradigm," Report on the conference at The MITRE Corporation McLean, VA, September 12, 2006, June 2007, Document Number 07-1220/ MITRE Technical Report MTR070244.

14 Robert B. Asprey, *War in the Shadows: the Guerrilla in History* (Garden City, NY: Doubleday, 1975), 56.

15 Ibid., 68-69.

16 Sean M. O'Brien, *Mountain Partisans: Guerrilla Warfare in the Southern Appalachians, 1861-1865* (Westport, CT: Praeger, 1999), XVI.

17 Ibid., XX.

18 Asprey, *War in the Shadows*, 111.

19 General George Crook, *The Apache Problem, by General George Crook* (Governors Island, NY: Military Service Institution of the U.S., 1882), 269.

20 Ibid., 263.

21 Colonel Billy J. Orr, General George Crook, *The Indian-Fighting Army, and Unconventional Warfare Doctrine: A Case for Developmental Immaturity* (Carlisle Barracks, PA: U.S. Army War College, 1992), 48.

22 David Tucker, and Christopher J. Lamb, *United States Special Operations Forces* (New York, NY: Columbia University Press, 2007), 72.

23 U.S. Army Center of Military History, *Medal of Honor Recipients*, website, Citation for Herman Henry Hanneken.

24 Asprey, *War in the Shadows*, 130.

25 Crook notes that with respect to securing useful Indian auxiliary forces, "the first difficulty was in overcoming the prejudices of army officers to command of this character and securing men properly qualified for such duty." General George Crook, *The Apache Problem, by General George Crook* (Governors Island, NY: Military Service Institution of the U.S., 1882), 263.

26 Department of the Army, *FM31-20, Doctrine for Special Forces Operations* (Washington, DC, Department of the Army Headquarters, April 20, 1990), 9-10, 10-2.

27 R. W. Komer, *Bureaucracy Does Its Thing: Institutional Constraints on U.S.-Gvn Performance in Vietnam* (Santa Monica, CA: RAND, 1972), viii.

28 *Report of the Defense Science Board Task Force on Understanding Human Dynamics*, 4.

29 In the 1990s it was common to recommend more area-specific training, including geography, language, culture and religion. See John O.B. Sewall, *Adapting Conventional Military*

Forces for the New Environment, in Arnold Kanter and Linton F. Brooks, *U.S. Intervention Policy for the Post-Cold War World: New Challenges and New Responses* (New York, NY: W.W. Norton, 1994), 95. Similarly, but specifically concerning the intervention in Haiti, another source notes "An area of significant weakness…was what we are labeling here as trans-cultural capabilities [to include] basic intelligence, language skills, and foreign area specialization." See Major General Anthony C. Zinni, *Non-Traditional Military Missions: Their Nature, and the Need for Cultural Awareness and Flexible Thinking*, in Joe Strange, *Capital "W" War: A Case for Strategic Principles of War (Because Wars Are Conflicts of Societies, Not Tactical Exercises Writ Large* (Marine Corps War College, 1998); and John T. Fishel and Andrés Sáenz, *Capacity Building for Peacekeeping: The Case of Haiti* (Washington, DC: Center for Hemispheric Defense Studies, National Defense University Press, 2007), 204. Many other examples could be cited.

[30]   James A. Winnefield, *Intervention in Intrastate Conflict: Implications for the Army in the Post-Cold War Era* (Santa Monica, CA: RAND, 2005), 112. Nonetheless, on the previous page the authors recommend: "Develop ways to expand the pool of soldiers with the requisite knowledge of language and culture associated with potential trouble spots around the world."

[31]   Colin S. Gray, "Irregular Enemies and the Essence of Strategy: Can the American Way of War Adapt?" *Monograph*, Strategic Studies Institute, March 1, 2006, 34.

[32]   David Kilcullen, "Twenty-Eight Articles: Fundamentals of Company-level Counterinsurgency," *Small Wars Journal* Edition 1, March 2006, 1-11.

[33]   FM3-24, *Counterinsurgency*, 4-3.

[34]   Ibid., 3-31 and 3-32.

[35]   Colonel Mark Bartholf, "The Requirement for Sociocultural Understanding in Full Spectrum Operations," *Military Intelligence Professional Bulletin* vol. 37, no. 4 (October-December 2011), 10. HTS supporting tasks are to "recruit, train deploy, and support an embedded, operationally focused sociocultural capability; conduct operationally relevant, sociocultural research and analysis; develop and maintain a sociocultural knowledge base." See also the current webpage, which is available at <http://hts.army.mil/>.

[36]   Chris King, *Human Terrain System and the Role of Social Science in Counterinsurgency*, PowerPoint, University of Hawai'i, Manoa, September 20, 2011.

[37]   NATO Task Forces, which have had HTTs attached to them, are typically commanded by generals.

[38]   These are not to be confused with CENTCOM's Human Terrain Analysis Team (HTAT). This staff element was created by CENTCOM in 2009 and located at its Tampa, Florida headquarters. It is now called the Human Terrain Analysis Branch, or "HTAB."

[39]   Ron Diana and John Roscoe, "The Afghanistan TCE and TSO: Administrative and Logistical Support to HTS Teams and Knowledge Management of HTS Information," *Military Intelligence Professional Bulletin* vol. 37, no 4 (October-December 2011), 20.

[40]   Diana and Roscoe, "The Afghanistan TCE and TSO: Administrative and Logistical Support to HTS Teams and Knowledge Management of HTS Information," 20.

[41]   Ibid., 21.

[42]   The Center includes HTS' Theater Coordination Element, the Defense Intelligence Agency, the National Geospatial Intelligence Agency, and the Atmospheric Program Afghanistan. Diana and Roscoe, "The Afghanistan TCE and TSO: Administrative and Logistical Support to HTS Teams and Knowledge Management of HTS Information," 21.

[43]   HTT Social Scientist, interviewed December 9, 2011.

[44]   "An HTS Social Scientist posted at ISAF coordinates Social Science Research and Analysis research efforts, collaborating with HTS teams and their supported units on the design of complex quantitative, qualitative, and mixed-method research projects that deployed HTS teams are not capable of executing due to logistical, resource, and security constraints." Diana and Roscoe, "The Afghanistan TCE and TSO: Administrative and Logistical Support to HTS

Teams and Knowledge Management of HTS Information," 22-23.

[45]   U.S. Army Training and Doctrine Command, Deputy Chief of Staff for Intelligence, *Human Terrain System*, PowerPoint, May 18, 2006.

[46]   Lieutenant Colonel Eric Rotzoll, Team Leader, AF2, interviewed October 10, 2011.

[47]   See James Douglas Orton, with Chris Lamb, "Interagency National Security Teams: Can Social Science Contribute?," *PRISM* 2, no. 2 (March 2011), 47-64.

[48]   Interviewee 44, December 10, 2011.

[49]   King, *Human Terrain System and the Role of Social Science in Counterinsurgency*.

[50]   HTT Social Scientist, interviewed December 14, 2011.

[51]   Ibid.

[52]   Colonel Mike Howe, Team Leader AF3, Jalalabad, interviewed November 10, 2011.

[53]   Paul Joseph, *Changing the Battle Space? How Human Terrain Teams Define "Success" in Iraq and Afghanistan*, Paper prepared for 7th Interdisciplinary Conference on War and Peace, (Prague, Czech Republic, April 30-May 2 2010), 15.

[54]   Ibid.

[55]   FM3-24, *Counterinsurgency* notes that "[t]raditionally, commanders use discrete quantitative and qualitative measurements to evaluate progress. However, the complex nature of COIN operations makes progress difficult to measure." FM3-24, *Counterinsurgency*, 2006, 5-26.

[56]   Costello also argues that an initial increase in IEDs is a sign that counterinsurgency operations in an area are going well. If the insurgents did not believe they were losing ground they would not bother attacking the patrols with IEDs. Mike Costello, "Counterinsurgency (COIN) & Human Terrain Techniques Combating IEDs in Afghanistan (CIED)," *Defense Update*, December 21, 2011.

[57]   A recent RAND study explores this issue well, and warns against a centralized assessment that removes local context and leads to poor findings and conclusions. The study recommends a combination of quantitative and qualitative contextualized analysis instead of a reliance on purely quantitative metrics. See Ben Connable, *Embracing the Fog of War: Assessment and Metrics in Counterinsurgency* (Santa Monica, CA: RAND, 2012), xv.

[58]   Cindy R. Jebb, Laurel J. Hummel, Tania M. Chacho, *Human Terrain Team Trip Report: A "Team of Teams,"* Prepared for TRADOC G2 by the USMA's Interdisciplinary Team in Iraq, unpublished, 2008.

[59]   Joseph, *Changing the Battle Space?*

[60]   CNA Analysis & Solutions, *Congressionally Directed Assessment of the Human Terrain System*.

[61]   Institute for Defense Analyses, *Contingency Capabilities: Analysis of Human Terrain Teams in Afghanistan—Draft Final Report*.

[52]   Jebb, Hummel, Chacho, *Human Terrain Team Trip Report, 3*.

[63]   Jebb, Hummel, Chacho, *Human Terrain Team Trip Report, 5*.

[64]   Orton with Lamb, "Interagency National Security Teams: Can Social Science Contribute?," 47-64.

3 HISTORICAL OVERVIEW OF HTS AND HTTS

The disadvantages of starting a critically needed program after military operations have already begun may seem self-evident. Certainly one would not expect U.S. forces to perform with great efficiency absent the required capability, which in this case was sociocultural knowledge. Beyond this general performance obstacle, however, are more specific constraints that complicated program management. Those challenges and how they affected the performance of HTTs in the field are not self-evident. It takes a well-balanced and detailed history of the program to identify them. Such a balanced history is difficult because the program was complicated, controversial and endured multiple achievements and disappointments. As former HTS director Colonel Sharon Hamilton observed not long ago, "The HTS story is one of challenges, rewards, stumbles, and successes."[1]

Moreover, much of the secondary literature on HTS and its HTTs is skewed, and even "extremely biased."[2] It tends to fall into one of two categories: uncritical promotion of the program because it is a worthy concept and overly negative condemnation of the program because it has encountered numerous problems during execution. In other words, advocates focus too much on the rewards and successes, and critics focus too much on the challenges and stumbles that Colonel Hamilton acknowledged. Building upon the few credible studies of HTS and numerous interviews with those who managed the program or were involved in its implementation, we tried to produce a balanced and thoroughly researched external history that recognizes program achievements without ignoring shortcomings. In doing so we found that the history of the program can usefully be broken down into six periods. The long first period is "gestation," during which Pentagon civilian and military leaders came to terms with the operational import of sociocultural knowledge.

Gestation

> *"This is not about another shiny object...."*[3]
> Karl Prinslow, Former Deputy Director
> Foreign Military Studies Office
> Ft. Leavenworth

The origin of the term "human terrain" is disputable, but arguably it made its way into the strategic studies realm amidst growing interest in military missions that take place in urban areas with dense populations. As one conference on the topic noted, in the decade following the dissolution of the Soviet Union, the "sight of American troops patrolling foreign cities ha[d] become common,"[4] and a key feature of such interventions was the importance of humanitarian operations and the need to manage relations with the civilian population well. Later Ralph Peters used the term "human terrain" in an article on urban operations, but he did not define it specifically.[5]

Following the terror attacks on September 11, 2001, the need to understand human terrain in order "to help narrow the search space for terrorists and terror groups"[6] became evident. General Robert H. Scales was perhaps the earliest, most persuasive person who emphasized this point. In October 2003, General Robert H. Scales highlighted the requirement for cultural awareness when he testified to the House Armed Services Committee on Operation Iraqi Freedom.[7] He wrote on the subject[8] and on July 15, 2004 again testified to Congress, making the case for an urgent investment in better sociocultural information capabilities for the U.S. military. Scales pointedly told Congress that the U.S. did not currently have the capability to conduct a counterinsurgency in Iraq because it lacked sociocultural knowledge of local human terrain.[9] Later, Scales would write that as previous world wars were defined by chemistry, physics, and information research, the current struggles in Afghanistan and Iraq would be won through social-science.[10]

Intelligence fusion cells designed to track terrorist leaders, in part by charting their social networks, were an early product of the Bush administration's war on terror.[11] It took some time for interest in this aspect of sociocultural knowledge to evolve into discrete programs. It is not clear when the first program began, but one relevant effort was a new intelligence program called SKOPE, established in late 2004 by the U.S. Special Operations Command, the National Geospatial-Intelligence Agency, and the U.S. Strategic Command.[12] The SKOPE cells were "small nine- to twelve-man teams composed of human terrain and geospatial intelligence personnel," that were "created to help [the Special Operations Command's] deployed teams more effectively locate potential targets." The program had to overcome "a great deal of skepticism and hostility from the intelligence and user communities," but in 2005 and 2006 they were proving their worth.[13] Meanwhile, as a result of ongoing operations in Afghanistan and Iraq, the term human terrain was being applied more generally in reference to conventional military operations. The gap between what the U.S. military knew and what it needed to know about Iraq's human terrain was evident.[14]

As Pentagon leaders became increasingly aware that sociocultural knowledge was a critical requirement for U.S. military forces, there was an explosion of interest in the topic. Conferences and a wide range of exploratory programs relevant to the subject were initiated.[15] Dr. Montgomery McFate organized one such conference on "Adversary Cultural Knowledge and National Security" in Washington, D.C. during November-December, 2004.[16] The conference was sponsored by the Office of Naval Research and the Defense Advanced Research Projects Agency. Andrea Jackson, a researcher at Quantum Research,[17] spoke on one of the conference panels. A few months later, in early 2005, at a meeting in Tampa, Dr. McFate and Ms. Jackson met Steve Fondacaro. He was a 1976 graduate of West Point with 30 years' experience in the Infantry and Special Operations Forces as a Ranger. Fondacaro was then working as a director of training initiatives for the Futures Center in the intelligence section of TRADOC. The three "got along great from the beginning" as they discussed sociocultural knowledge in this context of defeating improvised explosive devices (IEDs), which were by far the largest cause of U.S. casualties in Iraq and the most prominent operational problem confronting U.S. forces there.[18]

To counter IEDs, the Pentagon created a new organization in July 2004: the Joint Improvised Explosive Device Defeat Task Force. Under the command of Brigadier General Joseph Votel, the group was supposed to sidestep Pentagon bureaucracy and rapidly field new technologies that would protect soldiers from IEDs. After examining the problem at some length, the new Task Force increasingly emphasized the importance of countering the "bomb maker" and not just the bomb itself.[19] Identifying the network of contacts that supported bomb making and better understanding of what inclined people to make or fail to report bombs they knew about became a major focus of the Task Force. Indicative of this trend was a small program called *Cultural Preparation of the Environment* (CPE) that the task force launched in April 2005.

Lieutenant Colonel William Adamson, who served with Votel on the IED Task Force, had previously been a successful commander in Baqubah, Iraq. After Adamson left Baqubah, his successor's team experienced a large increase in IEDs. Adamson believed the knowledge that his soldiers accumulated about local social relationships, which was helpful for eliciting local cooperation in countering IEDs, was not organized and stored in a way that could be useful to the incoming soldiers.[20] Adamson and Votel funded the CPE tool to solve this problem. It was designed to be a portable, electronic guide to the human terrain. The device was to be a combination of Geographic Information Systems[21] and Social Network Analysis[22] software that would enable the user to visualize the complexities of the population in an area of operations.

The Joint Improvised Explosive Device Defeat Task Force provided $1.2 million for the creation and testing of the device between 2004 and 2006. The CPE tool was designed by MITRE Corporation under a program run by Dr. Hriar Cabayan, the science advisor to the Joint Chiefs of Staff, J3.[23] Cabayan tasked Dr. Nancy Chesser to lead the CPE project. Chesser in turn tapped McFate, still working as a defense consultant at the Office of Naval Research, and Jackson, who by now was working with The Lincoln Group as a field researcher in Iraq, to help develop the knowledge typology. McFate saw the link between successfully combating the IED threat and better understanding the human terrain: "[Social network analysis] can describe terrorist networks, anticipate their actions, predict their targets, and deny the insurgents the ability to act."[24] Jackson had a similar point of view, reinforced by her experience in Iraq.

The first phase of the project lasted from April to August 2005, cost $370,000, and focused on the creation of a sociocultural knowledge typology that could be used to organize field data.[25] Phase 1 CPE products included:

(1) a "detailed framework of social structure (key groups)" in Diyala Province in Iraq, where Adamson had served as a commander in the province's capital, Baqubah;
(2) "over 2,000 pages of research and analysis from journalists, social scientists and pollsters" with Global Information System data "where available";
(3) a "system framework on website," or knowledge typology; and a
(4) "stand-alone laptop CPE prototype" that was demonstrated on July 11, 2005.[26]

The CPE knowledge categories covered ethno-religious groups, tribes, individuals, security, economy and services, information environment, outside influences, formal political system, districts, and towns. After seeing a slide that illustrated the data layers of the CPE tool in 2005, General Abizaid at CENTCOM commented that with such knowledge, "we would know more about Iraq than we do the US."[27]

Following the meeting where McFate and Jackson met Fondacaro, McFate continued to work on the CPE project, briefing the State Department

Humanitarian Information Unit, the Army Civil Affairs and Psychological Operations Command, and the Marine Corps Intelligence Activity between March and July 2005.[28] She promoted the use of anthropology in particular, arguing that the "cultural knowledge gap has a simple cause—the almost total absence of anthropology within the national security establishment."[29] In a mid-2005 article, McFate and co-author Jackson proposed a new organization to meet the need for more sociocultural knowledge. They called it the "Office for Operational Cultural Knowledge," and suggested it could provide research support and conduct training for deploying units.[30] They argued the office could build upon the knowledge gained from the CPE program, and once instituted, would "solve many of the problems surrounding the effective, expedient use of adversary cultural knowledge."[31]

While McFate and Jackson were working with CPE and promoting sociocultural knowledge in publications and presentations, Colonel Fondacaro signed on with General Votel's IED task force. He was deployed to Iraq, where he served as the officer in charge of training support to all US units and validating success or failure of the IED task force projects deployed to Iraq.[32] He found himself working in close proximity with Andrea Jackson, who was assigned by The Lincoln Group to work for Multinational Command-Iraq headquarters on the CPE project.[33] During their time in Iraq, CPE was officially tested in Diyala Province, then under the responsibility of the 3rd Brigade, 4th Infantry Division. The CPE prototype was demonstrated on a classified laptop, including interactive Geographic Information System software, on October 31, 2005.[34] The test was seen by some observers as a failure, primarily because the Iraqi researchers in Diyala falsified data.[35] The issue with CPE, according to Fondacaro and McFate in a 2011 article, was that military personnel did not possess the "baseline knowledge" to accurately validate, obtain and enter data into the device.[36]

The same point—that a technological solution alone would not be sufficient—was made by Captain Don Smith from the Foreign Military Studies Office (FMSO) based at Fort Leavenworth.[37] FMSO had long championed better relationships between social science and the US military, but was skeptical it could be provided with new technology.[38] FMSO regularly listened in on Fondacaro's periodic briefings to the task force HQ on the status of CPE via videoconference. FMSO participants in a late spring (or early June) 2005 videoconference agreed that brigades in Iraq were not interested in "another gadget to support their mission."[39] In another summer of 2005 videoconference, FMSO participants again listened to the CPE discussion between Fondacaro and the task force,[40] and again concluded their organization did not need to get involved in a fruitless technology initiative. However, FMSO Director Dr. Jacob Kipp asked Captain Smith, one of his FMSO analysts, to listen to the next videoconference and provide his assessment.[41] Smith came back and argued that the requirement was not for new technology. Instead, he agreed with McFate and Jackson's recently published article that the need for sociocultural knowledge should be met with an organization that could "apply social science awareness and knowledge and understanding to support those soldiers."[42] Smith's "proselytizing within the FMSO directorate leadership" in August and September of 2005 made an impact.[43] In October, FMSO leadership approved the recommendation made by Smith and others for a program to provide sociocultural knowledge.

Concurrent with the efforts at FMSO, Fondacaro and Jackson worked closely in Iraq to prepare a briefing in summer 2005 for the new leader of JIEDDTF, Army General (ret.) Montgomery Meigs. Secretary of Defense Donald Rumsfeld appointed Meigs to replace Brigadier General Votel on December 6, 2005 and shortly thereafter the organization was expanded to become the Joint Improvised Explosive Device Defeat Organization (JIEDDO).[44] In a briefing to General Meigs in Iraq in the fall of 2005 Fondacaro and Jackson argued "technology is not the solution,"[45] and explained why CPE would not work. Fondacaro and his supporters believed the last thing soldiers in the field needed was "another gizmo."[46] Instead, commanders needed "angels on their shoulders"[47] because they could not analyze the situation in ways that productively accounted for the local population. They believed that only social scientists trained in the local customs and with local knowledge could provide that analysis. The solution, therefore, could "only be met by expert humans, on the staff, belonging to the commander, contributing to the [Military Decision-Making Process]."[48]

The briefing to Meigs was a key decision point. Meigs and his staff concluded a solution based on human expertise was needed. General Meigs returned to the JIEDDO headquarters in Washington, D.C. while Fondacaro and Jackson elicited the assistance of McFate and Smith to work on a human terrain concept and supporting organization. Meanwhile, Chesser and her colleagues at Cabayan's Strategic Multi-Layer Assessment Group at the Pentagon agreed to transition CPE to FMSO for further development after the end of the phase two of the project (at a cost of $898,000) in February 2006.[49] The project required a command to adopt it for further development, and FMSO was chosen "because they actually had anthropologists on staff."[50] Two years earlier the U.S. Special Operations Command had invested in human terrain-type analysis to better target terrorists. Now the Pentagon was about to invest in a new means of providing sociocultural knowledge to U.S. general purpose forces fighting a counterinsurgency.

Birth

"I approve release of $20.40M from the Iraq Freedom Fund (IFF) for the Human Terrain System."[51]
General Montgomery C. Meigs, Director, JIEDDO

The funding for CPE between 2004 and 2006 attracted attention to the topic of human terrain. In an October 24, 2005, meeting on CPE, 150 people from 25 organizations were identified as interested in CPE and human terrain projects.[52] The resources committed for niche technologies and the ballooning interest in the topic were not sufficient to launch HTS, however. Advocates needed a patron who appreciated the broader need for dedicated subject matter expertise. General Meigs became that figure when he agreed to help build the new human terrain organization. Even so, much work needed to be done. It was not yet clear how HTS would be organized, funded and operate, or where and how the concept would be tested. These issues would be resolved over time by personnel on Meigs' staff at JIEDDO and at TRADOC.

Maxie McFarland, a retired U.S. Army colonel working as the Deputy Chief of Staff for Intelligence, G2, at TRADOC, had called for more sociocultural awareness for military personnel in early 2005.[53] He moved for a year onto the staff of General Meigs at JIEDDO[54], and was present at the Baghdad briefing to Meigs by Fondacaro and Jackson. Meigs and McFarland concluded that a conceptual study to examine an organizational approach to the problem was worth studying, and McFarland volunteered to do it.[55] As FMSO was a direct reporting unit to TRADOC, and FMSO's leadership already had approved a conceptual design for HTS, McFarland gave FMSO the go ahead to take the lead. Over the course of early 2006 FMSO "was overseeing the creation of the Human Terrain System" for TRADOC.[56]

Between July 2005 and August 2006, Captain Smith at FMSO did the "practical work to implement the concept under the title Human Terrain System...."[57] Smith was assisted by senior FMSO leaders and researchers Jacob Kipp, Karl Prinslow, and Lester Grau. From November 2005 through June 2006, FMSO Deputy Director Karl Prinslow and Smith conducted a "Karl and Don road show" to secure JIEDDO support and funding, and solicit inputs for organization, training support, and operational applications by briefing various commands, agencies and departments.[58] By April 2006, the FMSO team had a draft of the design for the organization,[59] which they later published in *Military Review* under the title "The Human Terrain System: A CORDS for the 21st Century."[60] The fact that Smith's team felt comfortable linking their new concept to CORDS, a successful cross-functional program developed in an unsuccessful and controversial war, was an indication of how much Army thinking on counterinsurgency had changed since the invasion of Iraq. FMSO suggested the concept be tested through the deployment of five teams, and that a rigorous analysis of their successes and failures be conducted in order to determine whether or not the program should be continued or improved.[61]

In late 2005 the entire human terrain effort received a major boost when the 10th Mountain Division submitted an operational needs statement asking for a human terrain capability.[62] Army regulations require an operational needs statement from a field commander to launch the process of documenting the urgent need for a specific military capability. The goal is to determine within two weeks whether the need is legitimate, a high priority, and if so, how best it can be satisfied. With the Operational Needs Statement in hand, FMSO spent an estimated $700,000[63] worth of employee and Reservist hours, supplies and other logistical support, to develop a Human Terrain System "prototype." The FMSO group worked with the reservist community to create four groups. Two groups were recruited to serve as Reachback Research cells for Afghanistan and Iraq; the other two groups were to serve as deployable teams, one to Afghanistan and one to Iraq.[64] The FMSO team design called for a team leader that would have control over a civilian cultural analyst, a civilian regional studies analyst, a research manager and a human terrain analyst.[65] FMSO lacked the required funding to actually deploy teams, but it was able to begin training the team members. Individuals recruited by FMSO to deploy as team members tried to help by perusing the 2006 Quadrennial Defense Review looking for funding sources that might be tapped to move the project forward.[66]

Meanwhile, Steve Fondacaro returned from his temporary assignment for JIEDDO in Iraq to his "parent headquarters" at TRADOC near Newport News in Virginia.[67] After briefing Lieutenant General John F. Kimmons, the Army Deputy Chief of Staff for Intelligence, about HTS on May 18, 2006, Fondacaro secured approval for the experiment from the intelligence community, but a source for the requisite funding was not identified. Then, in a June 8, 2006, meeting, JIEDDO officially approved the HTS concept,[68] and the formal document transferring $20.4M from JIEDDO to create the Human Terrain System was signed by General Meigs on June 12, 2006.[69] HTS supporters finally had a source of funding to launch the program. Now they needed a management team to run the project.

On June 22, 2006, Maxie McFarland created a steering committee for the "Cultural Operations Research-Human Terrain System" (COR-HTS).[70] McFarland put Fondacaro in charge of the committee. On June 30, 2006, Fondacaro took his mandatory retirement after 30 years in the Army and accepted the position of Program Manager for the HTS program. The proposed leadership team for the new organization also included Program Manager (East) David Scott, Program Manager (West) Don Smith, and Business Manager Mike Morris.[71] Although Don Smith was retained as part of the leadership team, the institutional link with FMSO was broken.[72] Those present during this transition describe it as "a little rough," with too much "ego involved,"[73] but in any case the program leadership was set.[74]

The new leadership made some significant changes to the original FMSO organizational design. The new team identified development principles that shaped their efforts in creating the new HTS organization, including the need to "deploy capability now" and "spiral cultural solutions."[75] These principles meant that FMSO's "test the concept" approach would be implemented quickly. The HTS organization was supposed to be built over two years by collecting metrics and lessons learned from employment, continuously monitoring requirements, and analyzing training and organizational procedures during program execution.[76] In the short term, though, HTS determined that the five-team experiment (two teams to Afghanistan, three teams to Iraq) "had to be trained and deployed within the 2006-2007 fiscal year before their OMA [Operations and Maintenance, Army] funding disappeared."[77]

Fondacaro also brought a sense of urgency to the new HTS organization: "After 30 years of DOD service, I knew the monolithic Department of Defense bureaucracy was unable…to embrace change easily."[78] Fondacaro often told people that HTS program leaders had to be prepared to fight the bureaucracy, which tended to treat fresh ideas like "a virus that enters the body."[79] The problem was not Department of Defense officials as individuals, but "the bureaucratic funding system that cannot readily embrace innovation and change. There is no DOD Department of Innovation and New Ideas. All defense dollars are technically spoken for years ahead of each Defense budget."[80] In his view, HTS had to deploy some capability quickly to validate the concept in the field before funding was reapportioned for other priorities.

In addition, the new team put a priority on direct support to units on the ground rather than populating knowledge databases. Under the FMSO design, HTS products were intended to help populate the World Basic Information Library,[81] a FMSO-run repository of open source materials. The focus of the FMSO database was to use military reservists, who telecommute, to comb through the best open source products to answer intelligence community questions about all dimensions of emerging threats.[82] The human terrain data was to be fed directly into this database of open-source material. The new leadership team increased the focus on direct advice to ground units.

Another program change also took place during this period. In addition to tapping reservists to support its concept, FMSO had been able to obtain some funding from a unique interagency funded program, the Combating Terrorism Technical Support Office. Housed in the Pentagon's office that manages special operations and low-intensity conflict, the program follows a collective approach that serves multiple organizations by identifying interagency requirements and resourcing them. During 2005-2006, FMSO personnel from Fort Leavenworth were shuttling to Washington to engage representatives from multiple agencies to secure funding support for an experiment to test their concept.[83] In this regard, there was an interagency dimension to the HTS concept as worked out by FMSO. Interagency participation also "steadfastly remained an HTS goal" while Fondacaro led HTS.[84] However, once it was agreed that funding from JIEDDO would be administered by TRADOC, the immediate need for support from other agencies diminished and HTS focused on supporting ground units of the U.S. Army and Marines.[85]

The new HTS leadership team immediately turned its attention to successfully executing the five-team experiment that had been promised to JIEDDO. TRADOC G2 fleshed out a list of seven tasks for August 2006 that included developing, training, deploying and assessing the five experimental teams.[86] A Human Terrain integrated process team, co-chaired by the Department of Defense Under Secretaries for Policy and Intelligence, provided oversight to "ensure capabilities are achieved."[87] The Under Secretary for Acquisition, Technology, and Logistics oversaw the MAP-HT portion of the program. To speed the process along, the reservists that had been recruited by FMSO were supplemented by contractors paid through BAE Systems and their subcontractors, which had a standing contract with TRADOC.

Hiring 25 people to staff the first five teams was a high priority for TRADOC and BAE Systems. Even so, by August it was clear that the deployment of five teams in October and November 2006 would not be possible because so few people had been recruited, let alone trained, as team members.[88] Thus, by September 11, 2006, the five experimental teams had been scaled down to a single team to be fielded in the first quarter of FY07. The identification of a host military unit for the first HTT deployment became a priority. The 10th Mountain Division, which was scheduled to return to the United States in early 2007, was not able to host the HTT but other units were willing to do so.[89] In December 2006, Fondacaro's old boss from the IED task force, General Votel, presented an opportunity to place an initial team in Afghanistan. After leaving the IED task force, Votel had become the Assistant Division Commander for Operations of the 82nd Airborne. Votel told Fondacaro that an 82nd Airborne Brigade Combat Team was leaving for the Joint Readiness Training Center at Ft. Polk, Louisiana, in preparation for deployment to Afghanistan, and asked whether he could get a team to meet them there.[90] Votel also agreed to host a subsequent HTT in Afghanistan at CJTF-82 in Bagram.[91] Fondacaro hurriedly assembled a team and flew them to Fort Polk, Louisiana. The social scientist, somewhat apprehensive about the enterprise, missed her flight. Fondacaro purchased another ticket and persuaded her to take it.[92]

Getting the HTS program off the ground had proven difficult and time-consuming. It only managed to get under way because another new organization—JIEDDO—had been given the flexibility to push resources at new ideas that promised to rapidly meet requirements from commanders in the field. Even though JIEDDO was created to field new technology quickly, its leaders defined its mission broadly enough to allow them to justify pouring resources into what was essentially a personnel-intensive program. That, and aggressive leadership had set the stage for the first human terrain team experiment.

Tripartite Proof of Concept

> *"I remember the S3 called us his 'Human Google Machines.'"*[93]
> Major Robert Holbert

The 82nd Airborne's pre-deployment training at Ft. Polk provided the first opportunity to demonstrate that a cross-functional team of military leadership, civilian social scientists, technology-savvy research managers, and cultural analysts could be helpful to a brigade commander. Simultaneously the human terrain concept was being tested at two other levels as well. JIEDDO's funding challenged the HTS management team to demonstrate it could reverse the failed "technology" approach to providing sociocultural knowledge by quickly standing up an alternative human expertise-centric program. More broadly still, the entire population-centric approach to counterinsurgency, which HTS supported, was also being tested by the nation's leadership. About a month after the first HTT deployed to Ft. Polk, General Petraeus, the commander who published the new population-centric counterinsurgency doctrine, was given command of forces in Iraq. His selection represented a change in strategy that President Bush and Pentagon leaders hoped would reverse the deteriorating situation there. A lot was at stake on all three levels.

At Fort Polk the hastily assembled experimental Human Terrain Team met Colonel Martin Schweitzer and his 4th Brigade Combat Team, 82nd Airborne for the first time. The team members benefited from the exposure to military culture and operations, and the brigade staff was impressed by the team. The S3 Operations Officer began referring to the team members as "human Google machines."[94] Although it is has been reported that the experimental HTT trained together for four months,[95] in reality, the entire team did not train as a single unit. The team's social scientist, Tracy St. Benoit, did not join the team early enough to receive much pre-deployment training. St. Benoit, a West Point graduate, joined the team in late November 2006.[96] The team leader, retired Green Beret Rick Swisher, was coaxed out of retirement while the team was at Fort Polk. Fondacaro, who was the acting team leader at the time, called him the day after Christmas and convinced him to join the team at Ft. Polk on January 3, 2007. Similarly, Thomas Johnson did not train with the other members of AF1 at Ft. Leavenworth. Johnson deployed with the team and served for two months as its de-facto regional expert before returning to his academic post at the Naval Post Graduate School.[97]

The rest of the team had trained together for some time, however. Major Bob Holbert, Sergeant Britt Damon, and Captain Roya Sharifsoltani were all originally recruited by FMSO in 2006 along with other reservists who dropped out of the program. Holbert was a former social studies teacher who joined HTS in the middle of 2006.[98] Damon was a former military police officer and was working towards a degree in criminology.[99] Sharifsoltani, the team's cultural analyst, was of Iranian descent and a Medical Officer. She spoke fluent Dari and some Pashto, two languages vital to understanding Afghanistan.[100] Originally, FMSO had devised a 90-day training program (see Appendix One).[101] However, in the case of this first group of recruits, the training was largely self-education, and the period stretched to nearly six months at Ft. Leavenworth as management looked for authorization and funds to deploy the team.

The experimental HTT, designated AF1, followed Schweitzer's brigade when it deployed to Forward Operating Base Salerno in Khost, Afghanistan. AF1 arrived in Khost on February 7, 2007. Fondacaro accompanied Swisher and the other members of the team[102] and stayed with them for two weeks exploring ways the team could be used to good effect. Both McFate and Fondacaro note that they did not want to constrain the improvisational ability of the team to adapt to the needs of the brigade commander by specifying too precisely what the purpose of the team would be.[103] Swisher had the first Concept of Operations approved by HTS in January 2007 to guide him, but it did not provide much more detail than the original FMSO design.[104] Before boarding his aircraft back to Bagram, Fondacaro's parting instruction to Swisher was to "make things happen."[105]

Despite the brigade's interaction with the HTT at Ft. Polk, Schweitzer's staff struggled to utilize the HTT to its full potential once in Afghanistan. Initially they assigned the HTT to the brigade's intelligence section where, by all accounts, their talents were wasted.[106] They were then moved to the Effects Cell and were given an office near the psychological operations staff. They were told by the brigade to "define the human environment [the brigade forces] are operating in."[107] This purpose, however, was not concrete enough to assign responsibilities. Left to their own devices, the members of AF1 took up small initiatives to demonstrate their usefulness to the brigade, such as teaching English to local Afghan workers on base, rebuilding a mosque on the base that had fallen into disrepair,[108] and performing "participant-observation" studies while working with Afghans in their wheat fields and orchards.[109] They also:

> consulted with [psychological operations] on a media campaign to discourage Afghans from becoming suicide bombers. HTT helped pinpoint the most effective medium (radio), target demographic (fifteen- to thirty-year-old men), time slot (after dark, since most Afghan men work in the fields during the day), and even specific tastes ("they love drama"). The team polled mullahs in order to craft the message for maximum impact and enlisted some of them to do the voice-overs, because non-Muslims cannot quote the Koran. And they advised [psychological operations] to drop the part of the campaign that involved handing out copies of the Koran and prayer books. "You can't even touch the Koran if you're not Muslim!" Tracy said, shaking her head in amazement. "It could've been a marketing disaster."[110]

During June 2007, U.S., NATO and Afghan forces conducted Operation Maiwand, a 26-day operation to separate the Taliban from the population. It was "the first opportunity for the HTT to deploy outside the wire for an extended period of time" and turned out to be "a watershed moment for the HTT."[111] Before Operation Maiwand the HTT spent some time with Provincial Reconstruction Teams, and also some time with brigade elements in Gardez and Zormat conducting local operations. Based on these experiences, the HTT was able to put together a game plan for the brigade in Operation Maiwand that, according to the brigade's Fire Support Chief, amounted to a "forward cultural prep of the battle space."[112] The operation proved the value of the HTT to the brigade staff, and also allowed the team to coalesce into a strong single unit.[113]

Meanwhile, the HTS program management team back in the United States was being put to the test along with AF1. After Fondacaro returned from dropping off AF1 in Khost in February 2007, he learned that HTS requirements had suddenly increased exponentially. Some combat leaders had written Operational Needs Statements asking for human terrain teams. These requests for additional military capability coalesced into a single Joint Urgent Operational Needs Statement issued by Central Command in April 2007[114] (the Combined Joint Task Force 82 in Afghanistan signed another one) to support the surge of five brigades to Iraq that President Bush had recently approved.[115] This request for additional capability from Central Command demonstrated a sophisticated understanding of the requirement. It noted that the Human Terrain knowledge base "must be integrated into the theater information architecture to provide two way access both vertically and horizontally," and that HTTs "must be able to reach back to CONUS for supplementary information from subject matter experts outside the area of operations."[116] It also bluntly stated that the "key to success is hiring the right personnel." The HTTs would need individuals with "operational experience" and also "social science and/or regional expertise in the area into which they are being deployed to support the brigade." [117]

HTS staff had been monitoring the progress of CENTCOM's Joint Urgent Operational Needs Statement almost since the inception of the HTS program ten months earlier,[118] and now it had arrived. The CENTCOM Statement was the coalescing of requests from Iraq and Afghanistan theatre commanders. The request from Multi-National Corps-Iraq asked for a preliminary capability of five HTTs for the Multi-National Division in Baghdad to support "surge operations." A follow-on deployment of thirteen HTTs and four HTATs was also requested.[119] The Afghan Statement asked for a total of four teams. In short, the request asked for HTTs for every Army and Marine brigade-sized unit, and each divisional command in Iraq and Afghanistan: twenty-six teams.[120]

Instead of waiting to see how AF1 performed and was received, the HTS management team now had to build a program capable of rapidly fielding numerous teams and making those teams an enduring capability. On April 16, 2007, mere days after the Joint Urgent Operational Needs Statement was delivered, Fondacaro had to brief the committee set up to evaluate and fund urgent requests from the field: the Joint Rapid Acquisition Council. The seven Senior Executive Service civilians and general officers, with two more generals participating on video screens in Iraq and Afghanistan, approved the requirement and suggested initial funding of $16 million, which was eventually increased to $122 million for FY08.[121]

What had been envisioned as a five-team experiment became a shakedown cruise for a program that was headed for rapid expansion. With major

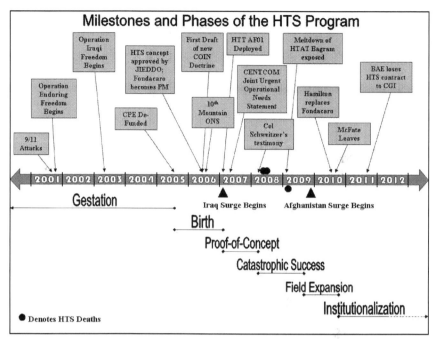

Milestones and Phases of the HTS Program

funding secured, the HTS organization was built up. Two Reachback Research Centers were created and staffed at Ft. Leavenworth and Fort Monroe (which later moved to Newport News); one each for Iraq and Afghanistan. In addition, a new training curriculum for HTT members was created. The top management team also evolved. Fondacaro and McFate remained on the east coast where they could work with the Army's Training and Doctrine Command, and senior officials in the Pentagon and Congress. McFate, as the Senior Social Scientist, was also responsible for certain theoretical and practical classes in the training program.[122] Deputy Program Manager Jim Greer and Chief of Staff (for western HTS operations) Karen Clark were hired at the Ft. Leavenworth training site in Kansas to oversee day-to-day operations and training of the teams.[123]

Up until this point, neither HTS nor AF1 had attracted much attention. But in June, during Operation Maiwand, the media learned of AF1's existence.[124] A *Stars and Stripes* reporter ran across Tracy St. Benoit in the Andar District of Ghazni, and published a flattering report on the encounter on June 28, 2007. In the article a company commander is quoted as saying, "I can't tell you how beneficial they are… They've got Ph.D.s in this stuff. They know all the cultural idiosyncrasies."[125] The *Christian Science Monitor*'s Scott Peterson[126] and *The New York Times*' David Rohde[127] followed up with similar reports from the field. As news of the HTTs existence spread reporters asked to be embedded with AF1. From this initial exposure in the media, attention to HTS and AF1 quickly spread. The budding program was being scrutinized just as it was getting off the ground,[128] which proved to be both an opportunity and a management challenge.

Meanwhile, HTS management sent a twelve-person team to evaluate, continue, and publicize AF1. The team arrived on July 2. In addition to the assessment personnel, it included four replacement team members who were there to observe and learn from the team's experience, and a journalist,[129] Steve Featherstone writing for *Harper's*.[130] Ann Marlowe writing for *National Review* was at FOB Salerno when the team arrived.[131] At the time AF1 was helping prepare for Operation Khyber, which was about to be launched. Due to the team's earlier success in Operation Maiwand, they were relied upon more by the brigade in the planning stage than previously.[132] Some brigade staff saw the assessment team as an inconvenient interruption of their duties. Some members of the AF1 felt the same way about the journalists, considering them part of a marketing campaign imposed on them by HTS management.[133]

Imposition or not, the assessment team's report was positive, indicating the value of the HTT. It listed eleven positive findings in a twelve-page section labeled "HTT Effects on the BCT"[134]:

(1) Decrease in Kinetic Operations
(2) More Effective Courses of Action
(3) Improved Situational Awareness
(4) Improved Ability to Recover from Mistakes
(5) Increased Support for the Host-Nation Government
(6) Improved Intelligence Collection and Analysis
(7) Improved Humanitarian Assistance
(8) Improved Village Assessments
(9) Improved Information Operations
(10) Decrease in Attacks on US Forces
(11) Decrease in Ordinary Crime in 4th BCT [Area Of Responsibility].

The report made twenty-nine recommendations to increase the program's effectiveness, often linking a recommendation with an anecdote, usually a quotation from the brigade commander, or a statement by a brigade combat team staff member.

For example, the fifth recommendation was that "HTTs should avoid embedding with [Tactical Human Intelligence Teams]" because, based on its experience during Operation Maiwand:

It quickly became evident that this created a perception within the local population that the HTT was part of the intelligence staff, thus undermining the credibility of the HTT. The focus of the HTT is on the local population rather than on the 'enemy.'"[135]

The Afghanistan assessment team left Salerno on August 10, 2007.[136] Replacement members for AF1 arrived over the next month or so, completely replacing the original team by the end of September.

The HTS management team's original model for developing HTTs changed with the sudden increase in demand for HTTs. Prior to Central Command's joint urgent operational needs statement, HTS management was focused on the need to create, field and test the experimental team in Afghanistan.[137] This approach was briefed to JIEDDO in June 2006, and was the plan HTS expected to follow throughout its experimental phase. However, after Central Command weighed in with an urgent request for 26 teams, adjustments in everything from recruitment to training and deployment practices had to be made. The HTS Concept of Operations was updated in collaboration with Central Command in April 2007, "reflecting the institutional learning of HTS as the program developed."[138] In essence AF1, which had been hastily assembled and deployed without the benefits of HTS training, became the pre-proof-of-concept team[139] that simply validated the potential contributions an HTT could make. According to one trainee at the time, "we were under the impression if that original team does well, more funding will be approved and then there will be this mad rush to get us out."[140] This in fact happened, and there was little time to analyze the AF1 experience critically. Instead, the replacement team for AF1 and five new teams that were quickly being trained and deployed to Iraq became the proof of concept effort that would guide the emerging HTS program.

In this context, the $20.4M from JIEDDO began to seem inadequate. The HTS program, working through the BAE Systems omnibus contract, was burning through money quickly because in addition to staff salaries it was paying large sums promised to team and reachback center members. Using Defense Department pay scales, Ph.D.-level social scientists on an HTT could envision making as much as $400,000 a year once danger pay and other bonuses for time in-country were added to base pay.[141] The program was also spending money on the residual technological effort mounted by CPE to facilitate access to human terrain data by the military, which under HTS was called "mapping the human terrain" (MAP-HT). The technology was considered of such value that the Office of the Secretary of Defense approved the MAP-HT tool kit as the second highest priority "Joint Capabilities Technology Demonstration" for fiscal year 2007.[142]

The MAP-HT toolkit was designed by Overwatch, a subsidiary of Textron Systems. It was designed to allow for "infrastructure management, web research, social network analysis and real-time collaboration to collect, store, process, analyze, visualize and share green data through all phases of the "civil information management process."[143] The MAP-HT toolkit was chosen over the more popular and widely used ArcGIS toolkit. Fondacaro explained that MAP-HT was selected because it would provide additional capabilities,[144] but cost was an issue as well. The ArcGIS software package for each computer would have cost $8,000, while MAP-HT was designed to be a lower cost solution.[145] In 2010 the MAP-HT team at Overwatch received a program of the year award,[146] but early versions of the product did not work well, and were described by one HTT member as being "literally a door jamb" because it could serve no other useful purpose.[147] The device apparently had power problems and would quickly overheat. When it did turn on, the software was not user-friendly and not compatible with the brigade's computer systems.

Colonel Schweitzer's Testimony

On April 24, 2008, subcommittees of the House Committee on Armed Services and the House Committee on Science and Technology held a joint hearing on "The Role of Social and Behavioral Sciences in National Security." As one attending Congressman noted, it was rare to have a joint committee hearing, and even rarer for Congress to pay attention to the subject of social science on the battlefield.[148] The testimony provided by the commander of the 4th Brigade Combat Team, 82nd Airborne Division, Colonel Martin P. Schweitzer, would become the high watermark for public approval of HTS.[149] Schweitzer explained that the HTT (AF1) played an invaluable role under his command in Khost, Afghanistan:

> HTTs do not merely serve as embedded cultural advisors for [Brigade Combat Team] commanders—but they assist commanders at every level to maneuver formations within tribal communities in such a manner that reduces the threat to all involved parties…. Using HTT capabilities, we reduced kinetic operations by 60 to 70 percent during our 15-month deployment.[150]

Schweitzer's statement on the large drop in kinetic operations made a favorable impression on the congressmen, but it was controversial.[151] Those supportive of the program use it as evidence of the effectiveness of HTTs, while critics regarded the statement as impossible to verify or not a representative estimate of likely HTT effectiveness.[152]

Meanwhile, Featherstone's and Marlowe's articles on the AF1 experience appeared. As if to presage the way opinion would polarize around HTS thereafter, the two journalists took decidedly different points of view. Featherstone's article was largely positive, while Marlowe's was largely negative. This mixed picture was further complicated by the performance of the five teams deployed to Iraq in a rush in late 2007. The performance of the five teams, IZ1 through IZ5, was decidedly mixed. HTS's own internal report, completed in August 2008 but never released,[153] details each team's challenges, problems, and outcomes. While the teams achieved some positive results, every team suffered from interpersonal conflict. In the case of IZ1, the level of conflict was "untenable," so much so that individual members left to work directly with battalions.[154] IZ5 proved to be a complete failure. Even though many positive comments are made about the team, the report acknowledges that "the BCT staff was unable to provide many examples of the HTT contributing to operational outcomes."[155] The team "fractured" and had to be withdrawn from the field. Reportedly the Team Leader openly engaged in "HUMINT collection and target analysis,"[156] while the rest of the team focused on the brigade's reconciliation effort.[157]

Problems related to MAP-HT also reduced team productivity. One team noted that they had been given the suite of software to use, but only the Team Leader had been trained to use any of it. Nor was the toolkit able to be connected to the brigade's network, meaning their work could not be directly fed into the decision making processes. Even then, one team found that the toolkit was irrelevant to the majority of questions and research requested by the brigade.[158]

In short, all the teams were believed to suffer from the same three problems:

(1) For operational reasons, the team members were split up and did not act as a cohesive entity, thus reducing their effectiveness to the brigade;
(2) They suffered from a lack of logistical or technological help from Ft. Leavenworth;
(3) Interpersonal problems plagued their capacity to operate well.[159]

In April 2008, McFarland met with some assessment team members and received an overview of their findings. One member thought the session failed to surface the problems the assessment team had uncovered,[160] but another member of the team thought McFarland was just being given the overview of the findings, and in any case seemed aware of the problems.[161] The actual report may not have stressed the "trenchant and hard-hitting"[162] evaluations of the teams, but neither did it ignore the problems. The report concludes by stating that "multiple programmatic changes are required to HTS recruiting, training, and ethics guidelines in order to allow the teams to fully reach their potential."[163]

One member of the Iraq assessment team particularly impressed Fondacaro: Dr. Janice Laurence. Laurence had a doctorate in organizational psychology, a senior position in the Department of Defense's Office of Personnel and Readiness, and a strong belief in the value of providing sociocultural knowledge to field units. Fondacaro stressed to Laurence that HTS was "mission-oriented," and that the mission was "deploying the Human Terrain Teams." She disagreed, arguing the HTS mission "was to deploy *effective* Human Terrain Teams." Taking this on board, Fondacaro asked Laurence to join HTS and address the team performance problems, which she was willing to do. She was brought into the HTS organization through the BAE contract and from February through April 2008 worked on improving HTS organizational practices, particularly in human resources. She ended up quite critical of BAE hiring practices, observing that BAE made money whether or not the people they recruited were effective. She also noted that HTS did not have a rigorous task analysis of what was required for team success in the field, which presumably made it difficult for BAE to hire to any clear standard. Her views were not well received by BAE or by those responsible for human resource management in TRADOC. After several months she left in frustration and took a position in academia.[164]

HTS management wrestled with these kinds of management and performance issues while remaining committed to fielding HTTs as quickly as possible. Given developments at the strategic level, the emphasis on building operational HTT capacity was understandable. The Pentagon was firmly backing new capabilities for irregular warfare in light of the terrorism threat and developments in Iraq.[165] When General Petraeus took command of Multi-National Force-Iraq (MNF-I) on February 10, 2007, the situation was dire. The level of violence in Iraq was escalating, "with up to 150 corpses being found daily in Baghdad."[166] It is not surprising that Petraeus and his staff wanted HTTs proliferated almost immediately to improve the Army's understanding of the local populations. Petraeus's approach and the importance of HTTs were affirmed by Secretary of Defense Robert Gates in a November 2007 speech at Kansas State University: "What new institutions do we need for this post Cold War world?....in Afghanistan the military has recently brought in professional anthropologists as advisors....And it is having a very real impact....".[167] Even after negative characterizations of the program emerged in the media and on Capitol Hill,

Gates backed the program. In April 2008, he dismissed criticism of the program, saying any missteps were "attendant growing pains"[168] common in new military programs. With Central Command, General Petraeus and Secretary Gates supporting the program, the nascent effort was safe for the time being.

Thus by April 2008, HTS had recorded a number of significant successes. It had successfully deployed the first team, received a massive boost in demand and an attendant increase in funding, and was widely perceived to be directly serving the new counterinsurgency campaign plan in Iraq. It also quickly fielded five new teams, replaced the members of the original AF1, and garnered some positive press. The growing pains acknowledged by Secretary Gates were significant, however. Program recruitment and training were substandard, contributing to poor performance of teams in the field. Moreover, the management and training of the HTTs was not based on any postulated, testable concept of how they could deliver high performance. Yet there was no time to stop and reassess the program's approach; a sense of urgency drove the program forward toward what its leadership would later call, a period of "catastrophic success."[169]

Catastrophic Success

> *"We referred to this 420 percent increase in the number of teams as a*
> *'catastrophic success'..."*[170]
> Dr. Montgomery McFate and Colonel Steve Fondacaro

In retrospect, the April 24, 2008 testimony by Colonel Martin Schweitzer, closely following in the wake of the April 14, 2008, speech by Secretary Gates, was a high-water mark for the HTS program. Even though the teams deployed to Iraq had received negative reviews, the program was set for major expansion with strong support from field commanders and the Secretary of Defense. On May 22, 2008, Congress included a section titled "Increased Use of Social Sciences in Irregular Warfare: Human Terrain Teams" in the FY2009 National Defense Authorization Act, declaring:

A key aspect of DOD's irregular warfare approach is the increased use of Human Terrain Teams. The bill authorizes $90.6 million for funding to meet CENTCOM's requirement for 26 teams and encourages DOD to expand the use of HTTs for other Combatant Commands.[171]

A follow-up Congressional hearing several months later on the importance of language and culture provided additional support for the HTS
program. Andrew Krepinevich, the Director of the Center for Strategic
and Budgetary Assessments Director, called for more programs like HTS
on July 9, 2008:

> In an era dominated by irregular warfare challenges, the United States
> military is more likely to undertake missions requiring irregular war-
> fare capabilities rather than traditional large-scale ground combat op-
> erations. A key component of military readiness will be the ability
> to understand the cultures of, and communicate with, people from
> many regions of the world.[172]

Assessments from such respected authorities on irregular warfare and
defense priorities helped to solidify congressional opinion behind HTS. At
the same hearing, McFate announced that the program would grow from
eleven teams to twenty-four teams by the end of September 2008, indicating
that HTS was making progress toward the congressionally approved fielding
of 26 teams.[173] She explained that the majority of these teams would be deployed to Iraq, but the number of teams in Afghanistan also would increase
to eight. HTS would also have to replace members of existing teams and
staff new ones as well, so there was an even higher requirement for quality
personnel than was immediately apparent.

As it turned out, McFate was overly optimistic about the timeline for
deploying teams. By the end of 2008 only seventeen additional teams had
been sent to Iraq and three additional teams to Afghanistan. This still represented a huge expansion from essentially a standing start (see chart at
right).[174] By the end of fiscal year 2009, the $20.4 million five-team ex-
periment purchased by JIEDDO in 2006 would be allocated more than
$234 million.[175] The program managers would later describe this period
of rapid growth as a catastrophic success.[176] "At the stroke of a pen, the
requirements for HTS went from a 5 team Proof of Concept to 26 team
operational need."[177]

In retrospect the sudden expansion in demand for HTTs seemed like
a pyrrhic victory to HTS program managers. However, at the time it
appeared to be an unqualified validation of the HTS vision, and HTS management continued to promote the program and its expansion. In particular, the advantages of deploying HTTs in peacetime and in advance of
potential military operations was much discussed and promoted with HTS
at this time. A journalist who visited HTS in early October 2008 reported
this optimism, saying HTS staff members believed that "Within the next

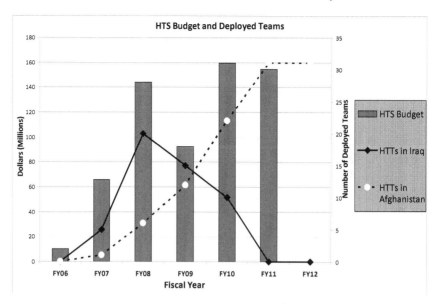

Source: Colonel Steve Fondacaro (ret.), Former HTS Program Manager, email on January 15, 2012; Center for Naval Analyses, Congressionally Directed Assessment of the Human Terrain System, 43.

few years, the number of Human Terrain teams will double around the world, deploying into Africa, Asia and Latin America."[178] Certainly the program was receiving a great deal of attention within the Department of Defense and elsewhere. From their heavy representation schedules at the time, it appears that outreach responsibilities were divided between Fondacaro and McFate. Fondacaro met the increasing demand for program overviews within the Pentagon and to military commands, where he knew the culture and many senior leaders. McFate's audiences were the media, academia, and prospective recruits.[179]

The demand for more teams from the field was an unquestioned success for the program, and outreach was a legitimate management responsibility, particularly as media attention brought mixed reviews of the HTT concept. However, HTS also faced a number of serious, traditional management challenges during this period that also required attention. Most immediately, HTS managers had to recruit, select, train and retain quality personnel, which proved difficult. In 2008 the program had a 30 percent attrition rate representing a loss of $7 million, or approximately 5 percent of the total program cost.[180] Only four percent of total recruits were fired, and it was hard to fail the training course, which had "no tests, no grades, and no measures of performance. Hence it is possible to sit through the course and not get dropped unless the student does something particularly egregious."[181] Thus the overwhelming number of trainees making up the 30 percent attrition rate just quit. Some trainees simply wanted the remuneration and security clearance they received during training and had no intention of actually deploying.[182] A lot of the personnel turbulence, however, was attributed to the inadequacy of the training program, and in particular, the poor relationship between the training and the tasks performed in the field.

Training was a particular challenge because the factors that produced high quality team performance were unknown and not clearly hypothesized for testing. HTS did not adopt a theory of small cross-functional group performance from management and organizational literature. Training therefore involved an element of "trial and error" as the HTS command history notes: "Because the HTTs were experimental, and their future job responsibilities during deployment on a [brigade] staff were unknown, the first iteration of training was based on a 'best guess' about what skills, techniques, and knowledge would actually be required."[183] HTS managers believed each team was a unique entity based on variable personalities and varying relationships with military commanders, something that could not be captured by standard measures of effectiveness:

> [E]very single team was idiosyncratic. It had different individuals, with different personalities, with different backgrounds, different academic training. Then there were the dynamics of any given team. And those teams were not deploying as a group; individual replacements [deployed] over time. At any given time, people were coming and going. And then the Brigades were changing over time and each brigade combat team has a different organizational culture and different missions and different security conditions and economic conditions in the area of operations.[184]

From McFate's point of view effectively evaluating HTT performance first required an understanding of the functions HTT personnel performed, functions that could not be postulated but that had to be validated from field experience.[185] With this objective in mind, HTS had a contractor complete a job analysis on HTT positions by interviewing current and former HTT members. The same contractor also analyzed the HTS recruitment and selection process that Laurence had criticized.[186] In February 2009 the contractor completed both efforts and turned in detailed reports. The reports made recommendations for getting better results within the context of TRADOC's current contract with BAE Systems (e.g. getting BAE to "use structured selection procedures"), and also outlined steps HTS and

TRADOC needed to take to create an effective human resource system for HTTs, such as hiring a Director of Human Resource Development, implementing a personnel tracking system, and creating a performance management system. The job analysis was not followed up with an ongoing effort to interview HTT members on their field experience but it did inform later efforts to reform training.[187]

Meanwhile, HTS management made repeated attempts to adjust the training curriculum based on their impressions of what worked well in the field.[188] Each new training cycle therefore had a different learning program than the one before it and the one after it. Trainees might be asked, for example, to interview random people at a Leavenworth bowling alley, or simulate interviewing members of an Alaskan fishing village.[189] Some trainees believed the instability in the training curriculum also reflected a "contractor mentality," whereby different things were tried to generate the impression of progress without certainty about what actually worked. In reality, the training changes were made not based on increasing knowledge of small cross-functional team performance or feedback on what worked well in the field.[190]

Without the ability to assess what a successful team would look and act like, the training could not be tailored for increasing relevance. Instead, the objectives of the training were more modest:

> With the training, we put together a four month training program, which I thought was pretty good for as rapidly as we had to put it together. It had to meet two requirements. The first one was to take the civilian social scientists and inculcate them into the Army culture and how they do things, so they can be effective downrange. The second was to take the military people, largely uneducated in the social sciences, and give them a largely anthropology overview so they can effectively integrate and support the social scientists downrange.[191]

The emphasis in training was on bridging the cultural gap between social scientists and the military, and HTS training managers believed "the feedback [received] from the units indicated that we probably had the training about right."[192] Those we interviewed, however, almost unanimously criticize the training from this period of the program. For many civilians the training seemed inadequate both in terms of its exposure to military matters and for preparing them for their specific field tasks. One long resignation letter crafted by an HTS recruit mere days before his scheduled deployment lamented that resignation was obligatory because the training left HTT members totally unprepared for fieldwork.[193] Another civilian HTT member found the military aspects of the training lengthy but superficial.[194] Most military trainees we interviewed also considered the training from this period inadequate.

HTS management was aware of the complaints and struggled to deal with the problematic training regime. They awarded Georgia Tech Research Institute (GTRI) an $8M contract on September 30, 2008, to redesign the training curriculum.[195] Fondacaro wanted to replace the BAE subcontractor, Echota, for two reasons. He believed they relied too much on basic training activities run by former Special Forces personnel, and did not focus on the academic topics necessary for field research. In addition, BAE had an established relationship with McFarland, who was trying to exert greater control over the program. Replacing Echota with GTRI would also increase the credibility of the program in the academic community and distance the program from McFarland's influence.[196] However, after months of work, the contract was cancelled, apparently for diverse reasons. McFate believed GTRI had been engaged in a number of unauthorized tasks and that they did not have the knowledge to accomplish the tasks they were assigned.[197] Fondacaro emphasizes that TRADOC required GTRI to increase contract deliverables by almost fifty percent without providing commensurate resources (essentially driving up the contract value from about $8M to $13M). In response, HTS and GTRI "threw up their hands" and terminated the contract.[198] In any case, the redesign of the training curriculum was set back. It would take more than two years before major progress was made on reforming the training program.

The quality of recruits vetted and supplied by BAE also was an issue. The rapid expansion of the program did not allow time for crafting a new contract that would serve HTS to best effect. Instead, HTS was obliged to use the existing omnibus contract TRADOC had with BAE Systems, which was later described as "totally and completely inadequate"[199] by Fondacaro. Recruits explaining the hiring process indicate the standards were flexible, if not incomprehensible. One recruit said his hiring interview was brief: "Can you wear a uniform? Can you carry a weapon? Can you carry 70lbs?"[200] The answer was yes to all three questions, and he was hired without further inquiry concerning his other qualifications relevant to human terrain mapping. Others recruits indicate they were contacted by recruiters who interviewed them over the phone without knowledge of their resume or having checked their references.[201] An April 2008 *Newsweek* article elevated public exposure of the program's recruitment woes when it contended HTS was unable to find enough qualified personnel.[202]

Over the next couple of years anecdotes about recruits unqualified to perform their duties would dog the program. There were also some examples of poor judgment by HTT members that raised questions about hiring practices, the most notorious of which was a report on Pashtun sexuality[203] that alleged widespread pederasty amongst Pashtun men. The reachback center attempted to repress the report, telling its author it would "humiliate"[204] HTS because of its poor methodology and reasoning. Most felt its content was not operationally relevant either.[205] The report became public and received significant media attention.[206] It discredited HTS so badly that the British would not allow HTTs to operate with their forces again until 2010.[207] Another example of poor judgment was a team leader who insisted that he accompany his female team members as they entered the female quarters of an Afghan home. He had to be forcibly restrained by the other military personnel present. The HTT leader's evident lack of appreciation for basic Afghan cultural norms discredited the team with the brigade staff.[208]

Even though by some accounts HTS was accepting questionable personnel, it struggled to fully staff the growing number of HTTs. The 30% drop out rate meant a training cycle had to be about fifty percent larger than absolute demand, but such numbers were difficult to raise and to accommodate. According to an HTS command history, "[a]ny cycle consisting of over thirty-five personnel strained HTS Training's capability to support with classrooms and instructors."[209] Yet, there were forty-seven students in the April 2008 cycle. Subsequent training cycles in the second half of 2008 were too small to yield the 25 people desired for deployment at the end of each cycle (July had 19, August had 22, September had 17). In the last months of 2008, however, class size stabilized with enough recruits to compensate for the average attrition rate without exceeding capacity (October and November classes had 34 recruits each).[210]

Recruiting Class Sizes, 2007-2009	
November 2007	31
2008	
March 2008	34
April 2008	47
July 2008	20
August 2008	19
September 2008	17
October 2008	34
November 2008	34
2009	
February 2009	17
April 2009	31
May 2009	41
June 2009	35
July 2009	46
August 2009	50
September 2009	17
October 2009	21
November 2009	30
December 2009	Null
2010	
February 2010	29
March 2010	21
April 2010	23

These are the number of recruits at the beginning of each training cycle and the month it began. On average, about 30 percent did not graduate, meaning that class size had to be about 32 to generate the desired 25 graduates needed to sustain teams. For each training cycle approximately four candidates would be lost through voluntarily departure; 2 through firing; 2 through failure to qualify; 2 for failure to qualify for a security clearance; and 3 for failing the medical screening.[211] Class size dipped below twenty during the summer of 2008, and again in early 2009 when the shift was made from contractors to Army civilians.

[Note: *The data for this chart were obtained from four semi-annual command histories that were internally created within HTS, as well as the report by CNA Analysis and Solutions.[212] Some interviewees recall different matriculation timelines and class sizes based upon their own experience during training. However, to ensure consistency in how training cycles are dated and counted, we used the HTS and CNA sources rather than individual testimonies.*]

In addition to stabilizing recruit class size, HTS management had to deal with the variations in multiple overlapping training cycles, each with their own training plan, training schedules, classrooms, and instructional support.[213] The training was also complicated by variation in class composition. It was not uncommon to have an incoming class with many more team leaders and research managers than social scientists or human terrain analysts. An uneven distribution made it difficult to assemble teams and have them train with brigades prior to deployment.[214]

HTS also faced a number of challenges at the team level. The individual replacement system adopted by HTS created a cohesion problem within each team. The high dropout rate during training, the poor reenlistment rate after initial deployment, the expanding number of teams, and above all else, the desire to keep a fully staffed team in country at all times to ensure continuity with a brigade, encouraged HTS to feed newly trained recruits to teams individually. Deputy Program Manager Jim Greer, based on his own observations as well as those of colleagues, assessed individuals' strengths and weaknesses throughout the training, and then assigned individuals to specific teams near the end of the training period.[215] The practice continued after Greer's departure until the creation of the Program Manager-Forward position in each theater, and then the team assignments were handled by that person.

For the most part then, the program trained individuals rather than teams. As one HTT member noted, teams always go through "forming, storming and norming"[216] phases, a reference to the popular management dictum that all small groups must get to know their membership, resolve conflicts and adopt behavioral norms that will allow them to be productive. Time was lost during the short nine-month individual rotations as teams constantly "had to go through the formation process again."[217] For example, when Michael Bhatia first arrived at AF1 he "wanted to turn everything on its head."[218] Despite the fact that the team had been performing well before his arrival, Bhatia wanted to change the HTT's processes, and even its mission objectives, which were the prerogative of the team's leader and the brigade commander. To resolve the problem, another team member suggested everyone take the Myers-Briggs personality profile test to better understand how other members perceived things. The team then "sequestered themselves for the better part of two days" and analyzed the results.[219] The resulting revelations allowed team members to better understand their differences, and from then on "it was full steam ahead."[220] However, if a team did not successfully resolve personal conflicts, its effectiveness and its reputation with the brigade could be compromised. The individual replacement system ensured this process occurred in-country, in the full view of the brigade the HTT was supposed to be supporting.

Another concern for team performance was the ongoing tension between the HTTs and the Social Science Research and Analysis program. The Social Science Research and Analysis teams were designed to collect survey data using indigenous locals that could be fed into the HTT system and used to leaven HTT productivity. APTIMA was awarded a $3 million contract for survey research in Afghanistan on July 1, 2008, and Sensor Technologies Inc. was awarded a contract for $22 million on September 28, 2008, for survey research in Iraq.[221] These were large outlays considering each HTT cost about

$2 million per year. The survey data were supposed to benefit HTTs but this did not happen often. According to one member of the Afghan reachback center, few teams contacted the reachback centers that housed the data and were supposed to be the focal point of all research.[222] Some teams did not utilize the reachback center because the quality of its research was suspect,[223] and data from internal command histories indicates that requests per team went down over time.[224] It is possible that the research center output was useful to higher command elements, but in any case, a significant amount of HTS's budget was allocated to conduct survey research that did not directly support HTT field activities.

The reachback centers and survey data were not available to recruits in training either. In 2008 HTS barred trainees from entering the reachback centers. Thus the trainees could not see the survey data or other HTT products in order to develop familiarity with the area where they would be deployed. HTS would later explain it excluded trainees from the centers because they lacked requisite security clearances. For a concept based on open source information, this struck trainees as a strange disqualification. Most of the data was not classified,[225] but program management did not find a way to make the information available to trainees.

Also, after two years of field experience, HTS began to suspect that a five-person team was not large enough. Five people were not enough to cover all the demands that a brigade commander and his staff placed upon a single team. In 2008, HTS projected it would need to begin fielding nine-person teams by mid-2009.[226] A team would then be composed of two Social Scientists, three Human Terrain Analysts and three Research managers, along with the Team Leader. This decision, if implemented, would exacerbate many existing problems: insufficient numbers of trainees, insufficiently qualified trainees, and high team turnover rates that reduced team cohesion.

Finally, HTT staff placement was highly variable, which could delay the ability of the HTTs to make a contribution. Where the "experimental" HTTs could best plug in to a brigade staff was not agreed upon. It was left to each commander to decide whether the HTT would report to him or some staff element, and if the latter, which one. If the HTT was moved from one command element to another, this also could delay the effectiveness of the HTT. Many believed that if the HTT was placed in a position where it appeared to support lethal targeting, as sometimes happened, the effectiveness of the HTTs was undermined.[227] Other HTT members were not bothered by such associations. Indeed, some willingly participated in lethal targeting.[228] Several HTT civilians, however, complained vociferously that their credibility with local Afghans was undermined when they were associated with lethal operations.[229] Later, in March 2009, HTS published a Commanders Guide[230] to assist brigade commanders in Iraq and Afghanistan to better understand how to use the HTTs, but commanders continued to place them at different locations on the staff according to their own preferences.

The management challenges were exacerbated by increasing public criticism and the deaths of several HTT social scientists. A small, vocal, and well-organized group of anthropologists focused their attention on the flaws—real and imagined—of HTS as early as October 2007, when the American Anthropological Association criticized five perceived ethical shortcomings of the Human Terrain System.[231] In May 2008 the Society of Applied Anthropology issued a statement expressing "grave concerns" about the program as well.[232] Even though few anthropologists served on the HTTs (about 6 out of the 49 PhD's hired by HTS as of April 2009 were anthropologists[233]), the negative publicity did not help the program.[234] As *Newsweek* and other prominent national news media were also beginning to level charges against HTS, program management was under increasing pressure to explain the bad press to senior officials. Fondacaro's time in the spring of 2008 increasingly was consumed by preparing for, traveling to, and responding to briefings in which he defended and promoted the rapidly growing program.[235]

The deaths of three HTS social scientists between May 2008 and January 2009 also shocked the program. In addition to the tragic loss of life, the media treated the deaths as prima facie evidence of incompetence. The fatalities repeatedly were used to criticize HTS and its training program.[236] (See shadow box, "When Social Science and War Meet.") Yet interest in the HTT capability remained high and the program was still entertaining opportunities to expand beyond Afghanistan and Iraq to Africa Command, the Pacific Command's Special Operations areas of operation, and to U.S. Forces, Korea.[237] For example, Fondacaro visited the Combined Joint Task Force-Horn of Africa in Djibouti at the invitation of Admiral Green, the task force's commander.[238] HTS management spent several days discussing the task force's requirements and whether the current HTS model could meet those needs before returning to the States via Stuttgart, Germany, where they briefed the newly established Africa Command.[239] Some within the HTS program, perhaps unfairly, thought the trip was an unnecessary expense and distraction at a time when the program needed less promotion and more attention to resolving internal problems.[240] What is clear is that by the end of the summer of 2008 the HTS program was under increasing pressure, with demand for HTTs rising, constraints impeding the quality and quantity of HTTs that could be fielded, and an increasing amount of negative media attention.

When Social Science and War Meet

Human Terrain Teams perform their social science mission in dangerous combat zones. Three deaths in less than a year made that reality abundantly clear. Michael Bhatia was first made aware of the HTS program by Tracy St. Benoit and would be her replacement as the social scientist on AF1. The people he trained with and his eventual teammates recognized his talent.[241] AF1 at the time was operating with a brigade that did not want civilians off base because there had been a recent increase in hostile activity. When an opportunity arose to leave the base, Bhatia strongly urged that he be allowed to go along and this permission was granted.[242] On the last day of the mission, May 7, 2008, he was killed by an IED.[243] The death of Nicole Suveges a month later robbed the program of another great HTT member. Suveges was a doctoral candidate at Johns Hopkins' School of Advanced International Studies. She was assisting a Provincial Reconstruction Team at the District Council building in Sadr City when a bomb exploded killing Suveges and eleven others. In her last email to the HTS management team Suveges wrote, "I love this job!"[244]

The third casualty HTS suffered was particularly shocking. In early November 2008 several members of AF4 were on a foot patrol near the village of Chehi Gazi. "Paula [Loyd] was in the middle of a city that they had been to every day. She was in a twenty minute conversation with a guy [Abdul Salam], discussing the high cost of things and inflation."[245] He grabbed a can of fuel, explained that it used to be twenty cents, but now was a dollar. Then he doused her with the fuel and set it on fire. Salam, who had a history of mental problems, was subdued and held at gunpoint. When Don Ayala, the leader of the three-member subset of AF4 learned that Loyd was seriously injured and might not survive her wounds, he "shot Salam in the head, killing him instantly."[246] Ayala was imprisoned in Afghanistan, convicted of manslaughter in Alexandria, Virginia, and sentenced to time served. Another member of the AF4 sub-team, Clint Cooper, accompanied Loyd to a burn unit in San Antonio, Texas, and then returned to AF4 in early December.[247] Paula Loyd died of her wounds on January 7, 2009.[248]

HTT members have suffered casualties besides these three deaths. A member of AF1 lost an eye after being struck by shrapnel during a mortar attack.[249] Multiple members of an HTT received injuries when an MRAP rolled over.[250] Two members of AF4 were wounded after an IED attack in Kandahar Province.[251] Colonel Hamilton's convoy in Afghanistan was ambushed in 2010,[252] and in Iraq, an HTT member was shot through the shoulder by a sniper.

The tragic deaths and multiple injuries experienced by HTS personnel underscored the obvious fact that HTT members were operating in a dangerous combat zone. U.S. media used the casualties to call attention to criticism of HTS and HTS management challenges. The Washington Post claimed that "the fatal attack on Loyd has aroused new criticism of the program," that "fewer and fewer are signing up" for work like HTS offered, and that, "several of Loyd's colleagues, once as highly motivated as she, say they will never go back."[253]

During this period McFate kept up her outreach efforts to the scientific community and broader public. She pursued the task with energy and what was widely recognized as a flamboyant style. In the last three months of calendar year 2008, Dr. McFate participated in at least 25 outreach events. She was interviewed by *USA Today*, *Military Officer Magazine,* an Italian newsmagazine, *Washington Post Magazine,* *Stars & Stripes,* a reporter from the UAE, and the *Dallas Morning News*. She gave HTS overview briefings to students at George Mason University, University of California Berkeley, and Wayne State University, and was interviewed by researchers at the UK Defense College, Harvard University, and Brown University. She represented HTS at events at the U.S. Pacific Command, Special Operations Command Pacific, Fort Bragg, the GEOINT Summit, Naval Postgraduate School, West Point, National Defense Intelligence College, II Marine Expeditionary Force, the Marine Corps Warfighting Lab, and the Deputy Undersecretary of the Army.[254] McFate was visibly passionate about the program, but some HTS employees began to believe the outreach effort was costing too much for the little good it seemed to achieve.[255]

Others argued that HTS needed to promote the program in order to counteract negative publicity and attract talented recruits. Given the program's unique nature and central importance in the population-centric counterinsurgency strategy, it attracted a lot of attention that had the potential to undermine HTT effectiveness. For example, one story attempted to discredit the HTT concept and undermine a specific team's effectiveness.[256] The article led to one member of the team being investigated by the Army.[257] Even though a significant portion of the article was considered "absurd and obviously untrue to anyone who has spent thirty-six hours in Afghanistan,"[258] the team members and HTS managers had to spend time correcting the record,[259] which led to more publicity and new allegations from the journalist.[260]

The program was controversial from the beginning, but it seemed like the tide of informed opinion was turning against it. The influential magazine *Nature*, for example, reversed its view of HTS. In its July 10, 2008, editorial, *Nature* had asserted that the program could be a win-win effort for Iraqis and Afghans on one side, and the U.S. military on the other.[261] Five months later, *Nature* called for the "swift close" of the program, saying "In theory, it is a good idea....In practice, however, it has been a disaster." *Nature* claimed that "The US Department of Defense's Human Terrain System...is failing on every level," and charged that:

> The immediate problems with the Human Terrain System can be traced to BAE Systems, the military contractor based in Rockville, Maryland, that screens potential employees, [and] then trains those it hires. It has failed in every one of those functions, and army management has failed in its oversight of BAE.[262]

Meanwhile, the program continued to experience difficult internal management challenges. While the trip to Djibouti was taking place, Deputy Program Manager Jim Greer left his position at Ft. Leavenworth for personal reasons, taking a job on the East Coast.[263] In an unusual move, McFarland immediately replaced Greer with Steve Rotkoff, without informing Fondacaro he was doing so. Normally, as HTS' program manager, Fondacaro would have handled hiring his own subordinates.[264] Fondacaro was hired under an Intergovernmental Personnel Agreement, which did not allow him to exercise full management responsibilities. Fondacaro thought the move was motivated by a desire to ensure that the training portion of the HTS program remained firmly under TRADOC control.[265] In any case, the decision seemed to signal declining confidence in HTS management and was resented by HTS management as unwarranted interference.

There were also management challenges in the field. Some teams were performing quite well. In one case, an HTT member learned how to read the signs the Taliban left on the side of the roads to warn local civilians about the presence of a bomb, and consequently could help direct military traffic away from the IED.[266] Another HTT reframed a commander's understanding of local attitudes toward insurgents. Instead of believing the Afghans in the area were passively accepting the insurgents, the team proved the locals were in fact fighting back, just not in an overt way.[267] Yet another HTT helped its brigade understand that it was not the Taliban who were burning down girls schools in its district but rather the locals themselves because they didn't want their women educated. This led the brigade to reconsider how it started development projects in the area.[268] Even while many HTTs were proving productive and useful to commanders, some were failing and notably so.

One of the most visible program failures was the attempt to insert a Human Terrain Analysis Team (HTAT) into Afghanistan in the summer of 2008. The team was located at Bagram Air Base, about a ten-minute walk from AF2. HTAT Bagram was assigned to the division level command of the 101st Air Assault Division. Early in the teams' tour, the team leader left the program and was replaced by the social scientist.[269] For some time he was the only person on the team, and he struggled to find a way to make himself relevant to the Division. Subsequently, he was twice accused of plagiarizing analysis,[270] and later, of alienating HTTs by trying to exert command authority over them.[271] The HTTs in Afghanistan strongly rebuffed his efforts, backed up by their brigade commanders. After his HTAT filled out, internal conflicts and the alienation of the division staff eventually led to the implosion of the team. The team leader, the research manager, and the social scientist for the team were all dismissed from the program in January 2009 for various reasons.[272] One HTT member in Afghanistan at the time believes this event, particularly the plagiarism charges, encouraged HTTs across the theater to distrust HTATs and made them "hesitant to send anything to [the] HTAT."[273]

The demise of this team, and the embarrassing details about the dismissed members' behavior, fueled further criticism of the program. HTS' most vociferous critic, amateur blogger John Stanton, posted numerous blogs condemning HTS for ineptitude. Anyone interested in HTTs could not search the topic on the internet without encountering his denunciation of the program. Stanton had been dismissed as a rumor-monger, someone who simply posted people's complaints without analysis or context. He was considered the "HTS [complaint] box" for those who were fired for incompetence,[274] didn't like the program, or wanted to have their say. The unraveling of the Bagram HTAT offered evidence that the program was, in fact, struggling. Even though the allegations by the HTAT's social scientist promoted in Stanton's blog[275] were later found by Army investigators to be groundless, they made their way to Congress where they further hurt the reputation of the program.[276]

Other HTS teams were having problems as well. In at least three cases in Afghanistan in 2008-2009, HTT members were kicked off of their forward operating bases by the brigade commanders they were supposed to serve. After the publication of AF6's work on Pashtun sexuality the team was left homeless for months, moving between Helmand and Nimroz Provinces with little support from commanders in the field who distanced themselves from the team.[277] After AF8's team leader insisted on trying to enter the female section of an Afghan home, he was expelled from the base and his team lost credibility with the brigade staff.[278] Finally, in September 2009, AF1's team leader behaved erratically in front of the brigade staff and criticized the brigade commander's plans. Fondacaro sent Mike Warren, who had recently been promoted as Program Manager Forward, to fire the team leader. When Mike Warren arrived at FOB Salerno the first thing he was told by the commander, in clear language, was to, "Get this…clown off of my base."[279] These events hurt the reputations and morale of HTTs across Afghanistan, to the point that some HTT members tried to disguise their affiliation with HTS when doing their work.[280]

Another major management challenge during this period of rapid expansion was the transition of HTT members from the contractor agreements they had signed before starting training at Leavenworth to direct employees of the Department of the Army. This transition from contractor to Army civilian status was imposed in January 2009. The proximate cause of the transition was the new Status of Forces Agreement signed with the government of Iraq on December 4, 2008.[281] The Agreement made U.S. contractors liable under Iraqi law, and required them to hand over all personal data to the requisite Iraqi government ministries. It was feared that the sectarian forces that controlled Iraqi government ministries might misuse this information to endanger the lives of the Iraqis working for HTS and their families. In effect, the agreement made it impossible for deployed HTT members to operate as contractors in Iraq. HTS decided it would not treat HTTs in Iraq differently than those deployed to Afghanistan, so every deployed HTS member had to have their status changed.[282]

Many HTT members thought cost savings were the real reason for the decision to transition from contractors to Department of Army civilians.[283] By December 2008, HTS was experiencing financial difficulties because of burgeoning costs, but also because congressional funding requests had been mismanaged. The FY2009 budget dropped to $90.9M from more than $144M for a complicated set of reasons. Congressional staffers were looking for an alternate source of funding for the program, and relying on Pentagon help to do so. The FY2009 figure was a rider on a much larger program bill that was approved by the House, but not the Senate, and there was a short window of opportunity to find an alternate source of funding. When the Army missed the opportunity to appeal the shortfall, it had to find a way to compensate. This ultimately happened but funding was delayed by four months, which caused numerous operational dislocations at a time when the program was under pressure to expand quickly, including the suspension of hiring and training for the January and February classes.[284]

With funding tight and criticism of profligate program spending growing, it would have been difficult to continue paying the large six-figure salaries, particularly as the number of teams had expanded greatly. In any case, the forced transition to Army civilian status led to an exodus of personnel from HTS. The salary reduction alienated many,[285] and others felt the situation was handled unprofessionally by HTS and TRADOC.[286] BAE Systems, which was conducting the recruiting for HTS, tried to emphasize the positive aspects of the change in status. It noted that civil service status "mitigates a number of issues currently detracting from mission execution":

- Medical care will be provided by local military medical services.
- Government term hires are afforded the same protections from prosecution by local national law as are uniformed military personnel.
- Government hires fall under the same legal requirements as uniformed personnel and with the support of the command may carry weapons if approved (see breakout box on HTTs and Weapons below).
- Creates a much closer relationship with the Soldiers in the units we support."[287]

Nevertheless, for many HTT members the change in status meant a pay cut of up to 50 percent, and many promptly quit.[288] Over the first few months of 2009 approximately 30 percent of all HTT personnel left the program,[289] leaving some HTTs and HTATs hollowed out with only one or two members remaining. Looking at the bright side, HTS managers noted that those who remained were the "true believers," but the exodus of experienced HTT members had a major impact. Since the dropout rate in training remained high, and negative publicity was an ongoing challenge as well, generating enough new recruits to fill the gaps was difficult.

Human Terrain Teams and Weapons

Most HTT members now carry weapons, even though doing so raised legal issues and questions about the members' proficiency with the weapons.[290] The practice developed over time and went through several stages; however the final authority always rested with the military units to which the HTTs were assigned. Initially, it was an unregulated decision. Some HTT members agreed with the American Anthropological Association that carrying weapons and dressing in military uniforms would affect their ability to conduct research objectively.[291] One social scientist refused to carry a weapon because "one of the symbols of power is a gun,"[292] and another social scientist signaled her benign, non-military purpose by attaching a stuffed animal to her flak vest: the Mission Monkey.[293] Other members decided to carry weapons and wear

---

military garb, citing the danger associated with operating in a war zone[294] and the fact that Afghans would assume someone not in uniform was a spy.[295] Allowing HTT members to carry weapons was also controversial for safety reasons. According to one HTT member: "The brigade never even looked to see if we had any experience, or if we had training. It was crazy dangerous to be around some of the people on the team when they were armed."[296]

During the expansion of the number of teams into Afghanistan and Iraq in 2008, brigades tended to restrict HTT members carrying weapons, predominantly because HTT personnel were not trained well enough to do so. If a unit allowed HTT members to carry weapons, it often trained them and provided the weapons. In many cases, HTT members went to weapons training classes on their own time while in training at Ft. Leavenworth.[297] Non-US military units rarely allowed HTT members to carry weapons. Finally, after the shift to a new training regime in 2011, HTT members received combat readiness training at Fort Polk, including training on a wide variety of weapons from certified Army trainers.

Some team members continue to believe that if HTT members are armed they can not maintain a benign reputation among Afghans. Others, however, argue that carrying a weapon is essential to the performance of their duties in a country like Afghanistan, which has a "Kalashnikov culture."[298] They do not think bearing arms inclined the Afghans to distrust HTTs. As one HTT member argued, "to talk to a Pashtun male while holding a gun is about as threatening as talking to a Brazilian child while holding a soccer ball."[299] Another HTT member declared that you "have to have your man jewelry in Afghanistan… [I]f you just show up with your notebook and no weapons," he asserted, the Afghans will not treat HTT members with respect.[300] One team leader even believed local Pashtun men approved of a female Pashtun-American HTT member who carried an assault rifle.[301] Similarly, a team leader and social scientist on one of the original Iraq HTTs both stated that having a weapon did not change the "dynamics of interactions with Iraqis or make them feel threatened."[302]

Some HTT members also felt weapons were necessary to work well with the U.S. and allied forces they served. Weapons were a "really easy way to integrate yourselves with the soldiers because you appeared to be less of a liability to them if you are armed."[303] Each HTT member that was given a ride on a convoy meant one less soldier who could cover a sector and fire back against the enemy. Even so, some civilian HTT members felt ill-prepared to deal with combat situations. One HTT member noted "we had to learn maneuver by fire under fire," and in such circumstances "the question—'was [the job] worth it'—comes up really quick."[304]

Also during this period, some sources within the U.S. military began to argue that the money spent on HTS could be spent more wisely on modifications to existing "organic" organizations—such as civil affairs, Special Forces, and psychological operations. The Marines had adamantly refused to endorse the HTS concept. The Marine representative to Pentagon meetings on sociocultural programs, then-Major Ben Connable, criticized the HTS approach in a *Military Review* article in the spring of 2009. Connable had two primary problems with the program. First, he argued that the hundreds of millions of dollars spent on the program could be better spent on training soldiers to productively interact with the same civilian population that the HTS civilian social scientists surveyed. He argued cultural training needed to be built into professional military education and warfighter training; otherwise it is not permanent and typically is dismissed when the war is over. Connable also complained that despite manifest problems with effectiveness, HTS leadership apparently was intent on costly expansion:

> The 15 July [2008] version of the HTS brief proposes growing the terrain teams to 10 members and greatly expanding the reachback cells. Although the cost of the program is classified, it is not difficult to determine the expense of hiring so many contractors, equipping them with computers, deploying them to combat zones, and sustaining the inevitable bureaucratic support staff that will flourish at Fort Leavenworth....We have been at war for eight years. When do the 'quick fix' solutions give way to long-term, doctrinally sound programs? It is time for HTS to give way.[305]

It is true that HTS managers considered expanding the size of HTTs,[306] but in reality, they were in no position to do so; it was enough of a challenge to fill the vacant slots in existing teams and meet the existing deployment schedule. More to the point, HTS management disagreed with Connable that other organic military organizations were capable of providing the sociocultural knowledge that commanders needed; thus expanding those programs would not solve the problem HTS was trying to address. Fondacaro, in response to Connable's critique, cited a Marine regimental commander who testified to him in early 2008 that "what you are doing is unique and needed."[307] The continued utilization of HTTs by Marine units in Iraq and Afghanistan suggests Marine field commanders found HTTs useful.

In summary, the year and a half period from Colonel Schweitzer's ringing endorsement of the HTTs to Congress on April 24, 2008, until the expulsion of AF1's HTT team leader under Colonel Howard on September 8, 2009, was a tumultuous time for the HTS program. At the strategic level the importance of the human terrain had been emphasized by General Petraeus, and then reemphasized by General Stanley McChrystal when the nation's focus shifted from Iraq to the Obama administration's population-centric strategy in Afghanistan. The HTS management team achieved some notable successes during this period of expanding demand for their product. It successfully expanded the use of HTTs beyond the Army to Special Operations Forces, the Marines, and U.S. allies in Afghanistan, and many of these teams were successful. For example, the first team supporting a Canadian brigade in Kandahar was described as a resounding success (see shadow box below on "How Canada Obtained a Human Terrain Team"). When General Petraeus visited the unit the HTT supported, and asked the U.S. battalion commander about his most important assets, the commander replied, "Truthfully? My HTT."[308]

How Canada Obtained a Human Terrain Team

In late 2006 polling showed that only 34 percent of Canadians believed the mission in Afghanistan would be successful.[309] In 2007 Prime Minister Stephen Harper called for an independent panel to study the question of whether Canada should stay committed to the mission. The resultant report, which was released on January 22, 2008, recommended that Canada should remain beyond February 2009, but that its mission should shift from combat to training the Afghan National Security Forces.[310] In response to the report and the likelihood of a Canadian withdrawal from Kandahar Province, a battalion of U.S. troops was attached to the Canadian command. Simultaneously, the Canadian commander "had been following HTS and asked for a team" to help the Task Force understand the population better.[311] The AF4 HTT that had deployed to Kandahar in September 2007 was now shifted to Canadian forces. After that, HTTs were attached to units commanded by other NATO allies: e.g. AF10 to the Germans, AF14 to the French, AF15 to the Spanish and Italians, and AF17 to the Poles.

The creation of the 2008 Human Terrain Team Handbook to help commanders use their HTTs to better effect was another success for the program.[312] The Handbook, released in September 2008, provided basic doctrine for the employment of HTTs in the field. It listed a set of Mission Essential Task Lists for each HTT position, and defined the purpose, functions, and duties, tasks and responsibilities of each team member. It also offered suggestions to commanders on how they could use HTTs, while emphasizing the flexibility commanders had to employ HTTs as they saw fit. Other successes included progress on correcting the poor performance of MAP-HT, the successor to the poorly functioning tool originally developed for JIEDDO to store and display sociocultural "green" data. In October 2008, the U.S. Army Research, Development and Engineering Command's communications-electronics center took over technical management of the tool[313] and began working on a declassified version that would improve the tools functionality.[314]

Nevertheless, these successes were overshadowed by some major challenges. Public criticism of the program had grown significantly, for both understandable and irrelevant reasons; rising costs were a cause for alarm; recruitment and retention of quality personnel were fundamental and continuing problems, and the original timetable for deploying HTTs had to be abandoned. HTS management did not know how to use training or other management tools to ensure more consistent performance by HTTs in the field, some of which were clearly struggling or even failing, and in some cases, egregiously so. Finally, in the face of these management challenges, TRADOC had signaled its intention to exert more control over the HTS program. The management tensions between TRADOC G-2 and HTS had been an ongoing program impediment, but they were about to come to the fore.

Field Expansion during Management Battle

> *"Even with three decades of special [operations] forces under his belt, [Fondacaro said] HTS 'is the hardest thing I've ever done.'"*[315]

The fall of 2009 to the fall of 2010 was a critical year for HTS. General McChrystal was taking command in Afghanistan, intent on implementing a population-centric counterinsurgency campaign plan that required in-depth knowledge of the human terrain to succeed. To meet high expectations for HTTs, HTS leaders had to resolve recruitment and retention problems, find a way to prevent performance disasters that alienated commanders and hurt the program's reputation, make new HTTs consistently capable of good performance, and counter negative publicity. They had to do all this while overseeing the drawdown of HTTs from Iraq, nearly quadrupling the number of teams in Afghanistan from six to twenty-two, and wrestling with TRADOC for management control of the then-$160M per year program. Given the renewed emphasis on human terrain and the controversies over HTS program management during the previous year, there was not much room for missteps.

General McChrystal spent the spring and summer of 2009 developing a new campaign plan for Afghanistan.[316] Strategic assessments were performed to support McChrystal's effort. At one workshop on tribal engagement, an analysis of the HTTs' studies of Pashtun tribes in Afghanistan concluded "the tribal system was weak in most parts of Afghanistan and could not provide alternatives to the Taliban or US control."[317] However, engaging the population remained important. In that regard, workshop participants believed that "Taliban strategists had a better feel for the complex social landscape and the various rival configurations of power in each region" than U.S. and international forces.[318] McChrystal agreed, and his new strategy emphasized the need to correct the situation: "Our strategy cannot be focused on seizing terrain or destroying insurgent forces; our objective must be the population....Gaining [the support of the population] will require a better understanding of the people's choices and needs." McChrystal concluded that "our conventional warfare culture is part of the problem," and that his forces had to "focus on protecting the Afghan people, understanding their environment, and building relationship with them."[319]

Thus when General McChrystal assumed command of International Security Assistance Forces in Afghanistan, all concerned knew that human terrain was the centerpiece of his new plan. What was uncertain was HTS's ability to help deliver the capability that McChrystal needed. Army leaders provided moral support to HTS and tried to help deflect negative publicity. For example, General Ed Cardon, the Deputy Commandant of the U.S. Army Command and General Staff College, said HTTs "give us not only the interrelationships on the ground, but the way that [Afghans] think." He argued that their value "continues to grow," and said he had "a lot of passion toward these small organizations, that have been stood up, as a result of these wars, that are giving us incredible capabilities."[320]

Congress also did its part by increasing funding for the program from $93M to $160M in FY 2010 (see chart at right)[321]—but not without some reservations. Initially it considered reducing funding given the drawdown in Iraq and news of HTS troubles. However, with the effort in Afghanistan picking up, Congress provided the funding, and signaled its concerns in a different manner. In the June 18, 2009, section of the National Defense Authorization Act for FY2010, Congress required the Under Secretary of Defense for Intelligence to commission a study of the management and organization of the HTS and deliver it by March 1, 2010. The House Armed Services Committee cited an abundance of both positive and negative anecdotal evidence surrounding the program as justification for requiring the study.[322]

When the due date for the report arrived almost a year later and was ignored by the Pentagon, Committee staff member Tim McLees held a meeting in the Rayburn Building on March 2 to warn of consequences.[323] He made it clear that if Pentagon officials were hoping the issue would be forgotten, they were wrong.[324] Following the meeting with McLees, the Under Secretary's office quickly contracted out the research to a small group of six analysts at CNA Analysis & Solutions, who finished the study in 90 days.[325]

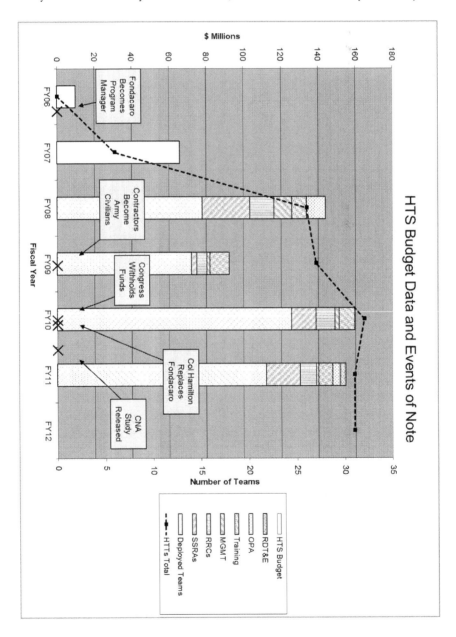

To drive the point home, the House Armed Services Committee inserted language in the May 19, 2010, FY11 Defense Authorization Bill, noting that it was "increasingly concerned that the Army has not paid sufficient attention to addressing certain concerns," and specified that "the bill limits the obligation of funding for HTS" until the Army completed three tasks: (1) submitting the "required assessment of the program," (2) revalidating "all existing operations requirements;" and (3) certifying "Department-level guidelines for the use of social scientists."[326]

While under pressure to assuage congressional concerns, HTS management also had to perform better to meet the expectations of field commanders. It was under pressure to produce more HTTs without the missteps that had previously damaged HTT reputations. Slowly, between July 2009 and December 2010, HTS managed to repopulate and expand the number of HTTs in Afghanistan. There were six teams in place in Afghanistan in May 2009 (AF1 through AF5, plus the HTAT Bagram), and seven teams by mid-November 2009. By December 2009 four additional teams had been deployed: AF7 (with the Marines), AF8, AF9, and a new group to administer and coordinate the teams in country, the Theater Coordination Element. [327] However, the new HTTs were not full teams. "It was onesies and twosies going out and being placeholders. They were not fully established, fully filled-out teams even though on paper it said we had teams in locations."[328] Eight additional teams—AF10 through AF17—were added by the end of March 2010, for a total of eighteen teams.[329] By this time HTT membership numbers had improved, but was still a mixed picture. AF1 through AF5 had an average of 7 members each; AF6 through AF10 had an average of 5 members each; and the brand new teams, AF11 through AF17, had an average of 1.3 members each.[330] HTS envisioned eight more teams—AF19 through AF26—being deployed before the fall of 2010, which would have brought the number of teams to twenty-seven.[331] Ultimately, though, the program could only manage to deploy twenty-two teams during this period.

Besides filling holes on teams and expanding their number, HTTs were appended to increasingly diverse types of military units. In addition to Army brigades, HTTs began working for the Marines, Special Operations Forces, and NATO allies. The first two HTTs to be deployed with Marine units were AF6, assigned to Camp Leatherneck in early 2009, and AF7, assembled by former Marine John Foldberg at Leavenworth, and deployed to Camp Dwyer in Helmand Province in the summer of 2009.[332] For the most part, the HTTs had to figure out the differences in military culture themselves. Foldberg was told before he deployed that "Marines have not bought into HTTs and you need to prove the concept to them."[333] Before deploying, Foldberg had the team practicing self-initiated "Marine culture" classes that helped them to adapt to their non-Army environment.[334]

The first HTT to work for a non-English speaking NATO ally was AF14, attached to the French Task Force Lafayette in Kapisa Province.[335] AF14 was lucky that one member of the team spoke French. Reasoning that English was a NATO official language and thus sufficient,[336] HTS management did not make a priority of sending HTT personnel with relevant foreign language skills to allied units. In many cases, an individual would speak the relevant language of of an ally, but be sent where that language capability was not useful.[337] HTS also gave no specific training to members assigned to allied military units so they would understand differences between U.S. and foreign staff structures.[338] Similarly, HTTs appended to Special Operations Forces were largely left to figure out the best working relationship themselves. Second-tour HTS social scientist, Chris Dixon, developed the relationship between his HTT, AF12, and Special Operations Forces at Bagram Air Base. The Special Operations Forces required each team member to have a previous tour as an HTT member, and to work independently rather than as a team. The HTT members also had to be ready to move anywhere in Afghanistan as a component of a special operations forces team.[339] A second HTT, AF16, would eventually be set up to work directly with other non-U.S. Special Operations Forces.

Through hard work and initiative, the HTTs began to repair some of the damage done to their image during the previous year. For example, one HTT succeeded in getting a brigade to realize that every time it fired artillery into a forest, it not only risked unnecessary collateral damage to people but also to their livelihoods and income. The brigade began to use artillery sparingly in that area after that.[340] It took many such small but successful interventions to establish a positive HTT image with the military commanders and their staffs, but HTT members felt they were making progress. One HTT member operating from Bagram said that when he began his tour, HTT work "was a scandalous thing," but over his time in theater the overall reputation of HTTs improved.[341] Even if progress was being made on correcting some of the worst impressions about HTTs, their performance remained variable. About this time HTS management admitted to internal TRADOC investigators that only about a third of the teams could be judged successful.[342] While HTS management worked to improve the reputation of HTTs and their actual performance, the management battle over control of HTS heated up.

General Martin Dempsey became the new TRADOC commander in December 2008. HTS senior managers heard that before arriving, General Dempsey had counseled McFarland to do more to help HTS become fully functional.[343] Later another member of HTS management said they believed that General Dempsey was not in favor of HTS being part of TRADOC, and that McFarland "had to justify its existence and thus had to become more involved."[344] Fondacaro, for his part, wanted HTS out from under TRADOC and managed either as a joint or interagency program.[345] Whether McFarland was motivated to help HTS improve its functionality or prevent its departure from TRADOC, he got more involved in assessing the program's progress and making decisions without the consent of program management.

To begin, McFarland arranged for outside assessments of HTS without the approval of HTS. In 2008, he requested that three members of the United States Military Academy at West Point faculty along with some of their students assess the program. Although the request was a surprise to HTS management, they supported the study effort. The team traveled to Leavenworth to meet trainees and then went to Iraq to interview brigade commanders and staff members. The West Point team's conclusions encouraged the Army to stay the course and be flexible on performance metrics.[346] Later, in March 2010, McFarland invited Dr. Paul Joseph of Tufts University to review the program. His assessment also provided a wealth of anecdotal evidence on the effectiveness of the teams and their impact on the military decision making process, but he did not recommend specific measures of effectiveness.[347]

Over time McFarland intervened more in program management. HTS management did not like the way the BAE contract was structured. The omnibus contract left them with little say over who was hired. McFarland, however, approved a new multi-million dollar contract with BAE for recruitment of HTT members without HTS approval or input.[348] While sticking with the BAE contract, McFarland moved to improve the quality of HTT personnel by approving detailed job descriptions for each of the roles played by HTT members.[349] The position descriptions were copy and pasted from a standard position description for a member of a Psychological Operations team.[350] These position descriptions were used in the Army's computerized recruiting system, the Defense Civilian Personnel Data System, which applied keywords to online job applications to determine whether or not applicants were qualified for various HTT positions. The result was that the Resumix computer program that matches job classifications to applicants increased the number of rejected applicants. Moreover, the new job classification system disqualified some recruits who were already in training and who were being transitioned to Department of the Army civilian status. HTS considered the job descriptions a disaster, believing they did not come close to accurately describing the desired characteristics of HTT positions. They had to be rewritten five months later by HTS management personnel.[351] The net impact was to reduce the number of personnel HTS could field at a time when they were under pressure to increase the number of HTTs, without any clear improvement in the overall quality of HTT personnel.

Meanwhile HTS was relying on people in the field to make good decisions and prove the worth of HTS, or be relieved from their duties. HTS's response to the HTTs who had performed poorly in the preceding year and helped generate negative publicity was to create Mike Warren's Program Manager Forward position.[352] In the early days of the HTS organization, the Deputy Program Managers, Jim Greer and Steve Rotkoff, acted as the liaison between the teams in the field and HTS. After Rotkoff left the organization in 2009, Fondacaro moved Mike Warren from his position as the AF4 Team Leader to the new position in Kabul to lead the Theater Coordination Element.[353]

In addition to firing ineffective HTT members, Warren worked with senior commanders to ensure them that HTS was monitoring and working to correct any program problems that arose in theater. One of Warren's most important contributions was his work with Major General Michael Flynn, General McChrystal's director of intelligence.[354] In a widely read and influential report published by a Washington think tank in January 2010 entitled, *Fixing Intelligence: A Blueprint for Making Intelligence Relevant in Afghanistan*[355] Flynn took the intelligence community to task for inadequate understanding of the human-socio context in Afghanistan. In this regard, Flynn was a natural ally of the HTS program, and Warren worked to make sure he was pleased with the program's direction. Flynn had complained that the HTTs operated at brigade level, and commanders at higher levels also needed visibility on the sociocultural context of operations. Warren worked to take control of the HTTs and HTATs in Afghanistan and make sure they helped support General McChrystal's new campaign plan.

Having a program management element in theater had other benefits as well. The Theater Coordination Element freed up staff back at Leavenworth to focus on the program rather than the day-to-day problems teams experienced in country. It was also in charge of placing the new recruits on teams. Being closer to the action than the HTS managers back at Leavenworth, Warren could do a better job of matching new members with units where their skills were most useful. However, both the CNA report and interviews with HTT members indicate this did not always occur.[356] Finally, Warren's forward HTS management team could help ensure that Social Science Research and Analysis contractor organizations conducted research that was more useful to commanders and the work of the HTTs.[357]

HTS management also continued to evolve. McFate had moved to Missouri to work on the HTS Operational Planning Team, where she could interact closely with Jeff Bowden who was leading the curriculum review.[358] However, in November 2009 she announced to her colleagues that she was limiting her role at HTS for personal reasons, and lowered her profile in HTS management.[359] Jen Clark was hired as McFate's deputy that same month and located in Newport News rather than Leavenworth. She quickly assumed most of McFate's duties. Several other components of the HTS program management also relocated from Leavenworth to Newport News.[360] When the Deputy Program Manager, Steve Rotkoff, and the Director of Operations, Mark French left the program in 2009, those two positions moved from Fort Leavenworth to Newport News.[361] Karen Clark, the long-serving original chief of staff for HTS operations in the west (i.e. Leavenworth) also left. Scott Mosher and Lieutenant Colonel Mark Bartholf came on to serve as Deputy and Chief of Staff, respectively in November 2009. They were located at Newport News where they "established effective procedures to route directors' issues through [the Chief of Staff] and hence to take the pressure of routine matters off of the [Program Manager]."[362]

As HTS management went through a substantial turnover, it came under increasing scrutiny. In addition to the CNA study mandated by Congress, two TRADOC investigations were initiated. TRADOC began an informal investigation of HTS in March,[363] and that spring TRADOC's Office of Internal Review and Audit Compliance also began an investigation to determine whether adequate contract management and oversight was in place. The investigation concluded that the program suffered from four major problems: "inadequate direct Government oversight, leadership, and management;" "an over reliance on contracted services and on contract vehicles that do not contain necessary standards and mechanisms for contractor accountability;" "growth [that] was and remains too rapid and too large in scope to be properly managed with the existing management structure;" and "inconsistency in the application of and inadequate standards for the selection of team members and in the quality of their preparation."[364]

In other words, and as the CNA report points out, TRADOC's internal review substantiated the long-running HTS management complaints about the BAE contract and recommended that it be rebid. However, it also highlighted program leadership issues arising from "frequent and lengthy absences," "a lack of consistent communication," and the tendency to "devote most...effort to selling the Project at the expense of leadership and effective management." The investigator noted that the latter observation was "made frequently by many interviewees."[365]

In addition, both the CNA and TRADOC investigation highlight the impropriety of contractors and personnel operating under Intergovernmental Personnel Agreements performing inherently governmental functions. As CNA notes, because government hiring is so slow, it is common to use contract personnel extensively when setting up a new program and then transition to government employees. In the case of HTS, and perhaps because of the problems identified in its internal review, TRADOC was slow to create civil service positions to manage the program. Instead, TRADOC retained ostensible responsibility for and control over many HTS management functions.[366]

Tensions between TRADOC and HTS leadership culminated in the decision by McFarland to ask for Fondacaro's resignation on June 10, 2010. When Fondacaro refused to resign, McFarland "gave him 24 hours to turn in his government-issued gear and clear out."[367] There was much speculation about the underlying reasons for the parting of ways. The Army had been willing to discount much of the unwelcome criticism that beleaguered the HTS program, but the growing sense that HTS was being mismanaged, or the mere Congressional interest in this possibility, seemed the proximate cause for Fondacaro's dismissal. Within HTS' small management circle, there was unified support for Fondacaro. Among HTT members more broadly, there was some resentment of the high profile Fondacaro and McFate maintained. Even some strong Fondacaro supporters say his charismatic leadership style was better suited for initiating the program than running it day to day. Fondacaro himself wanted more day-to-day management help, and moved to provide it over the course of the program. He also moved to initiate a training curriculum review designed to get at the heart of the HTT performance problems. However, given his personnel status he needed TRADOC approval for most of these changes, and felt he was blocked by TRADOC from making needed adjustments.

After the leadership change was announced both Fondacaro and TRADOC emphasized their fundamental management differences. McFarland acknowledged "We probably wouldn't be where we are today without him," but added "this is not his program. It is not about any one individual. It's about the young people and the units downrange."[368] Later, McFarland was more direct. He told *Wired's* Spencer Ackerman that Fondacaro was "not the right guy" to institutionalize the program: "Steve did a great job standing up the program," but "his skills are not the right ones to carry it to the next level."[369] Fondacaro believed TRADOC wanted to use funds intended for HTS for other purposes, something he had resisted.[370] He also believed TRADOC was ill-equipped to manage a new program the size and importance of HTS and that it should have been run as a joint or even interagency program: "This kind of work can't be done from inside the institution."[371] In fact, he worried that the innovative program he helped create would be swamped by bureaucracy, becoming "part of the very problem you were set up to address."[372] In an interview Fondacaro used an extended biological metaphor to explain his views:

Inside the monolithic DOD, he says, fresh ideas are treated like a virus that enters the body. First, they send out white blood cells to kill you. If you survive that, you move into a more dangerous, more insidious phase, where DOD stops trying to kill you but now tries to inject you with its DNA—to make you just like them. You have to keep fighting.[373]

In a succinct response that illustrated the different viewpoints both parties held, McFarland said he thought that "at some point, for any program to endure, it has to become part of the system."[374]

From their public comments, it seemed that Fondacaro and TRADOC had fundamentally different approaches to managing the difficult task of providing sociocultural expertise to deployed forces, and eventually the higher headquarters just imposed its view. In reality, the management differences between TRADOC and Fondacaro went deeper and involved numerous program management details.[375] Informally, TRADOC personnel suggest that in his rush to field HTTs, Fondacaro was willing to bend or ignore policy, ethics, and the law. The results of the TRADOC investigations and its rebuttal of the CNA report are not publicly available so there is no way to substantiate such charges. The CNA and TRADOC Internal Review and Audit Compliance results are available, however, and they substantiate Fondacaro's view that some elements of TRADOC responsible for contracting and personnel hiring performed poorly.[376]

In any case, Fondacaro's departed, and McFarland's deputy, Colonel Sharon Hamilton, was tasked to be the interim HTS leader. Later she was named the permanent director.[377] McFate formally left the HTS program in September 2010,[378] and in November Mike Warren resigned after nearly two years in Afghanistan, unhappy with the changes being made in HTS management.[379] Subsequent to Warren's departure the in-country HTS management team's authority was reduced and more decision-making was conducted at Newport News.[380] With Fondacaro, McFate, Clark, Greer, Rotkoff, and Warren all having been replaced, HTS now had a new management staff, and it was firmly under TRADOC control. The new HTS management team assumed control at a precarious time. HTT performance to date had delivered enough value to commanders that demand for the teams remained strong, but it also had been erratic enough to draw the attention of critics and congressional staff. What happened over the next couple of years would determine whether the program survived.

Institutionalization

> *"Problems in human resourcing and support have been evident in HTS for years—and little has been done to address them to date. As a result, we conclude that a more fundamental problem may exist: there may be a lack of TRADOC institutional commitment to making HTS a success."* [381]
>
> CNA Analysis & Solutions

Fondacaro had worried that HTS would become subject to bureaucratic norms that would reduce its effectiveness, but there also was the possibility that the program would be abandoned. There were some indications that the program was on probation. In a March 31, 2010 meeting with reporters, John McHugh, the Secretary of the Army, could not fully endorse the program, saying that he was "neither happy nor unhappy"[382] with HTS. McHugh indicated the Army was unsure about the future of HTS: "Whether it's a long-term solution or one in which we can glean short-term lessons and then move forward is still something we're not able to judge."[383] However, the Army's Deputy Chief of Staff, G-8 (programs), Lieutenant General Robert Lennox, expressed a more positive view of the program. In March he gave a lukewarm assessment to the House Armed Services Committee, saying, "Human Terrain Teams are out there trying to make a difference."[384] In May 2010 he was quoted as saying a TRADOC review team had studied the program and believed that HTS "was an enduring and valuable addition to a command," adding "we found that Human Terrain Teams have been very valuable in theater."[385]

McFarland and his hand-picked director of HTS, Colonel Hamilton, understood the program was on shaky ground. They had to reduce the negative publicity surrounding the program, reassure Congress, and make the case to Army leadership that HTS was an indispensable capability the Army needed for the foreseeable future. The most immediate problem McFarland and Hamilton faced were two ongoing reviews of the HTS program, the *Congressionally Directed Assessment* (henceforth, the CNA report) conducted by the CNA Analysis & Solutions and an internal investigation by TRADOC's own Office of Internal Review and Audit Compliance. The CNA report was a mixed blessing. On the one hand it concluded HTTs were useful to commanders; on the other, it identified problems in HTS management. Since the report focused on HTS management rather than HTT performance, its conclusions were worrisome. The report noted that most people who were interviewed regarded the hiring practices of BAE to be "substandard,"[386] and that this was due to the fact that HTS did not specify clearly enough the qualifications it sought in recruits.[387] The report also cited problems with the management relationship between HTS and TRADOC. It noted TRADOC might need an increase in staff to better handle the task of running HTS, but ultimately concludes that "there may be a lack of TRADOC institutional commitment to making HTS a success," and that HTS might function more efficiently if located elsewhere.[388]

When the first draft of the CNA report was delivered in mid-July 2010, just weeks after Fondacaro's departure, HTS, TRADOC, and the Under Secretary of Defense for Intelligence all challenged its findings. HTS provided a detailed critique of the report's factual errors and methodological flaws, and TRADOC complained that the "report focuses heavily on CONUS operations and support, with limited discussion of the team members and their contributions to tactical units in combat."[389] The Under Secretary of Defense also refused to endorse the report. Over the next two months changes were made to tone down some of the report's criticisms before it was delivered to Congress.

When the report was forwarded to Congress, the Office of the Under Secretary of Defense for Intelligence emphasized that HTTs were having a positive impact:

> The [CNA] report finds, and we do not doubt, that feed-back from unit leaders and staff has confirmed the positive operational impact that effective Human Terrain Teams can have on unit performance in the field.

At the same time, the Under Secretary's office admitted that it needed a performance assessment process that would illuminate the link between program inputs and HTT outputs to guide "continuous program improvement,"[390] and it promised it would not ignore the need for follow-up in this regard:

> This office intends to commit additional resources in FY11 to conducting a follow-on study to resolve the most critical of these differences and assess the progress that has been made as a result of the major HTS program leadership changes, and the institutionalization of the program in the Army base budget.[391]

The report arrived at the House Armed Services Committee in late September 2010, but did not receive focused attention from the Committee and its staff because of the mid-term congressional elections in early November. As a result of the elections, leadership of the committee passed from Democrats to Republicans, and the restructured House Armed Services Committee staff turned their attention to the drafting of a new defense budget. The CNA report had less of an impact in this context. It did not lead to demands for reforms; instead it was used to "unfence" the fifty percent of the HTS funding that the committee was withholding pending the insights into whether HTS improvements would be forthcoming. CNA had concluded some commanders found HTTs useful, some found them moderately helpful, and some found them unhelpful.[392] These findings were sufficiently encouraging for the Committee to continue HTS funding.

The CNA report also provided a glimpse of the earlier TRADOC investigation of the HTS program that revealed concerns about management of the program. Looking at the program prior to May 12, 2010, TRADOC's internal review found that a lack of detail in the initial Performance Work Statement "likely limited competition to the incumbent contractor" (i.e. BAE Systems). It also concluded that contractors played "too prevalent a role in the HTS workplace," performing "inherently government functions" of program management. Finally, it found the program suffered from the inability to assess performance at multiple levels. It lacked the mechanisms and metrics to 1) hold BAE Systems accountable for the performance of its recruiters, instructors, and students; 2) evaluate whether recruits obtained the skills necessary for successful performance in the field; and 3) "to determine the effectiveness or success of the training downrange" where HTTs conducted their work.[393] McFarland defended the contracting with

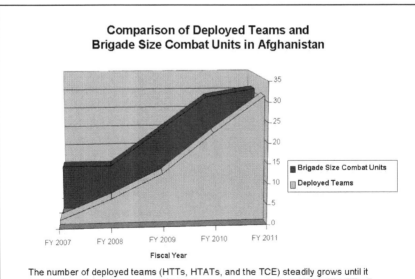

Comparison of Deployed Teams and Brigade Size Combat Units in Afghanistan

Fiscal Year

Brigade Size Combat Units
Deployed Teams

The number of deployed teams (HTTs, HTATs, and the TCE) steadily grows until it eventually matches the number of brigade size combat units in FY2011: 23 HTTs, 7 HTATs and one TCE. HTT data is take from the CNA study and combat unit data is from the Institute for the Study of War, available at: http://www.understandingwar.org/.

BAE, noting: "When you're starting something new and uncertain…you try to make performance work statements broad to give yourself flexibility to change and adjust."[394] The lack of metrics for assessing performance was harder to defend, except by noting that measuring sociocultural knowledge was inherently difficult.[395]

Ultimately HTS was saved from all the criticism it received by one thing: support from field commanders. Even though repeated assessments, internal and external to HTS, concluded that HTTs performance was erratic, there was enough strong and unequivocal support from brigade commanders to keep the program going—especially since senior commanders kept asserting the general importance of human terrain. General McChrystal was replaced by General Petraeus on July 4, 2010. Both men supported the population-centric approach to counterinsurgency, so the command change did not diminish support for HTS among the command staff in Afghanistan. Petraeus did not back away from his long-standing insistence that "the decisive terrain is the human terrain,"[396] either in confirmation hearings or his commander's guidance to his forces issued in August 2010. More importantly for HTS, when a journalist specifically asked him about the HTS program he responded by e-mail saying, "It is working. I hope it's here to stay."[397]

Backing up this assertion, HTS was given a green light from the U.S. Central Command in December 2010 to grow the HTT program from 22 to 31 teams by the summer of 2011. Understandably, Colonel Hamilton cited the decision by the U.S. Central Command as a key indicator of the HTS organization's prospects:

> I use that definitely as a metric for the success of our teams…The fact that Central Command increased the requirement for the number of teams they would like on the ground says a lot. CENTCOM has a limited amount of resources it has been allocated, so any time they request a human terrain team, it's a zero sum, there's something else they cannot request."[398]

HTS management kept working to meet the increased demand for HTTs, and to plug the holes in existing teams. They succeeded.

By March 14, 2011, thirty HTT members were deployed on the nine newest teams, for an average of 3.3 members per team.[399] By September 27, 2011, the number of people on these newest teams had grown to fifty-one individuals, for an average of 5.7 individuals. HTS reached its goal of thirty-one deployed teams in country[400] matching the number of U.S. brigade-sized units in country for the first time (see chart on previous page). Using open-source material and analysis,[401] as well as unclassified material posted on classified networks, we believe that by December 12, 2011, HTS had fielded 31 teams in Afghanistan (a Theater Coordination Element, seven HTATs and twenty-three HTTs), and that almost every single brigade-sized combat unit in Afghanistan had an HTT attached to it as of Spring 2012. Moreover, each of the seven regional commands had an HTAT attached to it. Two HTTs also were attached to Special Operations Forces command elements, and another two were also under the command of Provincial Reconstruction Teams. The Theater Coordination Element, which is attached to ISAF Headquarters, had an HTAT attached to it as well. Only the Air and Space Expeditionary Task Force, the Combined Joint Interagency Task Force, and the NATO Training Mission Afghanistan were without HTTs as of this writing.

HTS management tried to stabilize program effectiveness by establishing "policies and procedures in areas as diverse as ethical certification, human resources, peer product review, civilian evaluations, team product quality control, and individual position qualification."[402] HTS management also adjusted the training program by shortening the time at Leavenworth and increasing the time spent at Fort Polk, Louisiana for combat advisory training (see Appendix One).[403] A greater emphasis was placed on using returning team members to teach the new trainees, a process aided by the transition to Department of Army Civilians. Also, culture and language were approached in a more consistent fashion, incorporating the classes over a longer time period, as opposed to isolated blocks as was done in past versions of the training.[404] The second portion of training at Ft. Polk included certification for "combat lifesaving" and familiarization with basic Army equipment and life. The training includes constant outdoors exposure, qualifying on M4/M9, grenades, night vision driving, obtaining a driver's license for up-armored vehicles, etc.[405] In addition, the increased training for life in a combat environment was expected to make the transition to the field easier for recruits with no military experience. The training at Ft. Leavenworth had consistently been criticized as inadequate, too long, and unfocused, but these reforms helped mute many of those complaints.

In the summer of 2011, McFarland was replaced by Bob Reuss as TRADOC's G2, and as the overseer of the HTS organization. Shortly thereafter TRADOC's contract with BAE Systems was not renewed. Instead the contract went to CGI and its subsidiary Oberon.[406] Fondacaro had criticized the command's relationship with BAE and BAE's performance, claiming that an estimated 30 to 40 percent of the social scientists recruited by BAE had been unqualified:

> Dealing with BAE was extremely difficult… The contractor found it staggeringly difficult to provide 'what I needed in terms of people

and functions' for the program. That is, social scientists who both were physically and intellectually fit to operate in austere conditions in Iraq and Afghanistan, and who were 'flexible enough to work with a military organization.' But BAE struck Fondacaro as 'unwilling to do the hard work in terms of screening and testing, finding the people capable of working with the energy, the intellectual capacity and the competence for this exercise we were about to embark on.' In one case, BAE provided HTS with an octogenarian Iraqi-American for a job translating in Iraq. In another case, it gave HTS an applicant with a warrant out for her arrest for vehicular manslaughter…'Some of the people they were sending me were not up to par, and I had to let them go from the program,' Fondacaro says… 'They like to go out and get the lowest common denominator of people and charge the government an exorbitant price for them.'[407]

Such explicit criticism and the need to demonstrate changes in the midst of intense congressional oversight probably drove the decision to obtain the services of a different contractor.

HTS' approach to outreach also changed dramatically after the departure of Fondacaro and McFate. Far fewer efforts were made to engage the media. Instead, outreach efforts focused on military audiences. Journalists were not encouraged to embed with HTTs. Requests for assistance with external studies of HTS are routinely turned down. TRADOC also avoids publicity and help from interested outside parties. It provided minimal cooperation for the CNA report, and none at all for this and other studies it did not commission.[408] This approach has helped lower the profile of HTTs. The number of news articles about the HTS organization—pro and con—dropped significantly, to a trickle of news stories in the fall of 2011. Still, some media continue to raise questions about HTS. An October 18, 2011, *Nature* article revisited HTS, raising the issue of whether HTS social scientists participated in detainee interrogations.[409]

New HTS management also worked on the post-Afghanistan future of the program. HTS was tasked by the Office of the Under Secretary of Defense for Intelligence to develop an HTS concept of operation to support all combatant commands during peacetime (or Phase 0 as it is called by Pentagon planners).[410] The Undersecretary's office asked HTS to "take a step back … and look ahead and see how [one] could use the capability of Human Terrain System in other combatant commands, not while they're in conflict, but pre-conflict operations."[411] They could "provide information to commanders and staffs to then make decisions so that they understand second- and third-order effects [and] mitigation strategies before we ever get involved in a conflict."[412] Like the *pre-proof-of-concept* team deployed to Khost Province in February 2007, the new generation of HTS would begin with a small experiment. "With help and with funding from USDI…we'll actually do a pilot project with at least one of the combatant commands that would have a small footprint forward and as needed pull from our base of operations additional social scientists, research managers to go forward in support of their operations."[413] The objective is "to demonstrate the HTS Phase 0 capability in FY 2012."[414] Even though combatant commands already have a limited in-house sociocultural capability,[415] HTS management hopes to persuade them that it "can significantly enhance the [combatant command's] current sociocultural capability with the addition of trained personnel, reachback support, and specialized database structure and access to the Cultural Knowledge Consortium."[416]

Toward this end two pilot projects were initiated in 2011 and 2012. HTS deployed a two-person team to U.S. Army Africa elements located in Vincenza, Italy from June 2011 through September 2011. The team members—a leader and a social scientist—maintained a close interaction with the reachback research centers while deployed, and managed to produce 28 reports on multiple countries across the continent. The team reports were designed to support longer-term planning needs rather than immediate operational activities.[417] A second team embedded with Northern Command in April 2012 for a six-month pilot program funded by the Office of the Under Secretary of Defense for Intelligence. Again, the team consisted of a team lead and a social scientist, and this time the team was supported by two specific reachback cell analysts.[418] How well these pilot projects worked out, and what was learned from them is not known. However, at least one managed to catch the attention of news media and received some negative commentary.[419]

Meanwhile, in December 2011, Colonel Hamilton participated in the Special Operations Summit in Tampa, where she described the development of HTTs to work specifically with Special Operations Forces (SOF). She said that in 2011 and 2012 HTS began to work more closely with the SOF community. AF12 and AF16 are now specially designated SOF HTTs and based at Bagram Airfield where the Special Operations Command maintains a large presence. She described the SOF HTTs as a different type of team for a different mission: "They're smaller, they're more mobile, and we have to be able to pick our teams up in support…so what we've developed is a different construct so…we can help go out and assess what would be the most effective location and initial interactions with the village stability operations."[420] Hamilton's presentation suggested HTS will continue to court close cooperation with the U.S. Special Operations Command.

While the future being explored by Hamilton looked hopeful to some, she had a herculean task in the opinion of some former HTS personnel who were disillusioned by their experience in HTS. Some believed the program should be immediately shut down,[421] and others described the program as a failed experiment that hurt careers.[422] A large number of former team members, however, believe that the concept is valid, even if it was poorly executed. They want to see the capability maintained, although better executed and at a lower cost.[423] Some with this opinion returned to academia, in military educational institutions or elsewhere, and others left HTS to work in alternative organizations that are trying to provide sociocultural expertise to the military. There are many to choose from.

Proliferation

> *"There is a growing body of DoD investments in knowledge related to human dynamics…. However, this disparate set of programs shows signs of duplication as well as common shortfalls."*[424]
> Defense Science Board Study on Human Dynamics, 2009

HTTs were one of the earliest and best known attempts by the U.S. military to understand the human terrain in the current conflicts, but not the only one. With national strategy and senior military leaders like Petraeus and McChrystal emphasizing the importance of human terrain, the market for sociocultural advice grew exponentially. Other elements of the Department of Defense and other government agencies created a variety of new organizational constructs for analysis of human terrain (see chart on page 84).[425] Many of these organizations are manned or supported by contractors, who also provide a wide range of sociocultural services to government organizations, particularly training assistance for personnel deploying to Iraq or Afghanistan.

Some military organizations created variations on the HTS model. The Marines, for example, working from a recommendation by a female member of an HTT, pioneered Female Engagement Teams (FETs). Born out of Team Lioness—profiled in the 2008 documentary film, *Lioness*—Female Engagement Teams are comprised of active duty servicewomen who act as cultural liaisons to interact with Afghan females and children. Army Special Operations Command picked up on the concept and now has its own female engagement teams.[426] The teams receive a lot of media attention[427]—mostly positive—but also have critics. Some believe the teams transgress Afghan social norms by "driving around by themselves" in trucks, armed and interacting with women against the wishes of local patriarchs.[428] Others who have been deployed to Afghanistan suggest that "engaging women in Kabul or in Tajik areas can be done without too much risk." Attempting to do the same in the conservative Pashtun regions, however, can be "a major offense to their culture and be seriously counter-productive."[429]

The Pentagon made an attempt to keep track of the proliferating socio-cultural groups. The Defense Intelligence Agency created the Sociocultural Dynamics Working Group, which represented more than 30 organizations.[430] According to a Defense Science Board report, the group "evolved as the mechanism in the defense intelligence community to handle the requirement for integrating foreign population and cultural-focused functional areas crossing multiple organizational boundaries and analytical competencies." In this capacity, the working group was "the key component of the governance structure for developing a solution for managing sociocultural dynamics across the defense intelligence enterprise."[431] The intelligence community, through the Working Group, backed the creation of sociocultural knowledge capability.[432] In April 2007, the Working Group was being led by Patti Morrissey, who was helping HTS coordinate the funding "from JIEDDO...through the Army...and then through TRADOC down to us."[433]

Even though the Working Group was created to manage all the groups providing sociocultural intelligence, it struggled to achieve this. In a brief given by Morrissey in 2008, she admitted that "our efforts are disjointed and we are not maximizing resources."[434] Other observers agree that it was next to impossible to discover just who was doing what in the "human terrain" realm because no one "in DoD really knows what is out there, what has been paid for, and what the capability is because individual organizations tend not to share."[435] The situation is now less chaotic, but there are still diverse programs providing sociocultural analysis in the intelligence community and their future is uncertain.[436]

Programs to provide sociocultural knowledge also arose in other departments and agencies to assist their efforts in the field. For example, the Department of State created District Support Teams,[437] and the National Geospatial-Intelligence Agency created Human Geography Teams. Human terrain teams also are proliferating geographically. U.S. Africa Command, for example, created its own Sociocultural Research and Advisory Teams (SCRATs). The SCRAT program operates with 1-5 person teams on the ground conducting field research, which is fed back to the Social Science Research Branch in Stuttgart, Germany.[438] The purpose of the teams and research center are "to bring sociocultural insights and advice into the decision-making process, plans and engagement strategies in support of AFRICOM and all its constituencies."[439] Like HTS, the products SCRATs produce are intended to be unclassified; unlike HTS, team members are expected to

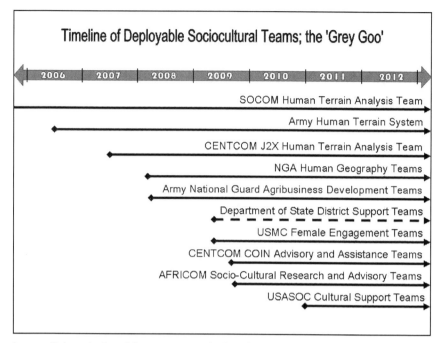

be proficient in local languages and already have regional expertise before deploying.[440] One interesting trait that sets the SCRATs apart from HTS is that they are not confined to a specific area of military operations, but rather form and dissolve based upon individual missions.[441] A second important difference between HTTs and SCRATs is that SCRATs are designed to operate independently from U.S. military forces, while HTTs are designed to deploy in the company of uniformed personnel.[442]

Some U.S. allies also fielded deployable sociocultural advisors. The British formed a Defense Cultural Specialist Unit on April 1, 2010 after a year of planning and preparation.[443] The purpose of their Cultural Advisors is to "help identify and understand issues relating to the local cultural, political, economic, social and historical environment to help commanders make better and more informed decisions."[444] The training regime for each individual is 15 months in length, and it is focused on specific areas. Unlike HTS, recruits are predominantly serving military officers and they are deployed to operate and act as individuals, not as teams.[445]

Canada also has sociocultural teams, called "White Situational Awareness Teams." At the same time that AF4 was deployed to the Canadian area of operations in Kandahar in 2008, Canada began to field these teams. Their purpose was to "map out the movers and shakers of [Kandahar] province and how the relate to each other."[446] The first team included three members of the Canadian Foreign Affairs Department and two intelligence officers of the Canadian armed forces.[447] The Canadian approach thus differs from HTS in that the teams are made up exclusively of uniformed military and government civilian personnel rather than civilian academics or ex-military personnel.

The common element in all these programs is that they provide some form of sociocultural engagement and/or analysis. The burgeoning field of sociocultural advising is now so prominent that some observers refer to it as "grey goo," an unflattering reference from nanotechnology literature that speculates on the possibility of endless, self-replicating miniature machines covering the entire planet in grey, machine goo until all life is extinguished.[448] Even some HTT members who support the HTS mission believe the program has metastasized into a huge field of sociocultural advisory services without much attention to quality:

> [In Afghanistan] it was amazing how many different shops were doing different things. It was always people with kind of an idea, "Hey, we're here to help you understand the local population." Everyone had a statement, but no clue what they were doing. For me, HTS is not exceptional; it's representative of the whole DoD system: getting people out there to be useful because we have [tons] of money to spend.[449]

The availability of resources for sociocultural analysis will no doubt change in the near future. With the drawdown in Iraq completed and the anticipated departure of most U.S. military forces from Afghanistan looming, immediate demand for sociocultural analysis will constrict dramatically. In addition, major cuts in the defense budget are forcing a careful reexamination of all defense programs, especially those perceived as niche capabilities created for recent operations in Afghanistan and Iraq. In fact, there are already indications that the HTS budget will be cut by 40 percent in the next fiscal year.[450]

In this competitive environment, sociocultural training programs and teams must convince senior leaders that they meet enduring requirements and do so efficiently. In the case of HTS, this requires a compelling explanation for past HTT performance variation. Without understanding the origins of past performance variation it will be hard for HTS to convince skeptics that it can manage the program to better, more consistent performance in the future. The brief history of the HTS program offered here makes a contribution to understanding HTS performance in several respects. It makes clear that:

- The Pentagon was slow to stand up a program for providing ground force commanders with sociocultural knowledge,[451] deploying the first HTT more than five years after Operation Enduring Freedom commenced. This delay impaired performance in the field.

- HTS only stood up because another new organization—JIEDDO— had the flexibility to push resources at promising new ideas, and defined its mission broadly to launch a personnel-intensive program in a system that primarily is focused on new technology.

- TRADOC, an organization that does not normally field units, did not have the appropriate management and contract vehicles in place to support such a program. It had trouble meeting the high demand for HTTs from commanders in the field, which further compromised performance.

- Residing in TRADOC should have generated at least one advantage for HTS; it should have made it easier to generate a theory of small cross-functional team performance based on other Army small team lessons learned. This hypothetical advantage never materialized. HTS never had a well-developed theory of HTT performance, much less one tested and validated by field experience, that directly informed its training program or explain to commanders the optimum role for HTTs.

- HTS survived because enough commanders and senior leaders valued the program and its fielded teams.

These insights from the history of the program are helpful but not sufficient for explaining the performance of HTTs. In the following sections we offer a more comprehensive and compelling explanation for HTT performance variation in the field; one that is consistent with the program's rich history, previous studies of HTS, commander assessments and our extensive interview data. We begin by examining the team attributes that affected field performance in the next chapter.

Notes

[1]   Colonel Sharon Hamilton, "HTS Director's Message," *Military Intelligence Professional Bulletin* vol. 37, no. 4 (October-December 2011), A1, A3.

[2]   Institute for Defense Analyses, *Contingency Capabilities: Analysis of Human Terrain Teams in Afghanistan –Draft Final Report*, 4-1.

[3]   Karl Prinslow, former Deputy Director, FMSO, interviewed October 14, 2011.

[4]   Daryl G. Press, *Urban Warfare: Options, Problems and the Future, Conference Summary*, Conference sponsored by the MIT Security Studies Program, Hanscom Air Force Base, Bedford, Massachusetts, U.S.A., May 20, 1998.

[5]   Ibid.

[6]   National Research Council (U.S.), *Experimentation and Rapid Prototyping in Support of Counterterrorism* (Washington, DC: National Academies Press, 2009).

[7]   Ike Skelton and Jim Cooper, "You're Not from around Here, Are You?," *Joint Force Quarterly* 36 (2004), 12.

[8]   Robert H. Scales, Jr., "Culture-Centric Warfare," *Proceedings*, United States Naval Institute vol. 130, iss. 10 (October 2004), 32-36.

[9]   Robert H. Scales, Jr., "Army Transformation: Implications for the Future," Testimony before the House Armed Services Committee, Washington, DC, July 15, 2004.

[10]   Robert H. Scales, Jr., "Clausewitz and World War IV—The Prussian Philosopher's Views Remain Valid on the Psycho-Cultural Battlefield," *Armed Forces Journal* (July 2006), 14.

[11]   Christopher J. Lamb and Evan Munsing, *Secret Weapon: High-value Target Teams as an Organizational Innovation*, Strategic Perspectives, Institute for National Strategic Studies, National Defense University, December 2010, 15-18.

[12]   Henry Kenyon, "Skope Cells Help Dispel Fog of War," *Defense Systems*, May 2, 2011.

[13]   Ibid.

[14]   One source indicates "the first Human Terrain Team, or HTT, had been deployed to Iraq in 2003," but provides no documentation for the assertion. Wahab, *In My Father's Country: An Afghan Woman Defies Her Fate*, 265.

[15]   A good overview of the many unclassified programs relevant to sociocultural knowledge can be found in *Report of the Defense Science Board Task Force on Understanding Human Dynamics*.

[16]   Montgomery McFate, "Anthropology and Counterinsurgency: The Strange Story of their Curious Relationship," *Military Review* (March-April 2005), 24-38.

[17]   Colonel Steve Fondacaro (ret.), Former HTS Program Manager, interviewed October 25, 2011.

[18]   See Iraq Coalition Casualty Count, <http://icasualties.org/Iraq/Fatalities.aspx> for breakdown of numbers of Coalition soldiers killed by IEDs.

[19]   Stephen J. Hedges, "U.S. Battles low-tech threat," *The Washington Times*, October 25, 2004.

[20]   Nancy Chesser, interviewed April 10, 2012

[21]   Geographic information system technology captures, stores, analyzes, and displays geographic data such as terrain population characteristics and man-made objects such as roads and buildings, in ways that reveal relationships, patterns, and trends in the form of maps, globes, reports, and charts. See <www.gis.com/content/what-gis>.

[22]   Social Network Analysis was initially created by social anthropologists as a tool to capture relations within a human society. See David Knoke and Song Yang, *Social Network Analysis*, 2nd Ed. (Los Angeles, CA: Sage, 2008). See Roger Mac Ginty, "Social Network Analysis and Counterinsurgency: a Counterproductive Strategy," *Critical Studies on Terrorism* iss. 3, no. 2, (2010), 209-226, for a critique of its use in current military operations. For more on mapping social networks see also the shadow box on "Defining Sociocultural Knowledge in the U.S. Military."

[23]   Cabayan has advocated the use of interagency "multi-disciplinary teams" employing "agile, federated approaches" to "do a better job of anticipating," predicting, and mitigating the effects of rare events such as IED and WMD attacks. Hriar Cabayan, 'Executive Summary,' in *Anticipating Rare Events: Can Acts of Terror, Use of Weapons of Mass Destruction or Other High Profile Acts Be Anticipated?: A Scientific Perspective on Problems, Pitfalls and Prospective Solutions*, Nancy Chesser, ed., *Topical Strategic Multi-Layer Assessment (SMA) Multi-Agency/Multi-Disciplinary White*

Papers in Support of Counter-Terrorism and Counter-WMD, November 2008, 2.

[24] Montgomery McFate, "Iraq: The Social Context of IEDs," *Military Review* (May-June 2005), 39.

[25] Nancy Chesser, interviewed April 10, 2012

[26] Nancy Chesser and S. K. Numrich, *CPE and Dynamic CPE (Cultural Preparation of the Environment)*, PowerPoint, October 4, 2005.

[27] Ibid.

[28] Montgomery McFate and Steve Fondacaro, "Reflections on the Human Terrain System During the First 4 Years," *PRISM* 2, no. 4 (2011), 67.

[29] Montgomery McFate, "Anthropology and Counterinsurgency: The Strange Story of Their Curious Relationship," *Military Review* (March-April 2005), 24-38.

[30] Montgomery McFate and Andrea Jackson, "An Organizational Solution for DOD's Cultural Knowledge Needs," *Military Review* (July-August 2005), 18-21.

[31] Ibid., 21.

[32] Colonel Steve Fondacaro (ret.), Former HTS Program Manager, email on April 30, 2012.

[33] Ibid.

[34] Ibid.

[35] Interviewee 29, October 19, 2011.

[36] McFate, Fondacaro, "Reflections on the Human Terrain System During the First 4 Years," 66.

[37] Karl Prinslow, former Deputy Director, FMSO, interviewed October 14, 2011.

[38] See Lester Grau, "Bashing the Laser Range Finder With a Rock," *Military Review* iss. 77, no. 3 (May-June 1997), 42-48; Lester Grau and Jacob Kipp, "Urban Combat: Confronting the Specter," *Military Review* iss. 79, no. 4 (July-August 1999), 9-17.

[39] Karl Prinslow, former Deputy Director, FMSO, interviewed October 14, 2011.

[40] Ibid.

[41] Interviewee 21, October 13, 2011; Karl Prinslow, former Deputy Director, FMSO, interviewed October 14, 2011; Nancy Chesser, interviewed April 10, 2012

[42] Karl Prinslow, former Deputy Director, FMSO, interviewed October 14, 2011. McFate and Jackson focused on an organizational solution that would operate from the continental United States, while Smith and FMSO advocated teams in the theater.

[43] Karl Prinslow, former Deputy Director, FMSO, interviewed October 14, 2011.

[44] "Gen. Montgomery Meigs Appointed to Lead Joint IED Effort," *The America's Intelligence Wire*, December 6, 2005; Deputy Secretary of Defense Memorandum, *Establishment of the Joint Improved Explosive Device Defeat Organization (JIEDDO)*, January 18, 2006, Department of Defense Directive 2000.19E, February 14, 2006.

[45] Colonel Steve Fondacaro (ret.), Former HTS Program Manager, interviewed November 1, 2011.

[46] Noah Shachtman, "Army Anthropologist's Controversial Culture Clash," *Wired: Danger Room*, September 23, 2008.

[47] Ibid.

[48] Colonel Steve Fondacaro (ret.), Former HTS Program Manager, interviewed November 1, 2011.

[49] Nancy Chesser and S. K. Numrich, *CPE and Dynamic CPE (Cultural Preparation of the Environment)*, PowerPoint, October 4, 2005.

[50] Nancy Chesser, interviewed April 10, 2012.

[51] Montgomery C. Meigs, *Memorandum For Record, Subject: Authorization to Released Joint IED Defeat Organization Funds for Human Terrain System*, Joint IED Defeat Organization, June 12, 2006.

[52] Nancy Chesser, *Cultural Preparation of the Environment (CPE)*, Brief given to the Joint IED

Defeat Task Force, PowerPoint, October 25, 2005.

[53] Maxie McFarland, "Military Cultural Education," *Military Review* (March-April 2006), 62-69.

[54] The Joint IED Defeat Task Force became the Joint IED Defeat Organization on February 14, 2006.

[55] Colonel Steve Fondacaro (ret.), Former HTS Program Manager, email on April 30, 2012.

[56] Kipp, Grau, Prinslow, and Smith, "The Human Terrain System: A CORDS for the 21st Century," 8-9.

[57] Ibid., Footnote 2, 15. The article credits McFate and Jackson as the originators of the broad concept for the program, but Smith as the one who did "most" of the practical work to make that vision a reality.

[58] Karl Prinslow, former Deputy Director, FMSO, interviewed October 14, 2011.

[59] Ibid.

[60] Kipp, Grau, Prinslow, Smith, "The Human Terrain System: A CORDS for the 21st Century," 8-15.

[61] Ibid. One long-time observer of HTS believes that the HTS design was "hopelessly flawed at its roots" because of "scarce resources." The initial design presumed the availability of more than 200 qualified, interested, and deployable social scientists at all times, a number that the interviewee believes the program was not able to reach. Interviewee 4, September 21, 2011.

[62] McFate, Fondacaro, "Reflections on the Human Terrain System During the First 4 Years," 67. There is some disagreement on when the 10th Mountain Division asked for the capability. The FMSO team says late-2005, while the 2008 HTS Yearly Report suggests the event took place in August 2006. It may be that FMSO obtained an early version of the needs statement and HTS worked from a later, formally approved version of the document. In any case, both FMSO and HTS note the importance of this initial operational needs statement for their initiatives. Karl Prinslow, former Deputy Director, FMSO, email on April 23, 2012; Colonel Steve Fondacaro (ret.), Former HTS Program Manager, email on April 30, 2012; Human Terrain System Program Development Team, *Human Terrain System Yearly Report*, Prepared for US Army Training and Doctrine Command, August 2008.

[63] Karl Prinslow, former Deputy Director, FMSO, interviewed October 14, 2011.

[64] Kipp, Grau, Prinslow, Smith, "The Human Terrain System: A CORDS for the 21st Century," 8-15. For more on the proposed deployment schedule as HTS became a stand-alone program, see Steve Fondacaro, *Providing Operationally Useful Information on the Human Terrain to the Theater*, PowerPoint, Draft, Social Science Operational Analysis Task 2.5.6, Brief given to The Office of the Under Secretary of Defense for Intelligence—Task Lead, August 7, 2006.

[65] Ibid. This design was previously conceptualized by McFate, Jackson and Smith on a drawing board at Johns Hopkins SAIS. Dr. Montgomery McFate, former HTS Senior Social Scientist, email on July 20, 2012.

[66] Britt Damon, Research Manager, AF1, interviewed January 4, 2011.

[67] Colonel Steve Fondacaro (ret.), Former HTS Program Manager, email on April 30, 2012.

[68] Colonel Steve Fondacaro (ret.), Former HTS Program Manager, interviewed November 1, 2011; Major Grant S. Fawcett, "Cultural Understanding in Counterinsurgency: Analysis of the Human Terrain System," *Monograph*, Fort Leavenworth, Kansas, School of Advanced Military Studies, United States Army Command and General Staff College, May 21, 2009, 24.

[69] "Authorization to Release Joint IED Defeat Organization Funds for Human Terrain System," Memorandum for Record, signed by JIEDDO Director, Montgomery C. Meigs, June 12, 2006.

[70] McFate, Fondacaro, "Reflections on the Human Terrain System During the First 4 Years," 67.

[71]   *Human Terrain System (HTS) Status Report*, Draft, June 28, 2006. This recommended management structure never materialized.

[72]   Of the many individuals that began FMSO training in the spring and summer of 2006 only Major Robert Holbert, Sergeant Britt Damon and Captain Roya Sharifsoltani eventually would be deployed as members of an HTT.

[73]   Major Robert Holbert, Research Manager, AF1, interviewed December 12, 2011.

[74]   According to current members of TRADOC, FMSO was never the logical place to set up an HTS-like organization since FMSO concentrates on foreign militaries, not indigenous populations. Similar reasoning could be applied to question whether TRADOC is any better suited to manage HTS. *TRADOC G2 Comments on the National Defense University paper titled "Human Terrain Team Performance: An Explanation," August 24, 2012*, Passed to NDU team, November 15, 2012, 4.

[75]   TRADOC Deputy Chief of Staff for Intelligence, and the Foreign Military Studies Office, *Human Terrain System Program for III Corps Pre-Deployment Conference, 11-13 July 2006*, PowerPoint, undated.

[76]   Ibid.

[77]   Colonel Steve Fondacaro (ret.), Former HTS Program Manager, email on April 30, 2012.

[78]   Ibid.

[79]   Joanne Kimberlin "Part I: New Weapon in an Old War in Afghanistan," *The Virginian-Pilot*, September 29, 2010.

[80]   Colonel Steve Fondacaro (ret.), Former HTS Program Manager, email on April 30, 2012.

[81]   Interviewee 21, October 13, 2011.

[82]   Karl Prinslow, "The World Basic Information Library Program," *Military Intelligence* iss. 31, no. 4, (October-December 2005), 51-53; Dr. Jacob W. Kipp, "FMSO-JRIC and Open Source Intelligence: Speaking Prose in a World of Verse," *Military Intelligence* iss. 31, no. 4, (October-December 2005), 47. The program's "founding premise was to better engage and utilize the civilian acquired skills of members of the Reserve Component (RC), especially members of the Individual Ready Reserve (IRR), by engaging them regardless of branch of service, military skills, rank or specialty, in research that supports the intelligence community requirements."

[83]   Karl Prinslow, former Deputy Director, FMSO, interviewed October 14, 2011.

[84]   Colonel Steve Fondacaro (ret.), Former HTS Program Manager, email on April 30, 2012. Early on, HTS collaborated with the Department of State's Human Information Cell to include joint trips in-theatre.

[85]   Colonel Steve Fondacaro (ret.), Former HTS Program Manager, interviewed October 25, 2011. Fondacaro and McFate preferred that HTS program be administered as a joint program, and hoped it would eventually become an interagency one. They pushed it forward as a joint effort, but the Marines had reservations and demanded that they be removed from sponsorship. Never achieving DOD-level joint status, they could not take the next step to interagency sponsorship.

[86]   Excel Spreadsheet of Tasks Constructed by Sarah Brown, August 14, 2006.

[87]   Unclassified excerpt from Briefing, *Irregular Warfare Quadrennial Defense Review Execution Roadmap Executive Committee Meeting*, secret unless otherwise marked, November 9, 2006.

[88]   Steve Fondacaro, *Cultural Operational Research/Human Terrain System*, PowerPoint, Joint IED Defeat Organization (JIEDDO), August 20, 2006.

[89]   II MEF and III Corps wanted to host HTTs during their upcoming deployments to Iraq; indeed Fondacaro notes that II MEF "actually wanted all five of our teams." Colonel Steve Fondacaro (ret.), Former HTS Program Manager, email on April 30, 2012.

[90]   Colonel Steve Fondacaro (ret.), Former HTS Program Manager, email on April 30, 2012.

[91]   Ibid.

[92] Colonel Steve Fondacaro (ret.), Former HTS Program Manager, interviewed November 1, 2011.

[93] Major Robert Holbert, Research Manager, AF1, interviewed December 12, 2011.

[94] Ibid.

[95] *The Human Terrain System Yearly Report 2007-2008*, 8, 10.

[96] Kristina Bjoran, "The Adventures of the Real Life Lara Croft in Afghanistan, and the Future of Smart Mobile GIS," *Geospatial Data Center*, Massachusetts Institute of Technology, November 10, 2010.

[97] Professor Thomas H. Johnson, Naval Postgraduate School, interviewed March 6, 2012.

[98] Laura L. Wynn, "The Story Behind an HTS Picture," *Laura L. Wynn*, September 28, 2008.

[99] David Glenn, "Anthropologists in a War Zone: Scholars Debate Their Role," *The Chronicle of Higher Education*, November 30, 2007.

[100] Steve Featherstone, "Human Quicksand for the U.S. Army, a crash course in Cultural Studies," *Harpers*, September 2008.

[101] Joint IED Defeat Organization (JIEDDO), *Cultural Operational Research/Human Terrain System (COR/HTS)*, PowerPoint, June 6, 2006.

[102] Colonel Steve Fondacaro (ret.), Former HTS Program Manager, interviewed November 1, 2011.

[103] Dr. Montgomery McFate, former HTS Senior Social Scientist, interviewed October 3, 2011; Colonel Steve Fondacaro (ret.), Former HTS Program Manager, interviewed October 25, 2011.

[104] *The Human Terrain System Yearly Report 2007-2008*, 5-7.

[105] Team Leader, AF1, interviewed November 1, 2011.

[106] Featherstone, "Human Quicksand for the U.S. Army, a Crash Course in Cultural Studies"; Interviewee 56, November 29, 2011; Interviewee 21, October 31, 2011.

[107] Interviewee 56, email on April 25, 2012.

[108] Matthew Hansen, "For Afghanistan: Brains, Not Bombs," *Omaha World-Herald*, September 11, 2009.

[109] HTT member, Afghanistan, interviewed October 4, 2011.

[110] Featherstone, "Human Quicksand for the U.S. Army, a Crash Course in Cultural Studies." Whether a non-Muslim can touch the Koran is disputed. It is agreed that only the "clean" may touch the Koran, but the definition of clean is a matter of dispute among Muslim scholars. See http://islam.about.com/od/quran/f/mushaf.htm.

[111] *The Human Terrain System Yearly Report 2007-2008*, 58.

[112] Ibid., 57.

[113] HTT member, Afghanistan, interviewed October 4, 2011.

[114] The Joint Urgent Operational Needs Statements from U.S. Central Command and Combined Joint Task Force 82 in Afghanistan are classified. Only the one from the Multi-National Corps—Iraq is unclassified. *Joint Urgent Operational Need Statement for Human Terrain Team Support to OIF Surge*, Lieutenant General Raymond T. Odierno, USA, Multi-National Force-Iraq, APO AE 09342-2001, April 7, 2007.

[115] LtCol Steve Chill, "One of the Eggs in the Joint Force Basket: HTS in Iraq/Afghanistan and Beyond," *Military Intelligence Professional Bulletin* vol. 37, no. 4 (October-December 2011),11.

[116] *Joint Urgent Operational Need Statement for Human Terrain Team Support to OIF Surge*, Lieutenant General Raymond T. Odierno, USA, Multi-National Force-Iraq, APO AE 09342-2001, April 7, 2007.

[117] Ibid.

[118] *Human Terrain System (HTS) Status Report*, Draft, July 18, 2006.

[119]   *Joint Urgent Operational Need Statement for Human Terrain Team Support to OIF Surge*, Lieutenant General Raymond T. Odierno, USA, Multi-National Force-Iraq, APO AE 09342-2001, April 7, 2007.

[120]   Colonel Steve Fondacaro (ret.), Former HTS Program Manager, interviewed November 1, 2011.

[121]   Colonel Steve Fondacaro (ret.), Former HTS Program Manager, interviewed October 25, 2011.

[122]   Dr. Montgomery McFate, former HTS Senior Social Scientist, email on July 27, 2012.

[123]   Jim Greer, former Deputy Program Manager, HTS, interviewed October 26, 2011.

[124]   Interviewee 21, October 31, 2011

[125]   Monte Morin "Cultural Advisers Give U.S. Teams an Edge," *Stars and Stripes*, June 28, 2007.

[126]   Scott Peterson, "US Army's Strategy in Afghanistan: Better Anthropology," *The Christian Science Monitor*, September 7, 2007, W11.

[127]   David Rohde, "Army Enlists Anthropology in War Zones," *The New York Times*, October 5, 2007.

[128]   Evan R. Goldstein "Professors on the Battlefield," *The Wall Street Journal*, August 17, 2007; Scott Peterson, "US Army's Strategy in Afghanistan: Better Anthropology," *The Christian Science Monitor*," September 7, 2007; Marina Malenic, "Pentagon Approves Funding for 'Human Terrain' Field Research," *Inside the Army* vol. 19, no. 39 (October 1, 2007); Montgomery McFate, David Price, Col. John Agoglia, Lt. Col. Edward Villacres, David Rohde, "Anthropologists and War," *The Diane Rehm Show*, Guest Host: Susan Page, National Public Radio, October 10, 2007; David Glenn, "Former Human Terrain System Participant Describes Program in Disarray," *The Chronicle of Higher Education*, December 5, 2007; Ann Marlowe, "Anthropology Goes to War: There Are Some Things The Army Needs In Afghanistan, But More Academics Are Not At The Top Of The List," *The Weekly Standard* vol. 13, no. 11, November 26, 2007; Noah Shachtman, "Army Social Scientists Calm Afghanistan, Make Enemies at Home," *Wired: Danger Room*, November 29, 2007; Sarah Sewall and Montgomery McFate, "A Discussion About Counterinsurgency," *Charlie Rose*, December 24, 2007.

[129]   *The Human Terrain System Yearly Report 2007-2008*, 74.

[130]   Featherstone, "Human Quicksand for the U.S. Army, a Crash Course in Cultural Studies."

[131]   Ann Marlowe, "Anthropology Goes to War: There Are Some Things The Army Needs In Afghanistan, But More Academics Are Not At The Top Of The List," *The Weekly Standard* vol. 13, no. 11 (November 26, 2007).

[132]   Britt Damon, Research Manager, AF1, interviewed January 4, 2011.

[133]   Interviewee 29, October 19, 2011; Team Leader, AF1, interviewed November 1, 2011.

[134]   *The Human Terrain System Yearly Report 2007-2008*, 44-55.

[135]   Ibid., 74.

[136]   Ibid., 23.

[137]   Ibid., 5-7.

[138]   Ibid., 5; Colonel Steve Fondacaro (ret.), Former HTS Program Manager, email on April 30, 2012.

[139]   Zenia H. Tompkins, former HTS trainee, interviewed December 9, 2011.

[140]   Ibid.

[141]   Noah Shachtman, "Army Social Scientists Calm Afghanistan, Make Enemies at Home," *Wired: Danger Room*, November 29, 2007. This figure is supported by the CNA report, which found "a senior social scientist with 1 year of field research experience could make $390K-$420K with differentials and overtime." CNA Analysis & Solutions, *Congressionally Directed Assessment of the Human Terrain System*, 88.

[142] Fondacaro and Central Command's J8 collaborated on sponsoring the JCTD. Colonel Steve Fondacaro (ret.), Former HTS Program Manager, email on April 30, 2012; Colonel Mark Bartholf, "The Requirement for Sociocultural Understanding in Full Spectrum Operations," *Military Intelligence Professional Bulletin* vol. 37, no. 4 (October-December 2011), 6.

[143] "MAP-HT: Mapping the Human Terrain" *Overwatch*, website.

[144] Colonel Steve Fondacaro (ret.), Former HTS Program Manager, email on April 30, 2012.

[145] Nancy Chesser, interviewed April 10, 2012.

[146] "MapHT—2010 JCTD Team of the Year," *Overwatch*, website.

[147] Major Robert Holbert, Research Manager, AF1, interviewed December 12, 2011.

[148] Brian Baird, Former U.S. Congressman, interviewed December 15, 2011.

[149] Colonel Schweitzer was promoted to Brigadier General on July 14, 2011.

[150] Joint Hearing of the Subcommittee on Terrorism and Unconventional Threats and Capabilities of the House Committee on Armed Services and the Subcommittee on Research and Science Education of the House Committee on Science and Technology; Subject: The Role of Social and Behavioral Sciences in National Security, April 24, 2008.

[151] Brian Baird, Former U.S. Congressman, interviewed December 15, 2011.

[152] David Price, "The Press and Human Terrain Systems—Counterinsurgency's Free Ride," Zero Anthropology, Maximilian Forte, May 29, 2009.

[153] The assessment was conducted in February 2008. McFate wrote the report while she still worked for the Institute for Defense Analyses. In an interview with *Inside the Pentagon*, Montgomery McFate said the report would be released in June 2008. Fawzia Sheikh, "Report on Anthropologists in Theater Tentatively Pegged for June," *Inside the Pentagon*, May 29, 2008.

[154] *The Human Terrain System Yearly Report 2007-2008*, 155.

[155] Ibid., 221.

[156] Ibid., 232-233. The report goes on to state that the Team Leader "was engaged in activities that violated the HTS mission. Many of the Team Leader's activities appeared to skirt various 'red lines' that the HTS program has tried to establish in order to avoid the involvement of HTTs in lethal targeting…." *The Human Terrain System Yearly Report 2007-2008*, 236.

[157] *The Human Terrain System Yearly Report 2007-2008*, 221.

[158] Ibid., 208.

[159] Ibid., 237.

[160] Civilian Joint Service Representative, interviewed February 9, 2012.

[161] Member of the HTS assessment team that visited Iraq in 2008, interviewed May 29, 2012.

[162] Civilian Joint Service Representative, interviewed February 9, 2012.

[163] *The Human Terrain System Yearly Report 2007-2008*, 237.

[164] She teaches at Temple University, where she has been an enthusiastic supporter for the HTS organization from a distance. She is currently co-editing a book on the Human Terrain System with Dr. McFate. Dr. Janice Laurence, interviewed June 12, 2012.

[165] A Pentagon briefing from this time period identifies the policy, doctrine and operational experiences propelling HTS forward: FM 3-24, chapter 3: Sociocultural Intelligence preparation of the battlefield for counterinsurgency; Irregular Warfare QDR Roadmap: DODD 3000.05, and the "GWOT." Operational experiences included those related in the joint urgent operational needs statements that documented that commanders were "frustrated by insufficient understanding of the target area population and its impact on operational decisions." Unclassified excerpt from *Briefing, Irregular Warfare Execution Roadmap, Irregular Warfare Tool Suite Plan EXCOM Outbrief*, 16 May 2007, secret unless otherwise marked.

[166] William A. Knowlton Jr., *The Surge: General Petraeus and the Turnaround in Iraq*, Industrial College of the Armed Forces Case Study (Washington, DC: National Defense University Press, December 2010), 1

[167]   Robert M. Gates, *Landon Lecture*, Manhattan, Kansas: Kansas State University, November 26, 2007.

[168]   Sharon Weinberger, "Gates: Human Terrain Teams Going Through 'Growing Pains'," *Wired: Danger Room*, April 15, 2008.

[169]   McFate and Fondacaro, "Reflections on the Human Terrain System During the First 4 Years," 68.

[170]   Ibid.

[171]   H.R. 5658, "National Defense Authorization Act for Fiscal Year 2009," *110th Congress*, 2009-2010, 475. Also for expanding to other combatant commands, see: Steve Fondacaro and Montgomery McFate, *Human Terrain System Information Briefing for Army G3*, PowerPoint, October 16, 2008.

[172]   Andrew F. Krepinevich, *Department of Defense Language and Cultural Awareness Transformation*, Testimony to the United States House of Representatives Committee on the Armed Service, Oversight and Investigations Subcommittee, July 9, 2008.

[173]   Montgomery McFate, Before the House Committee on Armed Services, Subcommittee on Investigations and Oversight, *110th Congress*, 2nd Session, United States House of Representatives, July 9, 2008.

[174]   CNA Analysis & Solutions, *Congressionally Directed Assessment of the Human Terrain System*, and Colonel Steve Fondacaro (ret.), Former HTS Program Manager, interviewed October 25, 2011.

[175]   CNA Analysis & Solutions, *Congressionally Directed Assessment of the Human Terrain System*, 43.

[176]   McFate and Fondacaro, "Reflections on the Human Terrain System During the First 4 Years," 68.

[177]   Colonel Steve Fondacaro (ret.), Former HTS Program Manager, interviewed October 25, 2011.

[178]   Lee Hill Kavanaugh, "Human Terrain Teams: Winning Hearts and Minds: Army Takes Human Terrain to Heart," *Kansas City Star*, October 14, 2008, 1.

[179]   The briefing and interview schedules are detailed in Human Terrain System, *Semi-Annual Command History, July—December 2007*; Human Terrain System, *Semi-Annual Command History, January—June 2008*; Human Terrain System, *Semi-Annual Command History, July—December 2008*; Human Terrain System, *Semi-Annual Command History, January—June 2009*.

[180]   United States Army Training and Doctrine Command, Office of Internal Review and Audit Compliance, Results Briefing, May 12, 2010; attached as Appendix G to the CNA Analysis & Solutions, *Congressionally Directed Assessment of the Human Terrain System*, 237-250.

[181]   CNA Analysis & Solutions, *Congressionally Directed Assessment of the Human Terrain System*, 93.

[182]   Ibid.

[183]   *The Human Terrain System Yearly Report 2007-2008*, 10.

[184]   Dr. Montgomery McFate, former HTS Senior Social Scientist, interviewed October 3, 2011.

[185]   "If you don't understand what teams are supposed to be doing, you can't evaluate how well they are doing it." Dr. Montgomery McFate, former HTS Senior Social Scientist, email on July 27, 2012.

[186]   The contractor, PDRI, complained that BAE would not make all of its subcontractor personnel available; it was able to secure less than 50 usable interviews. "Human Terrain System: Evaluation of the Human Terrain Team Recruitment and Selection Process," February, 2009, PDRI Technical Report 628; "U.S. Department of Defense—Human Terrain System (HTS): Job Analysis for Human Terrain Team Members in the Team Leader, Social Scientist, Research Manager, and Human Terrain Analyst Jobs," February, 2009, PDRI Technical Report 630.

[187] The HTS program has never instituted an effort to collect end of tour interviews with returning HTT members. In 2011 one HTS member began such an effort but was discouraged from continuing it. RRC Analyst, interviewed October 5, 2011; Joshua Foust, RRC Analyst, interviewed September 13, 2011; Social Scientist with an HTT, interviewed on February 15, 2012.

[188] Jim Greer, former Deputy Program Manager, HTS, interviewed October 26, 2011.

[189] HTT Social Scientist, interviewed December 14, 2011.

[190] RRC Analyst, interviewed October 5, 2011; Joshua Foust, RRC Analyst, interviewed September 13, 2011.

[191] Jim Greer, former Deputy Program Manager, HTS, interviewed October 26, 2011.

[192] Ibid.

[193] Social Scientist AF1, interviewed December 2, 2011.

[194] M. Mason, HTT member, Afghanistan, interviewed October 12, 2011.

[195] *Semi-Annual Command History, July—December 2008.*

[196] Colonel Steve Fondacaro (ret.), Former HTS Program Manager, email on January 15, 2012.

[197] Dr. Montgomery McFate, former HTS Senior Social Scientist, email on July 20, 2012.

[198] Colonel Steve Fondacaro (ret.), Former HTS Program Manager, email on March 6, 2012

[199] Colonel Steve Fondacaro (ret.), Former HTS Program Manager, interviewed October 25, 2011.

[200] M. Mason, HTT member, Afghanistan, interviewed October 12, 2011.

[201] Dr. Aileen Moffat, Social Scientist AF27, interviewed December 19, 2011; Research Manager, AF3, interviewed December 15, 2011.

[202] Dan Ephron and Silvia Spring, "A Gun in One Hand, A Pen in the Other," *Newsweek*, April 21, 2008.

[203] Human Terrain Team Report, *Pashtun Sexuality*, AF6.

[204] Joshua Foust, RRC Analyst, interviewed September 13, 2011.

[205] To this day some HTT members believe that the report, while obviously deleterious to the program, nonetheless contained important information for commanders' situational awareness. Social Scientist AF1, email on May 19, 2012. For a discussion on the meaning of 'operationally relevant' See Montgomery McFate, Britt Damon, and Robert Holliday, "What Do Commanders Really Want to Know?: U.S. Army Human Terrain System Lessons Learned from Iraq and Afghanistan," in Janice H. Laurence, and Michael D. Matthews, eds, *The Oxford Handbook of Military Psychology* (New York, NY: Oxford University Press, 2012), 102-103.

[206] Joel Brinkley, "Afghanistan's Dirty Little Secret," *The San Francisco Chronicle*, August 29, 2010; "Afghan Men Struggle with Sexual identity, Study Finds," *Fox News*, January 28, 2010.

[207] Major Michael Jacobson, U.S. Army Reserves, AF25 Team Leader September 2010—May 2011, interviewed October 7, 2011.

[208] Interviewee 24, October 17, 2011.

[209] *Semi-Annual Command History, January—June 2008.*

[210] *Semi-Annual Command History, July—December 2008.*

[211] *TAB 4—Human Resourcing & Recruiting*, Maxie L. McFarland, Memo, "Congressionally Directed Assessment—Human Terrain System (HTS) Initial Input," December 18, 2009, 23.

[212] *Semi-Annual Command History, July—December 2007; Semi-Annual Command History, January—June 2008; Semi-Annual Command History, July—December 2008; Semi-Annual Command History, January—June 2009;* CNA Analysis & Solutions, Congressionally Directed Assessment of the Human Terrain System, 92.

[213] *Semi-Annual Command History, January—June 2008.*

[214] HTS Program Development Team member, email on May 11, 2012.

[215] Karen Clark, former HTS Chief of Staff, interviewed October 24, 2011.

[216]   HTT Member, Afghanistan, interviewed October 25, 2011.

[217]   Tom Garcia, AF1, interviewed May 18, 2012.

[218]   HTT Member, Afghanistan, interviewed October 25, 2011.

[219]   Tom Garcia, AF1, interviewed May 18, 2012.

[220]   HTT Member, Afghanistan, interviewed October 25, 2011.

[221]   Steve Fondacaro and Montgomery McFate, *Human Terrain System Information Briefing for Army G3*, PowerPoint, October 16, 2008.

[222]   RRC Analyst, interviewed October 5, 2011.

[223]   HTT Research Manager, email on June 8, 2012.

[224]   Between July and December 2007, 133 Requests for Research (RFRs) were created, with six teams in the field in Iraq and Afghanistan, averaging of 22.1 requests per team. Between January and June 2008, 133 RFRs were created, with fifteen teams in the field, averaging 8.8 requests per team. Between July and December 2008, 224 RFRs were created, with twenty-seven teams in the field, averaging 8.2 requests per team. Between January and June 2009, 230 RFRs were created, with twenty-seven teams in the field, totally 8.5 per team. *Semi-Annual Command History, July—December 2007*; *Semi-Annual Command History, January—June 2008*; *Semi-Annual Command History, July—December 2008*; *Semi-Annual Command History, January—June 2009*. Despite the trend in declining requests, one source indicates that reachback centers produced a high volume of material: "in fiscal year 2008, the [Reachback Research Center] produced over 1,000 RFRs of varying length and complexity." Montgomery McFate, Britt Damon, and Robert Holliday, "What Do Commanders Really Want to Know?: U.S. Army Human Terrain System Lessons Learned from Iraq and Afghanistan," in Janice H. Laurence, and Michael D. Matthews, ed., *The Oxford Handbook of Military Psychology* (New York, NY: Oxford University Press, 2012), 103.

[225]   RRC Analyst, interviewed October 5, 2011; Kristen Farnum, Social Scientist, AF3, interviewed November 3, 2011.

[226]   Daniel Dali, *Human Terrain System Information Briefing for the 58th Annual Conference of the Civil Affairs Association Seminar on Intra-DoD Irregular Warfare Capabilities*, October 30, 2009.

[227]   Professor Thomas H. Johnson, Naval Postgraduate School, interviewed March 6, 2012.

[228]   Ibid.

[229]   AF1 Social Scientist, 2008-2009, email on April 19, 2012.

[230]   Nathan Finney, *Commander's Guide: Employing a Human Terrain Team in Operation Enduring Freedom and Operation Iraqi Freedom: Tactics, Techniques and Procedures* (Ft. Leavenworth, KS: U.S. Army Center for Army Lessons Learned, Number 09-21, March 2009).

[231]   American Anthropological Association, *American Anthropological Association's Executive Board Statement on the Human Terrain System Project*, dated October 31, 2007; Released November 6, 2007. The following month, in heated discussions of the program at the association's conference, a former HTS recruit was severely criticized for her participation with the program. See Zenia Helbig, *Personal Perspective on the Human Terrain System Program*, delivered at the AAA's Annual Conference, November 29, 2007.

[232]   Fawzia Sheikh, "Army to Boost Human Terrain Team Effort Despite Growing Pains," *Inside the Army* vol. 20, no. 22, (June 2008).

[233]   American Anthropological Association, *AAA Commission on the Engagement of Anthropology with the US Security and Intelligence Communities (CEAUSSIC)*, October 14, 2009, 12.

[234]   Roberto Gonzales, *The Counter-Counterinsurgency Manual* (Chicago, Il: Prickly Paradigm Press, 2009).

[235]   The command history of HTS from this period notes, for example, that the program manager was required to present four briefings in six days to three generals and an official at the Office of the Undersecretary of Defense for Intelligence. *Semi-Annual Command History, January—June 2008*.

[236] David Price, "Counterinsurgency, Anthropology and Disciplinary Complicity," *Counterpunch*, February 3, 2009; Lieutenant Colonel Eric Rotzoll, Team Leader, AF2, interviewed October 10, 2011.

[237] Steve Fondacaro and Montgomery McFate, *Human Terrain System Information Briefing for Army G3*, PowerPoint, October 16, 2008; *Semi-Annual Command History, July-December 2008*.

[238] Colonel Steve Fondacaro (ret.), Former HTS Program Manager, interviewed October 25, 2011.

[239] Africa Command was established on October 1, 2007, and activated on October 1, 2008. Africa Command ultimately opted in favor of creating its own sociocultural teams, the development of which HTS supported with a liaison officer.

[240] Karen Clark, former HTS Chief of Staff, interviewed October 24, 2011; Interviewee 29, October 19, 2011.

[241] HTT Member, Afghanistan, interviewed October 25, 2011.

[242] Ibid.

[243] Bhatia's tragic death and its impact are recounted in Wahab, *In My Father's Country: An Afghan Woman Defies Her Fate*, 306-311; and Robert Willey, "The Theory and Practice of War," *Boston Magazine*, May 2009.

[244] Steve Fondacaro, Montgomery McFate, TRADOC, "Nicole Suveges, A Funny, Kind Person, Has Died On An HTS Mission in Iraq," *Ethnography.com*, June 26, 2008.

[245] Program Manager Forward, Afghanistan, interviewed December 7, 2011.

[246] Matthew Barakat, "Army Contractor Pleads Guilty in Detainee Shooting," *The Washington Post*, February 4, 2009.

[247] Clint Cooper, Research Manager, AF4, interviewed November 22, 2011.

[248] Pamela Constable, "A Terrain's Tragic Shift," *The Washington Post*, February 18, 2009.

[249] John Stanton, "HTS Sergeant Wesley Cureton Wounded," *Cryptome*, December 10, 2009.

[250] HTS Employee, interviewed November 2, 2011.

[251] HTT Social Scientist, interviewed December 21, 2011; Mike Costello, "Counterinsurgency (COIN) & Human Terrain Techniques Combating IEDs in Afghanistan (CIED)," *Defense Update*, December 21, 2011.

[252] Program Manager Forward, Afghanistan, interviewed December 7, 2011.

[253] Pamela Constable, "A Terrain's Tragic Shift," *The Washington Post*, February 18, 2009.

[254] *Semi-Annual Command History, July—December 2008*.

[255] Research Manager on an HTT in Afghanistan, interviewed November 8, 2011; Interviewee 44, November 10, 2011.

[256] Robert Young Pelton, "Afghanistan: The New War for Hearts and Minds," *Men's Journal*, January 21, 2009; Lieutenant Colonel Eric Rotzoll, Team Leader, AF2, email on May 14, 2012.

[257] Captain Jeremy Jones, Research Manager, AF2, interviewed November 3, 2011.

[258] HTT member, interviewed October 27, 2011.

[259] Steve Fondacaro and Montgomery McFate, "U.S. Army Response to Robert Young Pelton's The New War for Hearts and Minds," *Men's Journal*, February 12, 2009.

[260] Robert Young Pelton, "Robert Young Pelton's Response to the U.S. Army," *Men's Journal*, February 12, 2009

[261] Editorial, "A Social Contract: Efforts to Inform US Military Policy with Insights from the Social Sciences Could be a Win-Win Approach," *Nature* iss. 545 (July 10, 2008), Published online July 9, 2008, 138.

[262] Editorial, "Failure in the Field: The US Military's Human-Terrain Programme Needs to be Brought to a Swift Close," *Nature* vol. 456 (December 11, 2008), Published online 10 December 2008, 676.

[263] Jim Greer, former Deputy Program Manager, HTS, interviewed October 26, 2011; Karen

Clark, former HTS Chief of Staff, interviewed October 24, 2011.

[264]   Interviewee 29, October 19, 2011.

[265]   Colonel Steve Fondacaro (ret.), Former HTS Program Manager, email on April 30, 2012.

[266]   HTT Social Scientist, interviewed December 9, 2011.

[267]   AF1 Social Scientist, 2008-2009, interviewed January 5, 2012.

[268]   Captain Jeremy Jones, Research Manager, AF2, interviewed November 3, 2011.

[269]   Colonel Steve Fondacaro (ret.), Former HTS Program Manager, email on April 30, 2012.

[270]   He reportedly plagiarized an article on *Small Wars Journal*, as well as a report written by a member of AF2. Joshua Foust, RRC Analyst, interviewed September 13, 2011; Lieutenant Colonel Eric Rotzoll, Team Leader, AF2, email on May 14, 2012; Social Scientist with an HTT, email on June 7, 2012.

[271]   Lieutenant Colonel Eric Rotzoll, Team Leader, AF2, email on May 14, 2012.

[272]   Maximilian Forte, "Reality check for Human Terrain System: Marilyn Dudley-Flores responds," *Zero Anthropology*, November 5, 2009.

[273]   HTT Research Manager, email on June 7, 2012.

[274]   Colonel Steve Fondacaro (ret.), Former HTS Program Manager, interviewed November 1, 2011.

[275]   John Stanton, "Death Threat Tarnishes US Army Human Terrain System," *Zero Anthropology*, February 26, 2009.

[276]   H.R. 2647, "National Defense Authorization Act for Fiscal Year 2010," *111th* Congress, 2009-2010, 155. A recent internal HTS report suggested that because HTS keeps many of its problems hidden from "internal and external" performance reviews, those operating within the program are more likely to engage with critics of HTS like Stanton. The report suggested a more open attitude would help in retaining good employees and substantially decrease negative discourse about HTS. HTS document containing interviews with returning HTT members, provided by a Social Scientist with an HTT, interviewed February 14, 2012, 6.

[277]   John Foldberg, Team Leader AF7, interviewed November 21, 2011.

[278]   Interviewee 24, October 17, 2011.

[279]   Program Manager Forward, Afghanistan, interviewed December 7, 2011.

[280]   Research Manager, AF3, interviewed December 15, 2011.

[281]   *Agreement Between the United States of America and the Republic of Iraq On the Withdrawal of united States Forces from Iraq and the Organization of their Activities during Their Temporary Presence in Iraq*, Ratified by Iraq, 27 November 2008.

[282]   Colonel Steve Fondacaro (ret.), Former HTS Program Manager, interviewed October 25, 2011.

[283]   This point was made repeatedly by many HTT members we interviewed, and vehemently denied by TRADOC sources. *TRADOC G2 Comments on the National Defense University paper titled "Human Terrain Team Performance: An Explanation," August 24, 2012*, Passed to NDU team, November 15, 2012.

[284]   *Semi-Annual Command History, January—June 2009*, July 31, 2009.

[285]   Research Manager on an HTT in Afghanistan, interviewed November 8, 2011.

[286]   Karen Clark, former HTS Chief of Staff, interviewed October 24, 2011.

[287]   BAE Systems, "Government Fact Sheet: Human Terrain System—Transition of personnel to Government Service": attached as Appendix E to the CNA Analysis & Solutions, *Congressionally Directed Assessment of the Human Terrain System,* 217-219.

[288]   David Axe, "War is Boring: After Setbacks, Human Terrain System Rebuilds," *World Politics Review*, November 25, 2009. According to one source: "If you were a competent HTA at this point you got a job somewhere else. HTAs took a disproportionate pay cut relative to everyone else because the HTAs were shifted to a GS12 position. The gap between GS13 and GS12 is pretty big. It made sense in a linear pay scale of GS15, GS14, GS13 and then

GS12, but when you look at the actual drop in the pay scale it's just huge. What you saw were the HTAs taking $120,000 to $180,000 pay cuts. There are a lot of different numbers and it depends on their contractor, but around $300,000 when they were contractors. Everyone was making around that amount." HTS Program Development Team member, interviewed May 11, 2012.

[289] CNA Analysis & Solutions, *Congressionally Directed Assessment of the Human Terrain System*, 76.

[290] Research Manager, AF27, interviewed October 25, 2011.

[291] CEAUSSIC, *Final Report on the Army's Human Terrain System Proof of Concept Program*, (Executive Board of the American Anthropological Association, Arlington, VA: American Anthropological Association, October 14, 2009), 23.

[292] *The Human Terrain System Yearly Report 2007-2008*, 134.

[293] Joanna Kimberlin "Part 3: Building Trust Amid Fear, One Mission at a Time," *The Virginian Pilot*, September 28, 2010.

[294] Colonel Steve Fondacaro (ret.), Former HTS Program Manager, interviewed October 25, 2011.

[295] AF1 Social Scientist, 2008-2009, email on April 19, 2012.

[296] Social Scientist AF1, interviewed December 2, 2011.

[297] Social Scientist AF1, interviewed December 2, 2011; HTT Social Scientist, interviewed December 14, 2011; Tom Garcia, AF1, interviewed May 18, 2012.

[298] Christopher Carr, *Kalashnikov Culture: Small Arms Proliferation and Irregular Warfare*, (Westport, CT: Praeger Security International, 2008).

[299] Social Scientist AF1, interviewed December 2, 2011.

[300] Major Robert Holbert, Research Manager, AF1, interviewed December 12, 2011.

[301] Dr. Ron Holt, Social Scientist AF1, interviewed September 28, 2011.

[302] *The Human Terrain System Yearly Report 2007-2008*, 134

[303] Social Scientist AF1, interviewed December 2, 2011.

[304] AF1 Social Scientist, 2008-2009, email on April 19, 2012.

[305] Ben Connable, "All Our Eggs in a Broken Basket: How the Human Terrain System is Undermining Sustainable Military Cultural Competence," *Military Review* (March-April 2009), 57-64.

[306] After two years in the field, HTS believed it would be beneficial to begin fielding nine-person teams by mid-2009. A team would then be composed of two Social Scientists, three Human Terrain Analysts and three Research Managers, along with the Team Leader. The increased team sized would allow HTTs to better cover the demands of brigade commanders and their staffs. This decision would have exacerbated many existing problems, particularly the insufficient numbers of qualified trainees the system could recruit, train and field.

[307] Colonel Steve Fondacaro (ret.), Former HTS Program Manager, interviewed October 25, 2011. Another source also cites a U.S. Marine Corps Regiment statement that they were able to "hit the ground running in large part because of this team was here and done solid work to document the human terrain." *VCSA Assessment Outcomes, 2 of 2*, PowerPoint, undated.

[308] Program Manager Forward, Afghanistan, interviewed December 7, 2011.

[309] "Public Support for Afghan Mission Lowest Ever: Poll," *CBC News*, September 5, 2008.

[310] "Canada's Military Mission in Afghanistan: Training Role to Replace Combat Mission in 2011," *CBC News*, February 10, 2009.

[311] Program Manager Forward, Afghanistan, interviewed December 7, 2011.

[312] Nathan Finney, *Human Terrain Team Handbook* (Ft. Leavenworth, KS: The Human Terrain System, September 2008).

[313] Kristen Kushiyama, "Sociocultural Data Collection Provides Insight for Commanders," *U.S. Army News Archive*, October 12, 2010.

314   Sean M. Gallagher, "Human Terrain System's transitional plans," *Sean M. Gallagher*, March 5, 2009.

315   Joanne Kimberlin "Part 1: New Weapon in an Old War in Afghanistan," *The Virginian-Pilot*, September 29, 2010.

316   General Stanley McChrystal, USA, *Commander's Initial Assessment*, August 30, 2009.

317   TRADOC G2 Human Terrain System, *My Cousin's Enemy is My Friend: A Study of Pashtun Tribes' in Afghanistan* (Fort Leavenworth, KS: United States Army, September 2009), 6.

318   Arif Ayub, "Tribal Engagement Workshop," *The Nation*, April 21, 2010.

319   General Stanley McChrystal, USA, *Commander's Initial Assessment*, August 30, 2009, 2-1.

320   "Department of Defense Bloggers Roundtable with Brigadier General Ed Cardon, Deputy Commandant, U.S. Army Command and General Staff College, Via Teleconference Subject: Military and Interagency Cooperation in Training and Education," *Federal News Service*, October 8, 2009.

321   CNA Analysis & Solutions, *Congressionally Directed Assessment of the Human Terrain System*, 43

322   H.R. 2647, "National Defense Authorization Act for Fiscal Year 2010," *111th* Congress, 2009-2010, 155.

323   Colonel Steve Fondacaro (ret.), Former HTS Program Manager, interviewed November 1, 2011.

324   Ibid.

325   CNA Analysis & Solutions, *Congressionally Directed Assessment of the Human Terrain System*.

326   H.R. 5136, "National Defense Authorization Act for Fiscal Year 2011," *111th Congress*, 2009-2010, 25.

327   Member of the HTS Social Sciences Directorate, interviewed October 5, 2011.

328   Ibid.

329   Kevin R. Golinghorst, "Mapping the Human Terrain in Afghanistan," *Monograph*, School of Advanced Military Studies, United States Army Command and General Staff College, Fort Leavenworth, Kansas, 27-28.

330   Reachback Research Center, *Map of HTTs in Afghanistan*, The Human Terrain System, March 16, 2010.

331   Golinghorst, "Mapping the Human Terrain in Afghanistan," 27-28.

332   Corey Flintoff, "Marines Tap Social Sciences in Afghan War Effort," Morning Edition, *National Public Radio*, April 5, 2010.

333   Member of AF7, interviewed September 30, 2011.

334   Ibid.

335   It was on a subset of AF2 that was then deployed with the French Task Force in Kapisa Province that Fondacaro and McFate appeared in the National Geographic documentary, *Talibanistan*. Filming took place on October 24-26, 2009. *Trip Report—HTS Program Development Team (PDT) Afghanistan, 17 October—7 November, 2009.*

336   Colonel Steve Fondacaro (ret.), Former HTS Program Manager, email on April 30, 2012.

337   Nicole Heydari, Human Terrain Analyst AF17, interviewed October 6, 2011; Dr. Amy Bursell, Social Scientist AF10, interviewed September 29, 2011.

338   Major Michael Jacobson, U.S. Army Reserves, AF25 Team Leader September 2010—May 2011, interviewed October 7, 2011.

339   HTT Social Scientist, interviewed December 21, 2011.

340   Social Scientist AF1, interviewed November 14, 2011.

341   Human Terrain Team Research Manager Raphael Howard, cited in Sgt Spencer Case, "Mapping Afghanistan's Human Terrain" *Combined Joint Task Force—82 PAO*, May 2, 2010.

342   United States Army Training and Doctrine Command, Office of Internal Review and Audit Compliance, Results Briefing, May 12, 2010; attached as Appendix G to the CNA

Analysis & Solutions, *Congressionally Directed Assessment of the Human Terrain System*, 237-250.

[343] Dr. Amy Bursell, Social Scientist AF10, interviewed September 29, 2011. Fondacaro also wanted HTS out from under TRADOC, preferring to see it managed on a joint or interagency basis. Colonel Steve Fondacaro (ret.), Former HTS Program Manager, email from April 30, 2012.

[344] Interviewee 10, October 3, 2011.

[345] Colonel Steve Fondacaro (ret.), Former HTS Program Manager, email from April 30, 2012.

[346] The report stated "Army culture must change to embrace process more than outcome in some cases, and steer clear of using measures of effectiveness that are solely outcome-based, such as money spent. While some quantitative metrics are useful, they alone do not paint the full picture." Jebb, Hummel, Chacho, *Human Terrain Team Trip Report*, 5.

[347] Both studies will be assessed and analyzed in the section, *Net Explanation for HTT Performance Variation.*

[348] Interviewee 10, October 3, 2011.

[349] "Appendix F: Position Descriptions for Human Terrain Teams," Documents include a February 2, 2010, job classification date; attached as Appendix G to the CNA Analysis & Solutions, *Congressionally Directed Assessment of the Human Terrain System*, 221-236.

[350] Colonel Steve Fondacaro (ret.), Former HTS Program Manager, email on April 30, 2012; HTS Program Development Team member, interviewed May 11, 2012; Member of the 2010 Curriculum Conference, interviewed March 22, 2012.

[351] Colonel Steve Fondacaro (ret.), Former HTS Program Manager, email on April 30, 2012. For example, according to Fondacaro, the team leader position descriptions were a word for word copy of a PSYOP detachment commander.

[352] The HTS Yearly Report called for the creation of an in-country management unit because "the HTS program manager is overburdened by CONUS and OCONUS management responsibilities." *The Human Terrain System Yearly Report 2007-2008*, 225.

[353] The position itself had originally been created six months earlier. The intent was to have the Team Leader from AF2, Mike Williams, take the position, but he declined it. Program Manager Forward, Afghanistan, interviewed December 7, 2011.

[354] Program Manager Forward, Afghanistan, interviewed December 7, 2011.

[355] Michael T. Flynn, Matt Pottinger, and Paul Batchelor, *Fixing Intel: A Blueprint for Making Intelligence Relevant in Afghanistan* (Washington, DC: Center for a New American Security, 2010).

[356] CNA Analysis & Solutions, *Congressionally Directed Assessment of the Human Terrain System*, 208; Nicole Heydari, Human Terrain Analyst AF17, interviewed October 6, 2011.

[357] Glevum & Associates, Human Terrain System, *Kandahar Province Survey Report*, March 2010.

[358] McFate's official position has been identified as "Senior Social Scientist." She is widely described by those we interviewed as the de facto co-leader of the program.

[359] According to one colleague, she "unofficially bowed out of the program." Member of the HTS Social Sciences Directorate, interviewed October 5, 2011.

[360] CNA Analysis & Solutions, *Congressionally Directed Assessment of the Human Terrain System*, 23.

[361] Karen Clark, former HTS Chief of Staff, interviewed October 24, 2011.

[362] CNA Analysis & Solutions, *Congressionally Directed Assessment of the Human Terrain System*, 45.

[363] An Army "AR 15-6" investigation is an informal but detailed fact gathering exercise that concludes with analysis and recommendations based on the facts obtained. An "investigation" is simply the process of collecting information for the command, so that the command can

make an informed decision. Informal investigations typically have a single investigating officer who conducts interviews and collects evidence, whereas formal investigations normally involve due process hearings for a designated respondent before a board of several officers. Office of the Staff Judge Advocate, *Investigating Officer's Guide for AF 15-6 Informal Investigations*, Joint Readiness Training Center and Fort Polk, undated.

364 Memorandum, "Findings and Recommendations, AR 15-6 Investigation Concerning Human Terrain Subject (HTS) Project Inspector General Complaints," May 12, 2010, For Official Use Only, redacted and released in response to a Freedom of Information request; available at <https://www.box.com/s/2mv0g54xsr41aegwbw9i>; February 19, 2013, 1.

365 Memorandum, "Findings and Recommendations, AR 15-6 Investigation Concerning Human Terrain Subject (HTS) Project Inspector General Complaints," May 12, 2010, For Official Use Only, redacted and released in response to a Freedom of Information request; available at <https://www.box.com/s/2mv0g54xsr41aegwbw9i>; February 19, 2013, 6.

366 CNA Analysis & Solutions, *Congressionally Directed Assessment of the Human Terrain System*. 42, 135 and Appendix G. CNA notes that the Internal Review and Audit Compliance investigation, which was completed in May, faulted TRADOC management of the BAE contract.

367 Joanne Kimberlin, "Part 4: In the Enemy's Lair, Fighting for Afghanistan's Future," *The Virginian Pilot*, September 29, 2010.

368 Ibid.

369 Spencer Ackerman, "Hundreds in Army Social Science Unqualified, Former Boss Says [Updated]," *Wired: Danger Room*, December 21, 2010.

370 Kimberlin, "Part 4: In the Enemy's Lair, Fighting For Afghanistan's Future"; Colonel Steve Fondacaro (ret.), Former HTS Program Manager, interviewed October 25, 2011.

371 Kimberlin, "Part 4: In the Enemy's Lair, Fighting For Afghanistan's Future."

372 Ibid.

373 Joanne Kimberlin, "Part 1: New Weapon in an Old War in Afghanistan," *The Virginian Pilot*, September 26, 2010.

374 Ackerman, "Hundreds in Army Social Science Unqualified."

375 Management differences did not preclude cooperation between HTS and TRADOC. For example, in February 2010, they worked together to create a "holding company" to provide a solution for personnel issues arising from the uncertain status of HTT members as they moved between deployment as Army civilians and contractor positions in the United States. It served as "the managerial unit that 'holds' HTS personnel who are in limbo between training and deployment and those who have recently returned from deployment." CNA Analysis & Solutions, *Congressionally Directed Assessment of the Human Terrain System*, 27.

376 To cite one example, starting HTS quickly meant using the available BAE contract. This contract was managed out of the Army's Space and Missile Defense Command located in Huntsville, Alabama, far removed from the TRADOC and HTS management offices. Thus the contracting officer was not even on site, which caused numerous complications over the course of the BAE contract implementation. Among other things, it was responsible for delayed funding when the contract hit its funding ceiling but TRADOC failed to note this fact. Colonel Steve Fondacaro (ret.), Former HTS Program Manager, email on April 30, 2012.

377 Initially there was speculation that a civilian would become the next permanent Director of HTS. Sharon Weinberger, "Human Terrain' hits rocky Ground: US Army Social-Science Programme Loses Director," *Nature* iss. 465, no. 220, Published online, June 22, 2010.

378 Dr. Montgomery McFate, former HTS Senior Social Scientist, interviewed October 3, 2011.

379 Program Manager Forward, Afghanistan, interviewed December 7, 2011.

380 Ibid.

381 CNA Analysis & Solutions, *Congressionally Directed Assessment of the Human Terrain System*, 3.

[382]   John McHugh, "Transcript: Defense Writers Group," *A Project of the Center for Media and Security New York and Washington, DC,* March 31, 2010, 10.

[383]   Sharon Weinberger, "Human Terrain' Hits Rocky Ground," *Nature* iss. 465, no. 220, Published online, June 22, 2010, 993

[384]   Hearing of the Subcommittee on Air and Land Forces of the House Armed Services Committee: *Army Acquisition and Modernization Programs,* March 10, 2010.

[385]   Noah Shachtman, "House Panel Puts the Brakes on 'Human Terrain'" *Wired: Danger Room,* May 20, 2010.

[386]   CNA Analysis & Solutions, *Congressionally Directed Assessment of the Human Terrain System,* 106.

[387]   Ibid., 107-108.

[388]   Ibid., 3.

[389]   Terry Mitchell, *Letter to Office of the Undersecretary of Defense for Intelligence,* August 19, 2010.

[390]   Office of the Under Secretary of Defense for Intelligence, *Response to the July 15, 2010 Draft of the CNA Report,* September 2010.

[391]   Ibid.

[392]   Section 344 of the House report on the Defense Authorization for 2011 would "prohibit the Secretary of the Army from obligating more than 50 percent of the remaining funds for the Army Human Terrain System (HTS) until several documents are submitted to the congressional defense committees [including] the independent assessment of HTS called for by the committee report (H. Rept. 111-166) accompanying the National Defense Authorization Act for Fiscal Year 2010." The CNA study has not yet been released formally to the public, but researchers studying the HTS and HTTs have had full access to the report since February 2011. Maximilian Forte, "Declaring the U.S. Army's Human Terrain System a Success: Rereading the CNA Report," *Zero Anthropology,* February 19, 2011.

[393]   United States Army Training and Doctrine Command, Office of Internal Review and Audit Compliance, Results Briefing, May 12, 2010; attached as Appendix G to the CNA Analysis & Solutions, *Congressionally Directed Assessment of the Human Terrain System,* 237-250.

[394]   Ackerman, "Hundreds in Army Social Science Unqualified."

[395]   Tony Bertuca, "Army Increasing Number Of Human Terrain Teams; Advising Allies," *InsideDefense.com,* December 10, 2010.

[396]   Spencer Ackerman, "Petraeus: I'll Change Afghanistan Rules of War," *Wired: Danger Room,* June 29, 2010; General David Petraeus, USA, *COMISAF's Counterinsurgency Guidance,* August 1, 2010.

[397]   Kimberlin, "Part 4: In the Enemy's Lair, Fighting for Afghanistan's Future."

[398]   Bertuca, "Army Increasing Number Of Human Terrain Teams."

[399]   Reachback Research Center, *Map of HTTs in Afghanistan,* The Human Terrain System, March 14, 2011.

[400]   Reachback Research Center, *Map of HTTs in Afghanistan,* The Human Terrain System, September 27, 2011.

[401]   The Institute for the Study of War, *Afghanistan—Order of Battle,* December 2011; *Ronna,* "HTS Teams and Locations"; CNA Analysis & Solutions, *Congressionally Directed Assessment of the Human Terrain System,* 73.

[402]   Colonel Sharon Hamilton, "HTS Director's Message," *Military Intelligence Professional Bulletin* vol. 37, no. 4 (October-December 2011), A1.

[403]   Dr. Chris King, *Human Terrain System and the Role of Social Science in Counterinsurgency,* University of Hawaii, Manoa, September 20, 2011.

[404]   Dr. Aileen Moffat, Social Scientist AF27, interviewed December 19, 2011.

[405]   Ibid.

[406] Federal Business Opportunities, R—TRADOC Human Terrain System, Solicitation Number: W911S011R0003, September 22, 2011.

[407] Ackerman, "Hundreds in Army Social Science Unqualified."

[408] Colonel Steve Fondacaro (ret.), Former HTS Program Manager, interviewed November 1, 2011.

[409] Fondacaro responded that it might have occurred but was not the purpose of the program, while Hamilton said it never happened because it was against the program's rules. Sharon Weinberger, "Pentagon Cultural Analyst Helped Interrogate Detainees in Afghanistan," *Nature* (October 18, 2011). Our interviews revealed just on case where a social scientist debriefed detainees at Kabul, not to obtain actionable intelligence but to help map the human terrain of the detainees' home province and villages in the HTT's area of operations. Interviewee 32, October 24, 2011. In retrospect, is possible that the author confused CENTCOM HTATs with HTS' HTATs.

[410] "Shape (Phase 0). Joint and multinational operations--inclusive of normal and routine military activities--and various interagency activities are performed to dissuade or deter potential adversaries and to assure or solidify relationships with friends and allies." Joint Publication 5-0, *Joint Operation Planning*, August 11, 2011, xxiii.

[411] "Human Terrain System," *YouTube*, December 23, 2011, accessed January 9, 2012.

[412] Ibid..

[413] Ibid.

[414] Colonel Sharon Hamilton, "HTS Director's Message," *Military Intelligence Professional Bulletin* vol. 37, no. 4, (October-December 2011).

[415] Colonel Mark Bartholf, "The Requirement for Sociocultural Understanding in Full Spectrum Operations," *Military Intelligence Professional Bulletin* vol. 37, no. 4 (October-December 2011), 9. "Each COCOM currently uses an independently developed sociocultural cell to provide analysis of the COCOM's area of focus, primarily through open source analysis."

[416] Ibid.

[417] Daniel Wierich, *After Action Review (AAR) for US Army Africa (USARAF) Human Terrain System (HTS) Pilot Project* (Newport News, VA: Human Terrain System, 2011), 8, in Major Steven J. Lacy, "Propping Open the Door: The Argument for Permanent Integration of Population-Centric Intelligence to Understand the Human Terrain" *Thesis*, National Intelligence University, July 2012, 66.

[418] Major Steven J. Lacy, "Propping Open the Door: The Argument for Permanent Integration of Population-Centric Intelligence to Understand the Human Terrain" *Thesis*, National Intelligence University, July 2012, 76

[419] Noah Shachtman, "*Que Curioso!* U.S. Army Cultural Advisers Now Eyeing Mexico," *Wired: Danger Room*, May 2, 2012.

[420] "Human Terrain System," *YouTube*, December 23, 2011, accessed January 9, 2012.

[421] Rafael Fermoselle, Social Scientist, Iraq, interviewed December 4, 2011.

[422] HTT Research Manager, interviewed January 3, 2012.

[423] HTS document containing interviews with returning HTT members, provided by a Social Scientist with an HTT, interviewed February 14, 2012, 4; HTT Research Manager, email on October 18, 2011.

[424] *Report of the Defense Science Board Task Force on Understanding Human Dynamics*, ix.

[425] Shad Eidson, "Sociocultural Research and Advisory Team Adds Community Perspective to CJTF-HOA," *CJTF-HOA Public Affairs*, July 15, 2010; Maureen Farrell, Former SCRAT Member, interviewed October 14, 2011; Regional Command Southwest, "Female Engagement Team (USMC)," *Regional Command Southwest Press Room*; USASOC Public Affairs, "Course trains cultural teams to work with women in theater," *U.S. Army*, January 21, 2012; Ronna, "CAAT History and Mission," *Ronna Web*; CNA Analysis & Solutions, *Congressionally Directed Assessment*

of the Human Terrain System, 213; George Mason University, "Geographic Information Systems Certificate Program," *Office of Continuing Professional Education*; "Agribusiness Development Team (ADT)," Pete Geren and George W. Casey, Jr., *A Statement on the Posture of United States Army 2008*, (Washington, DC: Department of the Army, February 26, 2008), 31; Joshua Foust, "District Development Teams Are a Go!" *Registan.net*, August 11, 2009.

[426]   Bryant Jordan, "Spec Ops Needs a Few Good Women," *Military.com*, February 14, 2011; Lolita Baldor, "Military Women to Serve Closer to the Front Lines, According to Pentagon Report," *The Huffington Post*, February 9, 2012; Matt Pottinger, Hali Jilani, and Claire Russo, "Half-Hearted: Trying to Win Afghanistan without Afghan Women," *Small Wars Journal*, February 18, 2010.

[427]   Bryant Jordan, "Spec Ops Needs a Few Good Women," *Military.com*, February 14, 2011; Lolita Baldor, "Military Women to Serve Closer to the Front Lines, According to Pentagon Report," *Huffington Post*, February 9, 2012; Matt Pottinger, Hali Jilani, and Claire Russo, "Half-Hearted: Trying to Win Afghanistan without Afghan Women," *Small Wars Journal*, February 18, 2010.

[428]   Dr. Amy Bursell, Social Scientist AF10, interviewed October 20, 2011.

[429]   Captain Benoit Paré, French CIMIC Officer, Afghanistan, email on May 8, 2012.

[430]   A new council has been created out of this working group: "In FY 2011, the Defense Intelligence Sociocultural Capabilities Council was established by USD(I) to develop and institutionalize sociocultural capabilities across the Defense Intelligence Enterprise." Colonel Mark C. Bartholf, "The Requirement for Sociocultural Understanding in Full Spectrum Operations," *Military Intelligence Professional Bulletin* vol. 37, no. 4 (October-December 2011),7.

[431]   *Report of the Defense Science Board Task Force on Understanding Human Dynamics*, 91.

[432]   Interviewee 94, March 6, 2012.

[433]   Colonel Steve Fondacaro (ret.), Former HTS Program Manager, interviewed November 1, 2011.

[434]   Patti Morrissey, *Developing a Human Terrain Knowledge Enterprise and Tradecraft for the USG*, PowerPoint, undated.

[435]   Interviewee 94, March 6, 2012.

[436]   A member of our research team visited National Geospatial Intelligence Agency headquarters on January 20, 2012, to receive an overview of NGA's significant investment in sociocultural research.

[437]   Kristina Wong, "Afghanistan Civilian Surge Could Last Decade," *ABC News*, March 4, 2010.

[438]   Christopher Varhola, *U.S. Africa Command Intelligence and Knowledge Development Social Science Research Center (SSRC)*, Information Paper, AFRICOM.

[439]   Maureen Farrell, Former SCRAT Member, interviewed October 14, 2011.

[440]   Christopher Varhola, *U.S. Africa Command Intelligence and Knowledge Development Social Science Research Center (SSRC)*, Information Paper, AFRICOM.

[441]   Maureen Farrell, Former SCRAT Member, interviewed October 14, 2011.

[442]   Maureen Farrell, Former SCRAT Member, email on April 23, 2012.

[443]   "Understanding Culture and Customs in Helmand," *British Army Website*, May 18, 2010.

[444]   "Military Develops its Cultural Understanding of Afghanistan," *Defense Policy and Business*, February 24, 2010.

[445]   "Understanding Culture and Customs in Helmand," *British Army Website*, May 18, 2010.

[446]   Tom Blackwell, "Mapping 'White' Afghans Aims to End Civilian Deaths," *National Post*, November 8, 2008.

[447]   Ibid.

[448]   K. Eric Drexler, *Engines of Creation: The Coming Era of Nanotechnology* (Garden City, NY: Anchor Press/Doubleday, 1986).

[449]   Interviewee 44, November 10, 2011.

[450]   Current indications are that these efficiencies will be achieved by cutting the position of Human Terrain Analyst and reducing the number of deployed teams. HTT member, Afghanistan, email on June 9, 2012. This topic has also been picked up in a recent blog posting quoting instructions disseminated to current HTS employees by then-current program manager, COL Sharon Hamilton. John Stanton, "Syria on the Horizon: Leadership, mission reboot at Army Human Terrain" *Intrepid Report*, June 21, 2012.

[451]   The U.S. Special Operations Command had some classified programs related to human terrain under way earlier. See the associated discussion on page 26.

4 ANALYSIS OF VARIABLES EXPLAINING PERFORMANCE

> *"It is more important that HTS build excellent teams who prove their effectiveness than to produce numerous ineffective teams."*[1]
>
> West Point Study on HTTs

To better explain HTT performance, we conducted over one hundred interviews with HTT members, HTS managers, and observers of HTS.[2] We concentrated on finding interviewees with experience on HTTs in Afghanistan from 2009 to 2011, but interviewee experience covered the entire range of the HTS program and experience with HTTs in both Iraq and Afghanistan (See Appendix Three). The interviews were structured around ten variables (see table on next page). The ten variables were extracted from a review of organizational and management research on small, cross-functional teams. Each variable is identified in the research literature as a significant determinant of small cross-functional team performance.[3] We asked each interviewee with personal experience on a team or in HTS management questions about each of the ten variables (see Appendix Four for a list of the basic questions). Interviewees often offered explanations that involved more than one variable. Therefore, after constructing transcripts of the interviews, we sorted the diverse insights offered by interviewees into the most appropriate variable category. From that data we could then construct a composite picture of the explanatory value of a variable. We separated out interview data on several teams widely acknowledged for their stellar performance, and also for several teams widely noted for having performed poorly.[4] The results from comparing the respective experiences of the best and worst teams strongly reinforced our general findings about the relative import of performance variables.

Postulated Determinants of Effectiveness in HTTs		
Level	**Variables**	**Defined**
Organization	**Purpose**	The broad, long-term mandate given to the team by its management as well as the alignment of short-term objectives with the strategic vision and agreement on common approaches within the team.
	Empower-ment	The access to sufficient high-quality personnel, funds, and materials, and an appropriate amount of authority, to allow for confident, decisive action.
	Support	The set of organizational processes that connect a team to other teams at multiple levels within the organization, other organizations, and a wide variety of resources the team needs to accomplish its mission.
Team	**Structure**	The "mechanics" of teams—design, mental models and networks—that affect team productivity.
	Decision-making	The mechanisms that are employed to make sense of and solve a variety of complex problems faced by a cross-functional team.
	Culture	The shared values, norms and beliefs of the team, manifested in behavioral expectations, level of commitment and degree of trust among team members.
	Learning	The ongoing process of reflection and action through which teams acquire, share, combine, and apply knowledge.

Individual	**Composition**	The mixture of characteristics that individual members bring to the group in terms of skill, ability, and disposition.
	Rewards	The material incentives and psychological rewards to direct team members towards the accomplishment of the team's mission.
	Leadership	The collection of strategic actions that are taken to accomplish team objectives, to ensure a reasonable level of efficiency, and to avoid team catastrophes.

The ten variables can be grouped by their scope, with the first three—purpose, empowerment, and support—considered to be organizational-level variables. Much of any cross-functional team's effectiveness is attributable to organizational factors beyond the team's immediate control (as the historical overview in the previous chapter suggests). The clarity of a team's purpose, the degree of a team's empowerment, and the quality of a team's support are primarily organizational-level team variables. Before a team is created, some higher authority usually determines what it should accomplish (purpose); whether the team will be given adequate resources, authority, and confidence (empowerment), and how the team will be inserted into and sustained by the larger organizational context in which it operates (support). These team attributes are often bestowed upon teams and beyond the ability of the teams to influence, but they can make a major impact on team performance.

In contrast, teams typically have more control over the next four team-level variables we consider: structure, decision-making, culture, and learning. Team-level variables are attributes and processes that help determine how the team operates. They are often the most salient characteristics to the casual observer because they regulate day-to-day operations. These variables also represent significant leverage points a team can most easily change to improve performance. Finally, three individual-level variables—composition, rewards, and leadership—capture individual team member attributes that may or may not be representative of the team as a whole but nonetheless affect its performance.

1. Team Purpose.

Team Founding	Strategic Consensus	Strategic Concept

Team purpose is defined as the broad, long term mandate given to the team by its management as well as the alignment of short-term objectives with the strategic vision and agreement on common approaches within the team.[5] **Team founding** is the initiating charter, mandate, or mission underlying the creation of the team. **Strategic consensus** is defined as basic agreement[6] among team members on the charter, mission, and goals of the team.[7] **Strategic concept** is the set of complicated, detailed, interconnected causal maps of the methodology that the team members employ to accomplish the team's objectives, such as agreement on how to do particular jobs,[8] how schedules will be set, what skills need further development, how the group will make team decisions,[9] and how continuing membership is earned.[10]

Teams are more likely to be successful when they have a single, coherent, and well-understood purpose. The broad, general purpose of HTTs was clearly stated early on and since then has been articulated consistently with only minor variations. However, the general mission statement is ambiguous in two respects that have handicapped a consensus on the purpose of the teams. In the following analysis we substantiated both these points, and make the case that greater clarity of purpose for the HTTs would benefit the entire HTS enterprise.

The Foreign Military Studies Office in 2005-2006 had a clear but broadly stated initial mission for its conception of the HTTs: map the human terrain. For many HTT members, mapping the human terrain meant basic data collection, not "higher level social science research." As we demonstrate later, the emphasis on data collection versus analysis was a persistent issue, and it was one that was never satisfactorily resolved. The guidance from HTS management to the first HTT in February 2007 left a lot of room for interpreting the team's purpose and how its work would be completed: "Just figure things out and then make things happen." This provided the team with "a blank check to operate how things need to be done,"[11] but left it unmoored from a more specific understanding of its primary goals and tasks. The five teams trained in Leavenworth in the summer of 2008 were given similar flexibility when they deployed to Iraq in fall 2008. After the six proof-of-concept teams (one in Afghanistan and five in Iraq) returned in early 2008, the HTS organization reviewed their experience and decided on a one-sentence description of their guiding mission that they taught to team members in their training cycle at Leavenworth:

> Conduct operationally-relevant, open-source social science research, and provide commanders and staffs at the brigade and division levels with an embedded knowledge capability, to establish a coherent, analytic cultural framework for operational planning, decision-making, and assessment.[12]

HTT members absorbed this generic team purpose well and often cited variations of it in interviews: "The overarching focus of HTS was to do culturally-specific, population-focused research in support of the unit that we were supporting."[13] Another HTT member said, "I pretty well stuck to the HTS doctrine: providing operationally relevant social science research to the unit."[14] Although the official HTT purpose statement has evolved slightly most HTT members recite its essential elements and believe that the HTS "vision was pretty damn clear."[15]

We believe, however, that this generic HTS statement of purpose begged two important questions that introduced confusion and uncertainty into the actual performance of HTTs: what is sociocultural knowledge, and what is operationally relevant? The generic definition of sociocultural knowledge is not clear, as we argued earlier (see shadow box on p. 7), and in the case of HTTs, there was much confusion over whether its boundaries intersected with military intelligence. Some HTT members who were not clear about their HTT's specific purpose were quite certain that it did not include providing information for lethal operations: "I should probably define what the mission wasn't—because that was defined more often than the mission—which is that we are *not* an intelligence gathering agency and we are *not* gathering targeting information for the S2 (intelligence officer) or for someone to act on kinetically."[16] In one case, an HTT shied away from a brigade commander who wanted it to participate in kinetic targeting, and consequently was considered ineffective by the commander.[17] In other cases, the aversion to supporting lethal operations amounted to denial by some social scientists that they were in a war zone trying to help one side win. As one HTT member noted, all HTS employees must "understand that we are [working] together to help win a war." Those who believed they would be insulated from combat, both physically and intellectually, could be "horrified at the realization of it, or just shut down."[18]

The proscription against working with "intelligence" seemed counterfactual. The HTS program was overseen by the Under Secretary of Defense for Intelligence, and the "G2" or Deputy Chief of Staff for Intelligence (DSCINT) at TRADOC. Also, as one student of HTS concluded, "All the talk of the Human Terrain System being simple 'open source' research was a polite fiction. The members of a Human Terrain Team worked for a military commander, they were located within a brigade headquarters, and information they shared, even if in the most general way, could help the commander sort out who was and was not the enemy."[19]

Nevertheless, HTS has asserted for years that the program was not a kinetic targeting intelligence asset. In keeping with this early guidance, some teams refused to work with intelligence officers. In one case:

> A three-star British General met with our team leader and the social scientist and said he wanted to use us. He had other atmospheric teams and told us to go out with them and report our findings to the S2 [intelligence officer]. He said he wanted us to have our information passed into the information cycle. The social scientist said, "We don't produce intelligence, and we won't talk to the S2 shop."[20]

The HTS resistance to identifying sociocultural knowledge as an input to intelligence operations has faded. Colonel Hamilton now refers to HTS as "an intelligence enabling capability,"[21] and in 2010-2011, an HTT was placed by its British commander in an intelligence cell, with a focus on non-kinetic information about the local population.[22]

The definition of operational relevance also was open to interpretation. HTS managers emphasized the importance of giving brigade[23] commanders a large amount of discretion on how they used the HTTs. Thus, in practice, commanders decide how HTT activities can be operationally relevant, and as we will demonstrate later, without a uniform appreciation derived from overarching counterinsurgency doctrine or a well-defined theater intelligence architecture. HTT members absorbed this reality, and frequently said in interviews that the purpose of their team was to be useful to and satisfy the brigade commander, or as one particular interviewee said, make him "happy."[24] As another HTT member explained, "There is no point in collecting this information unless you use it and influence the brigade," and doing so depended on the HTTs' relationship with the brigade commander.[25]

Consequently, commander views of what operationally relevant meant often dictated HTT purpose. Some commanders believed the purpose of their HTT was to help win popular support, which in turn would help win the war:

> The purpose of the team was to help that infantry commander better understand the Afghan people and culture so he can make the right decisions to win the war. And most of the time that doesn't involve killing bad guys, it involves winning over the good guys. I used to say 95 percent of the bad guys can be brought over, the rest just have to be killed. HTS was designed to do that, to win the people over.[26]

Other commanders believed HTTs served no useful purpose in this regard. One brigade commander, "did not appreciate any kind of touchy-feely understanding of the population," and "did not want the HTT getting in the way of the brigade's mission of trying to establish security in their Area of Operation."[27] Most disagreements over how HTTs could be operationally relevant, however, concerned the level of analysis provided by an HTT. We will explicate this point further in the following section of the report. However, to illustrate the issue, several HTT members thought they should conduct Ph.D.-level social science research while the HTT's brigade commanders they served wanted basic descriptions of the human terrain. These kinds of differences of opinion over what level of social science research were useful to operations were ultimately resolved in favor of the commanders' views, but not without some costs to efficiency as the common understanding was worked out.

In sum, the high degree of latitude given to brigade commanders to define operational relevance meant that HTTs could not jump straight to their tasks, but had to reach an accommodation with their commander before proceeding. Most HTTs were not able to translate the generic team purpose proposed by HTS in Leavenworth into a specific, shared team purpose that immediately allowed the team to proceed on task. This is why one HTT member complained that "HTS could never define what its mission was."[28] Without such a clear, specific and unambiguous team purpose, it was difficult for most HTTs to focus and perform quickly at a high level. Effective HTTs were able to resolve the system-level ambiguity about the definitions of sociocultural knowledge and operational relevance by adapting to the specific brigades they served, but this took time and reduced efficiency, especially given the year-long brigade tours for Afghanistan, which forced teams to repeatedly adjust their purpose to the preferences of new commanders.

These findings on team purpose are reinforced by examining the HTTs with the clear reputations for high and low performance. The most effective HTTs clearly were able to take the generic team purpose and, over time, adapt it to the commander's views to create a team-level strategic consensus about what the team should be and do. In contrast, the less effective teams could fracture over questions of whether they were in any way supporting lethal operations, and what level of research they ought to be performing in order to be operationally relevant.

2. Team Empowerment.

Structural	Resource	Psychological
Team empowerment can be defined as access to sufficient high-quality personnel, funds, and materials, and an appropriate amount of authority, to allow for confident, decisive action. **Team structural empowerment** is defined as the delegation of authority, responsibility, decision-making, task autonomy, power, control, and management to the team.[29] **Team resource empowerment** is defined as the budgeting of adequate resources for accomplishment of the team mission—personnel, funds, equipment, and other tangible resources.[30] **Team psychological empowerment** occurs when team members share a conviction that the team is capable of accomplishing its mission.[31]		

Cross-functional teams can fail if they are not empowered with resources, authority, and confidence to achieve their stated purpose. In general, the HTT members we interviewed did not believe the HTS organization empowered its HTTs with the effective allocation of resources. One team member said that, "In terms of resources, what HTS provided was disastrous."[32] Simple requests seemed impossible to fulfill. For example, one team created a reading list of 35 books on Afghanistan and got HTS managers to agree that each HTT in Afghanistan could benefit from having the collection in their workspaces. The team members, frustrated after a long waiting period and unconcerned about bureaucratic constraints sent a sarcastic explanation for how to overcome the problem: "Buy box, buy duct tape, buy a pen, put books in box, tape box, send to Afghanistan. Here's the address."[33] But it had no effect. Instead, the team spent its own money and had Amazon ship the books to its location in Afghanistan.

HTS did provide teams with hardware, software, and communications devices, but the consensus opinion is that these resources were not useful, at least in the early years of the program:

- "The MAP-HT literally was a door jamb; it did not work—it doesn't integrate with anything the brigade or the Army uses."[34]
- "MAP-HT is completely useless. The equipment HTS gave us was limiting."[35]
- "We had the MAP-HT computers that didn't really work, but we didn't really care because we had other systems and lines that came from the unit—pretty much everything came from the unit."[36]

- "We never had access to [classified internet] to communicate to share information with everyone else in the theater…so we could never discuss secret issues."[37]

A recent internal HTS report indicates the MAP-HT problems persist. The report, based on over 100 interviews with returning HTT members, conducted in early 2011 observed that, "there is not a single team using MAP-HT. Nor has any team ever effectively used it, though a couple of teams said they dabbled with parts of it for a short time. Most teams simply leave it in the box."[38] More recently usage rates have improved somewhat, but the large majority of teams still do not use the device.[39] HTTs dealt with other technological limitations besides MAP-HT. For example, HTS sent a stand-alone communications package to AF2 that was incompatible with anything the brigade, or the Army used. It also was unsecured, which posed a threat to operational security. The brigade S6 (Signals Officer) bluntly told the team lead they could not use the equipment.[40]

For the most part, however, HTTs were designed to live off of resources provided by their brigades, which again made the HTTs relationship with the brigade commander a matter of great importance. As one supervisor of multiple teams concluded: "It's how the team interacts with the brigade that determines what they are going to get."[41] In this regard, effective HTTs were able to convince their brigades to allocate the resources necessary to accomplish their tasks, including lodging, office space, mobility/security, interpreters, and food. If they performed well, and provided the brigade with valued information, they could receive even more resources. In addition, some HTTs benefited from special circumstances. For example, one HTAT that operated as an HTT noted that operating at a higher commander level had benefits: "We got what we wanted. We had our own vehicles. We were on missions and said, 'Let's go to this village' and they would say 'Here's a rifle platoon….' The whole purpose…was for us to collect information for them, and they would provide men for us…. It was phenomenal."[42] However, a member of HTAT Bagram had quite a different experience: "There were zero resources from the division."[43]

Most teams in the 2009-2010 period were being assigned to units that had never worked with an HTT before, and they met immediate and basic resources constraints. Some teams would arrive on base only to have the brigade staff question their orders because no one had told them the team was arriving.[44] Just finding a place to sleep could be a challenge,[45] as was office space: "We didn't have the office space we wanted. We had to hot-rack our desks"[46] so that everyone could use the equipment. Another team was repeatedly dislodged from its assigned space: "We went from two to a room, to four to a room, to six to a room. We just kept getting thrown out of billeting, and then we lost our office…. We had nowhere to meet and talk."[47] This HTT member said the inadequate work facilities were one reason they quit the program. Other teams accepted their makeshift billeting arrangements because the entire team was rarely on base at the same time. Yet another team found advantages in subpar office arrangements because it was less noisy than the brigade headquarters office: "We had a tiny office space around the back. Separated, but that was a good thing."[48]

It took time to establish a relationship with a brigade that generated resource support, and the relationship was not necessarily an enduring one. HTTs that received generous resources from a brigade were under pressure to perform well and if they did not, the resources could be pulled back. As an early team leader explained, "If you ask for all these resources, and you can't make it, your credibility goes downhill pretty fast."[49] In addition, even a good resource relationship came to an end when the brigade rotated out. One team member described how difficult it was to do his job after a change of command from one brigade that had provided excellent mobility to a new brigade that was not willing to provide the same mobility.[50]

There were additional resource limitations for some HTTs working with NATO allies. A member of a clearly ineffective team that was assigned to a NATO ally described the information, mobility and security resource constraints the HTT faced:

- "We never had access to the patrol reports. An American unit had arrived a year earlier. We should have turned those reports into baseline knowledge to put into MAP-HT. But we didn't have that either. We had no way to gather the data to say we had a basic idea of what is going on in the AO."[51]

- "We didn't have any vehicles even though the other units did. That limited our ability because of the restrictions placed on [NATO ally] movements for political reasons: to avoid casualties, and because the [NATO ally] also lacked vehicles. We did get out, but it was never ideal."[52]

Whether assigned to an American or allied unit, ineffective HTTs could find themselves in downward cycles where a lack of resources made it more difficult to demonstrate value, which in turn made it more difficult to get resources from the brigade.

In addition to resources, organizations also empower teams with delegated authority. Experts in cross-functional teams sometimes refer to such authority as "structural empowerment," i.e. the delegation of sufficient authority, control, and power to the team for the team to accomplish its mission. Most immediately, empowerment was often a function of the HTT's relationship with the commander. In some cases, the military backgrounds of HTT members helped secure respect and thus authority: "The brigade had confidence in us. Two team members were also former Special Forces. One team member was taken hostage by the Serbians. I'm a former Marine. One team member said he was with Naval Special Forces."[53] Other teams earned authority through their products and competent interaction with brigade commanders, so that "we were...considered one of his staff; he made time for us any time we really needed it."[54]

HTT leaders were also delegated authority from HTS. In the early years of the program, HTS managers made a point of allowing teams a great deal of latitude. Later, however, some interviewees noted that HTS managers would not back up team leaders trying to deal with problematic personnel: "If a team leader recommended to get rid of someone, [the HTS managers] would veto it if [they] liked them. [They] would say no. Without a chain of command that functioned, and without devolved authority to the lowest level, you were stuck with what you had."[55] The team leader continued by saying that he "didn't have the directive authority [from HTS] to require people to do things. I couldn't tell [the social scientists] to do anything."[56] Several team leaders found work-around solutions for their lack of authority over team personnel, such as sending problematic personalities to work by themselves on other Forward Operating Bases,[57] using less qualified team members to manage liaisons on base,[58] or allowing unmotivated team members to work on their own agendas.[59]

Other interviewees objected to micromanagement, either from HTS or HTATs. Complaints included asking the team to file specific reports on short notice, which interrupted their work for the brigade,[60] or moving team members between teams.[61] Most cases of HTS micro-management cited seem minor and representative of the normal irritations associated with work in a large organization rather than threats to team performance. Other micromanagement charges were leveled against some HTATs. HTATs operate at the division level, creating some ambiguity as to whether they in any way controlled the activities of the HTTs that operated at lower levels. According to one HTT member, different HTAT leaders interpreted their roles differently: "The first HTAT leader gave us support, and let us take our marching orders from the brigade, which is what he was supposed to do, but the second HTAT leader was constantly trying to push down [orders] to tell the brigade how to use their HTT, which was completely what they were not supposed to do."[62] The question of HTATs' proper role in supervising the use of HTTs was not resolved until the creation of the Theater Command

Element and subsequent codification of the HTAT role as an entity that was to remain at division level and focus on the creation of products through the convergence of all analytical sources.

Moving supervisory authority over the HTTs from Newport News to Kabul presumably makes the HTTs and HTATs more responsive to the theater commander. In any case, we believe HTS encouraged, and most teams discovered, that their local brigade commanders' authority made the greatest difference in their ability to perform well. Effective teams earned the trust of their brigades quickly and maintained that high level of trust across their tour. As teams produced products that commanders thought were helpful, their confidence grew and they redoubled their efforts. This type of energy is sometimes referred to as "psychological empowerment," a sense of competence, efficacy, and confidence. The converse was also true, however. Poor performance, or a reputation for poor performance, could destroy credibility with brigades and sap HTT morale.

3. Team Support.

Organizational Relationships	Supportive Contexts	Team-based Organizations

Team support is defined as the set of organizational processes that connect a team to other teams at multiple levels within the organization, other organizations, and a wide variety of resources that the team needs to accomplish its mission.[63] **Organizational relationships** refer to how the team, from its inception, is envisioned to relate and interact with other component parts of the system, including degree of network centrality, level of network embeddedness, and the types of organizational components in close network proximity.[64] **Supportive contexts** are defined as efforts by the larger organization to design, implement, and constantly improve mechanisms that reduce the amount of energy a team must expend in conflict with the larger organization, and maximize the amount of time that a team can spend on mission accomplishment.[65] **Team-based organizations** are characterized by freedom for teams to manage themselves, by recognition that different types of teams require different degrees of leadership intrusiveness, and a reliance on analytical tools to determine the structure of the network of teams in the organization.[66]

Team support, which is often referred to in the literature on teams as "team context," includes the broader organizational milieu in which a team operates; where the team is embedded within the host organization, how the team interacts with other parts of the organization, and what the relationships are between the team and other groups in the same space. Teams that are richly supported by the larger organizational apparatus have a much better chance of succeeding. Unfortunately, HTTs were not supported well by any of the three larger communities that they primarily drew upon and served, beginning with the academic community.

HTS was not formally tied to any academic institution, but the program was intended to bridge the gap between the academic and military communities that had evolved over the past decades. Early in the life of the program, one of the program's progenitors, McFate, associated HTS with a particular subset of academia and the social sciences: anthropology. Anthropology is a relatively small social science field, with only 11,000 members of the American Anthropological Association (compared, for example, to 137,000 members of the American Psychological Association).[67] Anthropologists have a long history of avoiding cooptation by the military, and take some pains to actively reject the nickname the field earned as "the handmaid of colonialism" from the days of the British Empire.[68] Moreover, at the time HTS was in its infancy, a well-organized subgroup of the American academy, the American Anthropological Association, was fighting the U.S. Government on its coercive interrogation policies.[69]

Thus the tendency for some members of the HTS management team to present HTS as an anthropology program[70] was controversial. McFate claimed to be "the most hated anthropologist in America,"[71] and warned some anthropologists she recruited to serve on HTTs that they would be unwelcome in academia for the rest of their careers.[72] The American Anthropological Association's negative reaction to the program created bad publicity,[73] and continues to be a powerful source of criticism of the program.

Even before the creation of HTS, there were signs it would be difficult to forge a partnership with the broader social science community. Some months after Operation Iraqi Freedom commenced, one military officer working on sociocultural knowledge attended a conference where he told representatives from academic communities that "we need your help…and they basically beat me up for two straight days."[74] The reluctance of many within the social science community to support military operations continues, with some even leveling charges of war crimes against HTT members.[75] It is difficult to know how widespread and significant the negative sentiments toward the HTS program were in academia. Other factors also complicated recruitment of regional experts, such as BAE's recruitment problems[76] and the sobering deaths of three highly-qualified regional experts in 2008—doctoral candidates Michael Bhatia, Nicole Suveges, and Paula Loyd.

However, anecdotal evidence suggests the academic resentment of HTS was substantial enough to complicate recruitment of qualified personnel,[77] which in turn forced HTS to roll back its expectations several times.

Part of the HTS plan for the reachback centers included a Subject Matter Experts Network (SMEnet).[78] After HTS received funding in 2006 and 2007 some of these external subject matter experts were pulled into HTS as faculty, observers, and team members (e.g. Tracy St. Benoit, Tom Johnson, and Michael Bhatia). Such talent proved hard to recruit and retain, so HTS had to use younger, less experienced analysts to work in the reachback research centers. In addition, HTS had to scale back expectations for HTT talent. The original HTT design called for two experts—one social science expert and one regional expert. Tracy St. Benoit and Tom Johnson deployed to Khost in February 2007, with St. Benoit playing the role of social science expert and Johnson playing the role of regional expert, but Johnson left Khost after a short period of time, and St. Benoit filled both roles for AF1 until her departure in September 2007. Only one of the five teams deployed to Iraq in Fall 2007 was able to field both a social science expert and a regional culture expert,[79] and the one regional expert left the program in December 2007.[80] Fondacaro said that because there were so few regional cultural experts HTS decided it would have to grow its own.[81] HTS then eliminated the position of qualified regional cultural expert from the HTT structure, reverting to a fall-back position of creating "cultural analysts"—human terrain analysts with some language or cultural expertise.

Although the lack of support for HTTs in academia was a problem, the more immediate and important source of support for HTTs was the HTS organization itself. Early on HTS was preoccupied with raising enough HTTs, and consequently tended to treat deployed HTTs with benign neglect. This detachment was sometimes interpreted negatively by HTT members: "I don't think anyone else at TRADOC or HTS cared about what the teams were doing. I think they only care if there is a problem. But they don't care about success."[82] Other HTT members noted charitably that HTS had many masters, which made it difficult to focus on HTT performance. It had to manage multiple organizational relationships with the Office of the Under Secretary of Defense for Intelligence (program approval and funding), Central Command (program consumers), TRADOC (program managers), and BAE Systems (omnibus contract holders until 2011). Some HTT members believed the management challenges associated with these complex relationships preoccupied HTS: "HTS had then, and had previously, and continues to have, some serious dysfunctions regarding its bureaucracy. It does not function well. It was constantly in a state of flux, based on the current whim of the people in charge."[83]

Either way, the result, many HTT members believed, was that HTS could not focus on HTT performance:

"HTS could have done more in setting us up for success, but they did nothing."[84]

"There weren't enough people to fill the jobs that were supposed to be filled. They were terrible at administration."[85]

"They could not figure out how to rehire someone. The team leader and I were writing letters to BAE trying to keep [an HTT member]. The brigade was requesting his return. They couldn't get it done. It was embarrassing."[86]

"Why am I going to the North when I speak Italian, and not the West? Then they took another guy who can teach German, and fluent in Dari, and sent him to the West. This is kind of [senseless]."[87]

"HTS has a big 'every man for himself' mentality. There is no emphasis on teams. None of that. Once you are there [in the field], no one from Leavenworth or Oyster Point is there to support you. Even if you send 50 emails, you are truly on your own."[88]

Deployed military units were the most immediate organizational milieu for HTTs, and they greatly affected performance as already noted. The HTT concept was supported by theater commanders like Petraeus and McChrystal, but not by all their subordinate commanders or military personnel more generally. Many interviewees noted traditional military culture is not supportive of the HTT concept.[89] The training regime encouraged new team members to believe that they would report directly to the brigade commander. In practice, the teams had to secure support wherever they could find it on the brigade staff. Some teams reported to deputy commanders because the commander himself was rarely on base: "When I went in, I introduced myself to the commander and gave him a brief. But understanding the dynamics of the brigade commander, who's on the FOB only 4-5 days per month, you discover the guy you have to go to is the [deputy commander]."[90] The executive officer was also considered a main point of contact.[91] Other teams reported directly to the operations officer, the S3: "You have to convince the S3 that everything you are doing is worthwhile. It's not unusual for a brigade commander to defer to the S3."[92] Some teams worked closely with other brigade staff sections, particularly

Civil Affairs, S9,[93] and Information Operations, S7.[94] Quite often, the teams were placed in Effects Cells where the information produced by the teams was combined with other sources to create a composite picture of the surrounding human terrain.[95]

Many HTT members believe that NATO allies were more supportive of the HTT concept than U.S. military personnel. HTT members worked with multiple NATO allies, some extensively so: "I [worked] with Norway, Latvia, Sweden and Finland, Hungary, US, Germans."[96] The other countries were generally seen as supporters of the HTS concept: "NATO allies loved the idea of Human Terrain Teams."[97] A team member noted that when he worked with the Canadians, he reported to a flag officer, which increased the HTT's influence.[98] Another team member noted the Germans insisted on adherence to their established protocols, "But if you respect the process, they are really easy to deal with."[99] More to the point, as another HTT member explained, "The Germans had Tactical HUMINT Teams, which are actually a hybrid of Civil Affairs and Human Terrain Teams. They were very receptive to some of us."[100]

In short, the HTTs were, in many respects, orphans bereft of sustained support. The academy did not embrace the HTS concept, and some disciplines strongly opposed it. The HTS organization was preoccupied with management challenges, and could not focus on HTT performance. Finally, the U.S. military culture provided varying levels of support. Enough flag officers and field officers supported HTTs to keep the program afloat and indeed, expanding. However, some field commanders were dismissive; almost all were skeptical, waiting for HTTs to prove themselves before embracing them.

4. Team Structure.

Design	Mental Models	Boundary Spanning
Team structure refers to the "mechanics" of teams—team design, team mental models, and team network dynamics. **Team design** covers the number of team members (i.e. team size), the tenure of the team, the job design that the team will perform, and the placement (co-location, concentration, or dispersion) of team members, in addition to the information and communications systems that are used to compensate for geographic dispersion. **Team mental models** are defined as complex maps of the network of specialized knowledge assets, in the form of people within the team, within the organization, and outside the organization.[101] **Team boundary spanning** is defined as a wide range of activities undertaken by team members to secure support from outside the team[102] through ambassadorial (upward) communications, lateral (horizontal) communications,[103] and probing/scouting (downward) communications.[104]		

Team structure refers to the "mechanics" of teams—team design, team mental models, and team boundary spanning. Effective cross-functional teams are structured to perform the task the teams are intended to accomplish. At Leavenworth the teams were originally organized around five functional positions with a clear hierarchy and the presumption that the team would report directly to the brigade commander.[105] Later, after cultural analysts proved difficult to attract and retain, the position was cut from the design and the teams were reduced to four functional positions. The cultural analysts' role was played by interpreters provided by brigades in the field.[106] Otherwise, the Leavenworth design was stable in principle.

It was less stable in practice. Most teams did not maintain the clean linear relationships between the team leader at the top, the social scientist, the research manager, and the human terrain analyst at the bottom. Many teams were redesigned in the field—by brigade commanders or team members—in ways that broke down the initial functional distinctions between team members. Thus, according to one HTT member, "The hierarchy on the website is almost completely thrown out the window when you get [in-country]."[107] Another team member noted that "HTS gives you the theory of the jobs, but when it comes down to it, everyone does everyone else's jobs."[108]

One major reason that teams moved away from their initial functional structures was that the brigade commanders demanded more geographic coverage. HTTs responded to these demands by splitting up their team into small subsets: "Often we would split into three different groups and have three different patrols going at the same time.[109] Commanders often encouraged HTTs and HTATs to deploy individuals away from large bases: "Why bring someone back to Bagram when he's doing such good work in the field?"[110] Similarly, the Jalalabad HTT chose to serve their brigade commander by dividing up the team along geographic lines: "There was only so much you could do sitting in Nangarhar. Our brigade had a massive area of operations. The structure was developed to provide what was best for the brigade. How can you cover Kunar if you are not there?"[111] The first Kandahar HTT also split into sub-teams serving different purposes and different clients in different geographic areas, with a research manager on base to coordinate the two sub-teams: "The team leader split the team up into two teams of three, stationed in the different areas with the companies. I stayed and coordinated everything between the two teams. I disseminated the reports to everybody, including the Canadians and the British."[112] The Wardak/Logar HTT also concluded that a geographic structure would be more valuable to their brigade commander than a functional structure, and split their team between two Forward Operating Bases.[113] In the most extreme cases of geographic dispersion, some HTT members were recruited onto Special Operations Forces teams and pulled off of their HTTs completely: "I was out with the ODA [Operational Detachment Alpha] alone. I wasn't working with the HTT guys."[114]

Another major reason the initial team design did not survive in the field was the management decision to replenish the HTTs through individual replacements rather than as complete teams. The frequent comings and goings of members forced some teams to cross-train in the field and require individuals to move between the different functions of the HTT. Other teams compensated for the instability by structuring themselves around the idiosyncratic skills of individual on the team. For example, one team told us that their team was structured, "entirely around the skills of the individual.... We had one guy who spoke Pashtu so we would use him to engage key leaders. Every individual was identified for their strengths and qualities."[115] One research manager noted that at other times, he worked "as a cultural analyst" while "there were times I was a subject matter expert on certain topics."[116] In the worst case, individuals were left alone to staff an HTT by themselves, which meant they had to perform all team functions themselves until new members arrived.[117]

Finally, even though HTS was clear about the role of each position, individuals sometimes arrived in theatre with their own and contrary expectations. One social scientist "initially thought he was there to do my job, and everyone else's job. I [the team leader] had to sit him down and tell him 'this is my job, this is your job.'"[118] Another HTT member noted that, "We didn't have a research manager. Our research manager refused to do that job. She wanted to be a fieldworker."[119] One human terrain analyst refused to leave the base so the team leader assigned them to remain on base in order to perform a liaison function with the brigade.[120]

The initial team design was a cross-functional one, intended to juxtapose different perspectives against each other to solve complex problems, but only a few teams developed common approaches that forced team members with different backgrounds and different team roles to collaborate. With team size and location highly variable, it was difficult for HTTs to adopt standard "task designs," or shared mental models on how tasks and technology should be used to maximize productivity. Teams understood they had a common set of products they could create, but the way they went about it was highly variable. For example, one team was expected to cover such a large area (four provinces) that it was forced to split the team up, leading one of the team's social scientists to observe that, "We did very little work as a team."[121]

Teams that were able to develop their own working processes could be quite effective, however. The first HTT in Afghanistan, which was widely acknowledged to be effective, worked as a tightly integrated cross-functional team:

> I used Holbert as the key focal point; he would assist Tracy with writing the reports. Roya was a language asset, and Damon helped Holbert a lot. They did a lot of engagement on the FOB, but when outside the wire, everyone was doing research. Tracy would do a debrief with the team and then she'd take that 20-page report, put it into a briefing, and we would give it to [the brigade commander].[122]

Less effective or ineffective HTTs typically did not come up with a working set of operating procedures. One member of an ineffective team lamented the lack of a working model for team activity, noting: "We never had a plan as far as I knew. We never knew how we would establish ourselves."[123] Some team members serving on teams that failed to work out the details of how they would operate once they were in the field were disillusioned by the experience and wanted more guidance from HTS: "There was no specific instruction on how the team should work, and what the chain of command would be. There was no discussion about how we would fit into the team when we showed up downrange."[124] The individual replacement system HTS employed exacerbated the problem, making it difficult for teams to establish protocols during training. It also seems, as we argue elsewhere, that HTS preferred to let the teams operate with greater flexibility to please commanders. HTS never developed an effective mechanism to gather, analyze, and respond to feedback from the field about best practices, nor did it have a model of team performance that postulated best practices.

Of course, geographic dispersion of HTT members, which accorded with the wishes of many commanders, often negated the need for team processes, regardless of their origin (HTS or the teams themselves). Instead members could individually pursue ways to contribute value to commanders:

> The team leader let me do pretty much whatever I wanted to do—he encouraged self-direction and self-starters. There is a lot of freedom downrange, and within that variable you need mature people to be able to do that, and incorporate what the brigade command teams or the battalions are interested in.[125]

Some team members preferred working as individuals, particularly those with strong academic backgrounds. On one team where this was the case, other team members felt the team was less effective than it should have been: **"I** think the research manager was [upset] because we were not functioning as a team; which we weren't. We were functioning as individual nodes."[126]

There also was variability in how the teams conducted networking, or team "boundary spanning." Team leaders were, by design, supposed to be the primary boundary-spanners for HTTs, first with the brigade commanders and staffs, and also with other organizations. If the team leaders were not respected, the entire team's credibility could be damaged. A previously effective HTT found that its ability to perform its task was limited by the arrival of a new leader who was not received favorably by the brigade staff: "He couldn't brief. He couldn't fit into his body armor. He was not able and not willing to go out. Immediately our credibility was gone."[127] On another team, "when the team leader presented [a brief], he would always take the lead and make himself look [bad].... In one instance the commander told him to be quiet. After the first month, they asked him not to come to meetings to brief."[128] Another ineffective team leader refused to join the brigade staff in their daily staff meetings because they were "painful" and "irrelevant."[129] Practically speaking, this meant the team had no understanding of the commander's intent regarding operations, and thus could not perform its duties well.

Yet, other teams benefited greatly from members who formed valuable relationships with the brigade staff and elsewhere. In many cases, these "boundary spanners" were not the team leader. One team left a member on base who, because of his age and experience, had contacts throughout the brigade, the division, Special Operations Forces and the Afghan security forces. He obtained the resources necessary for the team to continue functioning and would coordinate meetings and travel for every other team member for future missions as well.[130] Another effective team "sprinkled" their members across the entire brigade staff and other enablers to build the team's network of contacts. The team lead focused on the Task Force commander, executive officer and chief of staff; one human terrain analyst worked with the Psychological Operations section, while the other worked with the Provincial Reconstruction Team; and the research manager focused on the fusion cell that was established. The social scientist was described as a "floater" who could migrate across areas because of the rapport he had established in his time there.[131] Whether the networking was assigned to one individual or a distributed responsibility, it was a critical function for high team performance.

5. Team Decision-making.

Heterogeneous Perspectives	Conflict	Decision Implementation
Team decision-making is defined as the mechanisms that are employed to make sense of and solve a variety of complex problems faced by a cross-functional team.[132] **Heterogeneous perspectives** refers to the presence of diverse, coherent, belief systems on the team.[133] **Team conflict** is defined as the capability of the team to generate helpful conflict between divergent viewpoints.[134] **Decision implementation** requires a suppression of conflicting views in favor of sufficient strategic consensus to implement team decisions.[135]		

Cross-functional teams need to pay attention to the decision making process that turns the team's diverse perspectives into better overall team output. Typically high performing teams leverage heterogeneous capabilities and perspectives and exploit productive conflict to produce feasible and implemented solutions to complex problems. The key is to ensure that the decision-making integrates diverse capabilities and reconciles competing views in a productive manner. In general, the HTS organization paid little attention to how the teams would make decisions in Afghanistan. The team members we interviewed often could not remember "anything specific on how decision-making in the Human Terrain System worked."[136] The teams that deployed to Afghanistan largely were left to their own devices on productive decision-making processes, and the results were variable.

The underlying point of the HTTs was to leverage the conflict between a traditional military perspective and a population-sensitive social science perspective to help inform the military decision-making process. Most HTT members saw this natural tension as a positive factor, even the *raison d'etre* of the program:

> If you have someone with the military experience, and someone who has pure research experience, that conflict is what prepares you to brief the military and frame it to them. It's also the point of HTT, is trying to infuse information and point out the value of that information to people who have been trained to think in a certain way. I saw that tension as the natural byproduct, and a good thing.[137]

In addition, the civilian social science personnel were naturally a hetero-geneous group. Other than their experience in higher education, they lacked a common unifying experience. Instead, they came to their HTT positions with diverse experience and perspectives, which almost unanimously was seen as a source of strength by interviewees: "It helped to have people from different pasts;" "It was great to have incredible diversity;" "The diversity of experience was extremely important;" etc. As one HTT member said, given the complex environment, "if everyone is thinking the same thing," then it is likely "no one is really thinking."

Heterogeneous perspectives also are an acknowledged source of conflict. Often the conflicts arose between the social scientist and team leader. Sometimes it was a clash over authority and role confusion. In one recent case, a lieutenant wanted to move from a village because he suspected an attack soon, but the social scientist resisted, thinking his GS-15 rank entitled him to control such decisions.[138] In another case where the "biggest conflict was between the social scientist and the rest of the team," the conflict was ascribed to the fact that social scientists are "used to working as an individual," while on HTTs they were "forced to share everything, [which] caused some conflict." Similarly, another source argued social scientists who had been "sitting in the academy too long, had a difficult time...getting outside of that 'I' [and] the self-interest in their research, understanding 'we' and 'team' and what operationally relevant means."[139]

Some observers of HTS considered the conflict on teams unprofessional and something to be suppressed. On the contrary, it was natural and arguably built into the cross-functional structure of the teams. However, effective HTTs did have to find ways to resolve unproductive conflict. One team leader used the Myers-Briggs personality profile to help clarify underlying team conflicts. According to one participant, "it allowed people to see how the other perceived things and how they worked."[140] With relational, emotional, and destructive conflict over personality differences out of the way, the varying perspectives that each member brought to the table could be engaged fruitfully. When this happened, the team could experience "a lot of internal conflict" and "still [be] successful."[141] Other interviewees from successful HTTs made similar observations:

> "We had very open discussions. There was much wailing and gnashing of teeth, and then we would figure it out."[142]

> "We had a really wide variety of people. I think for the most part, it enabled creativity. There was some figurative chair throwing. But it enabled us to be creative."[143]

> "We would argue like cats and dogs. [Then we would use] dialectical reasoning to come up with the best idea; usually to a successful resolution."[144]

> "I could tell this group was a close family. They were very careful with who they brought in....They all had a lot of mutual respect...a lot of cohesion and trust. There were definitely disagreements. But they worked them out in a professional way." [An HTT member aspiring to join a high productivity HTT][145]

When teams were required to write together and review each other's documents, the level of productive conflict could go up:

> The decision-making became a little more problematic when it came to writing up reports for brigade commanders. Then sometimes we'd have pretty good arguments. Somebody would write a draft, and everybody else would tear it up. We shared products that we were writing, and people would tear those up. There was a fair amount of criticism at that level. Usually it was good-natured.[146]

The key in such circumstances was to keep the debate professional and not personal: "Our team was an ego-free environment. We would disagree frequently on research, but it would always be incredibly civil."[147] The decision to produce products as a team, rather than as a collection of products produced by geographically dispersed individuals, meant there was more conflict to manage. However, it also meant the products were more likely to survive brigade staff scrutiny, and therefore affect the military decision making process: "Within the team, we had our dissension, but there was more synergy when we worked together because we could put on a united front for briefings."[148]

In contrast, ineffective HTTs were more likely to avoid productive conflict through geographic separation, and reduced conversation among team members:

> There wasn't a road in between North and South Kapisa. To get to North Kapisa, I would take the northern route. To get to Southern Kapisa, the other social scientist would take the southern road. It was a geographic division. We had very different approaches and focuses. We never had any real conflict per se.[149]

Some team leaders avoided conflict between high-performing team members and lower-performing team members by isolating low-performers:

> Our team was very demanding of one another. The other research manager demanded a lot from you when asking you questions. The team leader had expectations for your output. That kind of culture is what continued and enabled us. When [poorer performers] showed up, we would give them a chance and if they couldn't perform we sent them away.[150]

Similarly:

> There was always a second tier consisting of people who just really weren't that good. It wasn't that they were stupid or lazy; you could just tell this wasn't the right environment and the right job for them to be doing. We didn't have the wherewithal to fire them. It was just better to say 'Okay, good idea, we'll keep it under consideration'— and then bin their idea as soon as you could, rather than dig in and engage them in an argument.[151]

Thus on some teams, conflict avoidance through delegation, geographic separation, walling-off or other means was not just a method of dealing with especially problematic personnel, but rather a management technique. When used in this manner, conflict avoidance reduced the effectiveness of HTTs by limiting the viewpoints that had to be considered while assessing and resolving complex issues.

The way teams reached decisions varied greatly, and had a lot to do with the team's leadership style (discussed below). At one extreme, some HTTs were told what to do by their autocratic team leader.[152] A team member of another ineffective team described their decision making process as "whatever [the team lead] told us to research, no matter how whimsical, how nonsensical, how unconnected to the overall mission."[153] In other cases team leaders were not so directive, but still dissuaded productive conflict by refusing to sanction it: "[The team lead] did not like to be questioned and did not like new or different ideas. I learned straight away to keep my mouth shut."[154] Another HTT leader permitted discussion but reserved the right to impose solutions: "You will have conflict, but I tell them we will reach a consensus decision [and that] I might have to overrule it and do what is in the interest of the battalion."[155] For another HTT, a similar model prevailed: "We would have a conversation, then [the team lead] made the call. He wasn't arbitrary."[156] And again: "We would discuss the problem or the issue, discuss what to do with the situation and then [the team lead] would make the final decision, but usually he made the decision that members already agreed to."[157]

Most HTT members were satisfied with a decision making process that allowed them to explain their views. For some HTT members, however, anything less than consensus decision-making was a problem. One team leader recounts how he explained his expectations to his team:

> I gave the team…what I expected of them and vice versa. Embedded in that was decision-making processes. I wanted it to be collaborative. I wanted their ideas and creativity because over the years I've seen great value hearing other options….I did expect that once I made the decision that everyone would pull in that direction. I had mixed success with that to tell you the truth.[158]

One HTT member, who had been absorbed onto a Special Operations Forces team, described the decision making there as more consensus-based: "Everyone had a real ability to speak because it is a small team. Everything depended on what we decided on as a team. Everyone had to understand the bigger picture. We always talked about getting 100 percent buy-in."[159] The more the decision making was consensus-based, the more conflictual and time consuming it could be. Still, it produced a team decision, as one member noted: "We would hash it out and sometimes it was loud, but it got done. I'm not saying I'd like to do that again, but it got the missions decided."[160]

In the review of leadership, we will examine again how leadership affected decision-making. Here it will suffice to note that successful teams overcame conflict stemming from internal differences and "generally were able to come to some common ground and create products that were beneficial from everyone's perspective."[161] Certainly this proved true on the best teams; they found a way to embrace different perspectives and resolve conflict productively to the benefit of the team. When traditional military professionals and social science experts were able to disagree, debate, and reconcile competing viewpoints, and then turn those discussions into militarily relevant products and advice, HTTs were effective; otherwise they generally were not.

6. Team Culture.

Climate	Cohesion	Trust
Team culture can be defined as the shared values, norms and beliefs of the team, which are manifested in behavioral expectations, level of commitment and degree of trust among team members. **Team climate** is "the set of norms, attitudes, and expectations that individuals perceive to operate in a specific social context."[162] **Team cohesion** is measured by the commitment of team members to the team's task, mission, and purpose; to the team itself; and to one another.[163] **Team trust** is "the shared perception by the majority of team members that individuals in the team will perform particular actions important to its members and that the individuals will recognize and protect the rights and interests of all the team members engaged in their joint endeavor."[164]		

Effective cross-functional teams have team cultures that are characterized by increasing degrees of trust. Often the first step is a team climate that encourages information sharing, which builds into team cohesion, and over time, develops into strong trust relations among team members. In any case, team performance requires some basic level of trust among team members, and HTTs had two problems to overcome in this regard: the team formation processes at Leavenworth and the recruitment of people with a low ability to work together in teams. Instead of forming teams upon their arrival at Leavenworth and keeping the teams intact through training, HTS typically did not tell recruits which team they would be part of until the recruits were about to be deployed.[165] Rarely did a team train together as a group,[166] especially from 2006-2009. Even as late as 2011, many new teams were still being formed with the team lead arriving weeks or months before any other team member arrived, and the team members only knowing one another if they happened to be in the same training cycle at Leavenworth, which often is not the case.[167]

In addition, because of the BAE contract constraints, HTS could not screen potential HTT members by demonstrated capacity to work on teams. Other attributes were accorded higher priority, perhaps for understandable reasons. However, one HTT member with experience over several years in the program believed that the recruitment of people who could not work well on teams helped explain the variable performance of HTTs:

> The one thing about HTTs is that it is very idiosyncratic. Personalities can make or break it. If you have the right group of people willing to work together, despite the circumstances, then you will be wildly effective. There were a lot of the extreme sides of each [type of performance]. Not much in the middle.[168]

Another self-effacing HTT member graded her own performance based on her ability to work as a member of a team. The first tour, she said: "I was a disaster." On the second tour, "I was less of a disaster," because she said, she began to work well with others.[169] Many HTT members, especially those without military experience, had to come to appreciate what it took to work well as members of teams; for many it was an on-the-job training experience.

HTTs in Afghanistan varied widely in their levels of cohesion, ranging from tightly-knit teams to those experiencing intense personal conflicts.[170] The military members (and in particular team leaders) generally appreciated the importance of a good team climate, appreciating the protection it could provide against splintering, sidetracking, and dysfunction: "We live and operate in small teams. Teams can splinter downrange. I think it's easy to get sidetracked because there is so much to do. That is why the atmosphere is important. Without that, you become a dysfunctional team."[171] Accordingly, some HTT leaders and teams worked hard to build team cohesion, making a point of eating together and enjoying what little recreation there was together.[172]

It is clear from close examination of the highly effective HTTs that they were able to create team cultures characterized by supportive team climates, with high cohesion and degrees of trust. An HTT member described the family-type bond that his team developed: "We had each others' back. It's like brothers and sisters. You can be rude to your brother and sister, but when someone else does it, then that's just wrong. We pick at each other, but if someone said anything, it was instant pack mode."[173] Often bonding was reinforced by the dangerous environment. Even people who experienced some degree of interpersonal tension in training sometimes later "bonded wonderfully in the field."[174]

Most teams, however, only had subsets of individuals who trusted one another, and thus mixed or weak team cultures. Many teams developed fissures and were only able to build cohesion among a subset of team members. Subgroups might form around high-performers, or in response to a member who was disliked: "Cohesion went up hugely when [the team lead] came in because it created this us versus him sense….So we all closed ranks."[175]

Given the workload and stressful environment, any major fissures in the team were likely to sidetrack productivity, or worse, make the team vulnerable to disintegrating under the pressures of a challenging task in a dangerous combat environment.[176] In some cases, HTTs succumbed to violent personal disagreements, leading to an environment that one team member described as "Lord of the Flies on crack."[177] One source observed, "You spend a lot of energy just trying to survive the dramas."[178] Another said, "We were unable to achieve what we were capable of due to dramas and problems that took 95 percent of our energy."[179]

For years the HTS program appeared to assume that high levels of team trust could be manufactured rapidly among people in a stressful environment who did not know each other well. This did not happen as a matter of course. As HTT members noted when asked about trust, "It's hard coming in with people that you don't know."[180] Absent having trained and deployed together, trust had to be built in the field. That meant that the importance of trust first had to be recognized and then pursued self-consciously, which is what effective HTTs did. Effective HTTs considered team trust a valuable resource that had to be constructed, nurtured and occasionally reconstructed throughout the team's deployment. Leaders knew the importance of "trust within the unit, within the team, and between the individuals. Who will do the right thing, all the time? This is why you must understand your team: to know who can do what missions."[181]

Several HTT members commented on the small-team trust culture that predominates in Special Forces, and which was a model of sorts for the HTTs, albeit one that was not always realized (see shadow box: The "SF" Connection). Special Forces do not automatically extend trust to all members of the team. Instead, each team member is watched closely and encouraged to earn the team's trust time and again by their actions and performance. Trust has to be earned, as some HTT members noted. In the best HTTs, this approach to trust prevailed and over time, helped the teams coalesce.

However, such an ideal was elusive. It was far more common for some members to develop deep bonds of trust while distrusting other members of the team, which limited the range of collaboration: "If you're in the trust tree, and you have different expertise, I will ask you for help."[182] Conversely, "it was a little difficult to deal with the team with the sub-groups in place."[183] Even capable members were ignored if they could not be trusted: "In SF, it's not your rank, it's your reputation. If you can't maintain that reputation, and guard it, then you're done. It's similar to that."[184] As some members noted, it takes time to build trust; there is rarely a shortcut for the process. In this regard the inability of the teams to train and deploy together as teams had a negative impact. Overall, teams where all members shared a bond of trust were rare, and consequently productivity was lower than it could have been.

The "SF" Connection

The Human Terrain System (HTS) has an enduring, informal connection to U.S. Army Special Forces. Special Forces are often described as the U.S. military's premier units for working "by, with, and through indigenous forces and populations," so it is perhaps not surprising that they are drawn to a program like HTS. HTS made a special effort to advertise for former Special Forces,[185] and in the early days of HTS, active and former Special Forces soldiers began filling the ranks of HTS as both teachers and team members. One individual who was with the program from the beginning said that early on, perhaps as much as 30 to 40 percent of HTS personnel had Special Forces backgrounds.[186] One primary source of former Special Forces talent for the HTS program was a pool of University of Tennessee alumni who spread the word about opportunities to serve in HTS.[187] Former Special Forces were involved in HTS training but also served as team leaders where they were respected by brigade commanders and staff more than "egg-head or Intel guys."[188] In general, former Special Forces had a reputation among HTT members for being the best HTT leaders.

It is not hard to see why. Special Forces culture presumably would be a good fit for an unorthodox program like HTS. Special Forces are known for unconventional, "outside of the box" approaches to problem solving. They pass through rigorous selection and training programs designed to determine whether they will be capable of operating as part of small teams far removed from the main body of U.S. military forces and in close proximity to indigenous forces and populations. They are expected to be self-reliant, creative, and politically savvy. With these attributes, it is not surprising that Special Forces see themselves as quite different from conventional forces, and in fact often "use the word 'conventional' as if it were a slur."[189] They like to work with a general mission, little oversight, and maximum flexibility; they are notoriously suspicious of bureaucracy. As the HTS program grew, however, so too did oversight, rules and regulations. Quite a few former Special Forces left the program as a result, but others have remained despite the declining flexibility, and the ups and downs of the program.

7. Team Learning.

Exploitation	Experimentation	Exploration
Team learning is defined as an ongoing process of reflection and action through which teams acquire, share, combine, and apply knowledge.[190] **Exploitation team learning** is defined as team practices that facilitate the transfer of knowledge from outside the organization to inside the team, the deliberate transfer of best practices between teams, team training activities, lessons-learned programs, and knowledge capture and storage programs.[191] **Experimentation team learning** is a different approach to team learning that envisions the cross-functional team as a laboratory in which multiple competing views are juxtaposed against each other in a sequence of novel experiments that require improvisation, flexibility, and reflection.[192] **Exploration team learning** expands knowledge to be used later in complex problem-solving—e.g. investment in wide knowledge networks, willingness to take risks, cross-organizational alliances, and buying knowledge through the acquisition of additional knowledge sources.[193]		

The rationale for cross-functional teams is that the juxtaposition of people with different perspectives allows for team learning in the form of sensemaking, debate, and improvisation. However, there is little evidence to suggest that HTS was, on the whole, a learning organization. There were multiple efforts by HTS to assess performance, but none that were systematic, rigorous and most importantly, sustained. Numerous bright and experienced HTT members went through HTS without being queried routinely for their insights on how to improve the organization. Many felt the organization did not care for their views.[194]

The single data point most indicative of HTS's inability to adapt to the demands of its environment is its training program. Training, especially in a nascent program feeling its way forward, normally benefits from a systematic effort to collect performance information in the field and turn it around quickly for the benefit of recruits still in the classroom. However, the 4.5-month training program in Leavenworth was criticized—often intensely—by nearly all of the people interviewed for this study, as well as internal audits of the program. One 2010 review concluded the training was "poorly designed and administered," and highlighted the fact that the program was "paying $1,200-1,500 per day for contract instructors who are receiving extremely negative student feedback." For example, the investigation cited student feedback from the fall of 2009 indicating that "56 percent of the students were dissatisfied with the training and 84 percent were dissatisfied with student support activities."[195] Numerous succeeding classes of HTT recruits repeatedly told HTS managers that the training needed improvement, but the training was not restructured significantly until 2011 (see Appendix A).

One HTT member summarized the training by observing that "The most I got out of Leavenworth was a sun tan."[196] Other representative comments include the following:

"There are no tests. People can take from that what they want, but the instruction is not intensive, and there is no accountability from what an individual takes from it. I think my team leader is an example of someone who sat through the courses and smiled and checked off that box. If he would have been tested, he might have performed better in the field. There needs to be a very minimal standard, especially for the team leader and the social scientist, so there is a uniform standard of what someone should know. There just isn't that."[197]

"I'm convinced that because people with personal agendas were given the opportunity to influence sometimes-naïve youngsters, the training contributed to a degradation of their ability to operate in the field, rather than an improvement."[198]

"My training amounted to nothing shy of an illegal or quasi-illegal example of gross waste, fraud and abuse of the American taxpayers' dollars."[199]

"We literally had people at the end of our training program crying because they didn't know what they were supposed to do when they got there."[200]

Even those providing the training early on were unenthusiastic, in one case reportedly telling their protégés, "You have had training, but you have not had relevant training."[201]

One interesting finding from our interviews is that many HTT members disapproved of their personal experience with HTS training but speculated that it improved one or two cycles after they departed. The program's training regimen has changed, and for the better as we explain elsewhere, but this observation emerges for HTT members from multiple training cycles as early as 2006 and persists through 2011. Interviewees said their personal training experience had been bad, but that they believed the training got better after they passed through it: "The training was absolutely rubbish for the most part, but I understand it has improved."[202] Similarly: "The training was inconsistent, insufficient, low quality, but I have heard they have completely overhauled the training since I went through it."[203] The most likely explanation for this common observation is that the nearly constant tinkering with the training program prior to the major revision in 2010 was known to interviewees, who then simply hoped the changes they heard about were for the better.

Three major themes emerge from critiques of the training. First, the training was found by social science personnel, and to a lesser extent military personnel, to be too elementary. Initially HTS management's major training objective was just to allow the two types of members to develop an appreciation for the other group's skills and culture. This required a delicate balance when introducing each group's competencies. Many civilians perceived the HTS attempts to teach them social science theory and methodology as too rudimentary, claiming it was even "insulting."[204] On the other hand, civilians tended to find the basic military training highly valuable and said that they appreciated it when it was included in the curriculum.[205] In contrast, some former military officers with decades of experience resented having to participate with the civilians in introductory military training.[206] For this reason, after the training regimen was overhauled later in the program, collective and individual training tasks were separated out to help provide more of an individual training experience as appropriate.

Second, the training was panned as irrelevant for the actual job the teams would be doing in Afghanistan. Some former military personnel, for example, perceived the social science training as too academic and disconnected from what their previous experiences in Iraq and Afghanistan suggested was needed. Civilians agreed, insofar as the training offered no exercises that would prepare them for life in a combat zone. "Flat out, there was no practical [field] training that ever occurred during the HTS training,"[207] which some found "irresponsible."[208] As late as 2009, some were surprised to find their only orientation to military culture in combat conditions, and "the only assigned full reading" [i.e. to be read in its entirety] was a copy of Robert Heinlein's science fiction classic: *Starship Troopers*.[209] In response, some trainees took it upon themselves to visit gun clubs for familiarization with weapons before deployment, and some team leaders conducted basic combat first aid classes for their teams after arriving in theater.

Third, civilians also doubted the relevance of the training for other reasons. One considered it too ethnocentric: "We had …Western-style negotiations training, which didn't help. I mean I can buy and sell used cars… now. But that doesn't help me anywhere I am going."[210] One civilian HTT member summed up his commentary on the relevance of the training by observing that after 4-5 months of training, "which cost a ton of taxpayers' money, [the trainees] would come out without any tangible skill sets."[211]

Despite these bleak assessments, there were two components of the training program that were widely lauded as having high value. Both were located outside of Leavenworth. A three-week Afghan immersion program taught at the University of Nebraska at Omaha was singled out as a valuable component of the training, despite its focus on the Dari language rather than the Pashto language. The training conducted with brigade staffs at the National Training Center in Fort Irwin, California, and the Joint Readiness Training Center in Fort Polk, Louisiana, also was appreciated by team members. That said, many team members expressed frustration that (1) they usually trained with *a* brigade, not necessarily *the* brigade they would be working with in Afghanistan;[212] (2) they usually trained with colleagues from their training cycle, not necessarily with members of the HTT that they would join;[213] and (3) they might train with a brigade heading to Iraq, on a scenario drawn from Iraq, even though they were headed to Afghanistan.[214]

We believe the criticism about the training is a symptom of a more fundamental learning problem. Our assumption is that the training was subpar because HTS management did not know how to measure HTT performance and did not have a process for collecting lessons learned systematically, as those charged with oversight of the program later admitted.[215] This would explain why the training was less relevant, and why HTS management did not move to improve it at an earlier date. In part the inability to identify performance metrics stems from the fact that the purpose of HTTs was variable, as explained above. Without a sharply focused purpose for the HTTs, it was difficult to develop job requirements for deployed HTT members, which in turn made it difficult to establish performance metrics. The HTS program sharpened its depiction of performance over time, doing a good job of explaining what needed to be done by individuals and HTTs collectively.[216] However, the program did not systematically collect information from returning personnel to help determine whether those job performance guidelines made sense, how good performance in the field came about, and how it could be better assessed. To our knowledge, there still are no clear performance metrics, qualitative or quantitative, that would differentiate effective HTTs from ineffective HTTs, metrics that would, help identify required knowledge, skills, and abilities that HTS could use to guide training of HTT members.

After the training ended in Leavenworth, HTT members moved to their new positions in Afghanistan, where they began in-theater learning in earnest as individual replacements for existing teams, or more rarely, as intact new teams in a geographic area. On-the-job team training in Afghanistan helped correct, supplement, and enhance the individual training received in Leavenworth. From the beginning of the program, leaders of effective HTTs found it necessary to establish supplementary training programs in theater to cover gaps in the HTS training provided at Leavenworth:

> When we were initially sent, we were told we weren't going to go outside the wire, so we didn't have the training to go outside the wire. We got onto a range and did a lot of firing. I got them training on how to get in a hello, how to hook up a seatbelt, how to hook up your intercom system, how to secure your equipment, how to get off the aircraft, and how to call in a [medical evacuation].[217]

He also leveraged nearby assets to get Combat Lifesaver training.[218] Other team leaders in Afghanistan also constructed on the job training programs to give team members the knowledge they needed to perform well in a combat environment.[219] From an experienced military man's perspective, this type of team training was rudimentary and remedial.

As we noted above, all HTTs had to learn how to win the confidence of their brigade commanders and staffs. In that sense learning was a prerequisite for becoming a successful HTT in the field. In an effort to be helpful to commanders, HTTs in Afghanistan had to be flexible and learn on the fly. Many HTTs were tasked by brigade commanders through a Commander Information Request system, and they had to answer a range of basic and complex questions. HTTs also were often asked, especially by curious lower-level officers, to provide responses to queries on a wide range of basic issues: "We were sort of like 'Ask Jeeves' out there. They would ask, 'What is this? What is that?' The lieutenants and the captains (who unlike majors and colonels didn't have the 'I know everything and I don't want you to teach me' mentality) were really good about asking questions."[220] HTTs also had to become more expert in their particular area of operations after arriving in Afghanistan. One HTT ordered books about Afghanistan from Amazon.com and built a small library on their Forward Operating Base in order to learn more about the region in which they operated.[221] Another way for HTTs to learn about the assigned area of responsibility was to comb through files of sociocultural documents left behind by previous brigades. In one case, a brigade commander asked his HTT to do this and it helped both the HTT and the brigade learn more about their area.[222]

Such learning by HTTs in the field basically amounted to exploiting other sources of information via, the Internet, books and other records. However, some HTTs also learned by exploration and improvisation. One person who had been a member of two different teams noted the contrast between the two in terms of their willingness to explore the sociocultural issues involved in different types of military missions. The person's first team threw themselves into a wide variety of activities: "The first team leader and social scientist, they were very open minded, very independent. They participated in every type of mission, even missions where they were going to houses and knocking down doors." [223] The person's second team was more circumspect, having "this sense that there were things we should not be involved in because they are bad. They had this ethics/moral limit…even though, as far as I know, there is no limit in the handbook that states we are not allowed to go on certain types of missions."[224] HTT exploration could lead to successful improvisation. For example, two veterans of previous HTTs helped build a new HTT attached to the Combined Joint Special Operations Forces-Afghanistan units. It took many months of work by HTS personnel individually proving their worth with Special Operations Forces in the field before any official relationship began, however.[225]

8. Team Composition.

Diversity	Competencies	Personality
Team composition is "what individual members bring to the group in terms of skill, ability, and disposition."[226] **Team diversity** covers a range of team member characteristics that are presumed to affect team performance, including attitudinal, demographic, and functional diversity. [227] **Team competencies**[228] is a template that uses team selection, team socialization, and team strategy processes to ensure that each team member has the necessary personality characteristics, goal orientations, or other individual-level attributes to contribute as a member of the team.[229] **Team personality** is the propensity of team members to contribute to team performance, sometimes referred to as "aggregated characteristics." For example, researchers have identified five personality characteristics that relate positively to team performance: team conscientiousness, agreeableness, extraversion, emotional stability, and openness to experience.[230]		

Team composition is "what individual members bring to the group in terms of skill, ability, and disposition."[231] Some individual skill sets on HTTs were rare and quite valuable. For example, some members had superb language capabilities, which were always in high demand even if not exploited well by HTS.[232] Others had extensive time overseas living in indigenous cultures, which allowed them to easily adapt to conditions in Afghanistan. Some team members were Muslim, which helped establish rapport with locals. In one case, an HTT had two members of Native American heritage who were perceived by other team members as especially sensitive to and understanding of tribal relationships: "That was a boon for us because they got the tribal thing from growing up with their parents. Even if they did not recognize it all the time because it's part of them, I could see it and how they interacted with the tribes. It was second nature to them."[233] By all accounts, the variance and diversity of such individual abilities varied greatly among HTT members.

HTTs exhibited three types of diversity that affected performance: civilian-military status, social science backgrounds, and gender diversity. The HTTs were designed to be diverse, and that diversity ensured a wide range of alternative views, which commanders appreciated. Diversity, along with the difficult and complex operating environment, also generated stress and in some cases revealed eccentricities that brought emotional conflict to the surface. A core belief among HTS managers in all time frames is that forcing two heterogeneous perspectives—military operations and social science—into productive conflict would stimulate insights helpful for conducting complex brigade-level counterinsurgency operations. In large measure this conviction was substantiated by experience. The vast majority of HTT members we interviewed, plus many brigade commanders,[234] believed the mix of civilian and military views on HTTs were valuable, and even essential for their productivity.

More debatable was the degree of social science diversity required on HTTs. The FMSO designers in 2005-2006 thought they would be able to find ten Ph.D.-level social scientists—five experienced regional experts on either Iraq or Afghanistan, and five social scientists—to staff the first five proof-of-concept teams. The HTS creators in 2006-2007 supported recruiting from a broader social science talent pool: "So you get psychologists, anthropologists, international relations, social workers—you just have [diverse] people."[235] This diversity ensured a wide range of skills and even viewpoints, but arguably also made it more of a challenge for teams to combine member skills sets in productive ways.[236]

In addition to the diverse social science backgrounds, many interviewees believed the HTS program managers wanted each HTT to have at least one female member. Gender diversity is a complex and largely unacknowledged factor in HTT effectiveness, but one that students of small team performance cannot ignore. It is not clear that gender diversity was a management goal, but if so, it was not uniformly achieved. Many HTT members were able to identify some teams that were all-male. It also is not clear what impact gender diversity had on HTT performance. There were cases of gender advantages, gender tension, gender and sexual attraction, and sexual harassment. The obvious advantage of female HTT members was that they could more readily approach and learn from Afghan women: "a woman will say things to a female that she couldn't say with her male relatives around; they are a good resource of information."[237]

In addition, several interviewees implied, and some stated explicitly, that injecting females into a brigade environment could enhance an HTT's ability to secure access and resources.[238] However, there were also cases of sexual attractions that could be disruptive. One team leader moved an HTT member to a distant Forward Operating Base to keep her away from a senior brigade staff member.[239] Some female HTT members described some younger female human terrain analysts as naïve about their sexuality, not understanding that their relationships could complicate team dynamics. Others were less naïve, but in either case, sexual attraction could quickly become a major management issue. In one case, a team leader recognized an HTT member's tendency toward flirting "and instead of ignoring it like many would in that environment because they don't feel comfortable handling it, he confronted it and the problem went away immediately."[240] Finally, there were allegations of sexual harassment. The notable example is the first HTAT in Bagram, which was investigated by the Army as a sexual harassment case, a contributing factor in the collapse of the team.

Gender diversity could raise management issues in less obvious ways as well. One example of complications arising from gender diversity was described by a female HTT member:

> My team leader is not sexist. He is famous for saying I care about your gray matter, not your gender. It's not that he thinks that women cannot do the job, but the fact was that he was senior to me, and he was concerned that something would happen to me. He tried very hard not to be patriarchal, but it was probably a bridge too far not to be patriarchal at least some of the time. He had daughters. I sensed some difficulty in trying to filter some of that stuff out.[241]

A male team leader acknowledged similar concerns: "For the most part, I couldn't be objective. She is closer to my daughter's age than anything else. I'm fifty and she's mid-twenties. It's hard for me to be objective. When she was in a situation, there was a fatherly, team leader instinct to take her side, but I tried to remain objective."[242] Some team leaders also were chary of letting female members take risks "outside the wire," and from the point of view of female team members who wanted to be treated equally, this attitude was an issue. As these examples illustrate, gender issues sometimes became management issues. However, in the main there is little evidence that gender affected team performance. The vast majority of close trust relationships, and conflict relationships between team members, were based on personality and performance factors unrelated to gender.

HTT composition varied greatly by individual background, skills and disposition, and also in terms of whether members were minimally qualified to perform their duties. Some of the people who made their way into the HTS organization were highly talented and well-recognized professionals; others were younger and inexperienced but intelligent and hard-working. Most interviewees asserted, however, that many HTT members were manifestly unqualified for their jobs; how much so is disputable and a matter of individual opinion. The former program manager made headlines when he said that "30 to 40 percent of the people" recruited into HTS "were not qualified."[243] This was a stunning assessment from the head of the program, but one echoed by many of the people we interviewed and not the harshest estimate we heard by any means.[244] Other assessments were less severe but still insisted there was a major problem: "The level of recruitment was uneven.... Of the 20-30 people in my class, 5-7 were qualified."[245]

The dominant explanation for problem personnel is that in the rush to expand the number of HTTs quickly, the contractor responsible for screening and hiring recruits did a poor job. Genuine experts on Afghanistan were in high demand by many organizations, so as a class they were hard to recruit. Moreover, since the program was being run on the basis of trial and error—at least initially—it was difficult to know what personnel profile was most conducive to successful field performance. The allegation made, however, is that the screening process lacked any rigor at all: "There is virtually no screening. The interview was on the phone [and completely inadequate]. I could have had six heads. I could have been a complete whack job."[246] Similarly, another social scientist described their recruitment process as superficial: "They don't get to know the people they hire before the decision is made. They don't check their references. So those who are unqualified or [have] difficult personalities make their way through and that created the team problems."[247]

The problematic personalities who slipped through the recruitment and screening process damaged HTT performance. Several of the people deployed to Afghanistan in 2008-2009 became notable examples of problem personalities, including the team member accused of plagiarizing research and creating a climate of sexual harassment that eventually led to the reassignment of at least three members of his team.[248] Another person deployed to Afghanistan was sent home for falsifying data.[249] For a while enough HTTs were having trouble securing the respect of commanders that researcher Paul Joseph of Tufts University, collecting data from HTT personnel in March 2010, considered it a minimal measure of effectiveness for the HTTs if they avoided being kicked off a base.[250] In the 2010-2011 period a team leader who had been kicked off a base in 2009 by a brigade commander, but remained with the program and redeployed with a new team, was "fired" by the other four members of his team. They produced a 17-page critique of his performance.[251] It failed to impress HTS managers, however. They retained the team leader and reassigned the team members or accepted their resignations.[252]

In most cases unqualified personnel did not precipitate team failure, but rather just diminished team productivity. Anecdotes on unqualified personnel abound, such as the assertion by one HTT member that some of the research managers were "computer illiterate" even though their primary function on the team required good computer skills.[253] In fact, HTT members regale each other with legends about unsuitable recruits that entered the program. One octogenarian HTT recruit had never seen a computer mouse before, and tried to apply it directly to the computer screen. Another HTT recruit was described as manifestly too pampered to succeed in the field: "there was no way she could deal with Afghanistan....You can't take those 42 pairs of shoes with you."[254] HTT members identified one recruit as mentally unstable, another as overweight to the point the person could not move with military units, and yet another as having the ulterior motive of evangelizing Afghans.[255] The extent to which such carping actually was justified and highlighted seriously unqualified personnel is difficult to say. Much depended on what the person would be asked to do. But such celebrated cases led many to conclude "BAE was just trying to get warm bodies" to meet its contract obligations.[256]

From numerous interviews, we have the impression that HTT personnel quality has improved over time. One HTT member observed that recent recruits "are extremely intelligent and brave, not like the earlier people.... they were in active shooting wars and had not been prepared for it. So to do research, in that environment, was impressive...."[257] Reportedly HTS is achieving better recruiting results now because it "has just started to do the same psychological testing as the CIA and Special Forces; pre-screening in fact. That will help weed out those prone to conflict."[258] We could not verify current screening procedures, but many of those we interviewed had the impression quality had improved and that better recruitment and screening were responsible for the improvements.

As previously noted, HTS policies reinforced individualism and complicated team building. The vast majority of established HTTs were replenished with individual replacements, reducing the ability of team leaders to choose quality members of their teams who could work well together. Some team leaders in Leavenworth were able to work the system to build what they hoped would become high-performing teams, but it was hard: "it was rare for [team leaders] to be hand picking people. My team leader managed to do that. But he had to fight to do it. It was a constant battle. Cajoling and charming people. It was a lot of horse trading."[259] One team leader who was able to recruit his team knew what he wanted: "I was looking for capability, capacity, adaptability and flexibility."[260] Those who managed to find the personnel they wanted and pull a preferred team together were protective of the team's composition, not wanting it to be disturbed.

Except for a few high performing (and in some cases hand-picked) teams, most HTTs did not have a distinctive personality. Those on ineffective teams often expressed the view, sometimes with colorful language, that their team personalities were dysfunctional. They believed poor performers and interpersonal conflict impeded positive team personality development, as did strong individual personalities. One interviewee, repeating a common observation, argued an HTT "had such disparate individuals that the team didn't have a particular personality."[261] Other high performing teams did not develop a strong personality *per se*, but rather a general commitment to openness, common purpose or high performance. For example, one team's personality was defined by its mission focus, a "common purpose…that allowed us to work with each other and those we needed to support."[262] Another team developed a general team appreciation for those who could endure some deprivation while getting the mission accomplished: people who "enjoyed the long days, field work, had a sense of humor and could withstand not showering for three weeks."[263] A few interviewees from effective teams thought their team personality reflected their leader,[264] whom they esteemed.

In short, HTT membership was diverse in many ways that could have been exploited for higher performance, but also presented a management challenge that was difficult to meet. More specifically, there is wide agreement that HTS found it difficult to populate HTTs with sufficiently qualified personnel, which complicated performance. Inadequate attention to team socialization processes made it even more difficult to exploit diverse individual skill sets. In theory, diverse individual skills and abilities can coalesce to generate effective aggregate team capabilities, and even team "personalities" wherein individual members learn from one another and adopt common attributes that serve the team well. But that happened only rarely on HTTs where, throughout the HTS program, including recently, interpersonal conflict has been a common problem,[265] one exacerbated by management decisions that complicated the ability of many HTTs to fully exploit the talent available to them.

9. Team Rewards.

Attractive Motivations	Active Incentives	Affective Impetus
Team rewards combine material incentives and psychological rewards to direct team members towards the accomplishment of the team's mission.[266] **Attractive motivations** are incentives that are sufficient to encourage qualified people to move from comfortable and often safer organizational positions into riskier cross-functional teams, and sometimes to filter out people with high needs for individual achievement, and to "filter in" people with high collectivism[267] personality characteristics. **Active incentives** are mission-based performance evaluation systems[268] that focus team members' attention on key effectiveness criteria[269] and create the additional motivation, energy, and persistence necessary to accomplish team objectives. **Affective impetus** is the feelings created by the convergence of individual emotions into a distinct affective state associated with members of the team at a specific time.[270]		

Effective cross-functional teams can be built in part through reward systems that attract individuals to join the teams, focus the team members' attention on critical success factors for team performance, and leverage powerful emotional commitments to the team's mission and the team itself. Although people often have multiple reasons for any behavior, HTT interviews reveal a number of primary motivations. One representative HTT member believed most HTT members fell into one of three categories that he labeled ne'er-do-wells, fantasists, and workers.[271] In general, ineffective HTTs were populated by ne'er-do-wells (who were there for the money) and fantasists (who were there for the adventure), and effective HTTs were populated by workers who initially or over time became committed to the mission.

Many HTT members were initially attracted to the program by the potential to make money: "It's a good paying position—the benefits are substantial as is the combat pay. Anyone who tells you it's not about the money, their nose might be growing."[272] Some team leaders and social scientists in 2007 and 2008 were reported to have made $400,000 a year in the program; research managers earned less; and human terrain analysts earned the least. "There were definitely monetary rewards. It's very lucrative."[273] Some civilian team members we interviewed saw the program as an excellent opportunity to pay off student loans, move to a larger home, or pay for necessary surgeries for uninsured family members. Often it is assumed that high remuneration correlates with high performance, but this was not the assumption among those we interviewed. On the contrary, those suspected of being attracted only by financial remuneration were often disparaged as unproductive, and sometimes singularly so.[274] As a class the "ne'er-do-wells" were mostly civilian because remuneration for active duty and reserve members of the military was limited to their regular military salary and combat pay. Ironically this meant that in some cases a uniformed team leader might be the lowest paid member of the team.[275]

Frequently, but not always, those who seemed primarily motivated by a desire for adventure were also considered less productive: "They could have been prior military or never been military, but wanted their…Rambo adventure….They didn't work. They just had their soldier adventure."[276] A few HTT members with this bearing were described positively as "forward-leaning" and practitioners of "derring-do" who needed to be reined in from time to time by older, wiser, and more mission-focused team members.[277] However, others who were described as adventure-seekers and adrenaline-junkies were seen as having abandoned the HTS mission to follow their own agendas: "He just liked to go out with the OMLTs [Operational Mentoring and Liaison Teams] and get shot at."[278] In general, the presence of adventure-seekers on HTTs degraded the teams' effectiveness levels because those motivated by adventure tended to perform less work that was relevant for the HTT mission.

"The workers" were defined as those attracted by the mission: "They clearly went to do the mission of sociocultural and socio-economic research."[279] People can have multiple motivations for behavior, and can do a job well for a variety of reasons. However, it perhaps is not surprising that those HTT members who believed in the mission were widely seen as more focused and harder working. Mission-minded HTT workers could be motivated by several different corollary objectives.

Many HTT members told us that they were attracted by the opportunity to have an impact on the outcome of the war. An HTT member explained his desire to have a positive impact:

> Mainly it was the chance to take what I had learned and apply it. I would be with soldiers on the tarmac waiting for a flight and I had at least three conversations where they would say, "What do you do?" I would say "I'm an anthropologist," and they would ask me to come along with them. "Why would I go there?" I would ask, and they would say they needed anthropologists. "Why?" "The tribal system there, the ethnic conflict, we don't know anything about it. We're getting crushed. None of us can figure it out."[280]

Other civilians we interviewed told us that they were motivated to join the HTS program because it provided them a rare opportunity, in the era of the all-volunteer force, to serve their country. One HTT member who served with Special Forces soldiers in Afghanistan said, "It was an honor to support them because I believe in what they are doing. There is also the patriotism thing. That was the biggest draw to get into HTS."[281] Another HTT member noted that one linguist joined the Army "out of gratitude" because their family had come to the U.S. seeking asylum.[282] Some of the younger social scientists and human terrain analysts told us that they needed the experience in Afghanistan to advance their career ambitions elsewhere.[283] Finally, several people told us they were attracted by the perception that they could counter-balance previous, more lethal activities by signing up for a program that emphasized non-lethality.[284]

The motivations of HTT personnel were put to the test when HTS had to reduce costs and ultimately transitioned its employees from contractor to Army civilian status. HTT members were contractors before 2009, and they billed by the hour, receiving pay for as many as 90 hours per week. Under financial pressures in early 2009, HTS managers were forced to reduce the generosity of the program significantly: "They went from assuming we worked 90 hours a week to paying for 80 hours, and then from 80 hours to 60 hours. In the end, it was a fairly sizable pay cut."[285] When HTT members eventually were told they would have to transition to Army civilian status, which involved further pay cuts, they had to decide whether or not to stay. Approximately one-third left: "For some people, especially at the human terrain analyst level, it pushed them to the point they left the program."[286] The program tended to experience high turnover anyway, but the departure of so many at one time was difficult to absorb. The exodus included many HTT members in the field, from training, and from the pipeline into training. Others stayed in the program despite being dissatisfied about the change.

Some HTT members, however, believed the reduction in salaries actually helped HTT performance. One HTT member believed that the pay cut removed the corrosive influence of large sums of money: "The pay scale that I went under in 2010 was about $100,000 lower than what it had been when my colleagues went in. I think the money was corrosive. I think it drew people that just wanted to make money, both in the upper levels and in all levels of the teams."[287] Another HTT member explained that the pay cut meant little to those motivated by the adventure or the mission: "I was like, let the chips fall. I would be criticized by people for saying this, but I was just going to do my job. I was pleased with my salary…people who were there to do the job, were happy with it, even as it was getting revised."[288]

Some motivations for persevering in the job transcended financial considerations. Members of effective HTTs reported that the most significant team rewards were deeply emotional commitments to the team itself, the team's reputation, and the team's mission. In other words, HTT members could be motivated by what some label team emotions, team mood, and team affect—the sub-variable of team rewards that we refer to as "affective impetus." The leader of an effective HTT explained that the highest possible reward for his team members was successful performance as a team: "I think the incentives are that you don't want to let the team down. I don't want to be the weak link."[289] A team member deployed in 2009 explained the nearly addictive nature of high performance: "There was a lot of appreciation directed at the HTT and we enjoyed some status. That created a cycle of positive reinforcement whereby the more recognition you get, you wanted to exceed expectations more. And that made it easy to get up in the mornings."[290] A recent HTT member described her team's high level of commitment to the mission: "When everyone is focused on how to solve a problem—for other people's sake, whether it's the local population or the troops—you might not derive as much personal satisfaction, but working the problem, you superseded all lack of food, resources, or whatever...you practically forget to eat lunch."[291]

In sum, effective HTTs in Afghanistan were blessed with mission-motivated personnel, or were able to replace other initial individual motivations with team rewards more tightly connected to the purpose of the HTTs. The change in pay structure in 2009 was a large disruption to team effectiveness in the short term, but it might have improved the performance of HTTs in the long term by removing the large monetary incentives for participation in the program. In a very small number of cases, we saw evidence of the emergence of powerful team emotions in which HTTs coalesced as a team, accomplished more than they thought they could, and thrived on the members' enthusiasm for the team experience.

10. Team Leadership.

Traditional	Coaching	Shared
Team leadership[292] is the collection of strategic actions that are taken to accomplish team objectives, to ensure a reasonable level of efficiency, and to avoid team catastrophes. **Traditional team leadership** is primarily top-down, directive, command-and-control authority applied from either outside the team or inside the team in order to overrule differences of opinion within the team, accomplish objectives set for the team, and ensure efficiency.[293] **Coaching team leadership** is defined as "direct interaction with a team intended to help members make coordinated and task-appropriate use of their collective resources in accomplishing the team's work."[294] **Shared team leadership**[295] is primarily "bottom-up," collaborative, shared sensemaking from many people outside and everybody inside the team[296] in order to accomplish team objectives, develop new capabilities, and avoid team catastrophes.[297]		

When cross-functional teams benefit from a well-understood purpose, are given the empowerment necessary to accomplish that purpose, are well-supported by the organizations in which they work, and operate in stable and unambiguous environments, team leadership is less important. In fact, in such propitious circumstances some think teams can be successful even with poor leadership. However, when so many small team performance variables are stacked against team success, as was the case with the HTTs, team leadership becomes the most critical variable. Desperate circumstances call for above-average leaders.

The HTTs in Afghanistan from 2007-2011 were led by team leaders with diverse military backgrounds and equally diverse reputations for success—some outstanding, some average, and some bad enough that they were sent home.[298] Some of the HTT leaders had an active interest in social science,[299] but most did not define themselves simultaneously as military professionals and social scientists. The leaders were Army or Marine reserve officers or retired active-duty officers with a wide range of career experience. Some had recent military service, and others had left the service decades ago to pursue other careers. For example, one popular and effective leader was a retired Green Beret with Vietnam-era and Central American experience in the 1980s.[300] Other team leaders had only recently retired.

These varying backgrounds among the HTT leaders were matched by a range of different leadership styles. One HTT member, who operated under multiple team leaders noted, "They were all different—some were bullies, some were passive, some were effective."[301] Several HTT members stereotyped their team leaders by categories of military service:

> I would say that O-6s from the conventional Army work the worst. The military sees O-6s as senior officers, just below general, so they get treated very well. The conventional O-6s come with some of that ego and want to be on par or equal to the regimental commander.[302]

Some HTT members thought reserve officers were more relaxed and adaptable than officers with recent active-duty experience:

> Reserves basically have a foot in…the reserve world and a foot in the civilian world. So they learn a skill set of how to interact with people. They don't necessary come with an ego…they've got a real world to deal with back home as a civilian.[303]

More than a few interviewees expressed the view that retired or active Special Forces officers and Marine Colonels were highly effective HTT team leaders:

> Active and former Special Forces officers are used to operating in different environments where there is no room for ego—of an 'I deserve this' mentality. A lot of times they are operating with local nationals and they know how to get down and get dirty. They are used to that.[304]

Similarly some interviewees extolled their Marine leaders for their ability to delegate, anticipate problems and an absence of "ego." [305]

Such typecasting was belied by numerous exceptions, however. A far more reliable predictor of good leadership emerged from interview data. What mattered most seemed to be the ability to employ the appropriate team leadership style—traditional, coaching, or shared—in the appropriate context. Traditional styles were appropriate in relations within the military hierarchy, in dangerous environments, or in situations calling for rapid action: "We agreed that when we were in the field, there was always somebody in charge. If things went bad, we went directly to the military model…You couldn't argue under fire."[306] Traditional styles were appropriate when quick recovery, rapid change or other decisive decision-making was required: "We had a member killed and everyone turned to me to fix it and clean it up, to do what needs to be done. That was my job and I did that. I can be a [expletive], but sometimes you have to get things done. You do what you have to do. I prefer to get input, but someone has to make a decision."[307] In these types of situations, there was broad agreement between the HTT members that a traditional command-and-control leadership style was necessary.

Coaching leadership styles were appropriate in contexts such as the persuasion of team members to agree on upcoming missions or to make the extra effort necessary to debate different perspectives within the team in order to get better solutions to complex problems. One exemplary leader was described as a superb coach who "saw the potential in every team member [and] provided support for them."[308] This team leader explained his theory of coaching leadership involved removing impediments: "If there are things you can't do that become mission stoppers, you must figure out ways to work around them...."[309] Similarly, another team leader described his job as asking his team members, "What can I do to facilitate your job?"[310] Another leader acknowledged that he was less scholarly-minded than the other members on their team, so he thought his role was "to create an environment where they can be successful...I provide the framework for them to be successful."[311]

In general, active Army officers were more likely to frame their role as traditional leaders, while effective reserve officers—perhaps because of their familiarity with working with non-military personnel and their specific idiosyncrasies—were more likely to see their role as coaching leaders. However, many effective HTTs were successful because their leaders combined coaching with directive decision-making as they thought circumstances demanded: "if you produce and you follow...stay in that corral...you have a lot of freedom. If you step out of the corral, I'll probably put you back in it."[312]

A shared leadership style that emphasized collaborative problem identification and decision making was more rare, but also evident in some circumstances. Shared leadership was more likely to emerge when leaders with military background felt subtle social science observations from diverse team members were required. As one leader noted, it was better to let those who do the ground research and create the product brief the brigade, in part "so they take pride and get the credit."[313] Another agreed that shared decision making made sense in some cases: "It's all situational dependent. I could elicit input on ideas, which I tried to do as much as possible, especially on an eclectic group."[314] Leaders who respected the skills of their team members naturally were inclined to share more leadership decisions, but sometimes circumstances made this a necessity. For example, in one case, a new team leader for an already well functioning HTT had to accept the fact that the other members on the team were far more knowledgeable about the area and the brigade than he was. That leader had to accept a high degree of shared leadership on his team, at least until he was up to speed on everything.[315]

The weight of interview data indicates that the most effective teams enjoyed leaders who could adapt their leadership style to circumstances. When we look at HTTs with undisputed reputations for effectiveness, it is quite clear that they had just such flexible leaders. They could operate as hard-charging Type A personalities, more facilitative Type B personalities, and when necessary step outside of their leadership roles to let other team members emerge as leaders in specific contexts. One such team leader said his leadership style depended not only on circumstances but also on the individual team members:

> ...it depended on the person. It was more coaching, some shared, and only traditional when necessary. I think for the most part it was coaching. With [the social scientist] out of deference to him, it was shared. Because the social scientist and the team leaders are co-equal. Certainly they drove the research. I supported that provided it was operationally relevant. On occasion, it might have been necessary for some traditional leadership, particularly with the younger members when it was appropriate. 'Do this and do not do that.' Coaching mostly; kind of a player-coach model. It was often like coaching basketball or football.[316]

At least three other high performing HTTs were notable for excellent leadership that used multiple leadership styles.

Team Leader Command Styles		
Traditional	**Coaching**	**Shared**
Top-down, directive authority to accomplish objectives set for the team, and ensure efficiency.	*Direct interaction with a team intended to help members make coordinated and task-appropriate use of collective resources to accomplish the team's work.*	*"Bottom-up," collaborative, shared decision-making in order to accomplish the team objectives...*

(Definition)

Positive Interviewee Comments	• "[He] was able to tamper down conflict simply through force of personality."[317] • "I considered it my task to make it work."[318] • "Things didn't come on their own. My team leader fought for them."[319]	• "'What can I do to facilitate your job?' I have numerous examples for how he [the team leader] showed that."[320] • "I could minimize conflicts by ordering people to do certain jobs."[321]	• "I knew what I wanted…so I made it clear with 3 rules: Do your work as best you can; don't embarrass the team; Always give 100 percent."[322] • "I never had to be directive….If a subordinate asked for permission, I would give it; as long it was not hair-brained."[323]
Negative Interviewee Comments	• "[He] started screaming at people at meetings. He had little interest in the mission."[324] • "When [he] didn't like my feedback, he stopped allowing me to go to the S3 meetings for a few weeks."[325]	• "He was a phenomenal supply officer. He would get stuff left and right; he was cutting deals. We always had food and snacks… He would dole them out. As in 'here, have a little something, you owe me.'"[326]	• "We were left [on] our own on what we would do. He did come out at least once…but he went after a few days."[327] • "He would say he would go out to see what we were doing, but never did."[328]

One high-performing HTT had a leader who was seen as an excellent traditional leader who did not use his rank as colonel to bully his team members or brigade staff around him, but rather worked more in a coaching leadership style.[329] Another effective HTT's leader was described as somebody who was able to switch back and forth between two leadership styles, depending on the circumstances he faced: "My team leader was laid back and had a good sense of humor. He was more about coaching and shared leadership. If you have people who are competent, you just have to direct them. If they are less competent, you have to coach them."[330] One team leader defined a shared leadership style: "It was co-leadership on the surface, which is usually a good way to go about it, and in training, they were training us this way. The social scientist was the academic team leader, and the team leader was the operations team leader. Together they decided the mission sets and resources."[331] All the HTT leaders described here were able to move back and forth between leadership types when necessary, and their teams worked better because of it. These leaders were also highly esteemed by their team members. Such leaders were often described as "the glue that held the team together" and a primary reason for team success.[332]

In contrast, ineffective HTT leaders often locked into one role—too authoritarian or too laissez-faire—and began to be seen over time by their team members as either dictators or lazy and perhaps clueless pushovers. In contrast to the adaptable and effective HTT leaders described above, some team leaders failed for lack of flexibility, often because they were locked into a traditional command-and-control leadership model in which they framed themselves as autonomous and powerful individuals, rather than part of a cohesive mission-driven team. These leaders could impair team productivity in a number of ways, but typically because they were not sufficiently engaged or were overly controlling:

- Some were perceived as disconnected from the mission, either because they did not understand the mission or were there primarily for the money: "I think he was just happy being a team leader making a salary."[333]

- Some exhibited an egregious lack of commitment: "He always had an excuse for not going outside the wire—sickness, he ate something bad, he had responsibility in the office. I followed up about it and he was just in his hooch playing video games."[334]

- Some alienated their colleagues: "The team leader pissed off everybody. The Norwegians kicked him out of their battle space with an email, 'Make sure [that person] is on a plane tomorrow.'"[335]

- Some punished team members who disagreed with them: "When my team leader didn't like my feedback, he stopped allowing me to go to the S3 meetings for a few weeks."[336]

- Some did not leverage the expertise of their team members to help them make good decisions: "He just didn't have a good feel for what Afghan culture was. One reason the social scientist was able to get off the team was because she catalogued numerous poor decisions he made in regards to Afghan culture. He had a temper and some of the things he did and advised…just were bad decisions."[337]

- Some were too controlling: "There is little place in the Army for a dictator….A good leader gets his people to want to help him get the job done. We didn't have that under [the team lead]. It was too much about him."[338]

In summary, poor team leaders could perform poorly in multiple ways, and the least capable often did. One of the more notable HTT leadership failures revealed multiple problems simultaneously. He was unable to see himself as a subordinate to his brigade commander: "The team leader was a retired military type. He had this chip on his shoulder about it. I remember when we would be having discussion with the colonel, and he would be telling the colonel where he thought the battalion should go. Okay, I know I'm a civilian, but even I know I shouldn't do that. And it was obvious the colonel did not appreciate it."[339] He also could not move into the role of a coach with his team members: "He spoke out of turns in meetings, he was brusque with people, he tended to yell at underlings about things that weren't mistakes at all—he just didn't understand them."[340] By contrast, good HTT leaders generally succeeded the same way; by artfully employing multiple leadership styles as circumstances warranted.

Notes

[1]   Jebb, Hummel, Chacho, *Human Terrain Team Trip Report*, 7.

[2]   This study conducted 105 interviews with 87 individuals. Individuals were interviewed multiples time because they either deployed on multiple teams, had in-depth knowledge of the program, or in only a few cases, the interview did not have sufficient time to finish on the first day. The interviews break out as follows: 57 with Afghan HTT members (11 team leaders, 28 social scientists, 13 research managers, 4 human terrain analysts); 4 with RRC analysts; 5 with Iraq HTT members, all social scientists; 13 with HTS management personnel; 2 with FMSO personnel; 1 with a (former) member of Congress; 7 with academic and defense community observers of HTS; 1 member of a SCRAT; 1 member of a Company Intelligence Support Team, 14 with military commanders (11 with brigade or Task Force commanders, 3 with brigade or Task Force command staff members).

[3]   Orton with Lamb, 'Interagency National Security Teams: Can Social Science Contribute?,' 47-64.

[4]   We identified teams at the ends of the spectrum of performance based upon a high degree of unanimity in HTT member assessments, commander assessments, and effectiveness assertions in secondary literature.

[5]   John R. Katzenbach and Douglas K. Smith, *The Wisdom of Teams* (Boston, MA: Harvard Business School Press, 1993).

[6]   D. Knight, C. L. Pearce, K. G. Smith, J. D. Olian, H. P. Sims, K. A. Smith, and P. Flood, "Top Management Team Diversity, Group Process, and Strategic Consensus" *Strategic Management Journal*, Issue 20 (1999), 445-465.

[7]   F.W. Kellermanns, J. Walter, C. Lechner, and S.W. Floyd, "The Lack of Consensus about Strategic Consensus: Advancing Theory and Research," *Journal of Management* iss. 31 (2005), 719-737.

[8]   L.L. Levesque, J.M. Wilson, and D.R. Wholey, "Cognitive Divergence and Shared Mental Models in Software Development Project Teams," *Journal of Organizational Behavior* iss. 22 (2001), 135-144.

[9]   J.E. Mathieu, T.S. Heffner, G.F. Goodwin, J.A. Cannon-Bowers, and E. Salas, "Scaling the Quality of Teammates' Mental Models: Equifinality and Normative Comparisons," *Journal of Organizational Behavior* iss. 26 (2005), 37-56.

[10]   J.E. Mathieu, T.S. Heffner, G.F. Goodwin E. Salas, and J.A. Cannon-Bowers, "The Influence of Shared Mental Models on Team Process and Performance," *Journal of Applied Psychology*, iss. 91 (2000), 273-283.

[11]   Team Leader, AF1, interviewed November 1, 2011.

[12]   A formal mission statement presented to a division staff in Afghanistan included this definition of the HTT team purpose. AF2 HTAT RC-East, *Human Terrain System: Human Terrain Team Organization and Capabilities RC(E)*, PowerPoint, undated.

[13]   John Foldberg, Team Leader AF7, interviewed November 21, 2011.

[14]   Interviewee 27, October 18, 2011.

[15]   Dr. Amy Bursell, Social Scientist AF10, interviewed September 29, 2011.

[16]   Team Leader, AF1, interviewed November 1, 2011.

[17]   Interviewee 24, October 17, 2011.

[18]   HTT Research Manager, interviewed January 3, 2012.

[19]   Nathan Hodge, *Armed Humanitarians: The Rise of the National Builders* (New York, NY: Bloomsbury, 2011), 254.

[20]   Interviewee 32, October 24, 2011.

[21]   "The mission of HTS, an intelligence enabling capability, is to: recruit, train deploy, and support an embedded, operationally focused sociocultural capability; conduct operationally relevant, sociocultural research and analysis; develop and maintain a sociocultural knowledge base to support operational decision making, enhance operational effectiveness, and preserve and share sociocultural institutional knowledge." Colonel Sharon Hamilton, "HTS Director's Message," *Military Intelligence Professional Bulletin* vol. 37, no. 4 (October-December 2011), A1.

[22]   Social Scientist, Afghanistan, interviewed November 18, 2011.

[23]   For purposes of simplification, we refer to divisions, regiments, brigades, battalions, and other organizations to which HTTs were attached from 2007 to 2011 as "brigades."

[24]   John Foldberg, Team Leader AF7, interviewed November 21, 2011.

[25]   Nicole Heydari, Human Terrain Analyst AF14, interviewed October 5, 2011.

[26]   HTT Team Leader, Afghanistan 2010-2011, interviewed November 15, 2011.

[27]   Interviewee 24, October 17, 2011.

[28]   Ibid.

[29]   J.E. Mathieu, L.L. Gilson, and T.M. Ruddy, "Empowerment and Team Effectiveness: An Empirical Test of an Integrated Model," *Journal of Applied Psychology* iss. 91 (2006), 97-108.

[30]   Bradley L. Kirkman, and Benson Rosen, "Antecedents and Consequences of Team Empowerment," *The Academy of Management Journal* vol. 42 no. 1 (February 1999), 58-74.

[31]   Ibid.

[32]   Research Manager, AF27, interviewed October 25, 2011.

[33]   M. Mason, HTT member, Afghanistan, interviewed October 12, 2011.

[34]   Major Robert Holbert, Research Manager, AF1, interviewed December 12, 2011.

[35] Social Scientist, Afghanistan, interviewed November 18, 2011.

[36] HTT member, interviewed October 27, 2011.

[37] Research Manager, AF27, interviewed October 25, 2011.

[38] HTS document containing interviews with returning HTT members, provided by a Social Scientist with an HTT, interviewed February 14, 2012, 16.

[39] TRADOC states that as of July 2012 at least "twenty-four percent of the teams in Afghanistan report they are using MAP-HT." *TRADOC G2 Comments on the National Defense University paper titled "Human Terrain Team Performance: An Explanation," August 24, 2012*, Passed to NDU team, November 15, 2012, 4.

[40] John Green, AF2 Team Leader, interviewed December 1, 2011.

[41] Program Manager Forward, Afghanistan, interviewed December 7, 2011.

[42] Human Terrain Analyst, Afghanistan, December 13, 2011.

[43] Dr. Marilyn Dudley-Flores, Social Scientist, HTAT Bagram, interviewed January 4, 2012.

[44] Major Michael Jacobson, U.S. Army Reserves, AF25 Team Leader September 2010—May 2011, interviewed October 7, 2011.

[45] Interviewee 24, October 17, 2011.

[46] Kristen Farnum, Social Scientist, AF5, interviewed October 17, 2011.

[47] Research Manager on an HTT in Afghanistan, interviewed November 8, 2011.

[48] Social Scientist, Afghanistan, interviewed November 18, 2011.

[49] Ibid.

[50] HTT Member, Afghanistan, interviewed October 25, 2011.

[51] Research Manager, AF27, interviewed October 25, 2011.

[52] Ibid.

[53] Research Manager, AF3, interviewed December 15, 2011.

[54] Kristen Farnum, Social Scientist, AF5, interviewed October 17, 2011.

[55] John Green, AF2 Team Leader, interviewed December 1, 2011.

[56] Ibid.

[57] HTT Research Manager, interviewed January 3, 2012; HTT Research Manager, email on June 7, 2012.

[58] HTT Social Scientist, interviewed December 9, 2011.

[59] HTT member, Afghanistan, interviewed October 12, 2011.

[60] Social Scientist, Afghanistan, interviewed November 18, 2011; HTT Social Scientist, interviewed December 21, 2011.

[61] Nicole Heydari, Human Terrain Analyst AF17, interviewed October 6, 2011; Kristen Farnum, Social Scientist, AF5, interviewed October 17, 2011.

[62] Social Scientist, Afghanistan, interviewed November 18, 2011.

[63] M.A. Campion, G.J. Medsker, and A.C. Higgs, "Relations between Work Group Characteristics and Effectiveness: Implications for Designing Effective Work Groups," *Personnel Psychology* iss. 46 (1993), 823-850; M.A. Campion, E.M. Papper, and G.J. Medsker, "Relations between work team characteristics and effectiveness: A replication and extension," *Personnel Psychology* iss. 49 (1996), 429-452.

[64] Prasad Balkundi and David A. Harrison, "Ties, Leaders, and Time in Teams: Strong Inference about Network Structure's Effects on Team Viability and Performance," *Academy of Management Journal* iss. 49 (2006), 49-68.

[65] G.M. Spreitzer, S.G, Cohen, and G.E. Ledford, Jr., "Developing Effective Self-managing Work Teams in Service Organizations," *Group & Organization Management* iss. 24 (1999), 340-366.

[66] Susan Albers Mohrman, Susan G. Cohen and Allan M. Mohrman, *Designing Team Based Organizations: New Forms for Knowledge Work* (San Francisco, CA: Jossey-Bass Publishers, 1995). Self-management finding is on, 74, 138; Conditions under which strong team leadership is

necessary are on, 144; Design tools finding is on 82-83.

[67]   For AAA figure, See <www.aaanet.org/about/Annual_Reports/upload/AAA-2010-AR. pdf>; for the APA figure, See <www.apa.org/about/index.aspx>.

[68]   Montgomery McFate, "Does Culture Matter? The Military Utility of Cultural Knowledge," *Joint Force Quarterly* 38 (2005), 42-48; Montgomery McFate, "Anthropology and Counterinsurgency: The Strange Story of Their Curious Relationship," *Military Review* (March/April 2005), 24-38.

[69]   Roberto J. González, *American Counterinsurgency: Human Science and the Human Terrain* (Chicago, IL: Prickly Paradigm Press, 2009).

[70]   Montgomery McFate and Steve Fondacaro, "Cultural Knowledge and Common Sense: Response to Roberto González," *Anthropology Today* vol. 24, no. 1 (February 2008).

[71]   Marjorie Censer, "Notes from the Annual Strategy Conference at the Army War College; April 9-10, 2008, Carlisle, PA," *Inside the Army* vol. 20, no. 15 (2008).

[72]   Social Scientist AF1, interviewed November 14, 2011.

[73]   Maja Zehfuss, "Culturally Sensitive War? The Human Terrain System and the Seduction of Ethics," *Security Dialogue* vol. 43, no. 2 (2012), 175-190.

[74]   Interviewee 94, March 22, 2012.

[75]   Social Scientist AF1, email on April 19, 2012.

[76]   Among the many people we interviewed, there is no point about which there is greater unanimity than the assertion that BAE used poor recruiting practices, and that includes the consensus view that HTS training up until 2011 was grossly inadequate.

[77]   See, Jason Motlagh, "Should Anthropologists Help Contain the Taliban," *TIME*, July 1, 2010. Motlagh notes "the prospect of getting blacklisted in U.S. academia has sapped the pool of seasoned anthropologists. Today recruits are more and more likely to have a degree in political science, history or psychology. Some only have a bachelor's degree."

[78]   See *Semi-Annual Command History, July—December 2007*, for a description of the efforts undertaken by HTS to create, increase and maintain the SMEnet during 2006 and 2007.

[79]   Appendix C of the HTT Handbook of September 2008 includes a project description that separates out the social scientist position played by Marcus Griffin from the regional cultural expert position played by Omar Al-Talib. Nathan Finney, *Human Terrain Team Handbook* (Ft. Leavenworth, KS: The Human Terrain System, September 2008), 104-112.

[80]   Dan Ephron and Silvia Spring, "A Gun in One Hand, A Pen in the Other," *Newsweek*, April 21, 2008.

[81]   Colonel Steve Fondacaro (ret.), Former HTS Program Manager, interviewed November 1, 2011.

[82]   Social Scientist, Afghanistan, interviewed November 18, 2011.

[83]   Major Michael Jacobson, U.S. Army Reserves, AF25 Team Leader September 2010—May 2011, interviewed October 7, 2011.

[84]   Interviewee 27, October 18, 2011.

[85]   AF1 Social Scientist, 2008-2009, interviewed January 5, 2012.

[86]   M. Mason, HTT member, Afghanistan, interviewed October 12, 2011.

[87]   Dr. Amy Bursell, Social Scientist AF10, interviewed September 29, 2011.

[88]   HTT Social Scientist, interviewed December 21, 2011.

[89]   Social Scientist, Iraq, interviewed October 12, 2011.

[90]   Team Leader, AF1, interviewed November 1, 2011.

[91]   Social Scientist, Afghanistan, interviewed October 19, 2011.

[92]   Kristen Farnum, Social Scientist, AF3, interviewed November 3, 2011.

[93]   Social Scientist AF1, interviewed November 14, 2011.

[94]   Research Manager, AF3, interviewed December 15, 2011.

[95]   Britt Damon, Research Manager, AF1, interviewed January 4, 2012; HTT Member,

Afghanistan, interviewed October 25, 2011; Member of AF7, interviewed September 30, 2011.

[96]   Human Terrain Analyst, Afghanistan, December 13, 2011.

[97]   Dr. Amy Bursell, Social Scientist AF10, interviewed September 29, 2011.

[98]   HTT Team Leader, Afghanistan 2010-2011, interviewed November 15, 2011.

[99]   Dr. Aileen Moffat, Social Scientist AF27, interviewed December 19, 2011.

[100]   Dr. Amy Bursell, Social Scientist AF10, interviewed September 29, 2011.

[101]   D. Wegner, "Transactive Memory: A Contemporary Analysis of the Group Mind," in G. Mullen and G. Goethals ed., *Theories of Group Behavior* (New York, NY: Springer-Verlag, 1986), 185-208.

[102]   Jennifer A. Marrone, "Team Boundary Spanning: A Multilevel Review of Past Research and Proposals for the Future," *Journal of Management* iss. 36 (2010), 911-940.

[103]   D. G. Ancona and D. F. Caldwell, "Bridging the Boundary: External Activity and Performance in Organizational Teams," *Administrative Science Quarterly* iss. 37 (1992), 634-665.

[104]   D. G. Ancona and H. Bresman, *X-Teams: How to Build Teams that Lead, Innovate, and Succeed*, (Boston, MA: Harvard Business School Press, 2007).

[105]   Nathan Finney, *Commander's Guide: Employing a Human Terrain Team in Operation Enduring Freedom and Operation Iraqi Freedom: Tactics, Techniques and Procedures*, (U.S. Army Center for Army Lessons Learned, Number 09-21, March 2009), 14.

[106]   Wahab, *In My Father's Country: An Afghan Woman Defies Her Fate*, 283.

[107]   Captain Jeremy Jones, Research Manager, AF2, interviewed November 3, 2011.

[108]   Ibid.

[109]   HTT Social Scientist, interviewed December 21, 2011.

[110]   M. Mason, HTT member, Afghanistan, interviewed October 12, 2011.

[111]   Research Manager, AF3, interviewed December 15, 2011.

[112]   Research Manager on an HTT in Afghanistan, interviewed November 8, 2011.

[113]   Kristen Farnum, Social Scientist, AF5, interviewed October 17, 2011.

[114]   HTT Social Scientist, interviewed December 14, 2011.

[115]   HTT Social Scientist, interviewed December 21, 2011.

[116]   Captain Jeremy Jones, Research Manager, AF2, interviewed November 3, 2011.

[117]   AF1 Social Scientist, 2008-2009, interviewed January 5, 2012.

[118]   HTT Member, Afghanistan, interviewed October 25, 2011.

[119]   Dr. Ron Holt, Social Scientist AF1, interviewed September 28, 2011.

[120]   HTT Member, Afghanistan, interviewed October 25, 2011.

[121]   Eli Corin Social Scientist AF2, interviewed October 13, 2011.

[122]   Team Leader, AF1, interviewed November 1, 2011.

[123]   Research Manager, AF27, interviewed October 25, 2011.

[124]   Social Scientist AF1, interviewed November 14, 2011.

[125]   M. Mason, HTT member, Afghanistan, interviewed October 12, 2011.

[126]   John Green, AF2 Team Leader, interviewed December 1, 2011.

[127]   Research Manager, AF3, interviewed December 15, 2011.

[128]   HTT Social Scientist, interviewed December 21, 2011.

[129]   Dr. Aileen Moffat, Social Scientist AF27, interviewed December 19, 2011.

[130]   Dr. Aileen Moffat, Social Scientist AF27, interviewed December 19, 2011.

[131]   Jeff McNichols, Research Manager, AF14, interviewed November 30, 2011.

[132]   R. A. Guzzo, E. Salas, & Associates, ed., *Team Effectiveness and Decision Making in Organizations* (San Francisco, CA: Jossey-Bass, 1995), 204-261.

[133]   DeWitt C. Dearborn and Herbert A. Simon, "Selective Perception: A Note on the Department Identification of Executives," *Sociometry* iss. 21 (1958), 140-144; A. I. Murray. "Top Management Group Heterogeneity and Firm Performance," *Strategic Management Journal*

iss. 10 (1989), 125-141; C. R. Schwenk, "A Meta-Analysis on the Comparative Effectiveness of Devil's Advocacy and Dialectical Inquiry," *Strategic Management Journal* iss. 10 (1989), 303-306.

[134]   S. E. Asch, "Effects of group pressure upon the modification and distortion of judgments", in H. Guetzkow, ed., *Groups, Leadership, and Men* (Pittsburgh, PA: Carnegie Press, 1951), 177-190; S.E. Asch, "Studies of Independence and Submission to Group Pressures: On minority of one against a unanimous majority," in *Psychological Monographs* iss. 70, no. 9, Whole no. 417 (1956); I. L. Janis, Victims of Groupthink , Second ed. (Boston, MA: Houghlin Mifflin 1982); Kathleen M. Eisenhardt, Jean L. Kahwajy, and L. J. Bourgeois, "How Management Teams Can Have a Good Fight," *Harvard Business Review* iss. 75, no. 4, (1997), 77-85; L. H. Pelled, K. M. Eisenhardt, and K. R. Xin "Exploring the Black Box: An Analysis of Work Group Diversity, Conflict, and Performance," *Administrative Science Quarterly* iss. 44 (1999), 1-28; 2 (definitions), 23 (findings); J. Keith Murnighan and Donald E. Conlon, "The Dynamics of Intense Work Groups: A Study of British String Quartets," *Administrative Science Quarterly* iss. 36 (1991), 165-186.

[135]   Paul C. Nutt, *Why Decisions Fail: Avoid the Blunders and Traps that Lead to Debacles*, (San Francisco, CA: Berrett-Koehler, 2002), 99, 118, 138, 272-273; A. C. Amason and D. M. Schweiger, "Resolving the Paradox of Conflict, Strategic Decision Making and Organizational Performance," *International Journal of Conflict Management* iss. 5 (1994), 239-253; H. Mintzberg, D. Raisinghani, and A. Theoret, "The Structure of Unstructured Decision Processes," *Administrative Science Quarterly* iss. 21 (1976), 192-205.

[136]   Social Scientist AF1, interviewed December 2, 2011.

[137]   Member of AF7, interviewed September 30, 2011.

[138]   HTS document containing interviews with returning HTT members, provided by a Social Scientist with an HTT.

[139]   AF1 Social Scientist, 2008-2009, interviewed January 5, 2012.

[140]   HTT Member, Afghanistan, interviewed October 25, 2011.

[141]   Britt Damon, Research Manager, AF1, interviewed January 4, 2011.

[142]   Major Robert Holbert, Research Manager, AF1, interviewed December 12, 2011.

[143]   AF1 Social Scientist, 2008-2009, interviewed January 5, 2012.

[144]   HTT Research Manager, interviewed January 3, 2012.

[145]   HTT Social Scientist, interviewed December 14, 2011.

[146]   Dr. Ron Holt, Social Scientist AF1, interviewed September 28, 2011.

[147]   Research Manager, AF27, interviewed October 25, 2011.

[148]   Social Scientist AF1, interviewed November 14, 2011.

[149]   Eli Corin, Social Scientist AF2, interviewed October 13, 2011.

[150]   Research Manager, AF3, interviewed December 15, 2011.

[151]   Social Scientist AF1, interviewed December 2, 2011.

[152]   Research Manager, AF27, interviewed October 25, 2011.

[153]   Dr. Marilyn Dudley-Flores, Social Scientist, HTAT Bagram, interviewed January 4, 2012.

[154]   Dr. Aileen Moffat, Social Scientist AF27, interviewed December 19, 2011.

[155]   Program Manager Forward, Afghanistan, interviewed December 7, 2011.

[156]   Social Scientist, Afghanistan, interviewed November 18, 2011.

[157]   HTT Social Scientist, interviewed December 9, 2011.

[158]   John Foldberg, Team Leader AF7, interviewed November 21, 2011.

[159]   HTT Social Scientist, interviewed December 14, 2011.

[160]   HTT member, interviewed October 27, 2011.

[161]   Research Manager on an HTT in Afghanistan, interviewed November 23, 2011.

[162]   John M. Mathieu, Travis Maynard, Tammy Rapp, and Lucy Gilson, "Team Effectiveness 1997-2007: A Review of Recent Advancements and a Glimpse Into the Future," *Journal of*

Management iss. 34, no. 3 (2008), 410-476, 427.

[163]   Ibid, 428.

[164]   Sheila Simsarian Webber, "Leadership and Trust Facilitating Cross-Functional Team Success," *The Journal of Management Development* iss. 21 (2002), 201-214, 205.

[165]   Karen Clark, former HTS Chief of Staff, interviewed October 24, 2011; Lieutenant Colonel Eric Rotzoll, Team Leader, AF2, interviewed October 10, 2011.

[166]   Member of AF7, interviewed September 30, 2011.

[167]   Major Michael Jacobson, U.S. Army Reserves, AF25 Team Leader September 2010—May 2011, interviewed October 7, 2011; Interviewee 27, October 18, 2011.

[168]   Britt Damon, Research Manager, AF1, interviewed January 4, 2011.

[169]   HTS employee, interviewed November 2, 2011.

[170]   Dr. Amy Bursell, Social Scientist AF10, interviewed October 20, 2011.

[171]   Team Leader, AF1, interviewed November 7, 2011.

[172]   Dr. Ron Holt, Social Scientist AF1, interviewed September 28, 2011; Wahab, *In My Father's Country: An Afghan Woman Defies Her Fate*, 295.

[173]   Major Robert Holbert, Research Manager, AF1, interviewed December 12, 2011.

[174]   Dr. Amy Bursell, Social Scientist AF10, interviewed September 29, 2011.

[175]   Social Scientist AF1, interviewed November 14, 2011.

[176]   In at least one case, shared suffering improved team trust. After Paula Lloyd was attacked some members of the HTT felt the team came together over the loss. Research Manager on an HTT in Afghanistan, interviewed November 23, 2011.

[177]   Dr. Amy Bursell, Social Scientist AF10, interviewed October 20, 2011.

[178]   HTS document containing interviews with returning HTT members, provided by a Social Scientist with an HTT, interviewed February 14, 2012, 7.

[179]   Ibid, 8.

[180]   Research Manager on an HTT in Afghanistan, interviewed November 23, 2011.

[181]   Team Leader, AF1, interviewed November 7, 2011.

[182]   HTT Research Manager, interviewed January 3, 2012. Another HTT member noted that "Right from the bat our team had problems here and there because the three of us were closer than the others...." Interviewee 53, November 22, 2011.

[183]   Interviewee 89, November 23, 2011.

[184]   HTT Research Manager, interviewed January 3, 2012.

[185]   Member of the HTS assessment team that visited Iraq in 2008, interviewed May 29, 2012; Zenia H. Tompkins, former HTS trainee, interviewed December 9, 2011.

[186]   Britt Damon, Research Manager, AF1, interviewed January 4, 2011.

[187]   Zenia H. Tompkins, former HTS trainee, interviewed December 9, 2011.

[188]   Britt Damon, Research Manager, AF1, interviewed January 4, 2011.

[189]   Anna Simons, "How Critical Should Critical Thinking Be? Teaching Soldiers in Wartime," in Robert Albro, George Marcus, Laura A. McNamara, and Monica Schoch-Spana, *Anthropologists in the Security Scape: Ethics, Practice, and Professional Identity* (Walnut Creek, CA: Left Coast Press, 2012), 234.

[190]   L. Argote, D. Gruenfeld, and C. Naquin, "Group learning in organizations," in M. E. Turner ed., *Groups at work: Advances in theory and research* (New York, NY: Lawrence Erlbaum, 1999); see also Mary Zellmer-Bruhn and Cristina Gibson, "Multinational Organization Context: Implications for Team Learning and Performance" *Academy of Management Journal* no. 49 (2006), 501-518.

[191]   James G. March, "Exploration and Exploitation in Organizational Learning," *Organization Science* no. 2 (1991), 71-87.

[192]   D. G. Ancona & H. Bresman, *X-Teams: How to Build Teams that Lead, Innovate, and Succeed* (Boston, MA: Harvard Business School Press, 2007).

193   Michael D. Cohen, James G. March and Johan P. Olsen, "A Garbage Can Model of Organizational Choice," *Administrative Science Quarterly* vol. 17 (1972), 1-25; James G. March, "The Technology of Foolishness," in J. G. March and J. P. Olsen, *Ambiguity and Choice in Organizations* (Bergen, Norway: Universitetsforlaget, 1976), 69-81; James G. March, "Bounded Rationality, Ambiguity, and the Engineering of Choice," *Bell Journal of Economics*, no. 9 (1978), 587-608.

194   "It seemed like they didn't really care what we thought as people going through the system. They were going to do whatever they wanted. We got that vibe…" Research Manager on an HTT in Afghanistan, interviewed November 23, 2011; Josh Foust, RRC Analyst, interviewed September 13, 2011; HTT Research Manager, interviewed January 3, 2012.

195   Memorandum, "Findings and Recommendations, AR 15-6 Investigation Concerning Human Terrain Subject (HTS) Project Inspector General Complaints," May 12, 2010, For Official Use Only, redacted and released in response to a Freedom of Information request; available at https://www.box.com/s/2mv0g54xsr41aegwbw9i; February 19, 2013, 6.

196   Research Manager, AF3, interviewed December 15, 2011.

197   Interviewee 24, October 17, 2011.

198   Major Michael Jacobson, U.S. Army Reserves, AF25 Team Leader September 2010—May 2011, interviewed October 7, 2011.

199   HTT Research Manager, interviewed January 3, 2012.

200   Interviewee 44, November 10, 2011.

201   HTS document containing interviews with returning HTT members, provided by a Social Scientist with an HTT, interviewed February 14, 2012, 14.

202   Research Manager, AF27, interviewed October 25, 2011.

203   Social Scientist, Afghanistan, interviewed November 18, 2011.

204   HTT member, Afghanistan, interviewed October 12, 2011.

205   Dr. Aileen Moffat, Social Scientist AF27, interviewed December 19, 2011.

206   Human Terrain Analyst, interviewed December 6, 2011.

207   Major Michael Jacobson, U.S. Army Reserves, AF25 Team Leader September 2010—May 2011, interviewed October 7, 2011.

208   Ibid.

209   M. Mason, HTT member, Afghanistan, interviewed October 12, 2011. In the book the use of social science to understand human society is criticized as "half…fuzzy-headed wishful thinking, half of it rationalized chemistry." Robert A. Heinlein, *Starship Troopers* (New York: NY, Berkley Medallion Books, 1959), 94.

210   Major Robert Holbert, Research Manager, AF1, interviewed December 12, 2011.

211   Interviewee 44, November 10, 2011.

212   John Foldberg, Team Leader AF7, interviewed November 21, 2011.

213   John Foldberg, Team Leader AF7, interviewed November 21, 2011; Member of AF7, interviewed September 30, 2011.

214   John Foldberg, Team Leader AF7, interviewed November 21, 2011.

215   See discussion on page 76 of this report.

216   The 2007 HTS concept of operations emphasizes the "proof of concept" status for HTS and that a commander should have "the maximum flexibility to employ this new and unique capability as he deems most appropriate." The 2008 HTT Handbook provides five specific responsibilities for the team and for a set for each position on an HTT. It also offers a paragraph under best HTT fieldwork practices that urges collaborative decision-making on the team, and advises commanders on the importance of integrating HTTs into brigade planning processes. However, it also emphasizes multiple organizational dispositions for HTTs, including consolidating the HTT, splitting it up, orienting different members toward subordinate units, etc. The following year the Center for Army Lessons Learned produced

a more polished version of the handbook called the *Commander's Guide for Employing HTTs in Operation Enduring Freedom and Operations Iraqi Freedom: Tactics, Techniques and Procedures.* See respectively, *Human Terrain System CONOP: Proof of Concept*, 4 April 2007, As Concurred on by HQDA G2, MNC-I, CENTCOM, & TRADOC, 6; Nathan Finney, *Human Terrain Team Handbook*, (Ft. Leavenworth, KS: The Human Terrain System, September 2008), 12ff; Nathan Finney, *Commander's Guide: Employing a Human Terrain Team in Operation Enduring Freedom and Operation Iraqi Freedom: Tactics, Techniques and Procedures*, (Ft. Leavenworth, KS: U.S. Army Center for Army Lessons Learned, Number 09-21, March 2009), 30ff.

[217] Team Leader, AF1, interviewed November 1, 2011.

[218] Ibid.

[219] Social Scientist AF1, interviewed December 2, 2011; Wahab, *In My Father's Country: An Afghan Woman Defies Her Fate*, 296

[220] Social Scientist AF1, interviewed December 2, 2011.

[221] M. Mason, HTT member, Afghanistan, interviewed October 12, 2011.

[222] Major Michael Jacobson, U.S. Army Reserves, AF25 Team Leader September 2010—May 2011, interviewed October 7, 2011; Social Scientist, Afghanistan, interviewed November 18, 2011.

[223] Nicole Heydari, Human Terrain Analyst AF17, interviewed October 6, 2011.

[224] Ibid.

[225] Social Scientist, Afghanistan, interviewed October 19, 2011.

[226] Greg L. Stewart, "A Meta-Analytic Review of Relationships Between Team Design Features and Team Performance," *Journal of Management* iss. 32 (2006), 29-54.

[227] F. J. Milliken and L. L. Martins, "Searching for Common Threads: Understanding the Multiple Effects of Diversity in Organizational Groups," *Academy of Management Review* iss. 21 (1996), 402-433; K. Y. Williams and C. A. O'Reilly, "Demography and Diversity in Organizations," Research in Organizational Behavior vol. 20 (1998), 77-140; S. E. Jackson, A. Joshi, and N. L. Erhardt, "Recent Research on Team and Organizational Diversity: SWOT Analysis and Implications," Journal of Management iss. 29 (2003), 801-830.

[228] T. Halfhill, E. Sundstrom, J. Lahner, W. Calderone, and T. M. Nielsen, "Group Personality, Composition and Group Effectiveness—An Integrative Review of Empirical Research," *Small Group Research* 36 (2005), 83-105.

[229] Ibid.

[230] S. T. Bell, "Deep-Level Composition Variables as Predictors of Team Performance: A Meta-Analysis," *Journal of Applied Psychology* iss. 92 (2007), 595-615.

[231] Greg L. Stewart, "A Meta-Analytic Review of Relationships Between Team Design Features and Team Performance," *Journal of Management* iss. 32 (2006), 29-54.

[232] Indigenous languages like Dari and Pashto were most in demand, but other languages could also be useful. For example, speaking Russian proved useful to one member who encountered Afghans who still spoke Russian and would share things with him for that reason alone. As noted elsewhere in the study, HTS did not make a point of assigning HTT members where their language skills would be most relevant. For example, one HTT member who spoke Turkic and Dari was assigned to a Pashtu region.

[233] Major Robert Holbert, Research Manager, AF1, interviewed December 12, 2011.

[234] See the discussion in this report on page 186.

[235] Interviewee 44, November 10, 2011.

[236] One interviewee believed certain social science backgrounds—e.g. psychology—were more likely to be hostile to the military ethos, which could exacerbate integration problems: "people with psychology background; I think they had an anti-military chip on their shoulder." Interviewee 7, September 28, 2011.

[237] HTT Team Leader, Afghanistan 2010-2011, interviewed November 15, 2011.

238 One interviewee stated bluntly what others acknowledged more tactfully: "Cleavage is the scarcest of scarce resources downrange. If you can control it, you can get what you want most of the time. That's how we got invited to the Special Forces barbecue every night." Social Scientist AF1, interviewed December 2, 2011.

239 John Green, AF1 Team Leader, interviewed December 1, 2011.

240 HTT Social Scientist, interviewed December 14, 2011.

241 Kristen Farnum, Social Scientist, AF5, interviewed October 17, 2011.

242 Interviewee 27, October 18, 2011.

243 Spencer Ackerman, "Hundreds in Army Social Science Unqualified, Former Boss Says [Updated]," *Wired: Danger Room*, December 21, 2010.

244 One estimate was that as many as 90% of the people deployed to Afghanistan on HTTs were unqualified: "In any organization there is a 10% default rate, and the rest are great. Flip that and you have HTS — 90% [is the] default and you could see it. There is so much drama and conflict and unprofessionalism, and it is corrosive." HTT Social Scientist, interviewed December 14, 2011.

245 HTT Research Manager, interviewed January 3, 2012.

246 Dr. Aileen Moffat, Social Scientist AF27, interviewed December 19, 2011.

247 Interviewee 50, November 18, 2011.

248 Dr. Marilyn Dudley-Flores, Social Scientist, HTAT Bagram, interviewed January 4, 2012.

249 HTT Member, Afghanistan, interviewed October 25, 2011.

250 Joseph, *Changing the Battle Space?*, 7.

251 Research Manager, AF27, interviewed October 25, 2011.

252 Dr. Aileen Moffat, Social Scientist AF27, interviewed December 19, 2011.

253 HTS document containing interviews with returning HTT members, provided by a Social Scientist with an HTT, interviewed February 14, 2012, 12.

254 Dr. Aileen Moffat, Social Scientist AF27, interviewed December 19, 2011.

255 HTT Research Manager, interviewed January 3, 2012.

256 Major Robert Holbert, Research Manager, AF1, interviewed December 12, 2011.

257 Major Michael Jacobson, U.S. Army Reserves, AF25 Team Leader September 2010—May 2011, interviewed October 7, 2011.

258 HTT Team Leader, Afghanistan, 2010-2011, interviewed November 15, 2011.

259 Social Scientist, Afghanistan, interviewed November 18, 2011.

260 John Foldberg, Team Leader AF7, interviewed November 21, 2011.

261 Kristen Farnum, Social Scientist, AF3, interviewed November 3, 2011.

262 Jeff McNichols, Research Manager, AF14, interviewed November 30, 2011.

263 HTT Team Leader, Afghanistan 2010-2011, interviewed November 15, 2011.

264 HTT Social Scientist, interviewed December 9, 2011.

265 HTS document containing interviews with returning HTT members, provided by a Social Scientist with an HTT, 4. The study noted concluded that "the primary focus of returning employees was conflicts within the team."

266 L.R. Gomez-Mejia, and D.B Balkin, "Effectiveness of Individual and Aggregate Compensation Strategies," *Industrial Relations* 28, (1989), 431-445; L.R. Gomez-Mejia, and D.B. Balkin *Compensation, Organizational Strategy, and Firm Performance*, (Cincinnati, OH: South-Western Publishing Co., 1992).

267 Jacquelyn S. DeMatteo, Lillian T. Eby, and Eric Sundstrom, "Team-Based Rewards: Current Empirical Evidence and Directions for Future Research," *Research in Organizational Behavior* vol. 20, (Greenwich, CT: JAI Press, 1998), 141-183.

268 Glenn M. Parker, *Cross-Functional Teams: Working with Allies, Enemies, and Other Strangers* (San Francisco, CA: Jossey-Bass, 2003), 136-7.

[269] L. R. Gomez-Mejia and D. B. Balkin, "Effectiveness of Individual and Aggregate Compensation Strategies," *Industrial Relations* 28 (1989), 431-445.

[270] S.G. Barsade, and D. E. Gibson, "Group Emotion: A View from Top and Bottom," in, D. Gruenfeld, E. A. Mannix, and M. A. Neale ed., *Research on Managing Groups and Teams* (Stamford, CT: JAI Press, 1998), 1, 81–102.

[271] M. Mason, HTT member, Afghanistan, interviewed October 12, 2011. Not all HTT members' explanations for why they joined the program can be sorted into these categories; for example, some people joined to get security clearances, some people joined as a way to recover from difficulties reintegrating into civilian life, and some people joined the program or stayed in the program for clearly personal reasons, such as personal relationships or wanting to collect data for a dissertation.

[272] HTT Team Leader, Afghanistan 2010-2011, interviewed November 15, 2011.

[273] Interviewee 24, October 17, 2011.

[274] One of many such observations along this line is the following: "They will earn a bunch of money, and not do anything. Those people would fall back on what they knew—intelligence work or watching movies." HTT member, Afghanistan, interviewed October 12, 2011.

[275] Lieutenant Colonel Eric Rotzoll, Team Leader, AF2, email on May 14, 2012.

[276] HTT member, Afghanistan, interviewed October 12, 2011.

[277] Dr. Ron Holt, Social Scientist AF1, interviewed September 28, 2011; Social Scientist AF1, interviewed November 14, 2011.

[278] Dr. Amy Bursell, Social Scientist AF10, interviewed September 29, 2011.

[279] M. Mason, HTT member, Afghanistan, interviewed October 12, 2011.

[280] Social Scientist AF1, interviewed November 14, 2011.

[281] HTT Social Scientist, interviewed December 14, 2011.

[282] Kristen Farnum, Social Scientist, AF5, interviewed October 17, 2011.

[283] Clint Cooper, Research Manager, AF4, interviewed November 22, 2011; Team Leader, AF1, interviewed November 7, 2011.

[284] Interviewee 32, October 24, 2011; Clint Cooper, Research Manager, AF4, interviewed November 22, 2011; Britt Damon, Research Manager, AF1, interviewed January 4, 2011.

[285] HTT member, interviewed October 27, 2011.

[286] Ibid.

[287] Interviewee 24, October 17, 2011.

[288] HTT member, Afghanistan, interviewed October 12, 2011.

[289] Team Leader, AF1, interviewed November 7, 2011.

[290] Social Scientist AF1, interviewed December 2, 2011.

[291] HTT member, Afghanistan, interviewed October 12, 2011.

[292] S. J. Zaccaro, A.L. Rittman, and M.A. Marks, "Team Leadership," *Leadership Quarterly*, iss. 12 (2001), 451-483.

[293] C.S. Burke, K.C. Stagl, C. Klein G.F. Goodwin E. Salas, & S.M. Halpin "What Type of Leadership Behaviors Are Functional in Teams? A Meta-analysis," *Leadership Quarterly* iss. 17 (2006), 288-307.

[294] J.R. Hackman, & R. Wageman, "A Theory of Team Coaching," *Academy of Management Review* iss. 30 (2005), 269-287.

[295] N. Bennett, J.A. Harvey, C. Wise, and P.A. Woods, *Desk Study Review of Distributed Leadership* (Nottingham, UK: National College for School Leadership, 2003).

[296] Katherine J. Klein Jonathan C. Zeigert, Andrew P. Knight, Yan Xiao, "Dynamic Delegation: Shared, Hierarchical and Deindividualized Leadership in Extreme Action Teams," *Administrative Science Quarterly* iss. 51 (2006), 590-621.

[297] Sean Hannah, Mary Uhl-Bien, Bruce J. Avolio, and Frances L. Cavaretta, "A Framework for Examining Leadership in Extreme Contexts," *Leadership Quarterly* iss. 20 (2009), 897-919.

[298]   HTT Social Scientist, interviewed December 9, 2011.

[299]   One reservist worked with social science researchers at his stateside job at the National Science Foundation, one team leader had a degree in theology and sometimes presented himself as a social scientist, and one enrolled in a doctoral program in social science after finishing his tour.

[300]   Kristen Farnum, Social Scientist, AF5, interviewed October 17, 2011.

[301]   AF1 Social Scientist, 2008-2009, interviewed January 5, 2012.

[302]   John Foldberg, Team Leader AF7, interviewed November 21, 2011.

[303]   Ibid.

[304]   Ibid.

[305]   Interviewee 44, November 10, 2011; Nicole Heydari, Human Terrain Analyst AF14, interviewed October 5, 2011.

[306]   Dr. Ron Holt, Social Scientist AF1, interviewed September 28, 2011.

[307]   HTT member, Afghanistan, interviewed October 25, 2011.

[308]   HTT member, Afghanistan, interviewed October 4, 2011.

[309]   Team Leader, AF1, interviewed November 7, 2011.

[310]   Nicole Heydari, Human Terrain Analyst AF17, interviewed October 6, 2011.

[311]   Interviewee 27, October 18, 2011.

[312]   Colonel Mike Howe, Team Leader AF3, Jalalabad, interviewed November 10, 2011.

[313]   Program Manager Forward, Afghanistan, interviewed December 7, 2011.

[314]   HTT Member, Afghanistan, interviewed October 25, 2011.

[315]   Nicole Heydari, Human Terrain Analyst AF17, interviewed October 6, 2011.

[316]   Interviewee 27, October 18, 2011.

[317]   Social Scientist, Afghanistan, interviewed November 18, 2011.

[318]   Major Michael Jacobson, U.S. Army Reserves, AF25 Team Leader September 2010—May 2011, interviewed October 7, 2011.

[319]   Nicole Heydari, Human Terrain Analyst AF17, interviewed October 6, 2011.

[320]   Ibid.

[321]   HTT Team Leader, Afghanistan 2010-2011, interviewed November 15, 2011.

[322]   Social Scientist, Afghanistan, interviewed October 19, 2011.

[323]   HTT Team Leader, Afghanistan 2010-2011, interviewed November 15, 2011.

[324]   Research Manager, AF27, interviewed October 25, 2011.

[325]   Interviewee 32, October 24, 2011.

[326]   Human Terrain Analyst, Afghanistan, December 13, 2011.

[327]   Clint Cooper, Research Manager, AF4, interviewed November 22, 2011.

[328]   HTT Social Scientist, interviewed December 21, 2011.

[329]   Kristen Farnum, Social Scientist, AF5, interviewed October 17, 2011.

[330]   HTT Team Leader, Afghanistan 2010-2011, interviewed November 15, 2011.

[331]   Kristen Farnum, Social Scientist, AF5, interviewed October 17, 2011.

[332]   Social Scientist, Afghanistan, interviewed November 18, 2011.

[333]   Interviewee 24, October 17, 2011.

[334]   HTT Social Scientist, interviewed December 21, 2011.

[335]   Dr. Amy Bursell, Social Scientist AF10, interviewed September 29, 2011.

[336]   Interviewee 32, October 24, 2011.

[337]   Interviewee 24, October 17, 2011.

[338]   HTT Team Leader, Afghanistan 2010-2011, interviewed November 15, 2011.

[339]   HTT member, interviewed October 27, 2011.

[340]   HTT member, interviewed October 27, 2011.

5 PERFORMANCE ASSESSMENT

"Twenty-first-century warfare is defined by information and intelligence, and the subcomponents of that are precision, perception, and understanding, more than speed, distance, and lethality."[1]

Major General Michael T. Flynn

Having completed the historical review of HTS and the analysis of performance variables that best explain HTT performance in the field, the stage is set to provide the reader with a net explanation for performance. Before doing so we need to need to explain an anomaly: why HTT experts are more critical of HTT performance than field commanders. In part the discrepancy might be explained by unfavorable publicity from ill-informed commentators.

In secondary literature a few egregious cases of poor performance are overly emphasized, and the largely positive testimonies from commanders for whom the HTTs worked are often downplayed or overlooked. Although the first six HTTs ran into problems, commanders early on began reporting back on the usefulness of the HTTs.[2] Even so, bias in secondary literature is not sufficient to explain the difference between commander assessments and other expert evaluations. Many expert sources agree HTT performance is highly variable,[3] including their own members, who tend to judge HTT performance more critically than field commanders.[4] Yet the large majority of commanders queried found the teams helpful. The disparate performance assessments and the strong testimony from commanders on the usefulness of HTTs both require explanation. Toward that end it is helpful to briefly survey previous studies, particularly with respect to how they characterize commander views, and then to examine more closely why commanders assessed HTT performance as they did.

Previous Assessments of HTT Performance

HTS conducted two early internal studies of HTT effectiveness, examining AF1 in July-August 2007 and then the initial five teams sent to Iraq in February 2008. HTS used the standard Army framework for military capability analysis, considering doctrine, organization, training, materiel, leadership, and education, personnel and facilities (i.e. DOTMLPF).[5] These internal reports are notable for being the only available sources of written documentation on what HTS thought of its own teams. The report on AF1 is strongly positive. It claims "the HTT has had a profound effect on the brigade [that] has been felt at all levels."[6] The Brigade Commander, Colonel Martin Schweitzer is quoted as saying, "without the HTT filter on the [courses of actions] and the alternative maneuver tools they identified to create the exact same effect, we would have lost double the lives and would have had double the contacts [encounters with armed enemy forces.]"[7] The report identified four specific vignettes that illustrated four ways AF1 helped the brigade:

(1) a decrease in kinetic operations;
(2) an improvement in Course of Action analysis;
(3) improved situational awareness; and
(4) improved information operations.[8]

We already provided a description of the HTS internal evaluation of the first five Iraqi HTTs in the history section of this report; here we just summarize its conclusions with respect to commander viewpoints. The report begins by stating "[e]ach of the HTTs in Iraq made contributions, some modest and some significant, to its respective brigade."[9] Specific commander quotations on HTT performance included in the report are overwhelmingly positive. The comments predominantly attest to the teams' ability to provide cultural context to military commanders for their actions. The report notes that 90 percent of respondents agreed the HTTs provided a unique and necessary capability, and 100 percent of respondents reported that the HTTs contributed to the brigades' ability to accomplish their missions.[10] One brigade commander is quoted as saying the HTT "gave us the background to achieve the right balance in kinetic and non-kinetic."[11] The Iraq report lists seven unique examples of significant contributions by HTTs as cited by brigade commanders or subordinate elements:

(1) facilitating the release of a falsely accused man;
(2) casualty avoidance;

(3) facilitating political reconciliation;

(4) course of action refinement;

(5) improved interaction with the local population;

(6) improved economic sustainability planning; and

(7) the identification of legitimate local authorities.[12]

However, the analytical sections of the report describe team performance problems that affected all five teams and in one case were severe enough that the team had to be withdrawn. HTS did not continue these internal reports, but several years later HTS management reported to TRADOC investigators that "anecdotal feedback suggests that one-third of the teams have been successful downrange, one-third have done okay, and one-third were unsuccessful."[13]

The next study of HTTs we consulted was *The Human Terrain Team Trip Report: "A Team of Teams,"* prepared in 2008 by faculty members at the United States Military Academy at West Point. The authors and their students traveled to Iraq in 2008 at the request of Maxie McFarland. Their assigned purpose was to determine the "value-added" from HTTs. The West Point team interviewed a number of HTS employees and managers, but the focus of the study was interviewing 4 brigades in Iraq that had HTTs, as well as one "null set" brigade that operated without a HTT. Personnel at all levels of the brigade, as well as the teams themselves, were interviewed for a total of over 100 interviews.[14] The individuals interviewed, questions asked, and responses received were not included in the 14-page report. The study findings are tentative insofar as it was just the beginning of what the authors noted should be a larger study on HTT effectiveness, one that was never completed.

The West Point report was notable in that all the commanders interviewed indicated they valued the work of the HTTs. One battalion commander said, for example, that "he would simply be ineffective without his HTT."[15] HTTs were deemed useful for providing:

(1) critical familial, tribal, and political linkage charts and analyses;

(2) continuity of knowledge between unit rotations;

(3) alternative perspectives in the planning process.[16]

The report found that, by comparison, "the continuity of knowledge and synchronization of staff processes concerning cultural knowledge seem limited" in the brigade that operated without an HTT.[17]

Despite the report's positive findings from commander interviews, it left the impression that HTT performance was actually more variable. It argued that while all commanders said they highly valued the HTT's work, "they only embraced HTTs once the HTTs proved themselves." The report then observes that "Key to the commander's buy-in concerning the HTT's value is the HTT's effectiveness," and concludes "It is more important that HTS build excellent teams who prove their effectiveness than to produce numerous ineffective teams."[18] By calling attention to the need for HTS to focus more on the quality than quantity of teams, the report implies HTT performance was known to be more variable than commanders reported. (In HTS's internal review of performance from the same time period, concerns about HTT performance variation were explicitly acknowledged.[19])

The West Point study does not offer a firm explanation for HTT performance variation. The authors concluded more research was necessary for "a more comprehensive and strategic view of the program" and to discern "longitudinal trends." However, the report does offer some preliminary thoughts about how performance could be improved. The findings are diverse, ranging from "ensuring that team members possess…adequate physical fitness" to using social scientists from a broader set of disciplines than anthropology, since that scholarly community had proven unreceptive to the HTS idea. It is difficult to extrapolate a singular explanation for variable HTT performance from the study observations, but the report did seem to put special emphasis on the quality of the team membership. The authors note that "Everyone we talked with mentioned that personality and attitude is everything," and they then list some of the "knowledge, skills and abilities" mentioned in their interviews as helpful for team performance. In this respect, the West Point study reinforced the HTS management's perspective that team performance was largely a matter of quality personnel and leadership, or "personalities."

The 2010 *Congressionally Directed Assessment of the Human Terrain System* was conducted by CNA Analysis and Solutions and funded by the Office of the Under Secretary of Defense for Intelligence. In requiring the report, the House Committee on Armed Services noted there was "anecdotal evidence indicating the benefits of the program" and "anecdotal evidence indicating problems." The CNA report found the same: that a review of internal HTS assessments indicated "pockets" of brigade commander feedback—some positive and some negative—over the past several years."[20] Precisely because HTT performance was reputedly variable, the Committee wanted a report that would "provide Congress with accurate and objective information on specific aspects of the HTS program and insight into HTS's operations and effectiveness."[21] The report focused on the management performance of HTS as opposed to HTT effectiveness, but included interviews with eighteen "customers" of HTS products, including seven brigade commanders and four battalion commanders.[22] Five interviewees interacted with HTTs in

Afghanistan, ten in Iraq, and one had experience with HTTs in both Iraq and Afghanistan. Five customers said their HTT was very useful; eight claimed variable HTT performance; three concluded the HTTs were not useful.[23]

CNA provides detailed charts on the questions commanders were asked and their responses, which are penetrating and varied. The commander responses defy easy summation. However, those who believed their HTT was useful said they helped commanders:

(1) understand the political make up of their area of operations;
(2) become experts on their area of operations;
(3) in non-lethal targeting meetings.

Those who claimed that their HTTs were not useful said the HTT leaders were inflexible on how they should be used, and that their products were not relevant. Concerning overall management of the program, the report concludes performance was handicapped by a series of unresolved problems within the HTS organization, especially HTS's relationship with TRADOC and human resourcing for both the teams and the program management.[24] Like the West Point study, the CNA report concludes the HTS program is successful. It "fills a gap for the war-fighter and therefore has made an important contribution to U.S. military operations in Iraq and Afghanistan."[25] Also like the West Point study, the CNA report does not proffer an explanation for HTT performance variation. Instead the report focuses on management issues.

The Institute for Defense Analyses' (IDA) report on Human Terrain Teams attempted to determine the conditions that "contribute to or detract from the effectiveness of Human Terrain Team/command relationship."[26] The IDA study utilized interviews with HTT members and commanders and support staff for a total of fifty-two "usable" interviews.[27] Nineteen of the interviewees were "military commanders" and thirty-three were HTS personnel.[28] Of the nineteen commanders, seventeen were brigade commanders, and the other two were staff officers who worked with HTTs on a daily basis.[29] IDA's metric for gauging effectiveness was the extent to which the HTTs provided the commander with "relevant sociocultural understanding for meeting his operational requirements."[30] However, because the West Point study emphasized the importance of commanders accepting and using HTTs to best effect,[31] IDA also compared the perspectives of both HTT members and military commanders on "whether or not the [HTTs] were used to the fullest extent possible."[32]

The focus of the IDA research was on the relationship between the brigade command team and the HTT, and indeed, the study concludes that "the Human Terrain Team's effectiveness may strongly depend upon its ability to develop a functional communication pattern and working relationship with the supported command."[33] Indicators of a poor relationship between the HTT and the supported command included "constrained participation in brigade staff meetings," "lack of frequent communication with the commander and/or his deputy," and "conflicts between the Human Terrain Team and brigade staff." IDA also found that conflicts *within* the HTTs were a significant factor in poor performance. IDA reasoned that conversely, building a fully functional, cooperative team should improve performance and thus "all the knowledge and lessons learned about forming effective small teams should be applied to creating a Human Terrain Team."[34]

Our research substantiates the IDA team's findings (and those of the West Point study as well) on the importance of HTTs forming harmonious relationships with the brigade commanders and staffs. However, we do not believe the conflict on the HTTs was *ipso facto* a negative influence on HTT performance. Insofar as HTTs were, by their very nature, cross-functional teams, a certain amount of conflict was inevitable and even desirable. The key performance issue concerns whether the team is able to resolve the conflict productively; i.e. in a manner that permits it to fulfill its mission effectively.

Finally, a recently released internal investigation by TRADOC into alleged management improprieties, conducted in 2010 also acknowledges performance variation in the teams. It found, "while some teams are reported to be providing significant value others are reported to have been or are currently ineffectively."[35] The report also references the "uneven quality of teams throughout Afghanistan," and attributes the uneven performance of teams to "the fact that there is no means to determine team effectiveness, a lack of standards for selection and team composition, uneven team leadership, and inadequate preparation and team building."[36]

Two other assessments of HTT performance in the field could not be obtained by the authors, but summaries of their conclusions offer no reason to believe they differ significantly from the other studies reviewed here.[37] Thus, all those who have studied HTTs closely tend to agree with the overwhelming majority of HTT members we interviewed and note that HTT performance varies from team to team. They do not, however, provide comprehensive or compelling explanations for the HTT performance variation. Instead they emphasize the fact that commanders are the primary HTT "customers," their perception of the usefulness of team output is disproportionately important, and commanders disproportionately assess HTTs as useful. Interestingly, the IDA study found that HTT members assessed the performance of HTTs more critically than commanders.[38] As we will show in the following section, one likely reason for this is that HTT members probably better understood the level of performance they were supposed to be providing.

Categorizing Commander Assessments of HTTs

Most studies based on commander assessments are notable for their small sampling of commander views, but arrive at the same two findings. The studies indicate commanders assess the performance of HTTs as variable, but also that most commanders are pleased with HTT performance and believe "they provided a level of insight [they] simply could not get from anywhere else."[39] Our study is no different, either with respect to its small sample size or the finding that most commanders valued HTT contributions. We were able to interview nine brigade commanders. Three rated their teams highly effective; one rated his team as completely ineffective; the rest identified their HTTs as having a mixed level of effectiveness. When all commander assessments from multiple studies are considered, it is clear that those who thought their HTTs were useful constituted the large majority (see chart below[40]).

Comparison of Studies Sampling Commander HTT Assessments			
	Successful	**Partial Success**	**No impact or Ineffective**
West Point Study	Highly valued		
	4		
CNA Study	Very useful	Varied usefulness	Not useful
	5	**8**	**3**
IDA Study	Success: the BCT could not have been successful without the HTT efforts	Partial Success: on balance, the HTT did more good than harm	No impact (regardless of reason)
	26	**9**	**1**

NDU Study	Effective	Mixed effectiveness	Not effective
	8	**4**	**1**

Operational needs statements from commanders were responsible for getting the HTS program off the ground, and positive assessments of HTT performance from commanders were critical for keeping HTTs in the field and increasing the number deployed. Given the importance of commander opinions, their reasoning on the value of HTTs is critical. We wanted to examine the widest possible range of commander comments to better assess the reasons why commanders liked or disliked HTT performance, and to determine if commanders had different levels of expectation on HTT performance. To increase the range of commander opinions we conducted our own interviews of commanders and collected all publicly available comments on HTT performance attributed to commanders by credible sources. To determine levels of commander expectations for HTT performance, we categorized commander praise and criticisms of HTTs in the three levels of cultural knowledge previously identified (see shadow box on page 7). The three levels roughly equate to the social science objectives of accurate description, explanation and prediction. They also establish a rough level of commander expectations:

- **Cultural Awareness**: basic familiarity with language and religion and an understanding and observance of local norms and boundaries. This roughly equates to good *description* of human terrain. It was often observed by commanders that such description is needed at *the tactical level*, down to battalion and company levels if not below.

- **Cultural Understanding**: the "why" of behavior embodied in perceptions, mindsets, attitudes, and customs. This roughly equates to *explanation* of human behaviors. Perhaps because brigade commanders were the focus of interviews it is not surprising that this level of understanding, which presumably is important at all levels, was emphasized at *the brigade level*.

- **Cultural Intelligence**: the implications of these behaviors and their drivers, including ways in which culture can shape *theater-level* decision-making. It might be a stretch to equate this highest level of cultural knowledge with *prediction*, but understanding what drives behavior and its implications allows commanders to anticipate developments in human terrain in response to their decisions.

The highest level of cultural intelligence was judged to be "a type of all-source analysis that relies heavily on open-source intelligence and human intelligence… the product of analysis rather than something that can be collected, [which] requires multi-disciplinary approaches and a multi-step process."[41] Generally social scientists agree that good description precedes accurate explanation, and that powerful explanatory frameworks for behavior are necessary before they can anticipate or make a prediction on human behavior in different circumstances. In this respect the postulated three levels of cultural knowledge are cumulative.

In practice, HTTs contributed to all three levels of cultural knowledge. Commander testimonies and our interviewees provide examples of each level:

Cultural Awareness: "[What] I wanted to do was human terrain mapping. Which was just rigorous data collection….I didn't want to do anything called social science research. All I wanted to do was consistent data collection about the local population….[The Team Leader] was very into this….From the beginning, we were focused on rigorous data collection, which was going to a village and profiling it…mapping out the boundaries of an ethnic group…it was routine, nothing fancy. That was all I wanted to do, so I never worried about coming up with research plans. I also never asked the brigade commander what he wanted."[42]

Cultural Understanding: "I held the team to an extremely high standard. There had been a HTT twice before that had flubbed and had tried to give them the bubblegum HT assessment crap. They just weren't having it. The British wanted advanced academic research from the field, not ASCOPE-PMSEII [a basic sociocultural typology[43]]. Fortunately I had selected a group of academics that were capable of that type of field research. The stuff we gave them back was impeccable….If you want to do advanced, in the field research, bring your institutions of higher learning into the field and do research there….back at [their Ministry of Defense], when they saw my team doing this, [the official] became such a believer."[44]

Most testimonies on HTT performance indicate the HTTs contributed at the first or second level of cultural knowledge. This makes sense because they were employed at the brigade level or below. HTATs, not HTTs, were supposed to provide the third level of cultural knowledge to U.S. forces. However, on occasion it has proven difficult to convince U.S. commanders that HTATs are necessary:

> What's frightening is that despite repeated explanations of our function, the first [HTAT] at Division in Iraq met with elements of a command that were almost as hostile as the small band of vocal cultural anthropologists at the American Anthropological Association…they didn't understand what we could contribute. They already had people doing <u>surveys</u>, and additional troops and enablers were obtaining atmospherics across the local population. What they didn't have was a team that could get data and information from trained social scientists from brigade level teams across Baghdad….[45]

In addition, some HTTs resisted passing their findings up the chain to the HTATs:

> Since there had never been an HTAT in theater these teams may have been concerned that we would try to play a supervisory role. HTS doctrine was at odds with this since we lacked tasking authority. When the teams didn't choose to share the products they were providing to the brigade commanders, our team leader and the division command tried to task the HTTs by having the division commander task the brigade commanders with special instructions to turn over the work products of the HTTs. These FRAGOs usually fell by the wayside since both the teams and the commanders saw this as an infringement on the brigade commanders' authority to task their teams. The result was that our team didn't get proper information flow from some of our most important assets."[46]

Even though it was easier for HTS to make contributions at the small unit and brigade level, some general officers from ISAF headquarters suggest that the cumulative effect of the HTT contributions leavened the decision making at higher levels, allowing them to anticipate the impact of alternative courses of action so they could choose the one that would produce the best outcomes:

> **Cultural Intelligence**: "…their ability to assess the population through engagement meetings with local officials, provincial government officials, and tribal leaders has increased ISAF's ability to better understand the average persons' perspective. This "grass-roots" per-

spective provided by HTTs offers a more robust and clear picture of the needs of the entire population, which is then incorporated into ISAF's decision-making processes to increase positive outcomes."[47]

Brigade commanders were not predisposed to believe HTTs would make contributions at one level of cultural knowledge or another. Commander testimonies, and previous studies, indicate that commanders generally had a "wait and see attitude" about HTT performance. Many positive commander comments on HTTs attest to their general value, but those commanders who provide more specific reasoning for why HTTs were helpful often credit HTTs with helping provide a good description of human terrain. In fact, the majority of positive explanations for HTT performance underscore their ability to provide better situational awareness for the brigade and subordinate units. Some commanders elaborated that HTTs provided:

- Continuity of situational awareness across multiple brigade deployments.
- Faster situational awareness than possible without an HTT.

Commanders also note that HTTs could help spread this basic situational awareness through their forces, for example by providing training on:

- Basic Afghan customs (do's and don'ts).
- How to collect information on human terrain effectively.

Some HTT members taught 'classes' before, after and even during operations. The HTT would teach soldiers better ways to engage with and understand Afghanistan, its people and the various dynamics soldiers would have to deal with while out on patrol.[48] An HTT in Kandahar delivered classes on the "five do's and the five don'ts" of Afghan culture in the area of operations. Multiple commanders observing these efforts came to believe HTTs were most effective at the Company level.[49] The consequences of better situational awareness on the command staff and throughout the force were also cited by commanders who believed that HTT insights:

- Countered common American prejudices about Afghans, and thus reduced hostility or disrespect.
- Introduced commander and/or staff to an alternative perspective that helped them see a problem differently (helping break down military group think).

Fewer commanders, and typically those who worked with the handful of widely acknowledged superlative HTTs, testified that the HTTs contributed at the second level of cultural knowledge. In other words, they not only helped describe the human terrain, they explained the behaviors in ways that helped commanders tailor their brigade operations. For example, a member of the British Task Force commented that the HTT input "caused…commanders to reassess ongoing operations, realign resources, undertake new population focused initiatives…."[50] In this vein, commanders said that with HTT help they could make decisions while better understanding their consequences, which facilitated course of action analysis. More specific benefits included:

- Reduced friction with the population (which in turn reduced casualties);
- Support for political reconciliation, by identifying who had power, trust, resources and what their motives were;
- Improved information operations, by helping tailor message content and style to reach Afghan audiences better;
- Better "damage limitation" when untoward events occurred that had to be explained and compensated for with the Afghan populace.[51]

When HTTs could better explain Afghan attitudes, decision making and behavior to commanders, it encouraged commanders to see problems differently, and solve them differently. Commanders were able to understand second and third order effects better, and act accordingly and faster. The most dramatic examples involved reductions in local violence. Although few commanders were willing to state that HTTs were directly responsible for a reduction in kinetic activity, some noted the correlation between HTT activities and reduced violence. In one case, an HTT member established a new shura between tribal elders and that led to the end of a tribal conflict.[52] In Eastern Afghanistan, the HTT identified for the commander who the real power players were in the region, which ran counter to the brigade's previous assumptions. The commander agreed to hold a shura with those leaders. The commander emphasized that all lethal activity stopped, "The. Next. Day."[53]

Rarely did brigade commanders assess HTT performance in ways that suggest they were capable of the third level of cultural knowledge, which provides deep insights on the origins and implications of Afghan behaviors and decision-making. While explaining Afghan observable behavior is important for course of action analysis, the ability to anticipate likely reactions to a course of action is invaluable. It is commonly understood that predicting behaviors in any particular circumstance is quite difficult. But at higher levels, where commanders must anticipate and estimate general Afghan re-actions rather than how any one particular individual leader or tribe might react, the need for such expertise is acknowledged by commanders even if it is not attributed to HTTs. The best explanation for why regional and theater commanders need the third level of cultural knowledge, and what it takes to get it, is a 2010 article by Major General Michael T. Flynn and other military officers entitled "Fixing Intel: A Blueprint for Making Intelligence Relevant in Afghanistan."[54] The article also articulates a cultural intelligence architecture that makes it possible to identify the ideal role for HTTs, and to better interpret commander reactions to HTTs in practice.

HTT Roles in an Integrated Cultural Intelligence Architecture

> *"The number one performance measure is whether I can pry them (HTTs) out of the commander's hands when I need to reallocate them on the battlefield. I can tell you I have not been successful, not once...there is a desire to have this capability in the battlespace."*[55]
> Major General Michael T. Flynn

Flynn and the other authors of "Fixing Intel" note that in counterinsurgency "the most salient problems are attitudinal, cultural, and human," and theater commanders need to keep abreast of these concerns on a daily basis:

> If relations suddenly were to sour between U.S. troops and an influential tribe...public confidence in the government's ability to hold the entire city might easily, and predictably, falter. In such a situation, the imperative to provide top Afghan and ISAF leaders with details about the tribal tension and its likely causes is clear. Leaders at the national level may be the only ones with the political and military leverage to decisively preempt a widening crisis.

Thus in a counterinsurgency small units supply key intelligence to higher commands rather than the other way around. In large unit conventional warfare:

> Satellites, spy planes, and more arcane assets controlled by people far from the battlefield inform ground units about the strength, location, and activity of the enemy before the ground unit even arrives. Information flows largely from the top down. In a counterinsurgency, the flow is (or should be) reversed. The soldier or development worker on the ground is usually the person best informed about the

environment and the enemy.

For this reason, all soldiers must be intelligence collectors who enable higher-level analysts to create "comprehensive narratives" for each district that "describe changes in the economy, atmospherics, development, corruption, governance, and enemy activity" and "provide the kind of context that is invaluable up the chain of command."

The Flynn article describes how the 1st Battalion, 5th Marines pacified Nawa with "two particularly farsighted decisions. First, they distributed their intelligence analysts down to the company level, and second, *they decided that understanding the people in their zone of influence was a top priority*" (emphasis added):

> By resisting the urge of many intelligence officers to hoard analysts at the command post, the S-2 and his deputy armed themselves with a network of human sensors who could debrief patrols, observe key personalities and terrain across the district, and—crucially—write down their findings. Because there were not enough analysts to send to every platoon, the infantry companies picked up the slack by assigning riflemen to collate and analyze information fulltime.

Yet this kind of approach is so alien to the conventional military that it cannot happen unless a small unit commander understands its utter necessity and throws his entire unit's resources into the effort. On this point Flynn cites the commander of another successful pacification effort who "had ordered his intelligence shop to support this effort by devoting their energy to understanding the social relationships, economic disputes, and religious and tribal leadership of the local communities." The commander explained his actions by noting "intelligence is a commander's responsibility," and that "Intel automatically defaults to focusing on the enemy if the commander is not involved in setting priorities and explaining why they are important."

In addition to arguing that success required pushing intelligence assets down to exploit a network of human sensors collecting from the many small units in direct contact with the population, Flynn argued that brigade level commanders:

> must authorize a select group of analysts to retrieve information from the ground level and make it available to a broader audience, similar to the way journalists work. These analysts must leave their chairs and visit the people who operate at the grassroots level—civil affairs officers, PRTs, atmospherics teams, Afghan liaison officers, female

engagement teams, willing NGOs and development organizations, United Nations officials, psychological operations teams, human terrain teams, and staff officers with infantry battalions—to name a few.

In short, primary collection is done at the small unit level where there are "many sensors," and analysis of the diverse descriptive inputs is done at the brigade level where there are more resources, and then passed along to the regional (or division) level to create a comprehensive composite understanding of the situation. At that level "specially trained analysts must be empowered to methodically identify everyone who collects valuable information, visit them in the field, build mutually beneficial relationships with them, and bring back information to share with everyone who needs it." Flynn elaborates:

> Once gathered, information must be read and understood. This select team of analysts would take the first pass at making sense of what they have gathered by writing periodic narrative reviews of all that is happening in pivotal districts: who the key personalities are, how local attitudes are changing, what the levels of violence are, how enemy tactics are evolving, why farmers chose to plant more wheat than poppy this winter, what development projects have historically occurred or are currently underway, and so on. Ideally, this would entail dividing their workload along geographic lines, instead of along functional lines, with each covering a handful of key districts.

These civilian analysts "would be information integrators, vacuuming up data already collected by military personnel or gathered by civilians in the public realm and bringing it back to a centralized location."[56] They would work in Stability Operations Information Centers at the regional command level.

Flynn's widely-applauded critique of how to do cultural intelligence in a counterinsurgency in Afghanistan makes it clear that HTTs won't be successful if employed as a substitute for a larger, more comprehensive effort to collect and analyze cultural intelligence. This point is not made in commander guidance provided by HTS. HTS management emphasized to brigade commanders that HTTs could conduct a wide range of cultural knowledge tasks for them, from basic data collection and field research to analysis that would support brigade decision making on courses of action.[57] Emphasizing HTT flexibility preserved maximum latitude for commanders to decide how to use HTTs. However, it also left commanders without a specific notion of how an HTT could best be utilized, or what else commanders must do to successfully obtain sociocultural understanding that is operationally relevant.

Judging by their explanations for HTT usefulness, most commanders employed HTTs primarily to increase their situational awareness; e.g.: "we basically went in blind and the HTT helped us get up to speed on local customs and culture."[58] Relatively few HTTs graduated to the second level of cultural understanding where they influenced commander decision making and courses of action. Yet when HTTs helped explain the behavior of local populations in ways that made U.S. military operations more effective, they were appreciated whether they were used at the brigade or smaller unit levels. According to one company commander:

> Without the HTT, our actions would not have been as precise. If they weren't there, I would have cordoned off the village, gathered local elders, and told them what we were doing, I would have told them to show me their personally-owned weapons, and if they didn't show us their weapons, we would have torn up the village and taken them. Because of the HTT, I understood my alternatives... Would I like a HTT? Absolutely—if you could have one for every company command, they would be a phenomenal asset.[59]

The primary problem with using HTTs at the small unit level is that there were too few of them to make much of a difference:

> We could have used four, one in every province.[60]

> You need guys like this at the company level...if you had a guy with the company they could...ratchet up the understanding at a level where you could make a difference and could measure it...[61]

> These teams were awesome, but they were 1/5th to 1/10th of what we needed to really have an impact.[62]

> What they touched, they gave added value to, but what they touched was so grossly inadequate, and even with 31 teams it still is...the single greatest improvement, if we are serious, is to increase the quantity.[63]

> [It's] criminal that we don't have HTT at the battalions or company level.[64]

Commanders who wanted to use HTTs at the small unit level and knew they could not cover the brigade's entire area of operations just tried to be selective in where they employed the HTT: "[P]utting them in every place where they are not the most needed is an ineffective use of the HTT."[65] Others believed it was necessary to use public polling because HTTs could not cover their entire areas well.[66]

While most commanders were thankful for the enhanced situational awareness HTTs provided even if they were aware that it was insufficient to meet their needs, some criticized the HTS program and HTT concept because of it. In fact, almost all negative comments from commanders about HTTs stem from differences of opinion about whether HTTs should be small-unit level data collectors who contribute to basic situational awareness or integrators of diverse cultural data sources who contribute to brigade commander decision making. Some commanders wanted to break up the HTTs and throw them at data collection, and were irritated when the HTTs resisted being used this way:

> They wanted to move as team—collect survey and data—[but] most valued added would have been to align [each individual HTT person's expertise] where needed, not as a team... [HTT] should let [the] command determine where each individual should go.[67]

Other commanders complained that HTTs used for local data collection were insufficient and thus their impact was questionable:

> The HTT could not cover the entire battle space and the papers were not what he needed to make decisions.[68]

> I didn't use their products....just wasn't what we needed...it was just too basic information. The team was a few years behind what the current operational demand was...[69]

In short, as one brigade commander commented, using HTTs as collectors was like using a squirt gun to fight a forest fire.[70] There is simply too much human terrain in a brigade area of responsibility for HTTs to build a comprehensive and current picture. No matter how well the HTT described portions of the local human terrain, they simply could not cover it sufficiently well to make a major difference for a brigade commander. Thus, as the Flynn article makes clear, collecting cultural knowledge at the village level is a small-unit commander responsibility in a counterinsurgency and requires a full-fledged effort to engage all available assets as collectors. Collecting cultural knowledge cannot be delegated to HTTs alone. HTTs can improve cultural awareness (the first level of cultural knowledge) but have too few members to make much of a difference if they are tasked to be the primary collector of cultural knowledge at the grass-roots level. Commanders needed to do as Flynn recommended, and so train and employ their troops and staff that they "armed themselves with a network of human sensors who could debrief patrols, observe key personalities and terrain" across their area of responsibility.

Some observers consider General Flynn's recommendation to use soldiers as sensors impractical, but others have validated the concept by simply executing it. Corporal Scott Mitchell, a member of a Company Intelligence Support Team with the 3rd Brigade Combat Team, 10th Mountain Division is one such example. Deployed to Kandahar Province between 2011 and 2012, Mitchell and the unit he was attached to, supported by two HTTs,[71] focused their efforts on a village situated in an unstable, violence prone area. Believing "everyone in the platoon is an intelligence collector,"[72] Mitchell wanted to collect "DMV-type" information from local Afghans to map the human terrain. Mitchell, who had received pre-deployment training from two early advocates of HTS, Don Smith and Andrea Jackson, acknowledged it can be difficult for soldiers to change their "warrior mindset." So he decided to work within their established ethos and make it a question of following orders. By attaching a short set of basic questions to 'request for information' orders, he obtained his information. Soon a village census emerged and over time, many insurgents were discovered and weeded out because the unit understood its human terrain. The village environment stabilized, and Mitchell's approach was institutionalized by the brigade commander who made it a standard operating procedure for all his units.[73]

Commanders who understood the need to employ soldiers as sociocultural data collectors had higher expectations for HTTs. They wanted HTTs to perform at the second level of cultural knowledge where they could make a contribution to explaining local human terrain to the command staff and facilitate command decision making. One brigade commander described how pleased he was that his HTT came to staff meetings and caused "helpful trouble,"[74] raising points no military officer could answer, and answering questions no military staff member could. Challenging prevailing command staff assumptions and even interpreting recent operations differently—"bringing a different lens on it"[75]—was an important HTT function for some commanders. The HTT's viewpoint could affect how a brigade operated. For example, one HTT identified how the brigade's operations in support of a road construction project were causing consternation amongst locals, and the brigade and its subordinate units changed their operating behavior.[76] Other brigades would use their HTTs to shape planning before any operation began, ensuring their comments, concerns and knowledge were fed into the process.[77]

Commanders who wanted HTTs to make a contribution to military decision making were frustrated when HTTs—for any reason—would not engage with their staff and the planning process. Sometimes the HTTs felt they needed to get up to speed first; other times the Team Leader insisted on being the only HTT voice in command staff meetings;[78] and still other times HTT members felt it was their duty to be removed from staff efforts that might have a lethal effects dimension. Commanders who wanted HTTs to integrate at the staff level and participate in decision making also complained that HTT products could be too basic. If an HTT arrived after a brigade had been working an area for some time, the commander might complain that the brigade knew more about the local human terrain than the HTT.[79] Some teams circumvented this problem by trying to isolate a key problem for the commander before getting around to basic data collection:

> Better teams would identify the biggest problem through interviews and research and build a database about what is affecting that problem and work backwards—learning about environment and what matters to the commander.[80]

Other teams rose to the second level of cultural knowledge over time and pleased their commanders with this capability:

> The HTT provides valuable cultural insight that goes beyond normal intel sources. The HTT takes the big picture outlook, from macro to micro. They give us a "forest from the trees" outlook. [The team leader] brings up 2nd- and 3rd-order effects issues that influence our planning. They act as an honest broker, and that information goes into the commander's decision making cycle.[81]

> They would get in there, into the wealth of assets available to them globally and give an assessment. That is what I used them for the most: to determine the root causes of the problems in the AO, not just the symptoms from someone without their depth of knowledge.[82]

> In accordance with the commander's guidance, the HTT…developed a Sadr City leadership chart to help the commander visualize the power structure within the society and identify legitimate local leaders. The brigade commander briefed GEN Petraeus, LTG Odierno, and MG Hammond on the chart (and provided copies to each of them), which eventually led to a major division operation called STEADFAST FALCON. In the words of the brigade commander, "The HTT empowered us to engage…It could have been a powder keg, but we opened discussions and prevented that. These discussions and

engagements had positive repercussions back to Najaf. The HTT empowered us to be much more effective with engagements, and the third-order effect was a strategic impact on the whole region."[83]

HTTs that found a way to integrate multiple data sources and explain local behaviors to the brigade commander, whether on a specific topic or more broadly over time, improved brigade command decision making and received the most effusive commander praise. Similarly, HTATs, operating a level up from HTTs, needed to help the division commander make sense of all sources of cultural knowledge across an even broader geographical swath of Afghanistan: "for HTATs it's not just about data collection; it's about making others understand the big picture."[84]

The Flynn explanation for how the entire force, aided by "select teams of civilian analysts" should produce cultural intelligence, helps make sense of the diverse commander assessments of HTT performance. Ideally, the few, small, and costly HTTs that were available needed to make a difference for brigade commanders at the second level of cultural knowledge rather than being used at the small-unit level as data collectors.

Net Explanation for HTT Performance Variation

> *"It is clear that the work and value of HTTs depends largely on the commander. The commander has to truly value diversity of ideas, through his actions as well as his words, and he has to truly value the criticality of cultural knowledge and the importance of non-lethal effects in general."*[85]
> West Point Study on HTTs

Having explained commander assessments of HTT performance, we can now provide a better overarching explanation for performance variation by postulating the ideal roles for HTTs and HTAT highlighted by Flynn's cultural intelligence architecture and using insights from the variable analysis provided in the previous chapter. Doing so makes it possible to see why the human terrain program, as configured, could not provide consistently high performance from HTTs. To operate as brigade advisors at the second level of cultural knowledge, HTTs should have had as much general expertise on Afghanistan as possible, and as much access as possible to specific information about the area they would operate in. Ideally, they should have been well-functioning teams of diverse expertise that trained together, and that bonded and found their place on brigade staffs prior to deployment or that relieved predecessors in the field with a period of overlap. They should have had extended periods of deployment to deepen their expertise on local conditions and to permit overlap with relieving HTTs and brigades. Almost none of these ideal but basic conditions and attributes pertain to HTS and HTTs as they were raised, trained and deployed, however. Instead, for intrinsic and extrinsic reasons HTTs were created and managed in such a way that it was difficult to impossible for them to quickly, if ever, serve as cultural knowledge integrators for brigade-level commanders.

To begin with, the larger organizational milieu and direction provided by HTS, theater command, and the Army was not propitious for HTT operations. The purposes ascribed to HTTs were too diffuse to communicate their ideal role to commanders. While allowing for commander discretion, HTS should have emphasized to commanders that the HTTs were too small to serve as primary collectors of data. HTTs should have focused on integrating diverse cultural data to facilitate commander decision making, and conducted spot research to clarify issues as needed. Instead, to magnify their potential value to commanders, HTS emphasized HTT versatility.

Early on HTS management noted that their first HTTs in Iraq were doing data collection and employment at the village level, and that commanders found this useful:

> Many of the Iraq teams felt that there was great value in being able to go to Combat Operating Bases and Joint Security Stations in order to support missions directly. In the words of one team member, "You get more bang for your buck going out with the company commander because he actually has to engage, and deal with council members and mediate. That's the person who values your information the most. The responsibilities at that level matter the most." As the S7 explained, "When the HTT operates below the brigade level (at company or battalion), they generate information that the brigade normally doesn't get. There's the potential for content filtering as the information goes through the normal reporting channels."[86]

This excerpt from an early internal HTS assessment of HTTs underscores two points about empowerment. HTTs serve at the pleasure of the brigade commander, and must win his confidence. In addition, the key resource HTTs needed most to advise commanders was information on the local area where they would be serving. In this regard HTTs would have benefited from knowing as soon as possible where they would be assigned so they could get up to speed on the area prior to deploying. They also needed access to pertinent cultural knowledge resources. These considerations were particularly important given the fact that HTS had trouble attracting the type of deep regional expertise it originally postulated as desirable. Instead, HTT members did not know where they would be deployed and were enjoined from using HTS Reachback Center information to develop even a general knowledge of the theater, much less specific knowledge of the area of operations they would be serving in. Once in the field, they needed access to good data. If it was not being produced by the larger organization, they would have to go collect it themselves.

The need for good data underscores the importance of the larger organization's support for HTTs. To be effective, HTTs needed to perform their role within a larger cultural intelligence architecture that was well understood by the entire theater command and particularly by brigade commanders, and which used diverse command assets to stream cultural knowledge to the HTT. Unfortunately, HTTs were relatively isolated; first from traditional academic culture, which was generally hostile to the activities they performed; from the HTS organization itself, which was preoccupied with management challenges in the United States; and most importantly, from the prevailing U.S. military culture. HTTs had to find ways to secure support from a wide variety of sources, but particularly from their own brigades, which was not easy. One commander said "[it] boggles my mind that there is talk about scaling down the human terrain teams....Commanders who recommend against it—I say they are ignorant on what the HTTs can bring, they must have had a personality conflict."[87]

But brigade commanders exercise great autonomy in how they will manage their areas of operation. If an HTT joined up with a commander who did not understand and condone the population-centric approach to counterinsurgency, then no matter how good the cultural knowledge produced by the HTT, it would likely be wasted. If, on the other hand, an HTT succeeded in educating an otherwise skeptical commander on the merits of the population-centric approach to counterinsurgency, they made the most elemental and direct contributions:

An hour later, the colonel arrives at this site. We haven't met him yet. So we walk up to the convoy, introduce ourselves, and chat for a few minutes. Then the analyst says, "Sir, can I speak to you for a second?" The commander says "Ok." So the analyst pulls him aside and says, "Sir, I saw this video [of the commander haranguing sheiks]. I'd like to offer you some suggestions if you don't mind. I know you're upset because you are getting rocketed. I know you are thinking of your soldiers but I would like to stress something. You cannot win this fight by being this aggressive. You need to make the sheiks your friends; you need to co-opt them. They have to see you as a human being. You are not going to stop them from rocketing unless you make them your friends." A year later, one night in dinner at the mess hall, I go to a table and there is the same colonel. He says… "I remember what your analyst said to me." And he does, he remembers the entire conversation word for word. Then the colonel says, "I need you to tell him that what he said changed the entire way I prosecuted the war….He was still aggressive but went out to meet sheiks, found a way to know them on a personal level, and found that it limited the amount of kinetic operations.[88]

Thus HTTs first had to have the good fortune to have a commander who appreciated the population-centric approach to counterinsurgency, or they had to work on making the commander a believer.

Even if the commander believed in the population-centric approach to counterinsurgency, the HTTs had to win the confidence of the brigade commander and his staff. All major studies of HTTs acknowledge this point because it was emphasized by commanders in their interviews:

> I'm a skeptic in that I don't [care] who you are. Once you come to the team you are going to be evaluated on what you will produce. So initially you will be distrusted. If that hurts your feelings, I'm sorry, but you have to prove you can provide some value; then you get trust. Until then, you get professional courtesy at best [laughter].[89]

> You have to earn trust. Had we had them 90 days prior, my staff would've trusted them better on the battlefield.[90]

Instead of plugging into a well recognized staff role, it was a matter of trial and error as each HTT had to find the best way to convince the commander that it was useful. Thus getting beyond data collection to the second level of cultural knowledge that could influence commander decision making took valuable time. HTTs that had internal conflict problems, or which could not quickly demonstrate their advantages to commanders, found themselves in a hole. One isolated HTT analyst who was unable to provide insights beyond the observation that "Afghan tribal relations are complicated," left his brigade command staff with the impression that the program was "a colossal waste of money for the United States Government."[91] HTTs that made such a poor impression would not receive the access and resources they needed to do their work, making it even harder to demonstrate their utility. Some HTTs were able to overcome initial poor impressions, obtain resources and win the confidence of the commander. Others never were accepted, and at best were used for basic data collection to increase the brigade's situational awareness.

Winning the confidence of a commander and finding their place within the larger cultural knowledge architecture was difficult for teams because they had so many handicaps at the team level to overcome. First, consistent with the purpose and role described above, HTTs should have been structured as part of the commander's staff and the theater commander's intelligence architecture[92] where their tasks should have focused on integrating diverse cultural intelligence collected at the small unit level. However, as a practical matter, HTTs had to give priority to pleasing commanders, and many commanders preferred to split HTTs apart and use them for data collection. Effective HTTs adapted to these requirements, restructured themselves and adopted different methods to compensate for the geographic dispersion of the team. In this way they were underutilized but able to please commanders. Other HTTs reached out beyond their brigades and found resources and outlets for their insights, but again, the failure to readily find a place in the brigade structure retarded the team's effectiveness.

Similarly, the way HTTs were raised and trained increased the likelihood of internal conflicts that could destroy a team's productivity. HTT members did not train together as teams for the most part, and what training they received was not based on a theory of HTT performance that could be tested from feedback from actual HTT performances in country. This point bears elaboration. As we document throughout the history portion of this book, and other sources emphasize as well, HTS management did not have a uniform understanding of performance variation and did not collect data that would have helped management identify sources of performance variation.[93]

From interviews, it seems some HTS managers assumed that performance variation was a function of "personalities." Others thought their experiment in civil-military teams was so unique they could not postulate performance criteria. Instead, they wanted to take the time to build up an empirical view of the team functions. To do so they paid a contractor to interview current and former HTT members. There were two problems with ignoring cross-functional team theory in favor of a bottom-up, exclusively empirical approach. As we have shown above, encouraging HTTs to do what commanders wanted (such as basic data collection) was not the best role for HTTs. The second problem was that it was slow, all the more so because HTS management never established a means of systematically securing feedback from personnel experiences in the field.

Absent a postulated theory of small cross-functional team performance and measures to assess its application in the field, the HTS program had no way to improve HTT learning and prepare teams for the variety of challenges they would face. Moreover, HTT members did not know who they would be serving with, but instead were individually assigned to teams after arriving in country. Therefore they did not have a chance to train as a team and get to know the other team members, much less brigade commanders and their staffs. For anyone familiar with military training, this approach to fielding HTTs was surprising:

> Before we go, we have everyone taking practice snaps, and guys figuring out where they go, what they do and how they act on the battlefield. And then you get to Afghanistan and something like an HTT, which everyone tells you is a valuable thing, and you drop in in the middle of the play. So automatically it throws everyone off…. [It] is inefficient at best, or just stupid.[94]

Without pre-deployment training as a team, HTTs could not work out team dynamics in a less stressful environment, or establish team decision-making processes until they reached the field. In the field, each new arrival potentially disrupted established productive team practices that had been built up. An early assessment by HTS recognized the shortcoming,[95] but it was not corrected.

Deploying the team members individually also inadvertently signaled to the members that they were valued as individual assets rather than as teams. Commanders expressed concern about the individualism of some HTT members: "Some of the folk were more loners, particularly the academics."[96] The tendency to do independent work absent a clear connection with operational needs was problematic because it could not be evaluated by multiple team members or integrated into the military decision-making process. One brigade staff member observed that whenever new members deployed "there is a constant tug between their desire to do academic research and my effort to focus them on something that will make a positive impact at the district level."[97] In some cases it could take months for an intractable HTT member to finally accept, if at all, that the purpose of the team was to provide operationally relevant information rather than an opportunity for collecting more data for a Ph.D. dissertation.[98]

In a stressful combat environment, the failure to gel as a team could be crippling. Some teams overcame their interpersonal conflicts and learned on the fly how to channel conflict over methods, products and conclusions into productive avenues that improved team performance, but often they did not. If teams could not resolve conflicts productively, they stood little chance of developing a cohesive team culture or trust. Fractured teams were prone to dysfunctions that could impair team productivity. Rather than deal with incessant interpersonal conflicts, some team leaders geographically separated team members, which reduced conflict but also the team's ability to play an effective role at the brigade level.

Finally, at the individual team member level, there were also significant impediments to team performance that were intrinsic to the program. The quality of HTT recruits was highly variable. It was hard for the program to establish the qualities it needed in recruits. Many recruits were alienated during training and left the program, or were involved for the wrong reasons and became problems for teams when they deployed. In many cases, team members were not conditioned, mentally or physically, to operate in hostile or austere environments.[99] Ideally, in addition to social science credentials, recruits would have been screened for their ability to succeed in group activities and not just individual endeavors. Experience in Afghanistan and Afghan language capabilities also would have been obvious advantages for HTTs expected to integrate and assess cultural knowledge, but these capabilities presumably were in short supply. Recruits also should have been screened for commitment to the mission. Instead, in the rush to institute the program, one of its major attractions was high individual member remuneration. Research consistently shows, and the military well understands, that job satisfaction on high performing small teams is more a function of team bonding and productivity than individual remuneration, but in the early years the program was structured to make the former difficult and rely on the latter.[100]

With so many impediments to high performance at the organizational, team and individual member levels, HTT performance was critically dependent upon stellar and versatile leadership. Interviews with HTT members strongly indicate that successful HTT leaders were ones who could exercise traditional, coaching and shared leadership appropriately as circumstances demanded. Those HTT leaders who were able to overcome the many impediments to HTT effectiveness were indispensable, heroic catalysts for HTT effectiveness who were much admired by their team members. The selection process for HTT leadership should have screened team leader candidates for these attributes and reinforced them in training. Instead, HTT leader performance seems to have been as variable as HTT performance in general. Autocratic team leaders were particularly out of place given the composition of the teams and their mission of cross-cultural knowledge, and they were a major factor in notable team failures.

In short, there were several preconditions for HTT productivity. HTTs had to:

(1) be appended to a brigade commander and staff that were committed to population-centric counterinsurgency—either from the beginning or because they were convinced by the HTT.

(2) prove to the commander that they could make a contribution, which took time.

(3) overcome the many intrinsic constraints on productivity that characterized the HTS program at the organizational, team and individual levels.

(4) have unusually stellar leadership to help the team gel and overcome productivity impediments in a difficult environment.

Finally, this all had to happen in a short period as the standard HTT member's deployment was only nine months. It also had to happen repeatedly since HTS deployed HTT members individually and in staggered timeframes rather than as teams. In such circumstances, the fact that most commanders appreciated HTTs for the contributions they made to their situational awareness, and that some commanders were able to use them for brigade decision making, is a testimony to the people that populated high performing HTTs and to the general lack of sociocultural knowledge in U.S. military forces, which made the HTT contributions so necessary and conspicuous.

Notes

[1] Major General Michael T. Flynn, cited in Robert Pool, *Sociocultural Data to Accomplish Department of Defense Missions: Toward a Unified Social Framework: Workshop Summary*, (Washington, DC: The National Academies Press, 2011). The book is a summary of presentations and discussions that took place on August 16-17, 2010, at a National Research Council public workshop sponsored by the Office of Naval Research.

[2] The commander of the first HTT, AF1, then-Colonel Martin Schweitzer, is the most notable example. He said his brigade did not begin to understand Pashtun culture until the HTT "plugged in their computers." Similarly, the commander of AF2 on Bagram Air Base, Colonel Scott Spellmon, quoted two years after the first team arrived in Afghanistan, said his brigade could not function well without understanding local dynamics in Kapisa province, and that after the HTT "talked to local elders" there was a reduction in violence. See respectively, Featherstone, "Human Quicksand for the U.S. Army, a Crash Course in Cultural Studies," 60-68; and Captain John Zumer, "Human Terrain Teams Build Friendships, Future," *American Forces Press Service*, March 2, 2009.

[3] Field Grade Officer in the U.S. Army with experience in intelligence and cultural issues and HTTs, interviewed May 21, 2012; Program Manager Forward, Afghanistan, interviewed December 7, 2011; HTT Research Manager, interviewed January 3, 2012; Dr. Montgomery McFate, former HTS Senior Social Scientist, interviewed October 3, 2011. See also discussion on pp. 137-161 of this report.

[4] Institute for Defense Analyses, *Contingency Capabilities: Analysis of Human Terrain Teams in Afghanistan—Draft Final Report*, 6-5.

[5] The DOTMLPF framework was recently updated to become DOTmLPF-P, defined as Doctrine, Organization, Training, Materiel, Leadership, and Education, Personnel, Facilities, and Policy. Chairman of the Joint Chiefs of Staff Instruction, *Joint Capabilities Integration and*

Development System, CJCSI 3170.01H, January 10, 2012, GL-1.

[6]   *The Human Terrain System Yearly Report 2007-2008*, 23.

[7]   Ibid., 24.

[8]   Ibid., 24-25.

[9]   Ibid., 108.

[10] Ibid., 136.

[11] Ibid., 109.

[12] Ibid., 161.

[13] United States Army Training and Doctrine Command, Office of Internal Review and Audit Compliance, Results Briefing, May 12, 2010; attached as Appendix G to the CNA Analysis & Solutions, *Congressionally Directed Assessment of the Human Terrain System*, 237-250.

[14] Jebb, Hummel, Chacho, *Human Terrain Team Trip Report*, 2.

[15] Ibid., 7.

[16] Ibid., 3.

[17] Ibid.

[18] The study also offers a plausible explanation for performance variation by noting that in the initial phase of HTS growth, the emphasis was placed on fielding as many teams as possible as fast as possible, which led to questionable hiring practices and imperfect training. Jebb, Hummel, Chacho, *Human Terrain Team Trip Report*, 3, 7.

[19] *The Human Terrain System Yearly Report 2007-2008*, 237.

[20] CNA Analysis & Solutions, *Congressionally Directed Assessment of the Human Terrain System*, 60.

[21] The complete study has not been made publicly available. A version of the report was available for a short period on the CNA website before it was removed. It is that version that circulates and is available on the web. CNA Analysis & Solutions, *Congressionally Directed Assessment of the Human Terrain System*, 2, 9.

[22] CNA Analysis & Solutions, *Congressionally Directed Assessment of the Human Terrain System*, 156-211.

[23] Ibid., 153.

[24] Ibid., 2.

[25] Ibid.

[26] Institute for Defense Analyses, *Human Terrain Team Study—Final Report*, Unpublished, 2011, 1-1.

[27] Ibid., 5-3.

[28] Ibid.

[29] Dr. P. M. Picucci, Research Staff Member, Institute for Defense Analyses, email on February 1, 2012.

[30] Institute for Defense Analyses, *Human Terrain Team Study—Final Report*, Unpublished, 2011, 5-1.

[31] Ibid.

[32] Ibid., 4-4.

[33] Ibid., 6-5.

[34] Institute for Defense Analyses, *Contingency Capabilities: Analysis of Human Terrain Teams in Afghanistan—Draft Final Report*, vi.

[35] Memorandum, "Findings and Recommendations, AR 15-6 Investigation Concerning Human Terrain Subject (HTS) Project Inspector General Complaints," May 12, 2010, For Official Use Only, redacted and released in response to a Freedom of Information request; available at <https://www.box.com/s/2mv0g54xsr41aegwbw9i>; February 19, 2013, 5-6.

[36] Memorandum, "Findings and Recommendations, AR 15-6 Investigation Concerning Human Terrain Subject (HTS) Project Inspector General Complaints," May 12, 2010, For

Official Use Only, redacted and released in response to a Freedom of Information request; available at <https://www.box.com/s/2mv0g54xsr41aegwbw9i>; February 19, 2013, 5-6.

[37] We were only able to obtain a few PowerPoint slides summarizing the reports. The first assessment was conducted at the behest of United States Forces-Iraq and was completed between August-December 2010. The second report was conducted by the U.S. Vice Chief of Staff of the Army, General Peter W. Chiarelli. Both summaries make it clear that commanders found HTTs useful. *United States Forces-Iraq Assessment of HTS (Completed Aug 2010)*, PowerPoint, undated; *Vice Chief of Staff of the Army Assessment Outcomes, 2 of 2*, PowerPoint, undated.

[38] Institute for Defense Analyses, *Contingency Capabilities: Analysis of Human Terrain Teams in Afghanistan—Draft Final Report*, 6-5.

[39] Commander, Task Force Helmand (UK), interviewed December 19, 2011.

[40] Jebb, Hummel, Chacho, *Human Terrain Team Trip Report*, 3; CNA Analysis & Solutions, *Congressionally Directed Assessment of the Human Terrain System*, 153; Data obtained from Dr. S.K. Numrich, Institute for Defense Analyses, email on April 18, 2012.

[41] Arthur Speyer and Job Henning, *MCIA's Cultural Intelligence Methodology and Lessons Learned* (Paper presented at the Socio-Cultural Perspectives: A New Intelligence Paradigm Conference, McLean, Virginia, September 12, 2006); cited in Lee Ellen Freidland et. al, MITRE Technical Report, *Socio-Cultural Perspectives: A New Intelligence Paradigm*, Report on the Conference at The MITRE Corporation, McLean, Virginia, September 12, 2006, Document Number 07-1220, June 2007.

[42] Interviewee 44, November 10, 2011.

[43] ASCOPE/PMESII (Areas, Structures, Capabilities, Organizations, People, Events. and Political, Military, Economic, Social, Infrastructure, Information) represents a 'crosswalk' of two separate categories of information that can be collected in the field as illustrated in FM 3-24, though the link is not explicitly shown in the field manual. The goal is to aid commanders in learning everything there is to know about their Area of Operations. Some interviewees expressed the usefulness of ASCOPE/PMESII in conducting field research.

[44] Major Michael Jacobson, U.S. Army Reserves, AF25 Team Leader September 2010—May 2011, interviewed October 7, 2011.

[45] Lawrence C. Katzenstein, Michael Albin, and Paul McDowell, "HTAT Arrives at Multinational Division Baghdad," *Military Intelligence Professional Bulletin* vol. 37, no. 4 (October-December 2011), 85-86.

[46] Ibid.

[47] Brigadier General David C. Gillian, Deputy Chief of Staff for Intelligence, ISAF Headquarter, August 2010. Cited on <http://humanterrainsystem.army.mil/>.

[48] Battalion Commander, Task Force Kandahar, interviewed November 28, 2011.

[49] Executive Officer, U.S. Army, Afghanistan, interviewed November 23, 2011.

[50] *Vice Chief of Staff of the Army Assessment Outcomes, 2 of 2*, PowerPoint, undated.

[51] For example, one senior British commander found his HTT particularly valuable in his military decision-making process for "preparing for consequence management" of his unit's operations. Commander, Task Force Helmand (UK), interviewed December 19, 2011.

[52] Executive Officer, U.S. Army, Afghanistan, interviewed November 23, 2011.

[53] Interviewee 56, November 29, 2011.

[54] Flynn, Pottinger, and Batchelor, *Fixing Intel*. Subsequent quotations come from this source.

[55] Robert Pool, *Sociocultural Data to Accomplish Department of Defense Missions: Toward a Unified Social Framework: Workshop Summary* (Washington, DC: National Academies Press, 2011), 11.

[56] Flynn, Pottinger, and Batchelor, *Fixing Intel*, 18.

[57] Nathan Finney, *Commander's Guide: Employing a Human Terrain Team in Operation Enduring Freedom and Operation Iraqi Freedom: Tactics, Techniques and Procedures*, (Ft. Leavenworth, KS: U.S.

Army Center for Army Lessons Learned, Number 09-21, March 2009). 1.

[58]   Battalion Commander, Task Force Kandahar, interviewed November 28, 2011.

[59]   *The Human Terrain System Yearly Report 2007-2008*, 44.

[60]   Major General Joseph L. Culver, Commander, 28th Infantry Division, Task Force Cyclone, interviewed November 17, 2011.

[61]   Program Manager Forward, Afghanistan, interviewed December 7, 2011.

[62]   Colonel Michael Howard, Commander, 4th Brigade, 25th Infantry Division, interviewed November 30, 2011.

[63]   Ibid.

[64]   CNA Analysis & Solutions, *Congressionally Directed Assessment of the Human Terrain System*, 161.

[65]   Colonel Michael Howard, Commander, 4th Brigade, 25th Infantry Division, interviewed November 30, 2011.

[66]   One commander noted a polling project "was pretty expensive but supplied us with data that was large enough to have real statistical value about the mindset of people in the whole area of operations. HTT would have never been able to compile so much data." Captain Benoit Paré, French CIMIC Officer, Afghanistan, interviewed December 2, 2011.

[67]   CNA Analysis & Solutions, *Congressionally Directed Assessment of the Human Terrain System*, 162.

[68]   Ibid., 211.

[69]   Ibid., 162.

[70]   Colonel Michael Howard, Commander, 4th Brigade, 25th Infantry Division, interviewed November 30, 2011.

[71]   One former HTT member has argued that HTT's can and should help orient soldiers toward useful data collection at the village level. Norman Nigh, *An Operator's Guide to Human Terrain Teams* (Newport, RI: United Stated Naval War College, 2012).

[72]   Corporal Scott R. Mitchell, 'Observations of a Strategic Corporal,' *Military Review*, July-August 2012, 58.

[73]   Scott R. Mitchell, former COIST Member, 3rd Brigade, 10th Mountain Division, interviewed August 1, 2012.

[74]   Colonel Michael Howard, Commander, 4th Brigade, 25th Infantry Division, interviewed November 30, 2011.

[75]   Colonel Randall P. Newman, Commander, Regimental Combat Team 7, 7th Marines, interviewed December 7, 2011.

[76]   Lieutenant Colonel Hubert Toupet (FRA), Chief of Information Operations, interviewed December 6, 2011.

[77]   Brigadier General William Roy, Former Commander Task Force Wolverine and 86th Infantry Brigade Combat Team, November 17, 2011.

[78]   Colonel Michael Howard, Commander, 4th Brigade, 25th Infantry Division, interviewed November 30, 2011.

[79]   CNA Analysis & Solutions, *Congressionally Directed Assessment of the Human Terrain System*, 162.

[80]   Ibid., 168.

[81]   *The Human Terrain System Yearly Report 2007-2008*, 183.

[82]   Colonel James Blackburn, Former Commander 2nd Stryker Cavalry Regiment, December 16, 2011.

[83]   *The Human Terrain System Yearly Report 2007-2008*, 113.

[84]   Chanelcherie DeMello, "Social Science: Saving Lives in Iraq," *Task Force Danger Public Affairs*, September 27, 2010.

[85]   Jebb, Hummel, Chacho, *Human Terrain Team Trip Report*, 4.

[86]   *The Human Terrain System Yearly Report 2007-2008*, 116-117.

[87]   CNA Analysis & Solutions, *Congressionally Directed Assessment of the Human Terrain System*, 161.

[88]   Joseph, *Changing the Battle Space?*, 9.

[89]   Colonel Randall P. Newman, Commander, Regimental Combat Team 7, 7th Marines, interviewed December 7, 2011.

[90]   Ibid.

[91]   Colonel James Creighton, Commander, Combined Team Uruzgan, September 2010—June 2011, interviewed December 16, 2011.

[92]   However, as Flynn argues, they should remain separate from the special operations forces fusion cells for high value targeting operations. Flynn, Pottinger, and Batchelor, *Fixing Intel*, 21.

[93]   The CNA report emphasizes the lack of HTS performance metrics. It notes HTS management valued commander responses on HTT effectiveness, but did not track such data "over time in any institutionalized fashion." CNA Analysis & Solutions, *Congressionally Directed Assessment of the Human Terrain System*, 60. The same issue is noted in TRADOC's internal AR-15-6 investigation, which found "there is no means to determine team effectiveness." Memorandum, "Findings and Recommendations, AR 15-6 Investigation Concerning Human Terrain Subject (HTS) Project Inspector General Complaints," May 12, 2010, For Official Use Only, redacted and released in response to a Freedom of Information request; available at https://www.box.com/s/2mv0g54xsr41aegwbw9i; February 19, 2013, 6.

[94]   Colonel Randall P. Newman, Commander, Regimental Combat Team 7, 7th Marines, interviewed December 7, 2011.

[95]   Ibid.

[96]   Colonel John Spiszer, Former Commander 3rd Brigade Combat Team, 1st Infantry Division, December 7, 2011.

[97]   Executive Officer, U.S. Army, Afghanistan, interviewed November 23, 2011.

[98]   RRC Analyst, interviewed November 21, 2011; Wahab, *In My Father's Country: An Afghan Woman Defies Her Fate*, 293.

[99]   Brigadier General William Roy, Former Commander Task Force Wolverine and 86th Infantry Brigade Combat Team, November 17, 2011.

[100]   Research Manager, AF3, interviewed December 15, 2011.

6 OBSERVATIONS

"[The intelligence section] is responsible for...the political, economic and social status of the occupied area, together with the attitude and activities of the civil populations and political leaders...In no type of warfare is the latest current information more vital....The goal is to gain decisive results with the least application of force and the consequent minimum loss of life... In major warfare, hatred of the enemy is developed among troops to arouse courage. In small wars, tolerance, sympathy, and kindness should be the keynote of our relationship with the mass of the population. There is nothing in this principle which should make any officer or man hesitate to act with the necessary firmness...whenever there is contact with armed opposition."[1]

U.S. Marine Corps *Small Wars Manual*

The primary purpose of this research was to explain HTT performance variation. The explanation provided in the previous section differs from conventional wisdom. For many observers, including those managing the program, the variable performance was a function of "personalities." In other words, they thought good leaders and talented HTT members performed well, and other less talented or inadequate leaders and personnel performed poorly. Similarly, many thought that whether HTTs and commanders worked well together was also a matter of personal chemistry, or again, a personality issue:

I've heard of two or three examples where the Human Terrain Team and the Brigade Combat Team... just wasn't a good match or marriage for whatever reason. Frankly, I don't get into the drama. I'm just disappointed that it didn't work because I know the potential that it can bring, or at least I think I know.[2]

There were innumerable personality clashes on HTTs, but as explained in the previous chapter, they do not adequately explain either HTT performance or whether the HTTs jelled with brigade commanders. The HTTs were small cross-functional teams, and multiple cross-functional team performance variables besides leadership and team composition are needed to understand their performance. Identifying the ideal role for HTTs in a larger cultural knowledge architecture, analyzing the management issues that the program faced throughout its life, and then using the ten cross-functional team variables (see chart on page 205) to explain why HTS could not field consistently high performing HTTs provides a more comprehensive and compelling explanation for HTT performance variation.

A multifunctional analysis of HTT performance demonstrates there were several preconditions and potential catalysts for HTT productivity. HTTs had to be appended to a brigade commander and staff that were committed to a population-centric counterinsurgency approach; they had to quickly prove to typically skeptical commanders that they could make a contribution; and, in doing so, they had to overcome the many intrinsic constraints on productivity that characterized the HTS program at the organizational, team and individual levels.

Ideally, HTTs should have been given more general expertise on Afghanistan and more access to specific information about the area they would operate in as early as possible. They should have been well-functioning teams composed of individuals with diverse expertise that trained together, bonded, and found their place on brigade staffs prior to deployment. They should have relieved predecessor teams in the field with a period of sufficient overlap to exchange knowledge, and not as individual replacements. They should have had longer periods of deployment to deepen their expertise on local conditions and to permit overlap with incoming HTTs and brigades. Almost none of these preconditions existed. Instead, HTTs were conceptualized, created and managed in a way that made it difficult for them to serve as cultural knowledge integrators for brigade commanders.

In particular, the purposes ascribed to HTTs were too diffuse to communicate their ideal role to commanders, who tended to dissipate their impact by allocating them for data collection rather than using their own troops for that purpose. HTTs should have plugged in to a larger cultural intelligence architecture that was well understood by the entire theater command and particularly by brigade commanders, but this architecture was itself under development and not universally embraced by brigade commanders. Commanders can use their assigned assets as they think circumstances demand, but they are well-trained to know the capabilities each type of unit provides. In the case of the HTTs, commanders did not understand the role they were supposed to play and took a wait-and-see attitude toward them.

HTTs thus had to prove themselves to skeptical commanders and secure their support, which wasted time and resources. It was a matter of trial and error for each HTT to find a way to convince commanders they could be useful, an exercise that was critically dependent on being paired with a commander who understood the population-centric approach to counterinsurgency. Some HTTs were able to overcome initial poor impressions, obtain resources and win the confidence of the commander. Others, at best, were used for basic data collection to increase the brigade's situational awareness. In this way they were underutilized but at least able to please commanders.

In other words, one major observation about the HTS and HTT experience is that the Army was not ready to field or exploit sociocultural knowledge in irregular war. HTS program managers were experimenting on the fly, which is laudable under the circumstances, but also inefficient and far less effective that it could have been. Program leaders could not recruit sufficient numbers of regional and cultural experts, so it had to try to develop them instead, which took time. In addition, HTS management could not authoritatively explain how the HTTs plugged into brigades or manage the development of the HTTs for consistently high performance. Similarly, brigades were not ready to receive the insights HTTs could produce. They were not sure how best to use HTTs and did not understand how to compliment or integrate their efforts with other brigade and higher headquarters activities. At a minimum this meant it took time for HTTs to begin to make contributions, and it usually meant their efforts were dissipated to lesser effect. After lauding HTS, Secretary of Defense Gates rightly expressed concern about the *ad hoc* nature of the program:

> I remain concerned that we have yet to create any permanent capability or institutions to rapidly create and deploy these kinds of skills in the future. The examples I mentioned have, by and large, been created ad hoc—on the fly in a climate of crisis. As a nation, we need to figure out how to institutionalize programs and relationships such as these."[3]

Gates' concern is well founded. The HTS experience demonstrates that trying to provide sociocultural knowledge in the midst of combat, without a well-established program and doctrine, is extremely difficult and perhaps impossible to do to great effect; certainly it cannot be done quickly, which is what such circumstances demand.

While we concentrated on explaining HTT performance variation, researching the history of HTS led us to some additional observations. The management tensions between TRADOC and HTS grew increasingly severe over time and were deleterious to the program. The sources of the problem merit explanation, if only to help others in the future avoid them. Based on the evidence available, we believe the explanation for the split between TRADOC and HTS management is three-fold.

First, some of the tension between TRADOC G-2 and HTS leadership was the result of honest differences over program management. Fondacaro and McFate carried a high profile, emphasized outreach and decentralized decision making as far forward as possible. They were frustrated by the bureaucracy that impeded what they wanted to do. TRADOC's preference was for lower profile, less controversial leadership and greater attention to the established chain of command and its existing procedures.

Second, given the results of various investigations, political pressure was building for management changes. Often in such cases management will simply choose new leadership, which at least communicates a willingness to make changes. In this case that happened; TRADOC G-2 released the program manager in 2010, and TRADOC's G-2 left the organization in 2011.

Third and most important in our view, most of the management difficulties can be traced back to contracting and hiring decisions that are endemic to government but were exacerbated by TRADOC G-2 management decisions.[4] In this respect, we agree with the CNA report's findings.[5] It is quite difficult to start a new program quickly in government. As Fondacaro has quipped, there is no "office of innovation and new ideas" in the Pentagon. All defense dollars are spoken for well in advance and securing control over how they are reallocated to meet emerging requirements is always contentious.[6]

In summary, the TRADOC-HTS management tensions ultimately help explain why it is so difficult to begin new, innovative programs and have them operate at peak efficiency and to good effect. In this regard the management troubles just underscore why it is particularly unwise to abandon difficult-to-acquire and hard-won sociocultural knowledge capability once it is built up. Unfortunately, as we detail elsewhere in this report, and as the Defense Science Board and many other sources note, the U.S. military has repeatedly done just that over the course of its history, and may well do it again by abandoning HTS during a period of budget cutbacks.[7]

Another major observation from this research is that the Army and HTS program leaders relied too heavily on their faith in the inherent value of civilian social science contributions, and not enough on the necessity of consulting organization and management best practices—and indeed, standard

Army practices—on how best to form small cross-functional teams. A Special Forces team may be given great latitude to improvise in the field. That makes sense given the diversity of Special Forces missions, their rigorous recruitment and selection process, and the time allowed for team bonding during training and other preliminary deployments. HTS and the HTTs they were deploying benefited from none of these advantages. HTS management should have postulated a theory of HTT performance, established systematic means to assess whether the performance theory worked well in the field, and then adjusted accordingly. They did none of these things.

Instead, HTS management decided to rely on field experience alone to identify what worked well for HTTs. Believing the HTS experiment in civil-military teams was unique, they put the teams in the field and then tried to assess what worked and what did not. Since the HTTs had to please commanders who used them differently depending on circumstances and their own predilections, it was difficult to acquire a clear picture of how the HTTs and their individual positions could best function.

Ironically, having decided on this approach and despite having initially promised rigorous metrics to evaluate success, HTS did not routinely collect feedback from HTT members after their tours. Instead, at one juncture. HTS had a contractor interview HTT members to see what functions they were performing, presumably believing whatever they were doing is what they should be doing. This approach relied too heavily on commanders who had no previous experience with HTTs and might not even agee with the population-centric approach to counterinsurgency. It also was slow, particularly since they were not routinely collecting data from individual HTT members' experiences.

Without a postulated theory of HTT purpose, functions and performance attributes, HTS could not postulate job requirements, recruiting standards or performance metrics. Most tellingly, without a postulated theory of small cross-functional team performance and measures to assess how well the theory worked in practice, it was difficult for HTS to devise a meaningful training program, which helps explain why the training was so consistently panned. HTS did not revise its training program to good effect until late in the program (during the 2010 training curriculum review; see Appendix One) and even then did not implement all the recommendations from that effort.

Comparison of Explanatory Variables in HTS Studies

		HTS 2008[8]	West Point 2008[9]	CNA 2010[10]	IDA 2011[11]	NDU 2012	
Organization		Doctrine		Mission	Mission	Purpose	
		Material	Information Management		Supporting information	Resources	Empowerment
				Policy restrictions	Direct liaison authority	Directive authority	
						Psychological Empowerment	
		Facilities	Relationships with Command	Relationships w/ Command & HTS	Relationships with Command	Support	
Team		Organization				Structure	
					Conflict	Decision Making	
						Culture	
		Training		Training	Training	Learning	
Individual		Personnel	Composition	Personnel	Composition	Composition	
						Rewards	
		Leadership	Leadership			Leadership	

Given the fact that HTS leaders were developing the program from scratch under tremendous pressure to field teams quickly, these shortcomings are understandable. Another exculpating factor is that HTS management efforts to tap subject matter expertise were handicapped by TRADOC's penchant for stiff arming expertise beyond the confines of the Army. Ultimately, however, the differences between TRADOC and HTS management over control of the program were not of great consequence. Neither HTS management before or after the wholesale leadership changes in 2010 demonstrated a coherent organizational approach to supplying brigades with HTTs. As Pentagon leadership acknowledged to Congress, HTT performance could not be engineered for consistently high performance until performance factors were identified, tested and modified in accordance with empirical testing. Absent these prerequisites for success, and as HTS management admitted, training and other HTS program adjustments could only be conducted on the basis of trial and error.

A final observation from this research is that in order to be effective, HTTs must plug in to a broader sociocultural knowledge architecture that is embraced by all field forces. Much of the debate surrounding HTS has been over the question of whether sociocultural knowledge should be "organic" to the force or supplied by outside expertise. The answer, as Major General Flynn and his co-authors argued, is both. In this regard, it is worth noting that HTS, no matter how well run, cannot alone win the battle for sociocultural knowledge. The entire force and command structure must be attuned to the population-centric counterinsurgency strategy and organized for sociocultural, intelligence-driven operations. As General Flynn and his co-authors argued, the most effective U.S. military officers in Afghanistan appreciated the critical importance of knowing the Afghan human terrain well. The same was true in Iraq. Colonel H.R. McMaster, one notably successful counterinsurgent, produced a 7-page reading list on COIN, Islam, Arab customs, and Iraqi history and politics, held discussion groups and sent two troopers per platoon to basic Arabic language courses at a local college prior to deployment.[12] Military leaders who understand the value of sociocultural knowledge can benefit from high-performing HTTs, as numerous commander testimonies illustrate:

[I]n one Afghan province the Taliban had regularly attacked US forces for over five years, despite a very aggressive outreach effort to village elders. The HTT questioned the use of kinetic [courses of action] in the area, observing that the true power brokers in the area were the mullahs, and not the village elders (who were mostly Taliban supporters). After redirecting their outreach effort to the mullahs, the brigade experienced a rapid and dramatic decrease in Taliban attacks. In the words of the brigade commander, "For five years, we got nothing from the community. After meeting with the mullahs, we had no more bullets for 28 days; captured 80 Afghan-born Taliban, 10 Pakistanis, and 32 killed or captured Arabs."[13]

Like George Crook, Herman Hanneken, Frederick Funston and other successful irregular warfare officers from the past, U.S. military leaders who perform the best in Iraq and Afghanistan understand the importance of human terrain, and are well-positioned to exploit HTTs effectively.

Unfortunately, too many commanders still believe the primary value of sociocultural knowledge is to find, fix and finish the enemy. As one well-known advocate of this point of view concludes:

> Network-centric warfare allows units to have an overwhelming, cascading effect on an adversary that causes his collapse and subsequent defeat. This effect is especially possible in an operating environment heavily populated by noncombatants *because the wealth of cultural and social data that is available, when properly databased*, is more readily obtainable and hence usable by a networked force than by an enemy who only has the information in his head. The confidence and improved performance brought by effective networking mitigates the cultural and social advantages that today's illiterate, ill-equipped indigenous adversary is routinely credited with having.[14]

Some officers believe modern sociocultural tools can lay bare the insurgents' organization right down to its individual members, thus exposing them to attack. This viewpoint is supported by a number of conventional force commanders and also some Special Operations Forces.[15] It disputes General McChrystal's "counterinsurgency mathematics," and the excerpts from the Marine Corps' Small War Manual that opened this chapter, both of which argue for giving priority to painstaking attempts to limit civilian casualties over inflicting damage on enemy forces. Instead, these officers believe it is possible to inflict enough attrition on the enemy that his clandestine organization will collapse. Alternatively, and just as problematic, some officers kept their forces concentrated in forward operating bases to minimize contacts with locals either to avoid irritating popular sentiment or to make force protection easier by concentrating U.S. forces on large bases. Not surprisingly, HTTs could not be effective working with officers who held these beliefs. The brigade commander cited above just wanted his HTT members to just stay out of the way while his brigade established security in its area of operations.[16]

Perhaps some inept insurgent or terrorist organizations can be eliminated through attrition, but it is a mistake to believe an insurgency that is well-established among the population can be easily identified and targeted. It is important to keep pressure on the insurgent's leadership and organizational structure so they remain on the defensive, and hopefully unable to mount tactical offensives, but not at the cost of alienating the population. The enemy is interwoven with the population, and allegiances and attitudes are in flux. Experience teaches that a principled approach to population security in such circumstances will ultimately win the day,[17] but it is a daunting task. It requires the utmost discipline and comprehensive sociocultural knowledge that informs commanders on how best to apply lethal force and when to restrain it.

Even isolated breakdowns in discipline and cross-cultural understanding cost U.S. forces dearly, and can have enduring effects. After a March 2012 rampage by a U.S. soldier left sixteen Afghan civilians dead, a former HTT member who operated in that locale noted the likely consequences: "I can't see this particular district recovering from this. I know first hand how hard it was for them to start working with us in the first place. I just can't see them coming back to the table."[18]

All errors in judgment that produce unnecessary casualties are lamentable, but some missteps are probably inevitable in a large, complex and enduring military operation. What is more alarming from an institutional perspective is the failure to successfully disseminate the military's preferred doctrine and approach to counterinsurgency throughout the force. In this regard, the *Military Review* article by Corporal Mitchell cited above is alarming. Published in the summer of 2012, Corporal Mitchell noted that "many of the soldiers in southern Afghanistan had not read FM 3-24;" and that "the basic principles of counterinsurgency were foreign to them." Soldiers "regarded courageous restraint as cowardice" and "they were more interested in killing the enemy than in key leader engagements."[19] Mitchell found a way to make an impact, but his account of the prevailing attitude among troops in the field reveals a major impediment to success. Commanders who believe the insurgency can be defeated through attrition alone are a major reason cultural knowledge has not spread through the entire force. As the amount of data collected on Afghanistan's "human terrain" by HTS and other programs has increased, so has the gap in cross-cultural understanding. It is particularly weak where one would think common purpose and shared sacrifice might make it strong: between ISAF and Afghan forces.

Between November 2010 and April 2011, intentional murders of ISAF forces by Afghan national security force personnel accounted for 16 percent of all combat deaths.[20] An Army study examining the rising tide of "fratricide-murders" describes the relationship as so bad that:

One group [ANSF] generally sees the other as a bunch of violent, reckless, intrusive, arrogant, self serving, profane infidel bullies hiding behind high technology; and the other group [ISAF] generally views the former as a bunch of cowardly, incompetent, obtuse, thieving, complacent, lazy, pot-smoking, treacherous and murderous radicals.[21]

The report, *A Crisis of Trust and Cultural Incompatibility*, concluded that Afghan security forces view American soldiers as "arrogant, bullying, unwilling to listen to their advice, and were often seen as lacking concern for civilian or ANSF safety during combat." Meanwhile, US soldiers saw Afghan security forces as highly unstable, corrupt, incompetent and dishonest individuals. They also saw civilians as insurgent sympathizers and cruel towards woman and children.[22]

The study concludes—as have many others before it—by recommending "improved cultural and human relations training and standards of behavior."[23] We believe more fundamental reforms are required. All military leaders involved in irregular warfare need to understand that the purpose of better sociocultural knowledge in irregular warfare is not more efficient attrition of enemy forces. Instead, the purpose is to employ U.S. forces in ways that minimize friction with the local population and maximize the willingness of the local population to partner with U.S. forces in defeating the insurgency. Whatever it takes to disseminate this knowledge must be given priority. If our forces cannot successfully disseminate understanding of basic counterinsurgency theory and learn to "maneuver" effectively over human terrain, then as Corporal Mitchell bluntly notes, "we will lose."[24]

Notes

[1] United States Government, *Small Wars Manual: U.S. Marine Corps, 1940* (Washington, DC: U.S. G.P.O., 1940), 19-20, 31-32.

[2] Interviewee 56, November 29, 2011.

[3] Robert M. Gates, *Landon Lecture*, Manhattan, Kansas: Kansas State University, November 26, 2007.

[4] It is not clear whether the problems uncovered by the CNA and TRADOC investigations were specific to TRADOC G-2, or more generally reflect the impediments that make government contracting and hiring so slow and unnecessarily difficult. It is impossible to say with certainty, particularly since TRADOC declines to share its experience and point of view. Based on the authors' experience, we suspect the latter.

[5] CNA concludes the relationship between TRADOC and HTS management was "problematic," and observes "it is possible that the HTS mission would be better served if HTS were located elsewhere." However, CNA also notes that many of the management problems

HTS encountered were typical for government. CNA Analysis & Solutions, *Congressionally Directed Assessment of the Human Terrain System*, 138.

[6]   Colonel Steve Fondacaro (ret.), Former HTS Program Manager, email on April 30, 2012.

[7]   *Report of the Defense Science Board Task Force on Understanding Human Dynamics*, 4. See Appendix B in particular.

[8]   *The Human Terrain System Yearly Report 2007-2008*; for doctrine, see 56; for material, see 72; for facilities, 83; for organization, 63; for training, 66; for personnel, 80; for leadership, 78.

[9]   Jebb, Hummel, Chacho, *Human Terrain Team Trip Report*: for information management, see 7; for relationship with commanders, see 5, 7, 9; for composition, see 8ff (West Point concluded effectiveness largely comes down to people, and identified issues for improving recruitment and training); and for leadership, see 9 where the study notes: "The vetting process should also include some measure of a potential HTT member to be a team player and for a team leader's ability to build and lead teams."

[10]   CNA Analysis & Solutions, *Congressionally Directed Assessment of the Human Terrain System*. CNA examined what Congress assumed was relevant to the effectiveness of HTS and by extension, the HTTs. However, the interview questions CNA researchers used reveal an interest in: mission (or purpose); training, and HTS support to HTTs. So it focused heavily on organizational-level variables (purpose, funding, support), but also touched upon training and personnel. For mission, see 18, 150; for policy restrictions, see 152; for relationship with commanders, see 152; for training, 152, and for personnel, see 151.

[11]   Institute for Defense Analyses, *Contingency Capabilities: Analysis of Human Terrain Teams in Afghanistan—Draft Final Report*; for mission, see 3-4, 3-5; for supporting information, see 6-15, 6-16; for direct liaison authority; for relationship with commanders, see 6-7, 6-8 (IDA also paid particular attention to HTT freedom of movement, which in large part was determined by the HTT relationship with the commander and his staff; 6-7, 6-10; for conflict and decision making and team culture, see 6-11; for training, B-1; and for team composition, see 7-1, 7-2, B-3..

[12]   Lieutenant Colonel James C. Laughrey, "Know Before you Go: Improving Army Officer Sociocultural Knowledge" in Harry R. Yarger, ed., *Short of General War Perspectives on the Use of Military Power in the 21ˢᵗ Century* (Carlisle, PA: Strategic Studies Institute, 2010), 142.

[13]   *The Human Terrain System Yearly Report 2007-2008*, 25.

[14]   Harry Tunnell, *Task Force Stryker Network-Centric Operations in Afghanistan*, Defense and Technology Paper #84, (Washington, DC: Center for Technology and National Security Policy, National Defense University, October 2011), 17.

[15]   Christopher J. Lamb and Martin Cinnamond, "Unity of Effort: Key to Success in Afghanistan," *Strategic Forum* no. 248, Institute for National Strategic Studies, National Defense University, October 2009.

[16]   Interviewee 24, October 17, 2011.

[17]   "Repression can win phases by dealing the insurgents a blow and making support for them more costly, but our data show that the vast majority of phases that were won with repression ultimately increased popular support for the insurgency and ended in a COIN defeat for the entire case." Christopher Paul, Colin P. Clarke, and Beth Grill, *Victory Has a Thousand Fathers: Sources of Success in Counterinsurgency*, (Santa Monica, CA: RAND, 2010), 98. See also Ben Connable and Martin C. Libicki, *How Insurgencies End* (Santa Monica, CA: RAND, 2010), 153.

[18]   Suze Knobler, "Vet patrolled Panjwai district," *Redlands Daily Facts*, March 16, 2012.

[19]   Corporal Scott R. Mitchell, "Observations of a Strategic Corporal," *Military Review* (July-August 2012), 59-60.

[20]   Jeffrey Bordin, *A Crisis of Trust and Cultural Incompatibility: A Red Team Study of Mutual Perceptions of Afghan National Security Force Personnel and U.S. Soldiers in Understanding and Mitigating the Phenomena of ANSF-Committed Fratricide-Murders*, May 2011, 4. Between 2009-May 2011 58 Western Personnel have been murdered. This number has increased by six in the wake of the

Qur'an Burning scandal of February 2012.

[21] Bordin, *A Crisis of Trust and Cultural Incompatibility*, 54.

[22] Ibid., 3.

[23] Ibid.

[24] Corporal Scott R. Mitchell, "Observations of a Strategic Corporal," *Military Review* (July-August 2012), 64.

7 CONCLUSION

"But whatever the outcome of these present conflicts [in Iraq and Afghanistan], this knowledge, both of substance and with respect to the importance of human dynamics, must not be allowed to slip away once again. The U.S. military must embrace the fact that human dynamics and war are now and forever inextricably intertwined."[1]

Defense Science Board, 2009

Some Army observers believe the need for cultural understanding is one of the "top 5" lessons learned from the post-9/11 wars.[2] It is a lesson that should have been learned much earlier given the history of U.S. military operations reviewed in Chapter Two. The military needs a standing capability to provide a baseline of sociocultural knowledge that can be rapidly expanded in wartime. HTS and the many other similar programs that stood up and proliferated during the wars in Afghanistan and Iraq could have been run much more efficiently if they had emerged from a standing sociocultural knowledge program designed for that purpose.[3] Unfortunately, the U.S. military has a tendency to ignore sociocultural knowledge of foreign forces and populations during peacetime, which is one major reason it is generally unprepared for irregular conflicts when they arise.

As our history of the Human Terrain System's experience illustrates, the effort to field HTTs fits perfectly with the broader U.S. military history on developing and using sociocultural knowledge. The Pentagon moved slowly with organizational innovations to provide sociocultural knowledge, and in doing so, downplayed human expertise in favor of technological solutions. Years after 9/11 the Department of Defense still had no dedicated organizational solution for providing desperately needed sociocultural knowledge. It would have taken longer than four years after 9/11 to initiate the HTS program if innovative leaders had not found a way to access funds intended primarily for the development of counterterrorism and counter-IED devices. Even though there was a substantial body of opinion in favor of developing cultural knowledge, getting a new organization off the ground for this particular purpose was a herculean task. The slow movement to develop and use sociocultural knowledge following 9/11 helps substantiate long-standing opinion that the predominant strategic culture in the U.S. military is not conducive to developing and using cross-cultural information.

HTS was an admirable attempt to overcome U.S. strategic culture. Innovative leaders envisioned, marketed, and implemented HTS on the fly in response to rising demand for human terrain knowledge. The program was instituted as a small civil-military team concept to leaven brigade-level command decision making, but it was managed in a manner more conducive to a small-unit data collection enterprise. Thus the ability of HTTs to perform at the level envisioned was compromised. Corrective action was not possible without a theory of small cross-functional team performance and associated measures of effectiveness that would allow HTS managers to improve performance based on experience and empirical observation. The training HTTs received was not based on a theory of HTT performance that was tested by feedback from actual in-country HTT performance. Thus the HTS program had no way to improve HTT learning and prepare teams for the significant challenges they would face.

There were performance costs to be paid for starting a sociocultural program from scratch, for fielding HTTs with no testable concept for high and reliable performance, and for managing a program in an organization that is not structured or ready for such an endeavor. In the words of one observer, "effective sociocultural education requires a significant investment in resources and there is no quick fix or shake-and-bake solution."[4] HTS was a quick fix for providing sociocultural knowledge. Its growing pains were to be expected, but they also must be identified and acknowledged if better performance is expected in the future. Assuming the program survives the current round of deep budget cuts, it needs to pay more attention to small-team performance factors in the future and find a place for itself in a broader sociocultural knowledge architecture.

The lack of a standing sociocultural knowledge capability handicapped U.S. counterinsurgency operations, but it is also true that being poorly prepared for counterinsurgency made it difficult for HTTs to perform well. There are limits to what any sociocultural program can do without a consensus among all brigade commanders on the critical importance of human terrain,[5] the role their own troops play in collecting human terrain data, and the analytic capability HTTs are supposed to provide to the brigade staffs as part of a larger, theater-wide human terrain-centric intelligence architecture. Absent a "whole force" approach to developing and using sociocultural knowledge, such as the one General Flynn envisioned, the ability of HTS or any other small sociocultural teams to make a difference is quite limited. Like the makeshift armor welded to Humvees in the first years of irregular warfare in Iraq, HTTs were an appliqué fix to a much larger problem. The concept was laudable, but not ideal, and not well implemented.

In the immediate future the program will retrench as its scope is curtailed to save resources. As of this writing, the number of teams deployed to Afghanistan has been decreased by one third; from 31 to approximately 20. New classes of incoming team members have been turned away, or allowed to graduate and then dismissed. Funding for most of the Human Terrain Team program comes from resources Congress made available to support the overseas contingencies in Iraq and Afghanistan, so it is not surprising that the number of teams is diminishing as U.S. forces disengage from those countries. The demands that gave rise to the program and the successes it demonstrated by finding merit with the large majority of field commanders it served, presumably make the case for institutionalizing the capability. The challenge now should be for HTS to transition to a standing peacetime sociocultural knowledge capacity, one that provides a different capability than the HTTs but that can expand quickly to generate HTT-like capability when U.S. forces go to war in the future. Recently a contract was awarded to a company to support HTS through the end of fiscal year 2013, so it appears the immediate future of the program is secure.[6]

Yet the long-term prospects for the HTS program are more uncertain given the pressure to cut back on defense spending in general and the historic tendency to abandon niche programs associated with irregular warfare. If the program does survive, it is not clear what its configuration will be. Colonel Sharon Hamilton, the program manager for the past several years, retired and was replaced in August 2012. The views of her successor, Colonel Stephen J. Bentley, and the marching orders he received, if any, are not known. Hopefully Colonel Bentley and the new managers who lead HTS into the future will benefit from a thorough understanding of how and why HTTs performed as they did over the past decade. If the program cannot learn from its past, or fades away for lack of support or other reasons, it is quite likely that the future of sociocultural knowledge in U.S. military forces will be much like its past—a story of too little knowledge, obtained and disseminated at great cost, and often too late to ensure success.

Notes

1 *Report of the Defense Science Board Task Force on Understanding Human Dynamics*, 4.

2 Colonel Robert Forrester, the Deputy Director of the Center for Army Lessons Learned, cited in Drew Brooks, "Lessons Learned in Iraq War will Apply in future Conflicts," *The Fayetteville Observer*, January 1, 2012.

3 For an argument for such a capability and the type of organization it would require, See David Tucker and Christopher Lamb, *Restructuring Special Operations Forces for Emerging Threats*, Strategic Forum, no. 219 (Washington, DC: Institute for National Strategic Studies, National Defense University, January 2006).

4 Lieutenant Colonel James C. Laughrey, "Know Before you Go: Improving Army Officer Sociocultural Knowledge," in *Short of General War Perspectives on the Use of Military Power in the 21st Century*, ed. Harry R. Yarger (Strategic Studies Institute, 2010), 139.

5 Not all unit commanders have embraced or supported a population-centric counterinsurgency campaign plan for the wars in Iraq and Afghanistan. To the present day, the debate over its value continues. See Elisabeth Bumiller, "West Point Is Divided on a War Doctrine's Fate," *The New York Times*, May 27, 2012.

6 Recently a $42 million contract was awarded to CGI Federal Inc. to support the Human Terrain System through September 27, 2012. See Defpro.news for Department of Defense contracts let by the U.S. Army, <www.defpro.com/news/details/38981/?SID=282fc322dd5 bdd89f6f1ca0b67f9ad84>.

EPILOGUE

"Soldiers and leaders have done a magnificent job over the past 10 years in understanding the human dimension. They are familiar with working with Soldiers of indigenous forces and other governments, learning the language and culture, all while operating in uncertain environments. The question facing us is, 'how do we build the structural imperatives necessary in the Army for these practices to continue?' Young Soldiers know the importance of people. The human domain must be the centerpiece of our future efforts."[1]
General Robert Cone, Commander, TRADOC

Looking to the future, it is difficult to predict what will happen to the Human Terrain System and the teams it fields. The program sits astride the path of two powerful countervailing crosscurrents in U.S. military thinking. One current is growing military appreciation for the importance of sociocultural knowledge, which is reinforced by several factors. To begin with, there was the searing failure to anticipate and properly prepare for post-conflict instability in Iraq, the amazing turn-around as U.S. military leaders found a way to partner with indigenous forces and population, and the way both of these developments underscored the critical importance of sociocultural knowledge. There also is the near consensus that irregular warfare will continue to be a primary feature of the future security environment, as will the imperative to preempt the threat of irregular forces employing weapons of mass destruction. In addition, most of those pondering future U.S. strategy alternatives, including General Cone and General Odierno, the current Chief of Staff of the U.S. Army, believe the United States will have to work much better with foreign forces and populations.[2] These factors all suggest that understanding the human domain will continue to be a critically important requirement for U.S. forces. It also helps that some members of Congress have shown sustained interest in ensuring the irregular warfare capabilities built up over the past decade are preserved.[3] Presumably, therefore, the U.S. military in general and the U.S. Army in particular should be loath to abandon the capability and knowledge base in the HTS program, especially given its relatively small cost.

But there is a countervailing force: organizational inertia. The U.S. military has a strong cultural aversion to irregular warfare and to devoting resources for sociocultural knowledge.[4] Historically this aversion has been demonstrated repeatedly as the military abandons sociocultural knowledge and the means to acquire it once the conflict that demanded its acquisition is over. The reason for this is not that the U.S. military is incapable of adaptation. The military adapts to the demands of its security environment, but it only embraces those adaptations over the long-term that most closely accord with its cultural predispositions; namely to find, fix and finish off the enemy. If this assertion is correct, we would expect the likely survival of several of the most prominent irregular warfare adaptations from the past decade to correspond with the contribution they make to destroying enemy forces.

For example, consider the Special Operations Forces' high-value targeting teams that killed or captured enemy leadership, the mine-resistant, ambush-protected vehicles that safeguarded soldiers as they moved, and now the Human Terrain Teams that informed commander decision making. One would expect Special Operations Forces direct action capabilities to survive because finding and attacking the enemy is most similar to what the U.S. military as a whole is raised, trained and employed to do. It also helps that these forces have a unified command that exists to ensure their capabilities are maintained. The existence of the mine-resistant vehicles is more precarious, however. They were fielded too late and at greater cost than necessary— like Human Terrain Teams—because they are a niche irregular warfare requirement, defensive in nature, and thus contrary to the prevailing military ethos. It is likely that these vehicles will be abandoned as U.S. forces leave Iraq and Afghanistan.[5] Mine-resistant, ambush-protected vehicles at least look like a military item and are demonstrably useful for protecting soldiers. The Human Terrain Teams, by contrast, are alien to military culture. In fact, it is hard to imagine anything more disagreeable to a professional military than civilian advisors on the battlefield. For this reason, and despite their value, they are the least likely irregular warfare capability to be institutionalized as a standing military capability and the most likely irregular warfare capability to be eliminated in a period of fiscal austerity. In this respect they might be likened to the proverbial "canary in the coal mine," the earliest possible indication of troubling trends; in this case, not bad air but a move to rollback irregular warfare capabilities.

Yet it is possible that Human Terrain Teams will survive. The kind of major institutional change they represent has happened before. The U.S. Army pioneered the training revolution of the 1970s in part by instituting rigorous after-action reviews to facilitate learning and commander decision making. Doing so was an uncomfortable transition that challenged prevailing notions of discipline and military virtue at the time, but the results have proven themselves. If a similar mindset animates future decision making on sociocultural knowledge in the military, Human Terrain Teams will have a future. Their future would be even more secure if the Army chose to house them in one of its organizations that is predisposed to value sociocultural knowledge.

When General Dempsey, the current Chairman, Joint Chiefs of Staff, commanded TRADOC, he reportedly argued the Human Terrain System was a poor fit for a command that focused on training and doctrine and that does not regularly deploy forces. One option for a better fit that should be studied is the U.S. Army's Special Operations Command. It meets the requirement for an organization that is familiar with what it takes to field high-performing, small cross-functional teams like Human Terrain Teams. If leaders in the special operations community could see the value of owning such a program, it would be more likely to thrive in an environment where sociocultural knowledge is understood to be an enduring requirement and forward deployment and high performance standards are the norm. There are also other reasons why it might make good sense to have the Army's Special Operations Command oversee the Human Terrain System.

Special Operations Forces are a force of choice in irregular warfare, and thus a primary consumer of sociocultural knowledge. Special Operations Forces have a long history of working with sociocultural expertise, including the Human Terrain Teams. As we note elsewhere in the book, Special Forces in particular valued the program, were drawn to work in the Human Terrain System and performed well with the Human Terrain Teams. Special Forces already use a female version of the human terrain teams,[6] as do the Navy SEALs,[7] so they understand the challenges of employing sociocultural advisors in combat zones. The special operations community also includes Civil Affairs and Military Information Support Operations units (i.e. psychological operations forces), both of which perform missions that are critically dependent upon good sociocultural knowledge.[8] Special Forces, Civil Affairs and Military Information Support units all belong to the Army's Special Operations Command, so housing the Human Terrain System there would be especially convenient for those forces.

Integrating the Human Terrain System within the special operations community also would support a new major initiative by the U.S. Special Operations Command to improve the ability of Theater Special Operations

Command to work with foreign governments and military forces on common security objectives. The Command refers to this initiative as "building a global Special Operations Forces network." It is providing more personnel, equipment and capabilities for the regional special operations commands, but ready access to expertise on local sociocultural norms and networks is even more important. As has been argued elsewhere, merging a new cadre of sociocultural experts with Special Operations Forces would effectively provide the United States with global scouts who could better identify and working on security problems "indirectly" through host nation forces:

> With their expertise in traditional social and communication systems, these personnel should be key advisors if American forces need to deploy to their country or region. They would help prepare Special Forces for their training missions and other deployments, alerting them to key figures in traditional networks. These specialists could assist the Embassy public affairs officers in shaping their messages. In operational settings, they would assist [military information support] personnel in the same fashion. They would serve as eyes and ears in places that U.S. and even local officials seldom visit...[9]

As this vision of an enhanced Army Special Operations Command capability set suggests, the Human Terrain System's personnel would support Special Operations Forces but also U.S. military forces more generally. Civil Affairs and Military Information Support Operations units have long supported general-purpose forces with minimum friction, and increasingly other Special Operations Forces elements benefit from close cooperation with general-purpose forces as well. There is slight risk that housing HTS in the Army's Special Operations Command would make HTTs less available to general-purpose forces during war. Depending on the circumstances, HTTs should also work closely with other agencies of the U.S. Government, as historically all Special Operations Forces have done. Whether or not the Human Terrain System is transferred to the Army's Special Operations Command, the capability it represents should be preserved and improved. If so, the chances of success against future irregular threats also will improve.

Notes

[1] David Vergun, "Leaders Look at Army of 2020 and Beyond," *Army News Service*, September 14, 2002.
[2] See also Dan Cox, "An Enhanced Plan for Regionally Aligning Brigades Using Human

Terrain Systems," *Small Wars Journal,* June 14, 2012; and also Sydney J. Freedberg Jr., "Army Makes Case for Funding Culture Skills Beyond Coin" *AOL Defense,* July 2, 2012.

[3] The House Armed Services Committee's Subcommittee on Emerging Threats and Capabilities has held hearings on this topic.

[4] See the book's introduction, but also Christopher Lamb, Matthew Schmidt and Berit Fitzsimmons, "MRAPs, Irregular Warfare, and Pentagon Reform," *Occasional Paper,* Institute for National Strategic Studies, National Defense University, June 2009.

[5] Ibid., 30ff.

[6] The U.S. Army's Special Operations Command uses "cultural support teams comprised of female Soldiers who serve as enablers supporting Army special-operations combat forces in and around secured objective areas." The possibility of housing HTS in this Command was raised in the prepared Statement by Christopher J. Lamb, on "The Future of U.S. Special Operations Forces," before the Subcommittee on Emerging Threats and Capabilities, House Armed Services Committee, *U.S. House of Representatives,* July 11, 2012.

[7] Dominique Casales, "NSW Cultural Support Teams: Females Fill Critical Battlefield Role," *Tip of the Spear,* U.S. Special Operations Command, June 2012, 22-24.

[8] Kevin R. Golinghorst, "Mapping the Human Terrain in Afghanistan," *Monograph* (Fort Leavenworth, Kansas: School of Advanced Military Studies, 2010), 6, 44. Golinghorst notes the potential synergy between the Human Terrain System and the Civil Affairs community, asserting "The U.S. Army must better integrate its existing capabilities and initiatives with both HTS and [Civil Information Management]," which is a core Civil Affairs mission.

[9] David Tucker and Christopher Lamb, *Restructuring Special Operations Forces for Emerging Threats,* Strategic Forum, No. 219, (Washington, DC: Institute for National Strategic Studies, National Defense University, January 2006), 3.

APPENDIX ONE: EVOLUTION OF HTS TRAINING

Early Training Concept

As the program was attempting to stand up, it relied on the knowledge of the trainees present. The first team to deploy, AF1, did not go through any official training other than final pre-deployment training at the Combat Readiness Center at Fort Polk where it joined the brigade it would be serving. The members of the program were asked to train themselves and each other as best as possible to accomplish the mission that they understood they would be performing in Afghanistan and Iraq. A 2006 COR-HTS briefing slide cites a theoretical training program for this phase, which included one week of Military Decision Making Process and Counterinsurgency studies, two weeks of regional studies, and three weeks of briefing, debriefing, and cross-cultural communication, though it wasn't implemented. After AF1 deployed the Iraq teams were temporarily scrapped due to funding issues.

HTS Training v. 1.0

When most former or current HTS members refer to poor training they are typically referring to the version of training that occurred in the mid-2007—2010 timeframe. According to McFate and others, this initial 16-week training program was designed in 2006 on the basis of an educated guess about what the supported military units wanted to know and what sort of training the teams would need.[1] To better understand why the training was considered inadequate, it helps to first describe the curriculum. Typically, the training covered a number of core courses. MAP HT was taught primarily to the Research Managers, who arrived to training before the rest of the trainees. The course showed the basics of the program and showed how to build a link diagram, but the training was not useful for several reasons. Most prominently, the course did not explain how to integrate the tool into the research process, and the first truly working version of MAP HT was not ready until 2010 in any case. After the rest of the new trainees went through in-processing, usually a weeklong process, the first course that everyone took was the HTT Capabilities (alternatively, "Program") Brief. This was several hours long, given by both Fondacaro and McFate, and designed to familiarize the trainees with the program and give them an idea of what they would be doing. Trainees would then go through a Military Culture and Army 101 course. The purpose of this course was to familiarize the trainees with the basics of how the military operates.

Subversion And Espionage Directed Against the U.S. Army (SAEDA) and an Intelligence Oversight course would usually follow the course on Army culture. These courses met the basic requirements for training on what should be classified and how to do it. All trainees also received training in Axis Pro and TIGR, both tools used for geo-spatial mapping, but again there was no instruction on how to incorporate these tools into the research process. The next course was a daylong Teambuilding Preparation course that prepared the trainees for the teambuilding exercise held the following day. The course taught the fundamentals of team skills. The teambuilding exercise itself went through a number of iterations. Typically the trainees would dress in full gear, then in groups go around the town of Leavenworth and interview citizens. The point was to give trainees a general sense of what they would be doing and how they would operate in a team.

Radical Islam was the next course and was designed to introduce students to Islam. The focus tended to be on the radicalization of Islam rather than the actual background, tenets, history, etc. of the religion. The students received a class on counterinsurgency theory that mostly helped them to build understand the basics of a population-centric campaign plan and its attendant vocabulary. Someone on post at Leavenworth typically taught this course.

One of the most popular courses during this time period was the Iraq/Afghanistan immersion course. The Afghan immersion took place at the University of Nebraska—Omaha and the Iraq immersion at University of Kansas. Following the immersion training, the students were given introductions to both Anthropology and Research Methods. Both classes were successful in teaching basics of the fields and were especially useful for trainees without a great deal of background in the social sciences. However, the major shortcoming was that the instructors could only teach at the conceptual level. As contractors with little to no Afghan field experience, especially conducting human terrain collection, they lacked the context to make the training experience relevant. Thus, when possible, a returned team-member was present in the classroom to facilitate the instruction. The popular program was eventually scrapped due primarily to cost constraints.

At this point, relatively late in the program, the teams received a class called Intro to HTS. Although it may seem odd that an introduction to HTS was so late in the training program, the purpose was to refocus the trainees on their mission now that they had been taught relevant skills. However, much like the Afghan immersion courses, the instructors lacked the context to show the students how to operationalize the knowledge.

One of the last courses taught was on the use of the INMARSAT, a satellite phone with a large enough bandwidth so that the user can connect a computer and gain access to the Internet. The course, like many of the others, was too short for a truly comprehensive overview, which led to a number of misuses and abuses in the field. Finally, the trainees received Defense Civilian Intelligence Personnel System (DCIPS) training, which teaches how to be a civilian government employee in an intelligence organization. A complaint about the class was that it taught trainees how to fill out the forms, but did not explain why the form was needed.

Although the schedule of training was modified throughout 2008—2010, it was largely unchanged in terms of core curriculum, which was not well received. To name a few of the common complaints about this curriculum, it was considered too theoretical, too simple, too repetitive, too time inefficient (with a lot of down time), and thought to provide poor explanations of team and individual purpose, teaching basics to team members that were already experts in that field (i.e. Military Culture to active duty team members and Intro to Research Methods to Ph.D.s and M.A.s). Another significant shortcoming during this period was a lack of accountability. There was no grading system, or mechanism to release poorly performing trainees. It was very difficult, if not impossible, to remove trainees from the program for incompetence or poor performance. "If you don't have specific tasks delineated, the only thing you can pull/fire people for is violation of social norms,"[2] one interviewee asserted. In this regard, some trainees were released because of sexual harassment complaints but for little else.

The most common net assessment of the training from this period was that when it came time to deploy, team members had no idea what their job *actually* was. The key issue behind this was a combination lack of specific training objectives based upon individual tasks for the four separate team member functions and a lack of contextual, operationally relevant training from experienced instructors.[3] Other major issues related to shortcomings in this training period were in regard to the instructors,

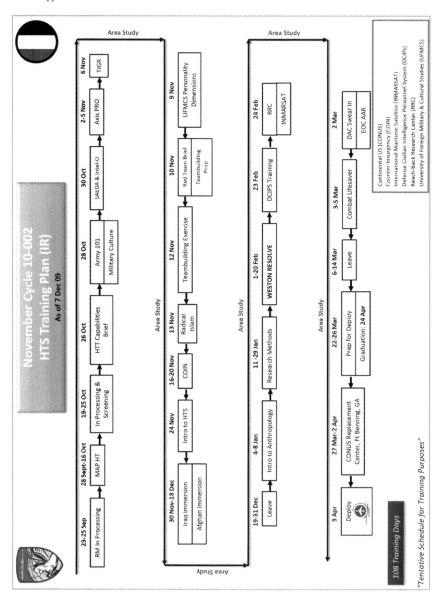

Source: HTS Program Development Team, *"The Future" Training Directorate Executive Overview*, PowerPoint, January 8, 2010. NOTE: There are multiple iterations of this graphic in existence as the training, the classes, and their titles were in flux.

as well. As contractors from a variety of backgrounds, the actual lessons tended to be highly varied. Also, due to contract restrictions on how many hours per week a contractor could teach and how many students at a time they could teach, there could be a great deal of downtime for students, especially in training cycles that were overfilled. A common result was that students would have half days, which provides a reason why some interviewees said the "most [they] got out of training was a suntan."[4] The net result from this training program tended to be unhappy trainees who felt unprepared to deploy to a combat zone.

HTS Training Reform Efforts

The beginning of efforts to reform the training can be traced to the publication of the HTT Handbook in October 2008.[5] The handbook, produced by the HTS Doctrine Development Team, delineated the Mission Essential Task Lists for the four roles of the HTTs—team leader, social scientist, research manager, and human terrain analyst, and then presented a list of five contributions[6] that the HTTs could make to the brigades they served in Iraq and Afghanistan:

Human Terrain System Teams Mission Essential Task List
1. Conduct a Cultural Preparation of the Operational Environment (CPOE)
Develop Human Terrain information requirements based on the Commander's CCIR and identified cultural knowledge gaps.
Assist Commander and staff by providing feedback on CCIR.
Design a Human Terrain Research Plan.
Develop the Human Terrain Collection Plan.
Coordinate cultural research activities.
Conduct social science field research.
2. Integrate Human Terrain into the Military Decision Making Process

Participate in unit MDMP by supporting planning staff with mission-focused Human Terrain information.
Assist in the development of culturally-astute Courses of Action.
Identify second and third order effects of proposed Courses of Action.
3. Provide Human Terrain Support to Current Operations
Identify cultural decision / adjustment points that impact the population.
Develop responses or mitigating strategies to gain or maintain support of the local populace.
Populate and maintain the human terrain component of the Common Operating Picture (COP).
4. Evaluate Human Terrain Effects
Assess the effect of friendly and enemy operations on the human terrain.
Assess the human terrain effects on friendly and enemy operations.
5. Educate the Supported Unit on Relevant Sociocultural Issues
Determine subordinate unit cultural knowledge requirements for their Area of Operations.
Develop tailored cultural information based on requirements.

Following the production of the handbook, the team used the reachback center to conduct a telephone survey of the deployed HTTs. In January 2009 they created an interview protocol. The document asked structured questions about the structure and composition of the teams in the field, their place in the host unit (section reporting to, staff meetings attended regularly, person that the team reports to, and person that the team receives "taskers" from), the amount of time the teams had been in the field, and the security environment faced by the teams.[7] The data collected was useful in understanding the evolving mission of the HTTs in the field. It is important to note that the HTS policy of interviewing team members has been contradicted by a number of former team members that claim no attempt was ever made to conduct interviews, sometimes even at the request of the returning team member.[8]

Continuing on the path toward training reform, HTS held a training curriculum review conference in 2010. The conference had been a long time in the making. Jeff Bowden, HTS' Training Manager had brought on Rob McLeary at the end of 2008 to try and fix the training. Both men had previously worked together at the U.S. Army's School of Advanced Military Studies at Ft. Leavenworth. During 2009, Mission Essential Task Lists had been created as an "interim fix", according to one member of the training development team, until the entire training curriculum could be overhauled.[9] This list was to define what each team member role was supposed to do and ensure that "research for research sake" was no longer conducted.[10] Members were supposed to focus on the purpose of HTS and engage in operationally relevant sociocultural research.

A 133 slide briefing entitled, 'The Future', presents an in-depth look at the problem analysis discussed at the conference.[11] The first point made in the slides—"Current Curriculum—the need for change"—indicates the intentions of HTS management. During the conference every aspect was of the training was critiqued, with working groups created to redefine and redesign the specifics of each position and how the training would help team members achieve maximum effect. The slides also provide a conceptual overview of a possible new training curriculum with individualized training for specific positions, training the members together for a number of weeks in between, and then team-focused training based on whatever element an individual would be sent to: HTT, HTAT or TCE. Another major objective of the conference was to better link the training to what a team would do in country. Thus the vast majority of those in attendance were returning team members, primarily social scientists with time in Iraq or Afghanistan.

During the conference metrics were created for all three HTS training goals identified in 2008, but the two metrics most relevant to HTT performance were focused on task 1.2—Provide Operationally Relevant Sociocultural Research and Analysis: (1) "Is all research tied to the unit's directed or implied requirements?", and (2) "Is the output of the research incorporated, in a timely fashion, with the unit's decision-making process?"[12] Moving toward a theory of effective HTT performance, HTS in 2010 proposed six subsidiary tasks necessary to provide/conduct operationally relevant sociocultural research, each with their own list of proposed measures of performance:

Task 1.2.1 **"Plan Research."**[13]

No.	Scale	Measure of Performance
1	Yes/No	Was research planning initiated prior to deployment?
2	Yes/No	Is the research plan designed to meet specific supported unit requirements?
3	Yes/No	Was a Research plan filed with the RRC for storage?
4	Yes/No	Was the research plan reviewed by the required oversight authority?
3	Yes/No	Did the RRC participate in the planning and design processes?
4	Yes/No	Was the research plan reviewed and altered as requirements, knowledge, or resources changed?
5	Time	To write the initial overall research plan
6	Time	To write each specific research design

Task 1.2.2. **"Conduct Research."**[14]

No.	Scale	Measure of Performance
1	Yes/No	Was the operational requirement for conducting research submitted by the host unit?
2	Yes/No	Was the operational requirement documented and stored?
3	Yes/No	Was a detailed risk assessment conducted to help determine the best research methodology for the operational environment?

4	Yes/No	Was the research design appropriate relative to the specific research objectives, team resources and capabilities and the operational environment?
5	Yes/No	Were detailed notes and data produced as a result of research activity?
6	Time	To conduct research systematic, empirical, complete, reliable, and valid research?
7	Percent	Of the team's time was devoted to conducting research and collecting data?

Task 1.2.3   "**Analyze Information.**"[15]

No.	Scale	Measure of Performance
1	Yes/No	Does the analysis incorporate data from HTS approved sources?
2	Yes/No	Did the analysis follow the research design?
3	Yes/No	Was the analysis performed in a scientifically rigorous manner on data appropriate to the chosen analytic techniques?
4	Yes/No	Did analysis address operationally relevant issues and stated research questions?
5	Time	How much time was required for analysis?

Task 1.2.4   "**Support Decision-Making.**"[16]

No.	Scale	Measure of Performance
1	Yes/No	Did the team regularly provide inputs throughout the MDMP?

2	Yes/No	Did the team actively pursue unit training support opportunities?
3	Time	How many hours per week did the team participate in mission analysis, COA development and mitigation strategies development?
4	Percent	What percentage of team support was provided to non-lethal targeting, civil military, psychological and information operations?
5	Area	What was the size of the operational area that the team directly supported?
6	Number	How many unit training events did the team support?
7	Yes/No	Did the team demonstrate an understanding of how to integrate into the commander's visualization process?

Task 1.2.5.   **"Assess Research Activities."**

No.	Scale	Measure of Performance
1	Yes/No	Did the team and project show understanding of how research has operational relevance to the unit?
2	Yes/No	Did the team regularly provide inputs throughout the MDMP?
3	Yes/No	Were the results of the assessment shared with the supporting unit and HTS PDT, RRCs, and Training Divisions?
4	Yes/No	Did the team implement the changes suggested by the assessment?
5	Number	How many assessments did the team generate?

| 6 | Percent | Were the team's inputs reflected in the unit's decision making process? |
| 7 | Percent | How many of the teams inputs were perceived to have a favorable outcome? |

Task 1.2.6 **"Report Research Activities"**:

No.	Scale	Measure of Performance
1	Yes/No	Did the team regularly report research activities?
2	Yes/No	Did the team report data in the HTS accepted formats?
3	Yes/No	Did the team store data utilizing HTS approved methods and storage areas?
4	Yes/No	Will the follow-on team have access to the team's knowledge base?
5	Time	How often does the team report research?
6	Yes/No	Did the team comply with HTS knowledge management SOPs and policies?

By January 2010, the doctrine and training personnel at Fort Leavenworth had created a 257-page document titled "Terminal and Enabling Learning Objectives." The report listed hundreds of desired actions by HTT members in theater, ranging from the macro-level (e.g. "provide operationally relevant sociocultural knowledge") to the micro-level (e.g. "prevent and/or resolve intra-team conflict"). The report's Appendix also specified who was assigned to perform the task (Common tasks, Individual tasks, or Collective tasks), provided a one-sentence to three-paragraph description of the desired action, the condition under which the action would be learned (e.g. "Acting as a member of a Human Terrain System team using lecture and discussion, in a classroom environment in small group practical exercises with time constraints"), the level of learning (knowledge, comprehension, evaluation, or application), and the standards that could be used to evaluate whether the HTT members had mastered the desired action. The long list of actions was broken into teaching modules, listed below:

In-Processing (pp. 12-14)
Introduction to Human Terrain System (pp. 14-33)
Team Dynamics (pp. 33-36)
The Research Life Cycle (pp. 36-55)
Introduction to Knowledge Management and Information (pp. 55-59)
Break-out Training [Team Leaders, Social Scientists, Research Managers] (pp. 60-78)
Research Design Practicum (pp. 78-102)
Depth Interviewing 1 (pp. 102-113)
Visual Ethnography (pp. 113-122)
Mixed Method Collection (pp. 122-131)
Imbedded Practicum 1 (pp. 131-140)
Surveys (pp. 140-150)
Depth Interviewing 2 (pp. 150-162)
Key Leader Engagements (pp. 162-172)
Imbedded Practicum 2 (pp. 172-181)
Direct Observation (pp. 181-190)
Participant Observation (pp. 191-201)
Imbedded Practicum 3 (pp. 201-209)
Group Interviewing and Focus Groups (pp. 209-219)
Secondary Source Research (pp. 219-230)
Imbedded Practicum 4 (pp. 230-239)
Pre-Capstone Review (pp. 239-249)
Human Terrain System Capstone Exercises and CTC Attendance (pp. 249-251)
Theater Specific Studies (pp. 251-253)
Area of Operations Specific Studies (pp. 253-247)[17]

This document provided a de facto roadmap for HTS reforms. If fully implemented, it would more than address the core complaint from HTT members that training gave them little idea of what they were supposed to do in the field.

The proposed timeline for the new HTS curriculum presumed it would start in October 2010. The HTS Curriculum Development Team created a roadmap that illustrated the steps they would need to take starting in January 2010 to make the curriculum redesign a reality.[18] The steps ranged from theoretical curriculum redesign to the administrative needs that would have to be addressed. However, the departure of Dr. McFate for personal reasons soon after the curriculum review conference, and the June replacement of

Colonel Fondacaro as Program Manager, delayed curriculum reform until January 2011. The training reformers were then able to leverage their work from the past two years to implement the current HTS training curriculum, with its increased focus on Department of the Army Civilian instructors with HTT experience; the combination of common, individualized, and collective training; and improved assessment of learning. Yet, due to a number of factors, including budget limitations, some of the suggested training changes were left unimplemented, including:[19]

- The integration of trainees into a metropolitan police unit to perform HTT duties as a team for a final exercise
- Bring control over trainee accountability to Leavenworth from the Program Management Office
- The development of a toolkit similar to MAP-HT but that is operationally relevant to the HTTs
- Publish a Social Science Training Handbook
- Publish an updated Commander's Handbook (Possibly forthcoming)
- Have a full capability Program Development Team to allow HTS to become a learning organization
- Improvement of HTS trainee recruitment

HTS Training v. 2.0

The current version of training is quite different from the previous versions. Many individuals have referred to the improvements in training, but most importantly the trainees that have gone through this iteration have talked about it positively.[20] Although the 2010 conference did not institute all suggested aspects of training reform, many important changes were made to the training. The most notable difference is in the length of the training. The core curriculum lasts only 50 days, as opposed to the previous training cycle of roughly 3 months. The 50 days are followed by 9 weeks of combat training at Fort Polk before deployment. The shorter training period means the courses are more focused and there is less downtime for the trainees. The 9 weeks of combat training provide substantial preparation for the teams of mostly civilians to deploy to a combat environment.

- **Department of the Army Civilian (DAC) instructors**: One of the most important changes was the use of returning HTT members as instructors. Using former team members as instructors provided exponential value as the instructors could now apply context to the lessons. Also, as Department of the Army Civilians, the instructors had a great deal more accountability to the program, as well as an actual motivation for and belief in the mission of HTS. As the instructors had a great deal of background knowledge, they were allowed a great deal more flexibility in developing materials and designing coursework.

- **Varied training**: Breaking up the training into common task training, individual task training, and collective task training was major advent to the training program. The previous training provided all trainees with only common task training, with the exception of the Research Managers who received 5 days of training in MAP-HT prior to the arrival of the other trainees. The focus on only common task training was a major factor in the common complaint of 'I just graduated training and don't know what my job is.' By training all students in the same functions there was by definition no cross-functionality. The addition of individual track training was critical to teaching each component of the HTT their specific function. In the collective task training section the trainees are then allowed to combine their common task knowledge with the individual training to operate together as a cross-functional team on a given training task.

- **Individual Task Training**: This section allows for each trainee to receive specialized instruction on the tasks they will be performing based upon their position on the team. Some trainees receive more instruction than others in this section, with Team Leaders and Social Scientists receiving the bulk of training, followed by Research Managers and the Human Terrain Analysts. Instructors are allowed a great deal of flexibility during this section and will often cross-train the various sections, so that a Team Leader not only learns their role, but also the role of a Social Scientist. Once again, the use of returned HTT members as instructors is very helpful to teaching the operational context of the concepts.

- **Improved learning assessment**: A number of other programmatic training changes were incorporated into the current training system. A grading system has been added to increase accountability among the trainees. It is now possible for trainees to be removed from the program for poor performance. This helps to ensure that any unqualified candidates that slip through the recruitment process don't end up deploying as they did in the previous cycle. Also, in place of a weeklong culture immersion "crash course," the trainees have culture and language training consistently across the 50-day training program. This helps to ensure that trainees remember more language and cultural dos and don'ts than they could have remembered from one week buried in the middle of a 3-month training program.

The new curriculum begins with 5 days of in processing. Incoming students are required to complete more administrative fundamentals than they were in the previous version of training allowing for a more streamlined transition at the end of training. In past cycles, if a student neglected any medical screening they may have ended up being delayed from converting to Department of the Army Civilian status and deploying. The Civilian Personnel Advisory Center qualifications are begun at this time to also ensure smooth transition and cut significant costs that are incurred when students go through the training and then fail qualifications resulting in termination.[21]

The next phase is considered the Introduction Period, where students receive foundation skills over the course of 10 instruction days. The courses in this section are focused on knowledge and skills that trainees will need to operate in a military environment. The teachers in this section are mostly seminar leaders and former Team Leaders with military backgrounds. Students are tested at the end.

The longest single section of instruction is the 20 instructional day Common Task Training section. Trainees are instructed largely in research operations. The purpose of this section is to train all students how to conduct operationally relevant sociocultural research and maintain that information. "Knowledge and skills addressed in this block of instruction fall under the following main headings: Introduction to the HTS Research Life Cycle in a military context, supporting Full Spectrum Operations; Tools to complete the Research Life Cycle, both qualitative and quantitative; and Applications to three sets of scenarios that experience in Afghanistan and Iraq have shown to be important to commanders, namely, Area Assessments (aka Sociocultural Preparation of the Operational Environment), specific COIN Stabilization projects, and a range of Other Requests, such as Key Leader Engagement (KLE) observation and short suspense projects."[22] As it is common task training, all trainees go through the same coursework. This section has an increased workload and requires 'homework' to be accomplished during free time. The purpose of this is to identify those that may have difficulty being self-motivated or operate independently.

The final learning portion of the 50-day training cycle is the 10-day Collective Task Training Section. This is an opportunity for the various components to come together and, with their combined knowledge; act as a cross-functional team in order to accomplish a real world scenario. The scenario varies, but requires a 'team' to brief a functional military staff. The process is a final opportunity for instructors to grade trainees and to differentiate between the strongest Team Leaders. Followed by this section is a 5-day Pre-Mobilization process between the graduation ceremony and deployment to Fort Polk. The period allows for downtime as well as time to accomplish any remaining administrative tasks/paperwork.

The current training program, although shorter in total length, is far more focused than the old program. The creation of a common tasks list was critical to creating this curriculum.[23] The condensed program means that students have more class-time that is relevant to their eventual deployment and the use of returning team members as instructors ensures that they are also receiving context as to *why* what they are learning is important. One former team member who returned to Leavenworth as an instructor explained how significant that context could be for new trainees. He explained the complexity of integrating into the military life, not only at the brigade level, but at the company level, while providing concrete examples. According to him the trainees found this knowledge valuable. "I would receive emails from people that would say they took it to heart and it helped them... I would have guys come back and say how that really affected the relationship."[24] The positive responses from team members are a good sign that the training is moving in the right direction.

Notes

[1] Montgomery McFate, Britt Damon, and Robert Holliday, "What Do Commanders Really Want to Know?: U.S. Army Human Terrain System Lessons Learned from Iraq and Afghanistan," in Janice H. Laurence and Michael D. Matthews, ed., *The Oxford Handbook of Military Psychology* (New York, NY: Oxford University Press, 2012).

[2] HTS Program Development Team member, interviewed May 11, 2012.

[3] HTS Program Development Team member, interviewed May 11, 2012.

[4] Research Manager, AF3, interviewed December 15, 2011.

[5] Nathan Finney, *Human Terrain Team Handbook* (Ft. Leavenworth, KS: The Human Terrain System, September 2008), 5.

[6] Ibid., 27.

[7] *Social Science Handbook Interview Form-v3_20090126*, produced circa January 26, 2009.

[8] Joshua Foust, RRC Analyst, interviewed September 13, 2011.

[9] Member of the 2010 Curriculum Conference, interviewed March 22, 2012.

[10] Member of the 2010 Curriculum Conference, interviewed March 22, 2012.

[11] Human Terrain System, *The Future: Training Directorate Executive Overview*, PowerPoint, January 8, 2010.

[12] *AppB Collective Task List Draft_20100209_U-FOUO.doc*, undated, 6.

[13] Ibid.

14 Ibid., 7.

15 Ibid., 8.

16 Ibid., 8-9.

17 Human Terrain System, *A: Terminal and Enabling Learning Objectives*, PowerPoint, ca. January 2011.

18 HTS Curriculum Development Team, The New HTS Curriculum Design, PowerPoint, March 5, 2010.

19 HTS Program Development Team member, interviewed April 19, 2012.

20 Dr. Aileen Moffat, Social Scientist AF27, interviewed December 19, 2011.

21 CNA Analysis & Solutions, *Congressionally Directed Assessment of the Human Terrain System*, Appendix G: IRAC Report.

22 U.S. Army TRADOC, *Human Terrain System Training Curriculum Overview Draft Copy*, August 3, 2011.

23 HTS Program Development Team member, interviewed April 19, 2012.

24 Tom Garcia, AF1, interviewed May 18, 2012.

APPENDIX TWO: RESEARCH METHODOLOGY

In Chapter Two we examined methodological alternatives for explaining HTT performance variation with primary sources. We noted that quantitative metrics are possible. Originally Human Terrain System leaders proposed such measures of performance and effectiveness.[1] However, as previous studies have noted,[2] HTT performance measures of effectiveness and quantitative data on HTT performance have not been used or collected by HTS. Only recently has anyone in the program begun systematically collecting qualitative assessments by interviewing HTT members after deployment, and that brief effort was soon discontinued.[3] Even if quantitative data were available, it would be difficult to validate the data and isolate the HTTs as the independent variable in subsequent analysis.[4]

Thus previous studies of HTTs rely on qualitative assessments from commanders of HTT performance.[5] We did the same, but to better understand HTT performance variation and commander assessments, we also took several additional steps to enhance our analysis. We:

(1) Researched the history of the program in-depth to establish key inflection points for program performance.

(2) Conducted extensive interviews with HTT and HTS members, concentrating on the recent 2009-2010 period in Afghanistan, to better understand HTT performance issues.

(3) Examined the data from interviews through ten organizational performance lenses to ascertain how each factor affected performance.

(4) Collected all available commander observations on HTT performance, categorized them, and derived a range of explanations for commander

satisfaction or dissatisfaction with HTT performance.

(5) Compared the insights from our historical, organizational, and commander assessments to produce the most compelling explanation for HTT performance variation.

The methodological approach we used is therefore similar to other studies in that it relies upon commander assessments to identify high and low team performance. However, it differs from other studies in that it 1) assesses commander evaluations of HTT performance in greater depth and augments those assessments with other data; 2) explains HTT performance variations by examining the teams themselves in greater detail with attention to performance variables substantiated by previous organizational studies of small cross-functional teams; and 3) generates a net assessment of HTTs by integrating the commander assessments and organizational performance analysis with the external historical realities that affected the performance of the HTS program. A more detailed explanation of our methodology follows.

Cross-Functional Team Performance Theory

The research method used in this book was pioneered for the study of interagency teams, most of which are cross-functional in nature. We conducted a thorough social science literature review—theoretical frameworks and empirical studies—to determine the factors that have been shown to create effective cross-functional teams. The results demonstrated that the research literature was sprawling, chaotic, and often logically inconsistent. (For example, theorists, researchers, educators, and practitioners often could not identify the differences between groups, teams, and cross-functional teams). In order to understand effective cross-functional teams (including, we believe, interagency national security teams as well as the Army's Human Terrain Teams) we first had to impose some order on the voluminous literature on effective cross-functional teams. From our review of the literature on cross-functional teams we extracted the 10 core cross-functional team performance variables explained in Chapter Four: purpose, empowerment, support, structure, decision-making, culture, learning, composition, rewards, and leadership. Each of these primary variables covers three additional, more precise, sub-variables.[6]

HTT Data Collection: The Literature

With that background on how we identified postulated performance variables, it is easier to describe the methodology we used in this study of HTTs.

We began data collection in August 2011. We cast a wide net using electronic databases and the key word "human terrain" to create a list of 1000 journal articles, trade journal articles, popular press magazine articles, and newspaper articles. This allowed us to chart the increasingly-frequent use of the term to refer to HTS and HTTs. From that starting point, we used a snowball literature review methodology, relying heavily on Google searches, to build our file of secondary data—all types of published literature, including books, academic journal articles, master's theses, conference papers, blog entries, comments on blog entries, and LinkedIn accounts. From that secondary data, we built a chronology of the HTS organization, emphasizing performance milestones and overall team performance assessments, and a preliminary list of team members for each of the 81 teams we identified. Our study is the first to identify specific HTTs and specific commanders. In any follow-on research the list of 81 HTTs in Afghanistan should be verified and supplemented by an equivalent list of HTTs in Iraq, and the complete set of commanders with knowledge about the performance of their HTTs should be interviewed in more detail. We then took on the difficult task of finding, contacting, and scheduling interviews with all known members of the HTTs in Afghanistan, starting with people identified in our secondary data and then adding to the contact list from information provided by our interviewees.

HTT Performance Standards

In all cross-functional team case studies some standards for performance must be determined in advance so the findings can be interpreted. A wide variety of effectiveness assertions are made in the secondary literature, where there is much confusion about what the HTTs were expected to accomplish. HTT effectiveness assertions found in the literature included the following: inserted females into near-combat environments, bridged the gap between the military and social science, reduced kinetic activity, served as an on-site cultural knowledge resource, served as a sounding-board for brigade commanders, reduced the loss of situational awareness as experienced brigades redeploy and new brigades take their place, and inserted new geo-spatial intelligence technologies into the battlespace. The natural place to begin, however, was with the performance objectives assigned to HTTs in the official program. Thus the diverse explanations for effective HTT performance gave way to a simple generic mission statement used by HTS: provide operationally relevant cultural knowledge to the brigade commander and the brigade. We determined, as did the CNA research team and the IDA research team before us, that the best metric for HTT performance was the subjective evaluation of brigade commanders about the performance of the HTTs. This meant there were potentially 81 different takes on HTT performance, one for each of the 81 commanders to whom the HTTs were assigned in Afghanistan.

It is important to emphasize here that the reliance on subjective brigade commander assessments of HTT performance is fraught with methodological limitations. A commander who frames his brigade's task as counterterrorism or lethal targeting could judge a high-performing HTT to be ineffective because they do not contribute to his perceived core mission. A commander who frames his brigade's task as collection of basic situational awareness for his Area of Operations could judge a high-performing HTT to be ineffective because it is such a small team. One brigade commander said that his team was effective, like a squirt gun is effective on a forest fire—it is helpful, but only a start. A commander who frames his brigade's core task as the creation of specific strategic actions that will accumulate into increased control of the Area of Operations, avoiding negative second- and third-order effects while creating positive second- and third-order effects, could judge a high-performing HTT to be ineffective because it does not contain the deep-level regional expertise necessary to manufacture those effective strategic options. In short, subjective commander evaluations of HTT performance are problematic, but we agreed with previous studies that they are the best available measure of performance. We recognized in advance that it would be important to obtain access to as many commander assessments as possible and to explore to the extent possible their rationale for their assessments, looking for common themes and reasoning, which is what we did.

HTT Data Collection: Interviews

The months of October, November, and December 2011 were primarily consumed by data collection through interviews with former HTT members. After a September 20, 2011, meeting in Newport News with the top management team of HTS, at which we learned that HTS would not participate in the study by providing access to former HTT members, we developed our own contact list of former and current HTT members and began interviewing them at a rapid rate. Most of the studies conducted by the National Defense University Organizational Performance Team from 2009 to 2012 are built on approximately 25-35 in-depth interviews, but the number of HTTs and their apparent performance variation required a much larger number of interviews. Ultimately, we conducted more than 100 interviews. The interviews ranged from one-half-hour to four hours. Most were conducted by telephone; many were conducted in person in our offices at National Defense University; a few were conducted offsite.

HTT Data Collection: Program History

An important element of the methodology is a detailed history of the HTS program and HTTs. Our history could not be either a "great man" history focused on HTS leadership, or a portfolio of independent "team biographies," but had to be a theoretically informed history of HTS performance in terms of its capacity to create effective HTT performance. In December 2011 and January 2012, using the secondary data and transcripts from the interviews, we constructed an 80-page chronology and drafted the first history of HTT performance. Several of our interviewees pushed us to explore the deep roots of HTS, rather than begin the history of HTS in February 2007, when the first team was deployed in Khost, Afghanistan. In response, one section of the history, "Gestation," captures the development of the HTS concept from 2001 to 2006. Other interviewees encouraged us to sort out a second segment of the history, the "Birth" section during which Steve Fondacaro and Montgomery McFate, in 2007, assumed control over a program that the Foreign Military Studies Office had built. Interviews helped us flesh out the "Proof-of-Concept" segment, which concentrates on the first HTT assigned to then-Colonel Schweitzer and initially led by Rick Swisher (February 2007 to September 2007) and subsequently by Pat Cusick (September 2007 to April 2008). The "Catastrophic Success" segment of the history covers the period from April 2008 to September 2009, during which the Khost team was replenished with new members and six additional teams were deployed to Jalalabad, Bagram (two teams), Kandahar, Helmand, and Zabul. Most of our interviews were targeted to cover the "Field Expansion" segment of the history from September 2009 to June 2010, when Steve Fondacaro was replaced by Sharon Hamilton as the program manager. Finally, several of our interviews are from HTT members downrange during the "Institutionalization" segment of the history, from June 2010 to December 2011.

HTT Data Analysis: Program History and HTT Performance

In January 2012, the team turned its attention to data analysis. We went through each interview transcript, using all four of our computers and all eight of our display monitors, coding each transcript into twelve categories. The first category of data from our data analysis was "history," allowing us to add detailed information to the draft history of HTS from people who were deployed on HTTs in Afghanistan. The second-through-eleventh categories were the qualitative equivalent of independent variables, data in which HTT members were asked initial and follow-up questions about each of the core variables that have been found to influence team performance. The twelfth category was "overall assessment," a category that we used as the qualitative equivalent of a dependent variable. Twelve composite documents, between 20 and 45 pages in length, were constructed by the research team in this manner, providing hundreds of data points for subsequent theory-guided analysis.

From early February to mid-April 2012, we translated the raw data for each of the ten team performance variables into a 50-page section of the report that presented theory-informed findings from the study. As mentioned earlier, each of the ten variables was buttressed by three more precise sub-variables. For example, the team culture variable was composed of sub-variables team climate, team cohesion, and team trust, and the core variable of team learning is broken down into the three sub-variables, exploitation learning, experimentation learning, and exploration learning. As individuals, we used the ten core variables and thirty sub-variables to carefully analyze the ten data documents carefully. We pushed ourselves at this stage of the study to move from "trees" (idiosyncratic observations by specific team members about determinants of team performance) to "forests" (recurring observations by multiple team members about facilitators of effective performance and impediments to effective performance). We then convened as a team to make a list of recurrent themes, discuss which themes had the most weight behind them in the data, and craft outlines for each of the ten variable analyses.

One helpful data analysis technique that we employed was a willing suspension of interactive complexity, meaning that at this stage we tried to isolate the impact of that one particular variable rather than the way it was linked to other performance variables. During the interviews, HTT members moved easily among the ten core variables—everything was connected to everything else. For example, good team leadership could trigger better team support, which could in turn lead to the creation of team resources that could be exploited to create team success, which could in turn help establish a team culture of effectiveness. By slicing the data into ten stand-alone data clusters, we were able to drill down on each of our ten core variables and produce non-obvious insights into determinants of effective HTT performance. A second helpful data analysis technique we used was a red-team/green-team analysis. We identified, from the 81 identified teams, several HTTs that were widely considered to be high-performing teams ("green" teams) and several HTTs that were widely considered to be low-performing teams ("red" teams). Interview data from the green teams was contrasted, for each of the ten variables, with interview data from the red teams. This technique helped us gain more clarity about the team attributes that led to high performance and the team attributes that led to low performance. A first draft of the variable analysis was completed, as scheduled, on February 29, 2012.

As discussed above, we realized that in addition to the interviews with HTT members on their team dynamics it would also be necessary to collect, analyze, and add to the knowledge base of brigade commander interview assessments of the performance of their HTTs. We interviewed nine commanders in order to help us better understand how different brigade commanders evaluated the performance of their HTTs. This sample, though, was not enough. We also collated all publicly available commander interviews into an approximately 40-page document and assessed the commander assessments for common themes and rationales.

HTT Data Analysis: Net Assessment

Concurrent with the writing of the variable analysis section from early February to mid-April 2012, our team wrestled with the creation of a net assessment, the "so what" of our study. Our previous data analysis techniques had separated the history of the HTS from the ten-variable analysis of the HTTs, and isolated the impact of each of the ten performance variables. In the net assessment, we integrated the historical analysis, the ten variable analyses, and the commander assessments in order to create our overall findings from the study. The commander assessments make clear that the majority found HTTs useful, but for different reasons, and our analysis of their comments explains why. In addition, the analysis of team performance variables explains why the 81 HTTs deployed to Afghanistan in 2007-2011 performed at varying levels of effectiveness.

HTT Data Analysis: Member Checks

We then conducted a "member check" of our study by sending a draft in April 2012, to the 84 individuals we interviewed (multiple people were interviewed twice because of their time spent on different teams, or because of their knowledge on the program) for a simultaneous "micro-check" and "macro-check." We communicated to our interviewees the interviewee numbers we had assigned to them and asked them to check all of our citations to their statements to make sure we had cited them correctly. As part of this "micro-check," we asked our interviewees whether they preferred to be identified by name, whether they preferred to be identified by position and location but not by name, or whether they preferred us to shield their anonymity as much as possible by not disclosing information that could be used to connect their comments to them as individuals.

Notes

[1] Steve Fondacaro, Program Manager, U.S. Army Training and Doctrine Command, Deputy Chief of Staff for Intelligence, Joint IED Defeat Organization—(JIEDDO), Cultural Operational Research/Human Terrain System (COR/HTS), *Human Terrain System Decision Brief Presented to Joint Integrated Process Team*, PowerPoint, June 8, 2006, August 20, 2006 version.

[2] For example, the CNA study notes "it does not appear that HTTs/HTATs have or used formal or standardized metrics in theater to assess their performance," and concludes CNA should keep better data on successes and failures of teams and individuals. Similarly, the IDA study identifies HTS program objectives but notes that no "standards, measures, or means of evaluation were ever developed or tested for these objectives." CNA Analysis & Solutions, *Congressionally Directed Assessment of the Human Terrain System*, 67, 107; Institute for Defense Analyses, *Contingency Capabilities: Analysis of Human Terrain Teams in Afghanistan—Draft Final Report*.

[3] HTS document containing interviews with returning HTT members, provided by a Social Scientist with an HTT, interviewed February 14, 2012,

[4] CNA study produced a list of metrics suggested by brigade commanders. While workable, it is evident that for many metrics it would be quite difficult to isolating HTTs as the independent variable. CNA Analysis & Solutions, *Congressionally Directed Assessment of the Human Terrain System*, 67.

[5] Institute for Defense Analyses, *Contingency Capabilities: Analysis of Human Terrain Teams in Afghanistan—Draft Final Report*.

[6] See Orton with Lamb, 'Interagency National Security Teams: Can Social Science Contribute?,' 47-64, for a preliminary presentation of the literature review on effective interagency national security teams.

APPENDIX THREE: AFGHANISTAN HTTS

We constructed a nominal list of 81 HTTs deployed to Afghanistan in the first five years of the HTS program. We constructed the list from open-source data, interviews, and unclassified map depictions of HTT deployments over time. The team numbers are adapted from the internal HTS numbering of the teams. For example AF1 was the designation of the Khost team at Forward Operating Base Salerno, but to facilitate computerized sorting of our data set, we renumbered the first nine teams as AF1 through AF9. Because the teams went through multiple generations as the brigade commanders changed, we designated these generations with additional tags; for example AF1-01 for Colonel Schweitzer's team, AF1-02 for Colonel Johnson's teams, AF1-03 for Colonel Howe's team, AF1-04 for Colonel Luong's team, and AF1-05 for Colonel Toner's team.

Not all of the names of the commanders to which the HTTs were assigned are known. Some of the commanders to which the teams were assigned were from NATO allies, and these nationalities are represented with the parenthetical notations of "CA" for Canada, "I" for Italy, "F" for France, "G" for Germany, and "P" for Poland. The start dates and end dates are estimated from an analysis of monthly updates to the Institute for the Study of War data base tracking the deployment of NATO assets in Afghanistan, and supplemented with interviewee data. The locations, like the commanders, are also largely estimated with assistance from interviewees. We chose not to present the team members column of our data set in this version of our document.

CURRENT ESTIMATED LIST OF 81 AFGHANISTAN HUMAN TERRAIN TEAMS (2007-2011)

TEAM NUMBER	COMMANDER LAST NAME	START DATE	END DATE	LOCATION
AF1-01	Schweitzer	2/2007	4/2008	FOB Salerno
AF3-01	Preysler	4/2007	7/2008	FOB Fenty
AF1-02	Johnson	6/2008	3/2009	FOB Salerno
AF2-01a	Spellmon	6/2008	9/2009	Bagram Air Base
AF2-01b	Division (HTAT)	7/2008	12/2008	Bagram Air Base
AF4-01	Hurlbut	6/2008	6/2009	Kandahar/FOB Ramrod
AF5-01	Brigade	11/2008	7/2009	Wardak/Logar
AF4-02	Thompson (CA)	2/2009	5/2009	Kandahar Air Field
AF6-01	Brigade	4/2009	3/2010	Camp Leatherneck
AF3-02	Spiszer	6/2008	6/2009	FOB Fenty
AF7-01	White	7/2009	8/2009	Camp Dwyer
AF4-03	Vance (CA)	7/2009	11/2009	Kandahar Air Field
AF5-02	Haight	7/2009	2/2010	Wardak/Logar
AF1-03	Howard	8/2009	4/2010	FOB Salerno
AF7-02	Newman	8/2009	8/2010	Camp Dwyer
AF2-02	Culver	9/2009	2/2010	Bagram Air Base
AF3-03	George	6/2009	6/2010	FOB Fenty
AF8-01	Tunnel	9/2009	9/2010	FOB Ramrod
AF9-01	Huber	10/2009	2/2010	Helmand HTAT
AF4-04	Menard (CA)	12/2009	5/2010	Kandahar Air Field
AF10-01	Leidenberger (G)	12/2009	6/2010	Mazar-e-Sharif HTAT
AF11-01	Division	1/2010	1/2011	Kandahar HTAT
AF5-03	Rohling/Johnson	2/2010	2/2011	Wardak/Logar
AF9-02	Durham	2/2010	2/2011	Helmand HTAT
AF12-01	SOF Commander	2/2010	2/2011	Bagram Air Base
AF13-01	Brigade	2/2010	2/2011	Kabul

AF14-01	Druart (F)/ Chavancy (F)	2/2010	8/2010	Kapisa
AF15-01	RC-West (I)	2/2010	11/2010	Herat
AF16-01	NATO SOF	2/2010	2/2011	Kabul
AF6-02	Brigade	3/2010	3/2011	Camp Leatherneck
AF17-01	Andrezejczak (P)	4/2010	10/2010	Ghazni
AF1-04	Luong	4/2010	8/2011	FOB Salerno
AF18-01	Regiment	4/2010	4/2011	Camp Leatherneck
AF2-03	Roy	2/2010	12/2010	Bagram Air Base
AF19-01	FOB Wilson	5/2010	1/2011	FOB Wilson
AF20-01	Brigade	5/2010	5/2011	Brigade
AF21-01	Brigade	5/2010	5/2011	Brigade
AF22-01	Brigade	5/2010	5/2011	Brigade
AF23-01	Brigade	5/2010	5/2011	Brigade
AF24-01	Brigade	5/2010	5/2011	Brigade
AF4-05	Vance (CA)	6/2010	10/2010	Kandahar Air Field
AF10-02	Fritz (G)	6/2010	2/2011	Mazar-e-Sharif HTAT
AF7-03	Furness	8/2010	9/2011	Camp Dwyer
AF14-02	Chavancy (F)/ Hogard (F)	8/2010	2/2011	Kapisa
AF2-04	Correll	9/2010	9/2011	Bagram Air Base
AF8-02	Blackburn	9/2010	8/2011	Zabul
AF25-01	Chiswell	9/2010	4/2011	Lashkar Gar
AF3-04	Poppas	10/2010	10/2011	Jalalabad Air Field
AF17-02	Bronowicz (P)	10/2010	4/2011	Ghazni
AF15-02	RC-West (I)	11/2010	5/2011	Herat
AF4-06	Milner (CA)	11/2010	7/2011	Kandahar Air Field
AF11-02	Clark	1/2011	7/2011	Kandahar HTAT
AF19-02	FOB Wilson	1/2011	8/2011	FOB Wilson
AF26-01	Brigade	1/2011	1/2012	Brigade
AF9-03	Sasmaz	2/2011	2/2012	Helmand HTAT
AF10-03	Kneip (G)	2/2011	2/2012	Mazar-e-Sharif HTAT
AF12-02	Schwartz	2/2011	2/2012	Bagram Air Base

AF13-02	Culver	2/2011	9/2011	Kabul
AF14-03	Hogard (F)/ Morin (F)	2/2011	10/2011	Kapisa
AF6-03	Kennedy	3/2011	7/2011	Camp Leatherneck
AF25-02	Davis	4/2011	10/2011	Lashkar Gar
AF17-03	General (P)	4/2011	10/2011	Ghazni
AF18-02	Regiment	4/2011	4/2012	Camp Leatherneck
AF27-01	German PRT (G)	4/2011	6/2011	Kunduz
AF15-03	RC-West (I)	5/2011	11/2011	Herat
AF20-02	Kolasheski	5/2011	5/2012	Brigade
AF21-02	Brigade	5/2011	5/2012	Brigade
AF23-02	Jenkins	5/2011	5/2012	Brigade
AF24-02	Brigade	5/2011	5/2012	Brigade
AF27-02	German PRT (G)	6/2011	11/2011	Kunduz
AF11-03	Crider	7/2011	7/2012	Kandahar HTAT
AF6-04	Smith	7/2011	7/2012	Camp Leatherneck
AF4-08	Wood	7/2011	7/2012	Kandahar Air Field
AF1-05	Toner	8/2011	8/2012	FOB Salerno
AF3-05	Kim	8/2011	8/2012	Jalalabad Air Field
AF8-03	Ortner	8/2011	8/2012	Zabul
AF5-05	Antonia	8/2011	8/2012	Wardak/Logar
AF13-03	Johnson	9/2011	10/2012	Kabul
AF13-04	Rynders	10/2011	11/2012	Kabul
AF27-03	German PRT (G)	11/2011	5/2012	Kunduz
AF13-05	Hammond	11/2011	11/2012	Kabul

APPENDIX FOUR: INTERVIEW QUESTIONS

Questions for HTT Members

Background:

(1) Could you provide a brief description of when you joined the Human Terrain program, where and during what period you served on an HTT, and when you left the HTS program (if you have)?

Team Purpose:

(2) What was the purpose of your team when you arrived in theatre? Did that purpose change over time?

Team Empowerment:

(3) Did your team members have the authority needed to accomplish the team mission effectively?

(4) Did your team have the resources to operate effectively? How much of your resources came from the Human Terrain System and how much came from the Brigade and/or other enablers?

Team Support:

(5) In what staffing section was the team placed?

(6) How much direct access to the commander did the team have?

(7) Who did the team liaise with most often to accomplish its missions and affect decisions?

Team Structure:

(8) How were the tasks divided among team members?

(9) How many reports did the team produce and what kind were they?

Team Decision-Making:

(10) How did the team make decisions about content and approval of individual, and collective, products?

(11) Did diverse perspectives help or hinder the effectiveness of the team decision making in your view?

(12) Were there any rules about the type of research to be conducted? If so, what?

Team Culture:

(13) If conflict occurred within the team, was it often? How was conflict managed and what effect did it have?

(14) Did the team develop trust among its members? If so, how and to what extent?

Team Learning:

(15) Did you consider the training at Ft. Leavenworth valuable and necessary?

(16) Did the team develop new ways to do its work? Can you provide examples?

Team Composition:

(17) How many members did your team have and what positions did they fill?

Team Rewards:

(18) Why did you join the Human Terrain System, and why did you stay in the program as long as you did?

(19) Why did you leave the program (if you did)?

Team Leadership:

(20) What leadership style most describes the Team Leader: traditional (as in directive); coaching (as in guiding members to better performance); shared (as in empowering collective decision making).

Overview:

(21) Of the products created by the team, how much of an impact on the brigade, the commander and the command staff did they have?

(22) Do you believe the team was effective in providing operationally relevant sociocultural knowledge to the brigade?

SELECTED BIBLIOGRAPHY

AAA Commission on the Engagement of Anthropology with the US Security and Intelligence Communities (CEAUSSIC), *Final Report on The Army's Human Terrain System Proof of Concept Program*. Executive Board of the American Anthropological Association, Arlington, VA: American Anthropological Association, October 14, 2009.

Aburezk, Kevin, "UNO Program Immerses Soldiers in Afghan Culture," *Lincoln Journal Star*, April 10, 2010.

Ackerman, Spencer, "Hundreds in Army Social Science Unqualified, Former Boss says [Updated]," *Wired: Danger Room*, December 21, 2010.

Ackerman, Spencer, "Petraeus: I'll Change Afghanistan Rules of War," *Wired: Danger Room*, June 29, 2010.

Afsar, Shahid, Samples, Chris, and Wood, Thomas, "The Taliban: An Organizational Analysis," *Military Review* (May-June 2008).

Agreement Between the United States of America and the Republic of Iraq On the Withdrawal of United States Forces from Iraq and the Organization of their Activities During Their Temporary Presence in Iraq, Ratified by Iraq, November 27, 2008.

Ake, David C., "Why Troops Love, and Sometimes Hate, the MRAP," *National Defense*, September 2011.

Albro, Robert, Marcus, George, McNamara, Laura A., and Schoch-Spana, Monica, *Anthropologists in the Security Scape: Ethics, Practice, and Professional Identity* (Walnut Creek, CA: Left Coast Press, 2012), 234.

Albro, Robert, 'Writing Culture Doctrine: Public Anthropology, Military Policy, and World Making, *Perspectives on Politics* vol. 8, iss. 4 (2010), 1087-1093.

Allison, John, "The Leavenworth Diary: Double Agent Anthropologist Inside the Human Terrain System," *Zero Anthropology*, December 7, 2010.

Alrich, Amy, *Framing the Cultural Training Landscape: Phase I Findings*, The Institute for Defense Analyses, December 2008.

American Anthropological Association, *Executive Board Statement on the Human Terrain System Project*, October 31, 2007.

Arnold, Matthew, "Improving the Coalition's Understanding of 'The People' in Afghanistan: Human Terrain Mapping in Kapisa Province," *Small Wars Journal*, September 2011.

Ashton, Adam, "A Commander Out of Step; Brigade Leader: Report Shows Col. Tunnel Twice Nearly Lost His Job," *The News Tribune*, October 16, 2011.

Asprey, Robert B., *War in the Shadows: the Guerrilla in History* (Garden City, NY: Doubleday, 1975).

Awan, Ayesha, "Institutionalized Ignorance," *University Wire*, October 17, 2007.

Axe, David, "War is Boring: After Setbacks, Human Terrain System Rebuilds," *World Politics Review*, November 25, 2009.

Axe, David, "Social Scientists Under Fire: How Anthropology and Other Social Scientists are Transforming the American Way of War in Afghanistan," *Miller-McCune*, February 17, 2010.

Ayub, Arif, 'Tribal Engagement Workshop,' *The Nation*, April 21, 2010.

Baba, Marietta, "Disciplinary-Professional Relations in an Era of Anthropological Engagement," *Human Organization* vol. 68, no. 4 (2009), 380-391.

Baier, Jeffrey K., *Mapping the Human Terrain: A Key to Operational Effectiveness For Future Peace Operations*, Master's Thesis for Peace Operations Training Institute, May 2010.

Baldor, Lolita, "Military Women to Serve Closer to the Front Lines, According to Pentagon Report," *The Huffington Post*, February 9, 2012.

Bailes, Alyson, Rene Dinesen, Hiski Haukkala, Paretti Joenniemi and Stephan De Spiegleleire, *The Academia and Foreign Policy Making: Bridging the Gap*, Danish Institute for International Studies Working Paper, May 2011.

Barakat, Matthew, "Army Contractor Pleads Guilty in Detainee Shooting," *The Washington Post*, February 4, 2009.

Bartholf, Colonel Mark, "The Requirement for Sociocultural Understanding in Full Spectrum Operations," *Military Intelligence Professional Bulletin* vol. 37, no. 4 (October-December 2011), 4-10.

Belasco, Amy, *Troop Levels in the Afghan and Iraq Wars, FY2001-FY2012 Cost and Other Potential Issues* (Washington, DC: Congressional Research Service, 2009).

Bellafiore, Dennis, and Bacastow Todd, "Human Terrain Data Infrastructure,"

The Speaker's Journal vol. 9, iss. 13 (Spring 2010), 181-186.

Belov, Nadya, Jeff Patti, and Angela Pawlowski, *Dynamic Context Maintenance in Human Terrain*, Advanced Technology Laboratories, Lockheed Martin, July 14, 2009.

Bertuca, Tony, "Army's Human Terrain System Program Under Review as Director Departs," *Inside the Army* vol. 22, no. 24 (June 21, 2010).

Bertuca, Tony, "Army Increasing Number of Human Terrain Teams; Advising Allies," *Defense News Stand*, December 10, 2010.

Bjoran, Kristina, "The Adventures of the Real Life Lara Croft in Afghanistan, and the Future of Smart Mobile GIS," *Geospatial Data Center blog.*

Blackwell, Tom, "Mapping 'White' Afghans Aims to End Civilian Deaths," *National Post*, November 8, 2008.

Boal, Mark, "The Kill Team: How U.S. Soldiers in Afghanistan Murdered Innocent Civilians," March 27, 2011.

Boot, Max, "Navigating the 'Human Terrain," *The Los Angeles Times*, December 7, 2005.

Bordin, Jeffrey, *A crisis of trust and cultural incompatibility a Red Team study of mutual perceptions of Afghan National Security Force personnel and U.S. soldiers in understanding and mitigating the phenomena of ANSF-committed fratricide-murders*, May 12, 2011.

Boykin, William, LTG, and Swanson, Scott, "'Operationalizing' Intelligence," *army.mil*, May 8, 2008.

Brinkley, Joel, "Afghanistan's Dirty Little Secret," *The San Francisco Chronicle*, August 29, 2010.

Brodie, Bernard, *War and Politics* (New York: NY, MacMillan Publishing Co., Inc, 1974).

Brooks, Drew, "Lessons Learned in Iraq War will Apply in future Conflicts," *The Fayetteville Observer*, January 1, 2012.

Bumiller, Elisabeth, "West Point Is Divided on a War Doctrine's Fate," *The New York Times*, May 27, 2012.

Burleigh, Nina, "McFate's Mission: Can a Former Punk Rocker Raised on a Houseboat Change the Way America Fights? Meet the Pentagon's Newest Weapon in the Wars in Iraq and Afghanistan," *More*, September 2007.

Cabayan, Hriar, 'Executive Summary,' in *Anticipating Rare Events: Can Acts of Terror, Use of Weapons of Mass Destruction or Other High Profile Acts Be Anticipated?: A Scientific Perspective on Problems, Pitfalls and Prospective Solutions*, Nancy Chesser, Ed., Topical Strategic Multi-Layer Assessment (SMA) Multi-Agency/Multi-Disciplinary White Papers in Support of Counter-Terrorism and Counter-WMD, November 2008.

Carr, Christopher, *Kalashnikov Culture: Small Arms Proliferation and Irregular*

Warfare (Westport, CT: Praeger Security International, 2008).

Cary, Peter, Youssef, Nancy, "JIEDDO: The Manhattan Project that Bombed," *iWatch News*, The Center for Public Integrity, March 27, 2011.

Caryl, Christian, "Human Terrain Teams," *Foreign Policy*, September 8, 2011.

Case, Spencer, "Mapping Afghanistan's Human Terrain," May 2, 2010.

Cardon, Ed, "Bloggers Roundtable with Brigadier General Edward Cardon, Assistant Division Commander, 3rd Infantry Division Moderator: Lieutenant Commander Brook Dewalt," *Federal News Service*, May 10, 2007.

Cardon, Ed. "Department of Defense Bloggers Roundtable with Brigadier General Ed Cardon, Deputy Commandant, U.S. Army Command and General Staff College, Via Teleconference; Subject: Military and Interagency Cooperation in Training and Education," *Federal News Service*, October 8, 2009.

Carroll, Kim, "Human Dimension explained at AUSA National Meeting," *TRADOC News Service*, October 6, 2008.

Cary, Peter, "JIEDDO: The Manhattan Project that Bombed," *iwatchnews.org*, September 29, 2011.

CBC News, "Canada's Military Mission in Afghanistan: Training Role to Replace Combat Mission in 2011," *CBC News*, February 10, 2009.

CBC News, "Ex-Canadian Forces Commander Menard Loses Rank," *CBC News*, July 21, 2011.

Censer, Margorie, "Notes from the Annual Strategic Conference at the Army War College; April 9-10, 2008, Carlisle, PA," *Inside the Army* vol. 20, no. 15 (April 14, 2008).

Chandrasekaran, Rajiv, *Little America: The War Within the War for Afghanistan* (New York: NY, Alfred A. Knopf, 2012).

Chandrasekaran, Rajiv, "Troops Face New Tests in Afghanistan," *The Washington Post*, March 15, 2009.

Chill, Steve, Lt Col., "One of the Eggs in the Joint Force Basket: HTS in Iraq/Afghanistan and Beyond," *Military Intelligence Professional Bulletin* vol. 37, no. 4 (October-December 2011), 11-16.

Clemis, Martin, "The "Cultural Turn" in U.S. Counterinsurgency Operations: Doctrine, Application, and Criticism," *Army History* (Winter, 2010).

Clinton, Yvette, Foran-Cain, Virginia, Voelker McQuaid, Julia, Norman, Catherine E. and Sims, William H. with Russell, Sara M., *Congressionally Directed Assessment of the Human Terrain System*, CNA Analysis & Solutions, November 2010.

Connable, Ben, "All Our Eggs in a Broken Basket: How the Human Terrain System is Undermining Sustainable Military Cultural Competence," *Military Review* (March-April 2009).

Connable, Ben, *Embracing the Fog of War: Assessment and Metrics in Counterinsurgency* (Santa Monica, CA: RAND, 2012).

Connable Ben, and Libicki, Martin C., *How Insurgencies End* (Santa Monica, CA: RAND, 2010).

Connable, Ben, *Military Intelligence Fusion for Complex Operations: A New Paradigm*, Occasional Paper (Santa Monica, CA: RAND, 2012).

Connelly, Donald, *The Unequal Professional Military Dialogue: American Civil-Military Relations and the Professional Military Ethic*, Paper prepared for US Army Command and General Staff College Professional Military Ethics Symposium, November 15-17, 2010.

Conroe, Andrew, "Whose Hearts and Minds? (Or, "Is There Reflexivity in Foxholes?")," *Critical Asian Studies* vol. 42, no. 3 (2010), 448-450.

Constable, Pamela, "A Terrain's Tragic Shift," *The Washington Post*, February 18, 2009.

Costello, Mike, "Afghanistan: COIN and the Human Terrain," *Defense Update*, September 4, 2012.

Costello, Mike, "COIN & Extreme Range Photography (EFR)," *Defense Update*, September 4, 2010.

Costello, Mike, "Counterinsurgency (COIN) & Human Terrain Techniques Combating IEDs in Afghanistan (CIED)," *Defense Update*, December 21, 2011.

Cox, Dan, "An Enhanced Plan For Regionally Aligning Brigades Using Human Terrain Systems," *Small Wars Journal*, June 14, 2012.

Cox, Daniel, "Human Terrain Systems and the Moral Prosecution of Warfare," *Parameters* (Autumn, 2011), 19-31.

Cox, Dan, "Understanding the Human Terrain in Warfare: A Clash of Moralities," *E-IR.info*, January 18, 2012.

Crook, General George, *The Apache Problem, by General George Crook* (Governors Island, NY: Military Service Institution of the U.S., 1882).

CS-JOCv1 *Military Contribution to Cooperative Security (CS) Joint Operating Concept* (Washington, DC: Department of Defense, Joint Chiefs of Staff, 2008).

Dali, Daniel, *Human Terrain System Information Briefing for the 58th Annual Conference of the Civil Affairs Association Seminar on Intra-DoD Irregular Warfare Capabilities*, October 30, 2009.

Denslow, James, "Scholar Soldiers in Afghanistan are on Dangerous Terrain: Using Social Scientists in Military Human Terrain Teams Blurs the Lines between Independent Academia and Partisan Militarism," *The Guardian*, June 11, 2010.

DeMello, Chanelcherie, "Social Science: Saving Lives in Iraq," *Task Force Danger Public Affairs*, September 27, 2010.

de Reus, Nico, Le Grand, Nanne, Kwint, Manfred, Renier, Frank, van

Lieburg, Anthonie, *Integrating Human Terrain Reasoning and Tooling in C2 Systems*, RTO-MP-HFM-202, 12-1-12-14.

Der Derian, James, Udris, David, and Udris, Michael, *Human Terrain: War Becomes Academic* (Oley, PA: Bullfrog Films, 2010).

Diana, Ron and Roscoe, John, "The Afghanistan TCE and TSO: Administrative and Logistical Support to HTS Teams and Knowledge Management of HTS Information," *Military Intelligence Professional Bulletin* vol. 37, no. 4 (October-December 2011), 21-23.

Dobel, J. Patrick, "The Ethics of Resigning," *The Journal of Policy Analysis and Management* vol. 18, iss. 2 (Spring 1999), 245-263.

Dreazen, Y.J., "Annie Get Your Gun: Women Are Fighting the Nation's Wars Like Never Before--And Paying the Price for Doing So," *National Journal* iss. 43, no. 45 (2011).

Drexler, K. Eric, *Engines of Creation: The Coming Era of Nanotechnology*, (Garden City, NY: Anchor Press/Doubleday, 1986).

Dudley-Flores, Marilyn, comment about Caryl, Christian, "Human Terrain Teams," in Forte, Maximilian, "Reality Check for the Human Terrain System: Marilyn Dudley-Flores Responds," *Zero Anthropology*, November 5, 2009.

Edelman, Eric, "Amb. Edelman's Remarks at the Department of State and Department of Defense Counterinsurgency Conference at the Ronald Reagan Building," Washington, DC, September 28, 2006.

Editorial, "A Social Contract: Efforts to Inform US Military Policy with Insights from the Social Sciences Could be a Win-Win Approach," *Nature* iss. 545 (July 10, 2008), (Published online July 9, 2008).

Editorial, "Cover Story: U.S. Army's Human Terrain Experts May Help Defuse Future Conflicts," *Defense News*, March 22, 2012.

Editorial, "Failure in the Field: The US Military's Human-Terrain Programme Needs to be Brought to a Swift Close," *Nature* vol. 456, (December 11, 2008), (Published online December 10, 2008).

Edwards, David B, "Counterinsurgency as a Cultural System," *Small Wars Journal*, December 27, 2010.

Eidson, Shad, "Sociocultural Research and Advisory Team Adds Community Perspective to CJTF-HOA," *CJTF-HOA Public Affairs*, July 15, 2010

Ellis, Richard F., Rogers, Richard D., Cochan, Bryan M., *Joint Improvised Explosive Device Defeat Organization (JIEDDO): Tactical Success Mired in Organizational Chaos; Roadblock in the Counter-IED Fight* (Norfolk, VA: Joint Forces Staff College, March 13, 2007).

Ephron, Dan and Spring, Silvia, "A Gun in One Hand, A Pen in the Other," *Newsweek*, April 21, 2008.

Eriksson, Johan and Ludvig Norman, "Political Utilisation of Scholarly

Ideas: The 'Clash of Civilisations' vs 'Soft Power' in US Foreign Policy," *Review of International Studies* vol. 37, (2011), 417-436.

Farris, Stuart L., "Joint Special Operations Task Force—Philippines," *Thesis* (Fort Leavenworth, KS: U.S. Army Command and General Staff College, undated).

Fawcett, Grant S., Maj., "Cultural Understanding in Counterinsurgency: Analysis of the Human Terrain System," *Monograph* (Fort Leavenworth, Kansas, School of Advanced Military Studies, United States Army Command and General Staff College, May 21, 2009).

Featherstone, Steve, "Human Quicksand for the U.S. Army, a Crash Course in Cultural Studies," *Harper's Magazine*, September 2008.

Federal Business Opportunities, R—TRADOC Human Terrain System, Solicitation Number: W911S011R0003, September 22, 2011.

Freedberg Jr., Sydney J., "Army Makes Case for Funding Culture Skills Beyond COIN," *AOL Defense*, July 2, 2012.

Finney, Nathan, *Commander's Guide: Employing a Human Terrain Team in Operation Enduring Freedom and Operation Iraqi Freedom: Tactics, Techniques and Procedures*, (Ft. Leavenworth, KS: U.S. Army Center for Army Lessons Learned, Number 09-21, March 2009).

Finney, Nathan, *Human Terrain Team Handbook* (Ft. Leavenworth, KS: The Human Terrain System, September 2008).

Finney, Nathan K., "Human Terrain Support in Current Operations," *Infantry* vol. 98, no. 2, (March-June 2009), 4-6.

Finney, Nathan, "Unity of Effort: A Culture of Cooperation and the Cooperation of Cultural Systems," *Armor & Cavalry Journal* (January-February 2009), 44-47.

Fishel, John T. and Sáenz, Andrés, *Capacity Building for Peacekeeping: The Case of Haiti* (Washington, DC: Center for Hemispheric Defense Studies, National Defense University Press, 2007).

Flintoff, Corey, "Marines Tap Social Sciences in Afghan War Effort," Morning Edition, National Public Radio, April 5, 2010.

Flynn, Michael T., Pottinger, Matt, and Batchelor, Paul, *Fixing Intel: A Blueprint for Making Intelligence Relevant in Afghanistan* (Washington, DC: Center for a New American Security, 2010).

FM31-20, *Doctrine for Special Forces Operations* (Washington, DC, Department of the Army Headquarters, April 20, 1990).

Fondacaro, Steve, and McFate, Montgomery, "U.S. Army Response to Robert Young Pelton's The New War for Hearts and Minds," *Men's Journal*, February 12, 2009.

Fondacaro, Steve, McFate, Montgomery, and TRADOC, "Nicole Suveges, A Funny, Kind Person, Has Died On An HTS Mission in Iraq," *Ethnography*.

com, June 26, 2008.

Fosher, Kerry, *Yes, Both, Absolutely: A Personal and Professional Commentary on Anthropological Engagement with Military and Intelligence Organizations*, in, Kelly, John D., Juaregui, Beatrice, Mitchell, Sean T., Walton, Jeremy, ed. *Anthropology and Global Counterinsurgency* (Chicago, IL: The University of Chicago Press, 2010).

Foust, Josh, "Is the Human Terrain System Worth Its Spit?," *Registan.net*, November 28, 2007.

Fox News, "Afghan Men Struggle with Sexual identity, Study Finds, *Fox News*, January 28, 2010.

Freedberg, Sydney, "Army Makes Case for Funding Culture Skills Beyond COIN," *AOL Defense*, July 2, 2012.

Freeman, Michael, and Rothstein Hy, ed., *Gangs & Guerrillas: Ideas from Counterinsurgency and Counterterrorism*, Naval Postgraduate School Technical Report, 2011.

Friedland, Lee Ellen, Shaeff, Gary W., and Glicken Turnley, Jessica, "Sociocultural Perspectives: A New Intelligence Paradigm," Report on the conference at The MITRE Corporation McLean, VA, September 12, 2006, June 2007, Document Number 07-1220/MITRE Technical Report MTR070244.

Fruhstuck, Sabine, "Where have All the Anthropologists Gone?," *Critical Asian Studies* vol. 42, no. 3 (2010), 434-436.

Gallagher, Sean M., "Human Terrain System's transitional plans," *Sean M. Gallagher*, March 5, 2009.

Gallagher, Sean, "Special Ops leads the charge for specialized data delivery," *Defense Systems*, May 21, 2010.

Garfield, Andrew, "Understanding the Human Terrain: Key to Success in Afghanistan," *Small Wars Journal*, July 16, 2010.

Gates, Robert M., *Speech to the Association of American Universities*, April 14, 2008.

Gates, Robert M., *Landon Lecture*, Kansas State University, November 26, 2007.

Geller, Adam, "Bridging the Gap," *The Associated Press*, April 8, 2009.

Geller, Adam, "From Campus to Combat: 'Professor' Pay Heavy Price," *The Associated Press*, March 10, 2009.

Gezari, Vanessa, "Afghanistan: The ethics of embedding anthropologists," *Pulitzer Center for Crisis Reporting*, September 9, 2009.

Gezari, Vanessa M. "Rough Terrain: The Human Terrain Program Embeds Anthropologists with the U.S. Military in Afghanistan," *The Washington Post*, August 30, 2009.

Glenn, David, "Anthropologists in a War Zone: Scholars Debate Their Role,"

The Chronicle of Higher Education vol. 54, iss. 14 (November 30, 2007).

Glenn, David, "Former Trainee in Human Terrain System Describes a Program in Disarray," *The Chronicle of Higher Education* vol. 54, iss. 16 (December 14, 2007), A8-A11.

Glevum Associates, *Kandahar Province Survey Report: March 2010* (Burlington, MA: Glevum Associates, March 2010).

Goldstein, Evan R. "Professors on the Battlefield," *The Wall Street Journal*, August 17, 2007.

Golinghorst, Kevin R., "Mapping the Human Terrain in Afghanistan," *Monograph* (Fort Leavenworth, Kansas: School of Advanced Military Studies, 2010).

Gonzales, Roberto J., *American Counterinsurgency: Human Science and the Human Terrain* (Chicago, IL: Prickly Paradigm Press, LLC, 2009).

Gonzales, Roberto J., Gusterson, Hugh, and Price, David, *The Counter-Counterinsurgency Manual: Or, Notes on Demilitarizing American Society* (Chicago, IL: Prickly Paradigm Press, LLC, 2009).

Gonzales, Roberto J., "Human Terrain: Past, Present and Future Applications," *Anthropology Today* vol. 24, no. 1 (February 2008).

Grau, Lester W., "Bashing the Laser Range Finder with a Rock," *Military Review* vol. 77, no. 3 (May-June 1997), 42-28.

Grau, Lester. W., and Jacob W. Kipp, 'Urban Combat: Confronting the Specter,' *Military Review* iss. 79, no. 4, (1999), 9-17.

Gray, Colin S., "Irregular Enemies and the Essence of Strategy: Can the American Way of War Adapt?," *Monograph*, Strategic Studies Institute, March 1, 2006.

Greanias, Jennifer Carol, *Assessing the Effectiveness of the US Military's Human Terrain System*, Thesis (Washington, DC: Georgetown University, November 19, 2010).

Griffin, Marcus, *An Anthropologist among the Soldiers: Notes from the Field*, in Kelly, John D., Juaregui, Beatrice, Mitchell, Sean T., Walton, Jeremy, ed. *Anthropology and Global Counterinsurgency* (Chicago, IL: The University of Chicago Press, 2010).

Griffin, Marcus B., "Research to Reduce Bloodshed," *The Chronicle of Higher Education*, November 30, 2007.

Gusinov, Timothy, "Almanac—Soviet Special Forces (Spetsnaz): Experience in Afghanistan," *Military Review* iss. 82, no. 2 (2002), 105.

Gusterson, Hugh, "Human Terrain Teams by Any Other Name?," *Critical Asian Studies* vol. 42, no. 3 (2010), 441-443.

Gusterson, Hugh, 'The U.S. military's quest for weaponize culture,' *Bulletin on the Atomic Sciences*, June 20, 2008.

Hajjar, Remi, "CULTURAL AWARENESS—The Army's New TRADOC

Culture Center—TRADOC's new Culture Center at Fort Huachuca is a key first step toward developing an Army-wide cultural awareness program," *Military Review* iss. 86, no. 6 (2006), 89-92.

Hamilton, Colonel Sharon, "HTS Director's Message," *Military Intelligence Professional Bulletin* vol. 37, no. 4 (October-December 2011), A2-3.

Hansen, Matthew, "For Afghanistan: Brains, not Bombs," *World-Herald Staff Writer*, September 11, 2009.

Hedges, Stephen J., "U.S. Battles low-tech threat," *The Washington Times*, October 25, 2004.

Heinlein, Robert A., *Starship Troopers* (New York: NY, Berkley Medallion Books, 1959).

Helbig, Zenia, "Human Terrain Systems Program; U.S. Army Training and Doctrine Command," *Memorandum to U.S. Congress*, September 13, 2007.

Helbig, Zenia, *Personal Perspective on the Human Terrain System Program*, Delivered at the AAA's Annual Conference, November 29, 2007.

Henry, William E., "Soldiers Meet with Leaders in Remote Afghan Province," *Armed Forces Press Service*, December 24, 2009.

Herlihy, Peter H., Dobson, Jerome E., Aguilar Robledo, Miguel, Smith, Derek A., Kelly, John H. and Ramos Viera, Aida, "A Digital Geography of Indigenous Mexico: Prototype for the American Geographical Society's Bowman Expeditions," *The Geographical Review* vol. 98, iss. 3 (July 2008), 395-415.

Hill Kavanaugh, Lee, "Army Takes Human Terrain to Heart," *The Kansas City Star*, October 14, 2008.

Hodge, Nathan, *Armed Humanitarians: The Rise of the Nation Builders* (New York, NY: Bloomsbury, 2011).

Hodge, Nathan, "Canucks Hop on 'Human Terrain' Bandwagon," *Wired: Danger Room*, November 11, 2008.

Hoffman, F. G., "Neo-Classical Counterinsurgency," *Parameters* no. 37, iss. 2 (2007), 71-87.

Holmes-Eber, Paula, and Barak A Salmoni., 'Concepts—Operational Culture for Marines,' *Marine Corps Gazette* iss. 92, no. 5 (2008), 72-77.

Holt, Ronald L., "Afghan Village Militia: A People-Centric Strategy to Win," *Small Wars Journal*, September 2, 2009.

Holt, Ronald L., "The Use of Pseudo-Operations in the AFPAK Theater," *Small Wars Journal*, September 15, 2010.

Horgan, Shea, *Navigating the Human Terrain: Cultural Awareness and the Adaptation of US Military Strategy*, Department of War Studies, King's College, 2011.

HTT AF04, *The Effects of Poppy Eradication in Southern Afghanistan*.

Human Terrain System homepage.

Human Terrain System, *Pashtun Sexuality*, Human Terrain Team (HTT) AF-6, 2011.

Human Terrain System Program Development Team, *Human Terrain System Yearly Report*, Prepared for US Army Training and Doctrine Command, August 2008.

Humes, William, MAJ, "Task Force Viking employs Human Terrain Teams," *DVIDS*, July 12, 2012.

Hunt, Jennifer C., "Center for Naval Analyses Report on Human Terrain Team Systems," *Seven Shots*, February 22, 2011.

Inskeep, Steve, "Marines Tap Social Sciences in Afghan War Effort," *NPR*, Morning Edition, April 5, 2010.

Institute for Defense Analyses, *Human Terrain Team Study—Final Report*, Unpublished, 2011.

Jackson, Jack A., S.K. Numrich, S.K., Picucci, P.M., Chase, CAPT Charles, Christope L. McCray, Christope L., Wright, Dominick, Hawkins Conrad, Mary, Johnson, Anthony, and Uhlmeyer, Maj. Kerri, *Contingency Capabilities: Analysis of Human Terrain Teams in Afghanistan, Draft Final Report*, The Institute for Defense Analyses, December 2011, IDA paper P-4-4809;Log: H11-001954/1.

Jager, Sheila Miyoshi, "On the Uses of Cultural Knowledge," *Monograph*, (Carlisle, PA: Strategic Studies Institute, U.S. Army War College, November 2007).

Jaschik, Scott, "Questions, Anger and Dissent on Ethics Study," *Inside Higher Ed*, November 30, 2007.

Jean, G.V., "'Culture Maps' Becoming Essential Tools of War," *National Defense* no. 95, iss. 675 (2010).

Jebb, Cindy R., Hummel, Laurel J., Chacho, Tania M., *Human Terrain Team Trip Report: A "Team of Teams,"* Prepared for TRADOC G2 by the USMA's Interdisciplinary Team in Iraq, unpublished, 2008.

Jelinek, Pauline, "Afghan Civilian Deaths Big Problem in War," *The Washington Post*, June 18, 2009.

Johnson, John P., Colonel, "DoD News Briefing with Colonel John P. Johnson from Afghanistan at the Pentagon Briefing Room," *DOD News*, Arlington, VA, November 21, 2008.

Jones, A., "Woman to Woman in Afghanistan: Female Engagement Teams join the counterinsurgency," *The Nation* no. 291, iss. 20 (2010), 11-16.

Jones D.M., and Smith M.L.R., "Whose hearts and whose minds? The curious case of global counter-insurgency," *Journal of Strategic Studies* no. 33, iss. 1 (2010), 81-121.

Jordan, Bryant, "Spec Ops Needs a Few Good Women," *Military.com*, February 14, 2011.

Joseph, Paul, *Changing the Battle Space? How Human Terrain Teams Define "Success" in Iraq and Afghanistan*, Paper prepared for 7th Interdisciplinary Conference on War and Peace (Prague, Czech Republic, April 30-May 2, 2010).

Joy, B., "Why the Future Doesn't Need Us Our most powerful 21st-century technologies—robotics, genetic engineering, and nanotech—are threatening to make humans an endangered species," *WIRED*, no. 8 (2000), 238-246.

Julardzija, Semir, *Human Terrain System in Peacekeeping Missions*, Peace Operations Training Institute, December 12, 2011.

Kahan, James P., Worley, D. R., and Stasz, Cathleen, *Understanding Commanders' Information Needs* (Ft. Belvoir: Defense Technical Information Center, 2000).

Kamps, Louisa, "Army Brat: How Did the Child of Peace-loving Bay Area Parents Become the New Superstar of National Security Circles?," *Elle* (April 2008), 309-311; 360-362.

Kanter, Arnold and Brooks, Linton F., *U.S. Intervention Policy for the Post-Cold War World: New Challenges and New Responses* (New York, NY: W.W. Norton, 1994).

Kaplan, Fred, "Rumsfeld's $9 billion slush fund," *Slate*, blog, October 10, 2003.

Kapisa Provincial Reconstruction Team Public Affairs Office, "Kapisa PRT, contractors pay road compensation," *RC East*, October 14, 2010.

Kapstein, Ethan B., "Measuring Progress in Modern Warfare," *Survival: Global Politics and Strategy* vol. 54, no. 1 (January 31, 2012), 137-158.

Katzenstein, Lawrence C., Albin, Michael, and Paul McDowell, "HTAT Arrives at Multinational Division Baghdad," *Military Intelligence Professional Bulletin* vol. 37, no. 4 (October-December 2011), 85-89.

Kelly, John D., Juaregui, Beatrice, Mitchell, Sean T., Walton, Jeremy, ed., *Anthropology and Global Counterinsurgency* (Chicago, IL: The University of Chicago Press, 2010).

Kenyon, Henry, "Skope Cells Help Dispel Fog of War," *Defense Systems*, May 2, 2011.

Khatchadourian, Raffi, "The Kill Company: Did a Colonel's Fiery Rhetoric Set the Conditions For a Massacre?," *The New Yorker*, July 6, 2009.

Kilcullen, David, "Twenty-Eight Articles: Fundamentals of Company-Level Counterinsurgency," *Small Wars Journal*, Issue 1, 2006.

Kimberlin, Joanne, "Part 1: New Weapon in an Old War in Afghanistan," *The Virginian Pilot*, September 26, 2010.

Kimberlin, Joanne, "Part 2: American Muscle Proves Futile in Land of Extremes," *The Virginian Pilot*, September 27, 2010.

Kimberlin, Joanna, "Part 3: Building Trust Amid Fear, One Mission at a

Time," *The Virginian Pilot*, September 28, 2010.

Kimberlin, Joanna, "Part 4: In the Enemy's Lair, Fighting For Afghanistan's Future," *The Virginian Pilot*, September 29, 2010.

King, Chris, *Human Terrain System and the Role of Social Science in Counterinsurgency*, Brief given to University of Hawai'i, Manoa, September 20, 2011.

King, Christopher, "Managing Ethical Conflict on a Human Terrain Team," *Anthropology News* no. 50, iss. 6 (2009), 16.

Kipp, Jacob W., 'FMSO-JRIC and Open Source Intelligence: Speaking Prose in a World of Verse, *Military Intelligence Professional Bulletin* (October/December 2005).

Kipp, J.W., and L.W. Grau. "Military Theory, Strategy, and Praxis," *Military Review* iss. 91, no. 2 (2011), 12-22.

Kipp, Jacob, Grau, Lester, Prinslow, Karl, and Smith, Don, Capt. "The Human Terrain System: A CORDS for the 21st Century," *Military Review* vol. 85, no. 5 (September/October 2006), 8-15.

Klicker, Karl, D. Capt., "Social Sciences: A Tool for COIN: These are not the droids you're looking for," *Marine Corps Gazette* vol. 96, no. 4 (April 2012), 58-61.

Knobler, Suze, "Vet patrolled Panjwai district," *Redlands Daily Facts*, March 16, 2012.

Knoke, David, and Yang, Song, *Social Network Analysis*, 2nd Ed. (Los Angeles, CA: Sage, 2008).

Knowlton, Jr. William A., *The Surge: General Petraeus and the Turnaround in Iraq*, Industrial College of the Armed Forces Case Study (Washington, DC: NDU Press, December 2010).

Komer, R W., *Bureaucracy Does Its Thing: Institutional Constraints on U.S.-Gvn Performance in Vietnam* (Santa Monica, CA: RAND, 1972).

Krepinevich, Andrew F., "Department of Defense Language and Cultural Awareness Transformation," Testimony to the United States House of Representatives Committee on the Armed Service, Oversight and Investigations Subcommittee, July 9, 2008.

Krulak, Charles C., "The Strategic Corporal: Leadership in the Three Block War," *Marines Magazine* (January 1999).

Kushiyama, Kristen, "Sociocultural Data Collection Provides Insight for Commanders," *U.S. Army News Archives*, October 12, 2010.

Kusiak, Pauline, *Culture, Identity, and Information Technology in the 21st Century: Implications for U.S. National Security* (Carlisle, PA: Strategic Studies Institute, 2012).

Kusiak, Pauline, "Sociocultural Expertise and the Military: Beyond the Controversy," *Military Review* vol. 88, no. 6 (November-December 2008), 65-76.

Lamb, Christopher, Schmidt, Matthew, and Fitzsimmons, Berit, "MRAPs, Irregular Warfare, and Pentagon Reform," *Occasional Paper*, Institute for National Strategic Studies, National Defense University, June 2009.

Lamb, Christopher J., and Munsing, Evan, *Secret Weapon: High-value Target Teams as an Organizational Innovation*, Strategic Perspectives (Institute for National Strategic Studies, National Defense University, December 2010).

Lamb, Christopher J., and Cinnamond, Martin, *Unity of Effort: Key to Success In Afghanistan*, Strategic Forum no. 248 (Washington, DC: NDU Press, October 2009).

Lamps, Jim, "Her Mission Orders in Afghanistan: Map the Human Terrain," *The Dallas Morning News*, March 13, 2009.

Landers, Jim, "Texas woman helps in Afghan war," *Dallas Morning Star*, March 14, 2009.

LaPlante, Matthew, D., "Utah Academic Weighs Ethics, Economics of Army Offer," *The Salt Lake Tribune*, February 21, 2010.

Laughrey, James C., "Know Before You Go: Improving Army Officer Sociocultural Knowledge," *Strategy Report Project*, U.S. Army War College, April 4, 2008.

Leymarie, Philippe, "Les anthropologies aux armee," *Radio France Internationale*, November 4, 2007.

Lucas, George R., Jr. *Anthropologists in Arms: The Ethics of Military Anthropology* (Lanham, MD: AltaMira Press, 2009).

Lujan, Fernando, "How to Get Afghans to Trust Us Once Again," *The Washington Post*, March 4, 2012.

Mac Ginty, Roger, "Social Network Analysis and counterinsurgency: a counterproductive strategy," *Critical Studies on Terrorism* iss. 3, no. 2 (2010), 209-226.

Macleod, Jenny ed., *Defeat and Memory: Cultural Histories of Military Defeat in the Modern Era* (New York, NY: Palgrave Macmillan, 2008).

Malenic, Marina, "Pentagon Approves Funding for 'Human Terrain' Field Research," *Inside the Army* vol. 19, no. 39 (October 1, 2007).

Marr, Jack, LTC, Chushing, John, MAJ, Garner, Brandon, MAJ, Thompson, Richard, CPT, "Human Terrain Mapping: A Critical First Step to Winning the COIN Fight," *Military Review* (March-April 2008), 18-24.

Marrero, Tony, "Task: Win Minds, Hearts of Afghanistan," *St. Petersburg Times*, January 1, 2010.

Marlowe, Ann, "Anthropology Goes to War: There Are Some Things The Army Needs In Afghanistan, But More Academics Are Not At The Top Of The List," *The Weekly Standard* vol. 13, no. 11 (November 26, 2007).

Maurer, Kevin, "In A New Elite Army Unit, Women Serve Alongside Special

Forces, but First They Must Make the Cut," *The Washington Post*, October 27, 2011.

McChrystal, Stanley, *COMISAF Initial Assessment*, August 30, 2009.

McFarland, Maxie, "A Center for Learning Innovation," *Military Training Technology* vol. 15, no. 4 (July 2010).

McFarland, Maxie, "Military Cultural Education," *Military Review* vol. 82, iss. 2 (2005), 62-69.

McFate, Montgomery, and Jackson, Andrea, "An Organizational Solution for DOD's Cultural Knowledge Needs," *Military Review* (July-August 2005), 18-21.

McFate, Montgomery, "Anthropology and Counterinsurgency: The Strange Story of their Curious Relationships," *Military Review* (March-April 2005), 24-38.

McFate, Montgomery, and Fondacaro, Steve, "Building a Rocket in the Garage: Reflection on the Human Terrain System During the First Four Years," *PRISM* 2, no. 4 (2011) 63-82,

McFate, Montgomery, *Culture*, in, Thomas Rid and Thomas Keaney, eds, *Understanding Counterinsurgency: Doctrine, Operations, and Challenges* (New York: NY, Routledge, 2010).

McFate, Montgomery, Price, David, Agoglia, John, Villacres, Edward, and Rohde, David, Interview with Susan Page, *The Diane Rehm Show*, NPR, October 10, 2007.

McFate, Montgomery, Before the House Committee on Armed Services, Subcommittee on Investigations and Oversight, *110th Congress*, 2nd Session, United States House of Representatives, July 9, 2008.

McFate, Montgomery, "Building Bridges or Burning Heretics: A Response to Gonzales in this Issue," *Anthropology Today* vol. 23, no. 3 (June 2007).

McFate, Montgomery, "Iraq: The Social Context of IEDs," *Military Review* (May-June 2005), 37-40.

McFate, Montgomery, "The Military Utility of Understanding Adversary Culture," *Joint Force Quarterly* 38, (3rd Quarter 2005), 42-48.

McFate, Montgomery, Damon, Britt, and Holliday, Robert, *What Do Commanders Really Want to Know?: U.S. Army Human Terrain System Lessons Learned from Iraq and Afghanistan*, in, Laurence, Janice H., and Matthews, Michael D., ed., *The Oxford Handbook of Military Psychology* (New York, NY: Oxford University Press, 2012).

McHugh, John, *Transcript: Defense Writers Group*, A Project of the Center for Media and Security New York and Washington, DC, March 31, 2010.

McLeary, Paul, "Human Terrain Teams," *World Politics Review*, October 14, 2008.

McManus, Doyle, "McManus: A smaller, smarter military: The best-equipped army in the world can still lose a war if it doesn't understand the people it's fighting," *The Los Angeles Times*, April 22, 2012.

Memorandum, "Findings and Recommendations, AR 15-6 Investigation Concerning Human Terrain Subject (HTS) Project Inspector General Complaints," May 12, 2010, For Official Use Only, redacted and released in response to a Freedom of Information request; available at https://www.box.com/s/2mv0g54xsr41aegwbw9i; February 19, 2013, 1..

Metz, Thomas F. LTG, *Statement by Lieutenant General Thomas F. Metz, Director, Joint Improvised Explosive Device Defeat Organization Before The House Appropriations Committee Subcommittee on Defense U.S. House of Representatives, Second Session, 110ᵗʰ Congress on the Joint Improvised Explosive Device Defeat Organization Mission*, February 14, 2008.

Mitchell, Scott R., "Observations of a Strategic Corporal," *Military Review* (July-August 2012), 58-64.

Mitchell, Sean T., and Kelly, John D., *The U.S. Military and U.S. Anthropology*, in, Kelly, John D., Juaregui, Beatrice, Mitchell, Sean T., Walton, Jeremy, ed., *Anthropology and Global Counterinsurgency* (Chicago, IL: The University of Chicago Press, 2010).

Mitchell, Terry, *Letter to Office of the Undersecretary of Defense for Intelligence*, August 19, 2010.

Ministry of Defence (UK), "CGS Outlines Rationale Behind Today's Army 2020 Announcement," *Defence Policy and Business News*, July 5, 2012.

Moore, Timothy, *Measuring the Role of Cultural Awareness in Tracing the Human Terrain* (Newport, RI: Naval War College, October 30, 2008).

Morin, Monte, "Cultural Advisers Give U.S. Teams an Edge," *Stars and Stripes*, June 28, 2007.

Mosser, Michael, "Puzzles Versus Problems: The Alleged Disconnect Between Academics and Military Practitioners," *Perspectives on Politics* vol. 8, no. 4 (December 2010), 1077-1086.

Motlagh, Jason, "Should Anthropologists Help Contain the Taliban?," *Time Magazine*, July 1, 2010.

Mulrine, Anna, "In Afghanistan, the NATO-led Force is 'Underresourced' for the Fight Against the Taliban," *usnews.com*, June 5, 2008.

Mulrine, Anna, "The Culture Warriors: The Pentagon Deploys Social Scientists to Help Understand Iraq's 'Human Terrain'," *US News and World Report*, November 30, 2007.

Mychalejko, Cyril, and Ryan, Ramor, "U.S. Military Funded Mapping Project in Oaxaca: Geographers Used to Gather Intelligence?," *Z Magazine*, April 2009.

Nagl, John, "The Evolution and Importance of Army/Marine Corps Field Manual 3-24, Counterinsurgency," *Small Wars Journal*, June 27, 2007.

National Research Council (U.S.), *Countering the Threat of Improvised Explosive Devices: Basic Research Opportunities, Abbreviated Version* (Washington, DC: National Academies Press, 2007).

National Research Council (U.S.), *Experimentation and Rapid Prototyping in Support of Counterterrorism* (Washington, DC: National Academies Press, 2009).

Naylor, Sean, "Stryker Soldiers Say Commanders Failed Them," *Military Times*, December 21, 2009.

Nigh, Norman, *An Operator's Guide to Human Terrain Teams* (Newport, RI: United Stated Naval War College, 2012).

Numrich, Susan K., *Human Terrain: A Tactical Issue or a Strategic C4I Problem?*, Institute for Defense Analyses, May 2008.

O'Brien, Sean M., *Mountain Partisans: Guerrilla Warfare in the Southern Appalachians, 1861-1865* (Westport, CT: Praeger, 1999).

Office of the Staff Judge Advocate, *Investigating Officer's Guide for AF 15-6 Informal Investigations*, Joint Readiness Training Center and Fort Polk, undated.

Office of the Under Secretary of Defense for Intelligence, *Response to the July 15, 2010 Draft of the CNA Report*, September 2010.

Orr, Colonel Billy J., *General George Crook, The Indian-Fighting Army, and Unconventional Warfare Doctrine: A Case for Developmental Immaturity* (Carlisle Barracks, PA: U.S. Army War College, 1992).

Orton, James Douglas, with Lamb, Chris, "Interagency National Security Teams: Can Social Science Contribute?," *PRISM* 2, no. 2 (March 2011), 47-64.

Ostrenko, Margaret, *Embedding HTS Pre-Deployment*, Human Terrain System, February 2011.

Ove, Torsten, "Afghan 'Poster Boy', Now an Adult, is Caught Between Two Worlds," *Pittsburgh Post-Gazette*, March 9, 2008.

Packer, George, "Knowing the Enemy: Can Social Scientists Redefine the "War on Terror"," *The New Yorker*, December 18, 2006.

Page, Julia, *Human Terrain Teams*, Masters Thesis, Virginia Tech University, February 23, 2012.

Paul, Christopher, Clarke, Colin P., and Grill, Beth, *Victory Has a Thousand Fathers: Sources of Success in Counterinsurgency* (Santa Monica, CA: RAND, 2010).

PBS Newshour, "Marines Get Crash Course in Afghan Culture," *PBS*, March 6, 2012.

Peters, Ralph, "Constant Conflict," *Parameters* no. 27, vol. 2 (Summer 1997), 4-14.

Peters, Ralph, "The Human Terrain of Urban Operations," *Parameters* iss. 30, no. 1 (Spring 2000), 4-12.

Peterson, Scott, "US Army's Strategy in Afghanistan: Better Anthropology," *The Christian Science Monitor*, September 7, 2007, W11.

Petraeus, David H., *Report to Congress on the Situation in Iraq*, September 10-11, 2007.

Pickett, M. Shands, "The Village Engagement Center: Stabilizing One Village at a Time," *Small Wars Journal*, September 30, 2010.

Pool, Robert (*Rapporteur*), "Sociocultural Data to Accomplish Department of Defense Missions," *Toward a Unified Social Framework: Workshop Summary*, National Research Council of the National Academies, 2011.

Porter, Patrick, "Good Anthropology, Bad History: The Cultural Turn in Studying War," *Parameters* no. 37, iss. 2 (2007), 45-58.

Pottinger, Matt, Hali Jilani, and Russo, Claire, "Half-Hearted: Trying to Win Afghanistan without Afghani Women," *Small Wars Journal*, February 18, 2010.

Press, Daryl G., *Urban Warfare: Options, Problems and the Future*, Conference Summary. Conference sponsored by the MIT Security Studies Program, Hanscom Air Force Base, Bedford, Massachusetts, U.S.A., May 20, 1998.

Price, David, "Counterinsurgency, Anthropology and Disciplinary Complicity," *Counterpunch*, February 3, 2009.

Price, David, "The Press and Human Terrain Systems—Counterinsurgency's Free Ride," *Zero Anthropology*, Maximilian Forte, May 29, 2009.

Prinslow, Karl, "The World Basic Information Library Program," *Military Intelligence Professional Bulletin* iss. 31, no. 4 (October-December 2005), 51-54.

Ramalingam, Ben, and Harry Jones, *Exploring the Science of Complexity Ideas and Implications for Development and Humanitarian Efforts* (London: Overseas Development Institute, 2008).

Renzi, Fred, "Networks: Terra Incognita and the Case for Ethnographic Intelligence," *Military Review* vol. 86, no. 5 (September-October 2006), 16- 22.

Report of the Defense Science Board Task Force, *Understanding Human Dynamics*, Office of the Under Secretary of Defense for Acquisition, Technology and Logistics, March 2009.

Reuss, Bob, *Human Terrain System Update for LTG Kimmons*, July 31, 2007.

Rice, Eric, "Caldwell Fears Cuts to Human Terrain Teams in Afghanistan," *Talk Radio News Service*, June 7, 2011.

Rid, Thomas, and Keaney, Thomas A., *Understanding counterinsurgency: Doctrine, Operations and Challenges* (Oxon, England: Routledge, 2010).

Roberts, Audrey, "A Unique Approach to Peacekeeping: Afghanistan and the

Human Terrain System," *Journal of International Peace Operations* vol. 5, no. 2 (September/October, 2006), 24-26.

Roberts, Audrey, "Embedding with the Military in Eastern Afghanistan: The Role of Anthropologists in Peace and Stability Operations," in, Walter Feichtinger, Ernst Felberbauer, and Erwin Schmidl ed., *International Crisis Management: Squaring the Circle*, Vienna and Geneva, July 2011.

Robertson, Jennifer, "*Reveille* For Anthropologists: Introduction-Anthologists in War," *Critical Asian Studies* vol. 42, no. 3 (2010), 425-433.

Robson, Seth, "A Woman's Touch: Engagement Teams Make Inroads with Afghanistan's Female Community," *Stars and Stripes*, October 9, 2010.

Rohde, David, "Army Enlists Anthropology in War Zones," *The New York Times*, October 5, 2007.

Rothstein, Hy S., *Afghanistan and the Troubled Future of Unconventional Warfare* (Annapolis, MD: U.S. Naval Institute Press, 2006)

Rubin, Elizabeth, "Battle Company is Out There," *The New York Times*, February 24, 2008.

Salmoni, B. A., "Advances in Predeployment Culture Training: The U.S. Marine Corps Approach," *Military Review* iss. 86, no. 6 (2006), 79-88.

Salmoni, Barack A. and Holmes-Eber, Paula, *Operational Culture for the Warfighter: Principles and Applications* (Quantico, VA: Marine Corps University, 2008).

Scales, Robert H., "Army Transformation: Implications for the Future," *Testimony before the House Armed Services Committee*, Washington, DC, July 15, 2004.

Scales, Robert H., "Clausewitz and World War IV—The Prussian Philosopher's Views Remain Valid on the Psycho-Cultural Battlefield," *Armed Forces Journal* vol. 143, no. 12 (July 2006), 14-24.

Scales, Robert H., "Culture-Centric Warfare," *Proceedings*, The United States Naval Institute vol. 130, iss. 10 (October 2004), 32-26.

Schivelbusch, Wolfgang, *The Culture of Defeat: On National Trauma, Mourning, and Recovery*, trans. by Jefferson Chase (New York, NY: Metropolitan Books, 2001).

Schwartzapfel, Beth, "Hearts and Minds," *Brown Alumni Magazine*, July 16, 2012.

Schweitzer, Martin, P., Col. Commander, 4th BCT/82 Airborne, United States Army. Before the House Armed Services Committee, Terrorism & Unconventional Threats Sub-Committee and the Research & Education Sub-Committee of the Science & Technology Committee , 110th Congress, 2nd Session Hearings on the Role of the Social and Behavioral Sciences in National Security, *United States House of Representatives*, April 24, 2008.

Schweitzer, Martin, Col., *DoD Briefing with Col. Schweitzer and Maj. Gen. Khaliq via Video Conference from Afghanistan in the Pentagon Briefing Room, Arlington, VA,* June 20, 2007.

Scully, Megan, and Kreisher, Otto, "Panel Sinks Navy's $2.5b Request for DDG-1000 Destroyer," *Congress Daily*, May 8, 2008.

Sepp, Kalev I., "Best Practices in Counterinsurgency," *Military Review*, May-June 2005, 8-12.

Sestokas, Jeff M., James A. Bell, David R. Manning, and William R. Sanders, *Training Methods to Build Human Terrain Mapping Skills* (Alexandria, VA: U.S. Army Research Institute for the Behavioral and Social Sciences, 2010).

Sewall, John O.B., "Adapting Conventional Military Forces for the New Environment," in Kanter, Arnold, and Brooks, Linton F., *U.S. Intervention Policy for the Post-Cold War World: New Challenges and New Responses* (New York, NY: W.W. Norton, 1994).

Sewall, Sarah, and McFate, Montgomery, "A Discussion about Counterinsurgency," *Charlie Rose*, December 24, 2007.

Shachtman, Noah, "Army Anthropologist's Controversial Culture Clash," *Wired: Danger Room*, September 23, 2008.

Shachtman, Noah, "Army Social Scientists Calm Afghanistan, Make Enemies at Home," *Wired*, November 29, 2007.

Shachtman, Noah, "House Panel Puts the Brakes on 'Human Terrain' (Updated)," *Wired: Danger Room*, May 20, 2010.

Shachtman, Noah, "How Technology Almost Lost the War: In Iraq, the Critical Network are Social—Not Electronic," *Wired*, iss. 15.12, November 27, 2007.

Shachtman, Noah, "'Human Terrain' Called Year's Biggest Euphemism," *Wired: Danger Room*, January 8, 2008.

Shachtman, Noah, "*Que Curioso!* U.S. Army Cultural Advisers Now Eyeing Mexico," *Wired: Danger Room*, May 2, 2012.

Shane, Leo, III and Baron, Kevin, "Petraeus Confirmation Hearing, Live," *Stars and Stripes*, June 29, 2010.

Shapiro, Mark, *The Human Terrain System: A Question of Ethics and Integrity*, in Forte, Maximilian C. eds, *The New Imperialism: Militarism, Humanism, and Occupation, Volume 1.* (Montreal, Canada: Alert Press, 2010), 69-77.

Sheikh, Fawzia, "Army to Boost Human Terrain Team Effort Despite Growing Pains," *Inside the Army* vol. 20, no. 22 (June 2, 2008).

Sheikh, Fawzia, "Bolstered Army Human Terrain Effort Expected with Afghanistan Surge," *Inside the Pentagon* vol. 26, no. 11 (March 18, 2010).

Sheikh, Fawzia, "Next Human Terrain Team Phase Aims to Institutionalize Practices," *Inside the Army* vol. 21, no. 6 (February 16, 2009).

Sheikh, Fawzia, "Report on Anthropologists in the Theater Tentatively Pegged for June," *Inside the Pentagon* vol. 24, no. 22 (May 29, 2008).

Sherman, Jason, "DOD seeks $102 Million in FY—09 Budget for Immediate Warfighter Needs," *Inside the Navy* vol. 21, no. 6.

Shweder, Richard A., 'A True Culture War," *The New York Times*, October 27, 2007.

Silverman, Adam L., "The Why and How of Human Terrain Teams," *Inside Higher Ed*, February 19, 2009.

Silverman, Barry G., "Human Terrain Data: What Should We Do With It?," Presented at *Winter Simulation Conference '07*, December 1, 2007.

Simons, Anna, "Anthropology, Culture and COIN in a Hybrid Warfare World," in, Paul Brister, William Natter, and Robert Tomes ed., *Hybrid Warfare and Transnational Threats: Perspectives for an Era of Persistent Conflict* (New York: Council for Emerging National Security Studies, 2011).

Simons, Anna, "Asymmetries, Anthropology, and War," *Pointer* vol. 37, no. 2 (September 2011), 56-64.

Simons, Anna, "Got Vision? Unity of Vision in Policy and Strategy: What It Is, and Why We Need It," *Advancing Strategic Thought Series*, Strategic Studies Institute, July 2010.

Simons, Anna, *How Critical Should Critical Thinking Be? Teaching Soldiers in Wartime*, in, Robert Albro, George Marcus, Laura McNamara, & Monica Schoch-Spana ed., *Anthropologists in the Security Scape* (Walnut Creek, CA: Left Coast Press, 2011).

Simons, Anna, *The Company They Keep: Life Inside the U.S. Army Special Forces* (New York, NY: The Free Press, 1997).

Skelton, Ike and Cooper, Jim, "You're Not from Around Here, are You?," *Joint Force Quarterly* 36 (2004), 12-16.

Slaikeu, Karl A. "Winning the War in Afghanistan: An Oil Spot Plus Strategy for Coalition Forces," *Small Wars Journal*, May 18, 2009.

Sorrentino, Diana, *Sociocultural Intelligence: Understanding the Theories, Practice and Importance of the Sociological and Cultural Discipline as it applies to your Collection and Analysis of Intelligence Data*, BRG Research Group, February 10, 2011.

Spellmon, Scott, *DoD News Briefing with Col. Spellmon From Afghanistan*, February 4, 2009.

Spellmon, Scott, *DoD News Briefing with Colonel John Spiszer, Via Teleconference from Afghanistan, at the Pentagon Briefing Room, Arlington, VA*, November 18, 2009.

Speyer, Arthur and Henning, Job, *MCIA's Cultural Intelligence Methodology and Lessons Learned*, cited in Lee Ellen Friedland, Gary W. Shaeff, Jessica Glicken Turnley, "Sociocultural Perspectives: A New Intelligence Paradigm," Report on the conference at The MITRE Corporation McLean, VA, September 12, 2006, June 2007, Document Number 07-

1220/MITRE Technical Report MTR070244.

Spiszer, John M. "Counterinsurgency in Afghanistan Lessons Learned by a Brigade Combat Team," *Military Review* vol. 91, iss. 1 (January-February 2011), 73-79.

Spillius, Alex, "NATO Chief Tells US to Stop Attacking European Allies," *Telegraph.co.uk*, September 29, 2009.

Spradlin, Jennifer, "Human Terrain Teams: Mapping a Course for a Peaceful, Prosperous Iraq," *Soldiers* vol. 65, iss. 10 (October 2010), 6-7.

Stannard, Matthew B., "Montgomery McFate's Mission: Can One Anthropologist Possibly Steer the Course in Iraq," *The San Francisco Gate*, April 29, 2007.

Stanton, John, "All American Human Terrain System 2012: Arrogance & Incompetence & East Money," *Pravda*, June 8, 2012.

Stanton, John, "Death Threat Tarnishes US Army Human Terrain System," *Zero Anthropology*, February 26, 2009.

Stanton, John, "Iran Should Release Amir Hekmati," *Pravda*, January 1, 2012.

Stanton, John, "Pentagon's Phase Zero Intelligence Human Terrain Program: Foreign internal defense, diversion or drug war?" *Intrepid Reporter*, May 2, 2012.

Stanton, John, "Syria on the Horizon: Leadership, mission reboot at Army Human Terrain," *Intrepid Report*, June 21, 2012.

Stanton, John, "US Army 101st Airborne Investigative Report on Human Terrain System: *Toxic at Headquarters and in Bagram*," *Zero Anthropology*, April 2, 2009.

Star, Alexander, "Afghanistan: What the Anthropologists Say," *The New York Times*, November 18, 2011.

Star, Alexander, "Applied Anthropology: Can the Study of Politics, Power and Culture at the Local Level Reshape Efforts to Rebuild Afghanistan?," *New York Times*, Sunday, November 20, 2011.

Stemets, Bill, "Anthropologists at War: New Military Program that Embeds Anthropologists with Soldiers has Academics up in Arms," *In These Times*, June 19, 2008.

Strange, Joe, and Zinni, Anthony C., *Capital "W" war: a Case for Strategic Principles of War: (Because Wars are Conflicts of Societies, not Tactical Exercises Writ Large)* (Quantico, VA: Marine Corps University, 1998).

Tan, Michelle, "Report Blames Lapses on Stryker Commander," *Army Times*, November 27, 2011.

Tarzi, Amin, and Lamb, Robert D., "Measuring Perceptions about the Pashtun People," *The Center for Strategic and International Studies*, March 2011.

Tett, Gillian, "Interrogation is not a social science," *Financial Times*, November

4, 2011.

Thomas, T. L., "Grozny 2000: Urban Combat Lessons Learned," *Military Review* vol. 80, no. 4 (2000), 50-58.

Thompson, Jonathon D., "Integrating the BCT Human Terrain Team with the Maneuver Company," *Infantry* iss. 99, no. 4 (November-December 2010), 9-12.

Tolk Andreas, Davis, Paul K., Huiskamp, Wim, Klein, Gary W., Schuab, Gary, and Wall, James A., "Towards Methodological Approaches to Meet the Challenges of Human, Social, Cultural, and Behavioral (HSCB) Modeling," *Proceedings—Winter Simulation Conference*, 2010, 912-924.

Trachtenberg, Marc, *Social Scientists and National Security Policymaking*, Speech given to the Notre Dam International Security Program, April 22-23, 2012.

TRADOC G2 Comments on the National Defense University paper titled "Human Terrain Team Performance: An Explanation," August 24, 2012, Passed to NDU team, November 15, 2012.

Tucker, David and Lamb, Christopher J., *United States Special Operations Forces* (New York, N.Y.: Columbia University Press, 2007).

Tunnell, Harry, *Task Force Stryker Network-Centric Operations in Afghanistan*, Defense and Technology Paper #84 (Washington, DC: Center for Technology and National Security Policy, October 2011).

Tzu, Sun, *The Illustrated Art of War*, trans. Thomas Cleary (Boston, MA: Shambhala, 1998).

Umble, Amy Flowers, "Priest leads a full life," *Fredericksburg Free Lance-Star*, May 13, 2007.

U.S. Army Center of Military History, *Medal of Honor Recipients*, website, Citation for Herman Henry Hanneken.

United States Government, FM31-20, *Doctrine for Special Forces Operations*, (Washington, DC, Department of the Army Headquarters, 20 April 1990).

United States Government, *Marine Corps Vision & Strategy 2025*, (Washington, DC: U.S. Marine Corps, 2008).

United States Government, *Report of the Defense Science Board Task Force on Understanding Human Dynamics* (Washington, DC: Office of the Under Secretary of Defense for Acquisition, Technology, and Logistics, 2009).

United States Forces-Iraq Assessment of HTS (Completed Aug 2010), PowerPoint, undated.

United States Forces-Iraq HTS Assessment DEC 2010, PowerPoint, undated.

United States Civilian Board of Contract Appeals, *CBCA 2230-TRAV In the Matter of Audrey Roberts*, June 21, 2011.

United States Government, Field Manual 3-24/Marine Corps Warfighting

Publication 3-33/5, *Counterinsurgency* (Washington, DC: Department of the Army, December 2006).

United States Government, House Armed Services Committee, *H.R. 5136, National Defense Authorization Act for Fiscal Year 2011*, Executive Summary.

United States Government, *Small Wars Manual: U.S. Marine Corps, 1940*, (Washington, DC: U.S. G.P.O., 1940)

Vandiver, John, "AFRICOM building research center," *Stars and Stripes*, June 15, 2009.

Varhola, Christopher, *U.S. Africa Command Intelligence and Knowledge Development Social Science Research Center (SSRC)*, Information Paper, AFRICOM.

Vergano, Dan, and Wise, Elisabeth, "Should Anthropologists Work Alongside Soldiers?," *USA Today*, December 9, 2008.

Vice Chief of Staff of the Army Assessment Outcomes, 2 of 2, PowerPoint, undated.

Vine, David, "Enabling the Kill Chain," *The Chronicle of Higher Education* (November 30, 2007), B9-B10.

Vlahos, Kelley, "Can I get You Some Team with That Airstrike?," *The American Conservative*, blog, September 21, 2010.

Voa News, "European Governments Restrict their NATO Forces in Afghanistan," *VoaNews.com*, March 4, 2010.

Wahab, Saima, *In My Father's Country: An Afghan Woman Defies Her Fate* (New York, NY: Crown Publishers, 2012).

Warren, Tarn, "ISAF and Afghanistan: The Impact of Failure on NATO's Future," *Joint Force Quarterly* 59 (4th Quarter, 2010), 45-51.

Weinberger, Sharon, "Gates: Human Terrain Teams Going Through 'Growing Pains,'" *Wired: Danger Room*, April 15, 2008.

Weinberger, Sharon, "'Human Terrain' Hits Rocky Ground," *Nature*, Volume 465 (June 2010), 993.

Weinberger, Sharon, "Pentagon Cultural Analyst Helped Interrogate Detainees in Afghanistan: 'Experiment' raises alarm among social scientists," *Nature*, October 18, 2011.

Weinberger, Sharon, "The Pentagon's Culture Wars: What Began Several Years Ago as an Attempt to Recruit Social Scientists to Help the Military has Sparked a Broader Debate About Militarizing Academia," *Nature* vol. 455, (October 2, 2008), 583-585.

White, Nathan, *Developing U.S. Intelligence Capabilities for Population-centric Counterinsurgency and Stability Operations: Learning from Iraq and Afghanistan*, 2011.

Whitlock, Craig, "Members of Stryker Combat Brigade in Afghanistan accused of killing civilians for sport," *The Washington Post*, September 18,

2010.

Willey, Robert, "The Theory and Practice of War," *The Boston Magazine*, May 2009.

Winnefield, James A., *Intervention in Intrastate Conflict: Implications for the Army in the Post-Cold War Era*, (Santa Monica, CA: RAND, 2005).

Wong, Kristina, "Afghanistan Civilian Surge Could Last Decade," *ABC News*, March 4, 2010.

Wynn, Lisa, "The Story Behind an HTS Picture," *Culture Matters: Applying Anthropology*, September 22, 2006.

Yarger, Harry R. ed, *Short of General War Perspectives on the Use of Military Power in the 21st Century* (Carlisle, PA: Strategic Studies Institute, 2010).

Yingling, Paul, LTC, "A Failure of Generalship," *Armed Forces Journal*, May 2007.

Young Pelton, Robert, "Afghanistan: The New War for Hearts and Minds," *Men's Journal*, January 21, 2009.

Young Pelton, Robert, "Robert Young Pelton's Response to the U.S. Army," *Men's Journal*, February 12, 2009.

Zehfuss, Maja, "Culturally Sensitive War? The Human Terrain System and the Seduction of Ethics," *Security Dialogue* vol. 43, no. 2 (2012), 175-190.

Zimmerman, Laura A., Sestokas, Jeff M., Bell, James A., Manning, David R., Sanders, William R., *Training Methods to Build Human Terrain Mapping Skills*, Research Report 1933 (Fort Knox, KY: U.S. Army Research Institute for the Behavioral and Social Sciences, October 2010).

Zumer, John, "Human Terrain Teams Build Friendships, Future," *Armed Forces Press Service*, March 2, 2009.

INDEX

9/11 (see September 11)
101st Air Assault Division, 59
10th Mountain Division, 32, 34, 186
II Marine Expeditionary Force, 57
5th Marines,
1st Battalion, 182
4th Infantry Division,
3rd Brigade, 29
82nd Airborne
4th Brigade Combat Team, 34-35, 42
Abizaid, John, 28
academia, 44, 47, 82, 119, 120
Ackerman, Spencer, 74
Adamson, William , 28
Adversary Cultural Knowledge and National
    Security, conference on, 27
Afghan Security Forces/ Afghan National
    Security Forces, 18, 64, 126, 209
AF1, 36-45, 68-69, 81, 120, 246
    St. Benoit's replacement by Bhatia, 56;
    Bhatia's leadership of, 53;
    casualties, 56;
    Combat Readiness Center training, 221;
    expulsion of team leader, 60, 64;
    evaluation by human terrain system of,
        40-41, 170;
    support to Schweitzer's brigade, 36-37,
        42
AF2, 59
    incompatible communications, 115;
AF4
    Ayala's shooting of Salam, 56;
    casualties, 56;
    IED attack in Kandahar, 56;
    Loyd's death, 56;
    Salam's attack on Loyd, 56;
    shift to Canadian forces, 64, 84;
    team leader transfer to theater coordi-
        nation element, 71
AF6
    deployment with marines at Camp
        Leatherneck, 68;
    Pashtun Sexuality report (see Pashtun
        Sexuality, report on), 59
AF7
    Foldberg's marine leadership of, 68-69
AF8, 59, 68
AF9, 68, 246
AF10, 64, 68
AF12
    special operations forces relationship,
        69, 81
AF14
    support provided to the French by, 64,
        69
AF15
    support provided to the Spanish and
        Italians by, 64
AF16
    work with non-U.S. special operations
        forces, 69, 81
AF17, 68
    support provided to the Poles by, 64
Afghanistan, 1-2, 6, 12-14, 18, 21, 26-
        27, 32-39, 41-42, 44, 46, 53, 55-
        57, 59-60, 62-66, 68-69, 71, 74,
        78-80, 82-83, 85-86, 107, 110,
        113-114, 125, 127, 133, 138-142,
        144-145, 149-151, 173-174, 179-
        181, 183, 188, 193-195, 201, 206-
        208, 212, 214, 217, 221-222, 225,
        227, 235, 238, 240-242, 244, 246
    human terrain team creation of reading
        list on, 114
Afghans, 20, 66, 145, 179, 186
    human terrain team contribution to
        water management solution for,
        18-19;
    lethal operations undermining U.S.
        forces credibility with, 54;
    non-overt means of fighting back Tali-
        ban by, 58;

participant-observation studies on, 37;
reputation of armed human terrain
teams among, 62;
U.S. forces cross-cultural tensions with,
1, 209
Africa Command, 55, 83
creation of Sociocultural Research and
Advisory Teams (SCRATs) at, 83
Air and Space Expeditionary Task Force, 79,
American Anthropological Association
(AAA), 61, 178
negative reaction to human terrain
teams by, 55, 119
Andar District, 39
Apache Indians, 10
APTIMA
survey research contract, 69
ArcGIS, 42
Army Civil Affairs and Psychological Operations Command
cultural preparation of the environment
project involvement by, 29
authorities, 59, 61, 74, 108-109, 114, 116-
118, 128, 151, 154, 178, 205
Axis Pro, 222
Ayala, Don
killing of Abdul Salam, 56
BAE subcontractor, Echota
effort to replace, 50
BAE Systems contract, 34, 41, 44, 48, 58,
70, 77-80, 119-121, 132, 145
contractors, 50;
hiring process, 44, 48, 50, 61, 70, 75,
132, 145;
loss, 79;
performance, 58, 72, 75, 77-80, 119
Bagram Air Base, 35-36, 59, 68, 115, 124,
143, 242
AF12 relationship with special operations forces at, 69, 81
Balkans, 11
Baqubah city, 27-28
Bartholf, Mark, 72
Battle of Monongahela, 8
Bhatia, Michael
death, 56, 119-120;
team leadership, 53
Bowden, Jeff, 71, 227
Braddock, Edward, 8
British colonists

use of sociocultural knowledge by, 8-9
British Empire, 9, 119
Brown University, 57
Bush administration, 26, 35, 38,
Cabayan, Hriar, 28, 30
Camp Dwyer, 68
Camp Leatherneck, 68
Canada, 84-85, 124
human terrain team support to, 64, 122;
see also White Situational Awareness
Teams
Cardon, Ed, 66
Central Command, 28, 38, 41, 45, 78, 120,
expansion of HTTs beyond, 45, 80-81;
see also JUONS
Center for Strategic and Budgetary Assess-
ments, 46
Chehi Gazi village, 56,
Chesser, Nancy, 28, 30
Chiarelli, Peter, 6
Christian Science Monitor, 39,
civil affairs, 16, 20, 29, 63, 122, 182, 218-219
Civil War, 9
civil-military teams, 192, 204
Clark, Jen, 72, 74
Clark, Karen, 39, 72
CNA, 20, 52, 67, 71-72, 74-77, 80, 172-173,
175, 203, 205, 240
see also Congressionally Directed As-
sessment of the Human Terrain
System
Cold War, 11, 44
combat advisory training, 79
Combat Lifesaver training, 140
combatant commands, 45, 80-81
Combating Terrorism Technical Support
Office, 34
Combined Joint Interagency Task Force, 79
Combined Joint Special Operations Forces-
Afghanistan, 141
Combined Joint Task Force 82, 38
see also JUONS
Combined Joint Task Force-Horn of Africa,
55
Commander Information Request, 140
commander relationship with HTTs, 1-3
assessments of HTTs, xv, 2-3, 20-21,
86, 157n4, 169, 175-188, 238-239,
241, 244
expectations, 65, 68, 150, 176, 186

HTT commanders, ix, xiii, xiv, 1-3, 16, 18, 42, 48, 55, 59, 63-65, 71, 75, 77-78, 111-113, 117-118, 121-129, 135, 140, 142, 145, 164n216, 169-195, 197n37, 200-204, 246-249

Human Terrain Team Handbook and improvement in, 64,

Schweitzer and AF1, 36-37, 42, 170, 195n2, 242, 246

ordering of an HTT team leader off the base, 2, 156

team leaders and commanders, 2, 16, 60, 64, 112, 126, 135, 145, 157, 178, 187

use of HTTs for kinetic targeting, 43, 54, 93n156, 111,

Common Task Training, 234-235,

Company Intelligence Support Team, 3rd Brigade Combat Team, 10th Mountain Division

Scott Mitchell's village census, 186

composition, team, 16, 109, 141-146

competencies, 141, 144-146

defined, 109, 141

diversity, 142-144

personality, 146

skill, 141-144

team member qualifications, 144

Concept of Operations

approval of first HTS Concept of Operations, 36;

update in collaboration with Central Command, 41

Congress, U.S./ Capitol Hill, xv, 10, 39, 45

criticism of HTTs heard by, 59, 74, 206

funding HTTs, 60, 66

Krepinevich testimony on importance of language and culture, 46

McFate on HTS, 46

Office of the Undersecretary of Defense for Intelligence response to, 2-3, 66, 76

Petreaus testimony on human terrain, 1

Scales testimony on sociocultural information, 26

Schweitzer testimony on HTTs, 2, 42, 63

Senate, 60

see also Congressionally Directed Assessment of the Human Terrain

System; House Armed Services Committee; House Committee on Science and Technology; House of Representatives, U.S.; National Defense Authorization Act for FY2009; National Defense Authorization Act for FY2010

Congressionally Directed Assessment of the Human Terrain System, 75, 172

data on HTS budget, 47, 67

data on HTS class sizes, 52

data on number of HTTS and brigade-size combat units, 77

commanders assessments of HTTs, 175-176

TRADOC investigation, 72-73

HTS management, 76

see also HTT evaluation

Connable, Ben

criticisms of HTS program, 63

Consolidated Stability Operations Center, 15,

Cooper, Clint, 56

Costello, Mike

measures of effectiveness for evaluating local sympathies, 19

counterinsurgency

U.S. adoption of, xiv, 12,

importance of human terrain/sociocultural knowledge in, xv, 1, 26, 65, 181, 185

doctrine, 2, 6, 208-209

attudinal data and, 19, 181

HTS serving, 3, 20, 32, 35, 45, 57, 78, 112, 142, 190-191, 194, 201-204, 213

see also U.S. Army/Marine Counterinsurgency Field Manual (FM/FMFM 3-24)

Crook, George, 9-10, 207

cross-functional teams, ix, 3

cultures of, 107, 132

decision-making in, 108, 127-128

design of, 125, 192, 204, 213, 234

HTTs as, 16-17, 35, 125, 174, 201, 236

learning in, 108, 136

performance variables, 49

purpose in, 108

organization theory of, 48, 86, 107, 239-240

rewards systems in, 109, 147

structural empowerment of, 108, 116,

123
culture, team, 132-35
    SF connection; 135
cultural intelligence (see sociocultural)
    definition, 8, 176, 178;
    architecture, 181, 188, 190, 192, 201;
    see also Fixing Intelligence: A Blueprint
        for Making Intelligence Relevant
        in Afghanistan; sociocultural
Cultural Knowledge Consortium, 81
Cultural Operations Research-Human Ter-
    rain System (COR-HTS), 32, 221
Cultural Preparation of the Environment,
    27-31, 41
    project on, 27-29;
    tool, 28
curriculum (see HTS Core Curriculum)
Dallas Morning News, 57
Damon, Britt, 36, 125
Dari, 36, 121, 139
decision-making, team, 108, 127
    civil-military relations, 127-128
    conflict, 127-131
decision implementation, 127-131
    heterogeneous perspectives, 127-131
    Myers-Briggs, 128
Defense Advanced Research Projects
    Agency, 27
Defense Cultural Specialist Unit (UK), 84,
Defense Intelligence Agency, 83
Defense Civilian Intelligence Personnel
    System (DCIPS), 223,
Defense Science Board, 8, 83, 203,
    see also Understanding Human Dy-
        namics
Dempsey, Martin,
    HTS at TRADOC, 69-70, 218
Department of Defense, U.S./Pentagon
    Bureaucracy, 27, 33
    creation of new constructs for human
        terrain analysis, 8
    Office of Personnel and Readiness, 44
    Office of the Secretary of Defense, ix,
        41
    Office of the Undersecretary of De-
        fense for Intelligence, 2
Department of State, U.S.
District Support Teams, 83;
    Humanitarian Information Unit, 28-29
detainee interrogations, 80

Dixon, Chris, 69
Diyala province, 28-29
Djibouti, 55, 58
doctrine, organization, training, materiel,
    leadership, and education, personnel
    and facilities (DOTMLPF), 170
doctrine, 63, 218
    counterinsurgency, 2, 12, 13, 51, 112,
        208;
    HTS doctrine, 64, 111, 170, 178, 202;
    Special Forces, 11;
    see also HTS doctrine development
        team, Training and Doctrine
        Command
embedded reporters, 39, 80
Embedded Training Teams, 16
empowerment, team, 114-118
    MAP-HT problems, 115
    Mobility, 115-116
    problematic personalities, 117
    psychological empowerment, 114
    reliance on brigade, 114-118
    resource empowerment, 114
    structural empowerment, 114
Featherstone, Steve, 40, 43
Female Engagement Teams, 16, 82
*Fixing Intelligence: A Blueprint for Making Intel-
    ligence Relevant in Afghanistan*, 71
Flynn, Michael, 71, 169, 181-183, 185-186,
    188, 206, 214
Foldberg, John, 68
Fondacaro, Steve
    authority under Intergovernmental
        Personnel Agreement;
    becomes HTS Program Manager, 32-33
    IED Task Force and, 32
    management of HTS, 33-73
    meeting with McFate and Jackson at
        CPE, 27-31
    resignation, 73
    selection of GIS toolkit, 42
Foreign Military Studies Office (FMSO), 26,
    29-34, 36, 110, 142, 242
Fort Bragg, 57
Fort Irwin, 139
Fort Leavenworth, 14, 26, 29, 34, 36, 39, 43,
    49, 58, 60-63, 68, 70-72, 79, 110, 113,
    121, 123, 132, 136-137, 139-140, 146,
    222, 227, 231, 233, 236
Fort Monroe, 39,

Fort Polk, 62, 79, 139, 221, 233, 236

Forward Operating Base Salerno, 36, 40, 41, 60, 264

French units, 64, 69
    attached HTS units to, 64;
    see also Task Force Lafayette

French and Indian wars, 9

French, Mark, 72

funding
    CPE tool, 28-29
    JIEDDO, 31-32
    Department of Defense bureaucracy, 33
    Combating Terrorism Technical Support Office, 34
    Joint Rapid Acquisition Council, 38
    mismanagement of congressional funding requests, 60
    coordination with Sociocultural Dynamics Working Group, 83
    see also Congressionally Directed Assessment of the Human Terrain System

Funston, Frederick, 10, 207

Gardez city, 37

Gates, Robert, 44-45
    concern for HTS, 45, 202;
    support for HTS, 44-45

gender diversity, 142-143

Geographic Information Systems, 28
    see also CPE; MAP-HT; ArcGIS

GEOINT Summit, 57

George Mason University, 57

Georgia Tech Research Institute (GTRI), 50

Germans, 122
    attachment of HTT to, 64;
    Social Science Research Branch, 83;
    Tactical HUMINT teams, 122

Ghazni province, 55

Glevum Associates, 16

Global Information System, 28

Grau, Lester, 31

Greer, Jim, 39, 53, 58, 71, 74,

grey goo, 85

guerillas, 9

Haiti, 10-11

Hamilton, Sharon, 25, 75, 78, 82, 112
    ambushed, 56;
    HTS leader, 74-75, 242;
    presentation at Special Operations

Summit in Tampa, 81;
    retirement, 230

Hammond, Jeffrey, 187

Hanneken, Herman, 10, 207,

Harper, Stephen, 64

Harper's Magazine, 40

Harvard University, 57

Helmand province, 59, 68, 242

high-value targeting teams, 217

Holbert, Robert, 35-36, 125

House Armed Services Committee, U.S.
    commission of study on HTS, 66, 92, 172;
    FY11 Defense Authorization Bill, 68;
    Scales testimony on, 26;
    Lennox testimony on, 75;
    see also House Committee on Science and Technology

House Committee on Science and Technology
    joint hearing on "The Role of Social and Behavior Sciences in National Security", 42

House of Representatives, U.S.
    FY 2009 HTS program rider approval by, 76

HTS casualties, 56, 119-120

HTT member shot by sniper in Iraq, 57;
    Bhatia killed by an IED in Afghanistan, 56;
    Suveges killed by a bomb in Sadr City, 56;
    Loyd burning incident, 56-57

HTS Core Curriculum,
    adjustments to, 49
    assessments of, 71, 73, 138, 204
    creation of training curriculum, 39
    curriculum development team, 232
    description of, 221-236
    Georgia Tech Research institute redesign of training curriculum, 50
    Fondacaro training curriculum review/2010 curriculum conference, 71, 73, 204

HTS Doctrine Development Team, 225, 231

HTS management, 14, 16, 35, 38, 40-41, 44, 46, 49-50, 52, 55-58, 63-81, 102n376, 107, 110, 119, 138-139, 171-172, 183, 189, 192, 199n93, 202-204, 206, 209n5, 227

AF1 assessment team, 41
assessment of HTTs performance, 48-49
attempts to stabilize program effectiveness, 79
creation of management team, 32-33
guidance to first HTT, 36
HTS management structure 2010, 13, 72
    request for Fondacaro's resignation, 73
    new HTS management, 74, 80
    post-Afghanistan future of HTS, 80
    tensions with TRADOCG2, 65, 73, 203
    transfer of HTT members from contractor agreements to Department of the Army, 60
    see also Congressionally Directed Assessment of the Human Terrain System; COR-HTS
HTS Reachback Research Center, 32, 81
    availability to recruits, 54
    Fort Leavenworth, 14, 39
    Fort Monroe, 14, 39
    reaction to Pashtun sexuality report, 51
    Subject Matter Experts Network (SMEnet), 120
    telephone survey of HTTs, 226
    utilization by HTTs of, 54
HTS recruiting
    BAE approach to, 61
    class sizes, 52
    standards, 44, 70, 142, 145
    see also Human Terrain System Yearly Report 2007-2008;
HTS training cycle, 49, 51-52, 110, 132, 137, 139, 225, 233-35
HTT evaluation, 44
    commander evaluations, 20
Human Terrain System: Evaluation of the Human Terrain Team Recruitment and Selection Process, 48
    Joseph study, 20, 70, 145
    see also Congressionally Directed Assessment of the Human Terrain System; Contingency Capabilities: Analysis of Human Terrain Teams in Afghanistan; Human Terrain System Yearly Report 2007-2008, The; Human Terrain Team Trip Report: A "Team of Teams"
HTT job description, 70

HTT performance, 74, 177-180, 188, 192, 200, 204, 206, 213
    difficulty of assessing, 2, 4, 25, 43, 48, 77, 139
    methodology used to assess, 3, 20-21, 107, 238-245
    recruitment and training, 45, 65, 73
    standards/requirements/measures of, 17, 19, 47, 86, 139, 172, 174, 227, 231
    variables of, 108-157, 169, 173, 201
    variation in, 2, 69, 78, 83, 113, 171-175, 194, 203
    see also BAE Systems contract; for studies, HTT evaluation
HTT weapons, 61-62, 138
Human terrain
    combating IEDs and, 27-35, 58
    cultural preparation of the environment and, 41
    decisive terrain of counterinsurgency, 1-2, 64, 65, 78, 206, 213
    historical use of, 9
    origin, 26-27
    software, 34, 41-43, 65, 114-115
    synonym for sociocultural knowledge, 2, 7-8
    see also sociocultural knowledge
Human Terrain Analysis Teams (HTATs)
    composition of, 14, 16, 61
    empowerment of, 117-118
    HTAT Bagram, 59, 143, 178, 188
    structure of, 79, 124
Human Terrain System (HTS)
    academia and, 47, 82, 119-120
    American Anthropological Association criticism of, 55, 61, 119, 178
    Establishment, 26-35
    media attention, 39-40, 44, 47, 51, 55, 57, 80-81
    mission, 6-21
    resources, 44, 50, 78-79, 85, 86, 114
    roles/job descriptions, 70
    training, 3, 14, 17-18, 33-37, 39, 41, 44-45, 47-55, 58, 60-65, 69-71, 73, 79, 110, 121, 125, 132, 135-140, 149, 194, 204, 206, 213, 221-236
    TRADOC G2 relationship with, 31-33, 43, 50, 58, 69-70, 73-79, 171
    use of capability in combatant com-

mands, 45, 80-81
  see also, BAE Systems contract;
      Civil Affairs; USASOC,
      Commander's Guide, Concept
      of Operations, COR-HTS; for
      studies, HTT evaluation; JUONS;
      FMSO; funding; MAP-HT; HTS
      Reachback Research Center;
      Special Forces; Theater Coordina-
      tion Element (Kabul); training
      cycle
Human Terrain Team Handbook, 64
Human Terrain Teams (HTTs)
  AFRICOM use of, 55
  cross-functional teams, xiii, 14, 16-17,
      21, 35, 49, 86, 107, 109, 116, 123-
      125, 132, 136, 147, 151, 174, 192,
      201, 204, 213, 218, 234, 236
  authority delegated by HTS, 109, 114-
      118, 178
  brigade-size combat units in Afghani-
      stan and, 77
  composition, 16, 109, 141-146, 174,
      194, 201, 226
  determinants of effectiveness, 19-20,
      40, 42-44, 48, 53-54, 57, 108-109,
      130, 142, 145, 148, 150, 172-176,
      192, 194, 213
  diversity in, 128, 141-146
  formation process, 53, 132
  group dynamics, xv, 48, 123-127, 143,
      193, 244
  brigade staff structure, 16, 36-40, 48,
      54, 60, 121, 126-129, 174
  HTAT Bagram sexual harassment case,
      143
  influence on Female Engagement
      Teams, 82
  lack of resources, 114-118
  leaders, 2, 16, 32, 36, 43, 51-52, 59-60,
      62-64, 71, 116-117, 123-141, 143-
      157, 187, 193-194
  Schweitzer's endorsement of, 2, 42
  NORTHCOM use of, 81
  personnel issues, 47-51, 61-62, 65, 70-
      74, 114-118
  purpose of, 110-113
  Lennox endorsement of, 75
  Sociocultural Research and Advisory
      Teams (SCRATs) differences with,

      83-84
  SOCOM use of, 57, 81, 218
  tensions with Social Science Research
      and Analysis (SSRAs) program,
      53, 71
  weapons and, 61-62
  non-Army units (Marines, SOF, NATO
      allies) and, 37, 63, 64, 68, 69, 79,
      82, 116, 122, 182, 246
  see also commander relationship with
      HTTs; for studies, HTT evalua-
      tion; HTS; JUONS; MAP-HT;
      Pashtun Sexuality, report on Hu-
      man Terrain Team Trip Report:
      A"Team of Teams"
improvised explosive devices (IEDs)
  attacks on HTTs;
  HTS and defeating;
  IED Task Force, 27, 29, 34
information operations, 13, 18, 40, 122, 170,
      180
INMARSAT, 223
Institute for Defense Analyses, 20, 173-175,
      205, 240
Institute for the Study of War, 246
intelligence
  HTT relationship with, 16, 37, 40-41,
      111-112, 177-178
  sociocultural knowledge and, 7-8, 9-13,
      33, 83, 176-177
intelligence architecture, 181-188
  see also Fixing Intelligence
intelligence fusion cells, 26, 127
interagency, 34, 70, 73, 79, 239
Intergovernmental Personnel Agreement,
      58, 72
internal/interpersonal conflict (on HTTs),
      43, 59, 129, 146, 191-193
International Security Assistance Force
      (ISAF), 79, 178
  ANSF murders, 208
  COMISAF campaign plan, 71
  Flynn as J2 in, 71, 181
Iraq, 1, 4, 6, 12-14, 19, 26-33, 35, 38-39, 41,
      43-47, 53, 55, 57-58, 62-66, 70,
      80, 82, 85, 107, 110, 120, 138-139,
      142, 206-207, 212, 214, 216-217,
      221-222, 225, 227, 235, 240,
  HTT performance in, 44-45, 170-171,
      173, 178, 189;

Iraq Freedom Fund (IFF), 31;
  Status of Forces Agreement, 60;
  see also HTTs, IED Task Force
      irregular war, 4, 44-46, 207, 214,
          216-218
      American experience with, 9;
      Krepinevich on, 46;
      sociocultural knowledge in, 4, 45, 202,
          209, 217-218
Italian units, 64, 121
Jackson, Andrea, 27-31, 186
  first meeting with McFate and Fon-
      dacaro, 28;
  proposal for new organization, 29-31
Jalalabad city 124, 242
Johns Hopkins' School of Advanced Inter-
      national Studies, 56
Johnson, Thomas, 36, 120, 246
Joint Capabilities Technology Demonstra-
      tion (JCTD), 41
  Program of the Year Award, 42
Joint Chiefs of Staff
  J3, 28
Joint Improvised Explosive Device Defeat
      Organization (JIEDDO), 30-32,
      34-35, 41, 83, 86
  briefing on CPE, 31
Joint Readiness Training Center (JRTC), 35,
      139
Joint Urgent Operational Needs Statement,
      38, 41, 176
  10th Mountain Division submission of,
      32;
  2007 CENTCOM submission of, 38;
  Combined Joint Task Force 82 submis-
      sion of, 38
Joseph, Paul, 20, 70, 144-145
Kabul city, 14, 71, 83, 118
Kandahar province, 19, 56, 64, 84, 124, 179, ✗
      186, 242
Kansas State University, 44
Kapisa province, 69, 130, 195,
Khost province, 18, 36, 38, 42, 81, 120, 242
Kimmons, John F., 32,
Kipp, Jacob, 29, 31
Krepinevich, Andrew, 46
Kunar province, 124,
Laurence, Janice, 44, 48,
leadership, team
  coaching, 151-155, 194

command styles, 154-155
leaders with military experience, 151,
    153, 235
styles, 151-155, 157, 194
learning, team
  exploitation learning, 136, 243
  experimentation learning, 136, 243
  exploration learning, 136, 140-141, 243
  HTS training, 136-141
  performance metrics, 139
  see also HTS Core Curriculum; HTS
      management; HTT performance
Lennox, Robert, 75
Logar province, 124
Loyd, Paula, 56-57, 119
MAP-HT, 34, 41-43, 65, 114-116, 233-234
Marion, Francis, 9
Marlowe, Ann, 40, 43
McChrystal, Stanley, 64-66, 71, 78, 82, 121,
    207
McFarland, Maxie, 31-32, 43, 58, 69-70, 73-
    75, 77, 79, 171
  approval of job descriptions by, 70;
  asks for Fondacaro's resignation, 73;
  BAE contracting and, 50, 70
McFate, Montgomery, 36, 39, 45-48, 50, 57,
    71-74, 80, 119, 203, 221-222, 232,
    242
  combating IEDs through understand-
      ing the human terrain, 27-30;
  conference on "Adversary Cultural
      Knowledge and National Secu-
      rity", 27;
  cultural preparation of the environment
      project, 28-30;
  first meeting with Jackson and Fon-
      dacaro, 27;
  GTRI and, 50;
  Outreach, 57
McHugh, John, 75
McLeary, Rob, 227
McLees, Tim, 67
Meigs, Montgomery, 30-32
  assisting HTS, 32;
  2005 Fondacaro and Jackson briefing
      to, 30
Military culture, xiii-xiv, 36, 68, 121-122,
    135, 138, 154, 190, 213, 217
  course on, 49, 222-223;
  Fondacaro's knowledge of, 47;

HTTs alien to, 68, 121, 190, 217;
  McChrystal on conventional warfare in,
    66;
  on need to change, 20;
  see also Special Forces
Military Decision-Making Process, 30, 193,
    226
  social science informing, 128
military information support operations,
    218-219
Military Officer Magazine, 57
Military Review, 31, 63, 208
Mine-resistant, ambush-protected vehicles
    (MRAP), 217
  HTT casualties/injuries in, 56
Miskito Indians, 10
Mission Essential Task Lists, 64, 225, 227,
Mitchell, Scott, 186, 208-209
MITRE Corporation, 28
Morris, Mike, 33
Morrissey, Patti, 83
Mosher, Scott, 72,
Multinational Command-Iraq, 27
Myers-Briggs Personality Profile, 53, 144
Nangarhar province, 124
National Defense Authorization Act for
    FY2009, 45, 61
National Defense Authorization Act for
    FY2010, 66
National Defense Intelligence College, 57
National Geospatial-Intelligence Agency, 26
Human Geography Teams, 83
National Review, 40
National Training Center, 139
Native American scouts, 10
Native Americans, 8-10, 142
NATO, 1, 37, 64, 116
  HTTs embedded with, 64, 68, 69, 116, 122,
    246
NATO Training Mission Afghanistan, 79
Nature, 58, 80
Naval Postgraduate School, 57
Nawa district, 182
Newport News, 14, 32, 39, 72, 74, 118, 241
Newsweek, 50, 55
Nicaragua, 10
Nongovernmental organizations (NGOs),
    183
Northern Command, 81,
Odierno, Ray, 3, 187, 216

Office for Operational Cultural Knowledge,
    29
Office of Naval Research, 27-28
Office of the Deputy Undersecretary of the
    Army, 57
Operational Mentoring and Liaison Teams
    (OMLT), 148
open source, 33, 54, 78, 111, 177
Operation Iraqi Freedom, 26, 119,
Operation Khyber, 40
Operation Maiwand, 37, 39-40
Operational Detachment Alpha (ODA), 124
organization
    adaptation, xiv-xv, 217
    JIEDDO, 30-35, 41
    Learning, 41, 108-109, 136-141
    Performance, 238-244
    Relationships, 238-244
    team-based, 108-109
    variables of, 108-109
Overwatch, 42
Pacific Command, 55, 57
Pashto, 36, 139,
Pashtun Sexuality, report on, 51, 59
Peters, Ralph, 26
Peterson, Scott, 39
Petraeus, David, 1-2, 6, 35, 44-45, 64, 78, 82,
    121, 187
Philippines
    nationalist insurgency, 10
Polish units, 64
polling, 16, 20, 64, 185
Prinslow, Karl, 26, 31
problem personalities, 144
Provincial Reconstruction Teams, 16, 20, 37,
    79, 182,
public opinion, 16
purpose, team
    founding, 110-113
    strategic concept, 110-113
    strategic consensus110-113
    Quantum Research, 27
Rangers, 27
Rangers, Robert's, 9
    resource constraints, 116
    HTT dependence on brigades, 115
Resumix, 70
Reuss, Bob, 79
rewards, team
    attractive motivations, 147-149

active incentives, 147-149
affective impetus, 147-149
HTS financial pressure, 149
HTT serving with Special Forces, 148
salary reductions, 149
Rohde, David, 39
Rotkoff, Steve, 58, 71-72, 74,
Rules of Ranging, 9
Sadr City, 56, 187,
Salam, Abdul, 56
Salaries, 41, 60-61, 147-150, 156,
reductions in, 149-,150
Scales, Robert H., 26, 41
School of Advanced Military Studies, 227
Schweitzer, Martin
brigade command, 170;
AF1 support to, 35-37, 242;
testimony endorsing HTTs, 2, 42, 45,
63
Scott, David, 33,
Sensor Technologies Inc, 53
Sharifsoltani, Roya, 36
Shuras, 19, 180,
SKOPE, 26
Small Wars Manual: U.S. Marine Corps,
1940, 7, 200
Smith, Don, 29-31, 33
Mitchell's training with, 186
social network analysis, 12, 28, 42,
social science
community, 29, 119
controversial use of, xiv-xv
personnel, 16, 38, 120, 132, 138, 142,
151, 153, 194
research, 14, 110-111, 113, 176
sociocultural knowledge as a sub-category of, 7-8, 30
war and, 42, 56, 111, 128
Social Science Research and Analysis (SSRA)
unit, 16, 53, 71
Society of Applied Anthropology, 55
sociocultural knowledge
American West use of, 8-9
FM 3-24 on, 2, 6
ASCOPE-PMSEII, 177
Civil War use of, 9
collectors of, xiv
conference on "Adversary Cultural
Knowledge and National Security", 27
countering IEDs and, 27-29, 35

defense intelligence community and, 83
Defense Science Board on, 8
deficiency in Iraq of, 12, 26, 119
deficiency in post-Cold War operations
of, 11-12
deficiency in the Vietnam War of, 11
defining, 7-8, 111
DIA Sociocultural Dynamics working
group, 83
HTS justification by, 14, 111, 213
HTTs providing, 19, 78, 113, 206, 212
importance of, 3, 6, 20, 25, 203, 208-
209
intelligence operations use of, 26, 112
Laurence belief in, 44
McFarland on need for, 31
Flynn on, xi-xii, 71, 214
official interest in, 30, 44
organic military capabilities, 63
Scales's testimony on, 26
U.S. military ignorance of, 12-13, 26,
195, 202, 213
U.S. military and, xiv-xv, 2, 4, 8, 206-
207, 212
see also CPE, cultural intelligence, Fix-
ing Intelligence
Sociocultural Research and Advisory Teams
(SCRATs), 83
Somalia, 11
Soviet Union, 11, 26
Spanish units, 64
Special Forces/ Green Beret, 134, 145, 204,
218
"connection", 135
irregular warfare and, 11, 63
members of HTTs who were, 50, 117,
149, 152
Special Operations Forces (SOF), 27, 64,
68-69, 79, 81, 124, 126, 131, 141, 207,
217-219
Special Operations Summit, 81
St. Benoit, Tracy, 36, 39, 56, 120
Stability Operations Information Centers,
15, 183
Stanton, John, 59
Stars and Stripes, 39
Strategic Multi-Layer Assessment Group, 30
Stuttgart, Germany, 55, 83
structure, team
boundary spanning, 123-127

design, 123-127
mental models, 123-127
Subject Matter Experts Network (SMEnet), 120
Subversion And Espionage Directed Against the U.S. Army (SAEDA), 222
support, team
  anthropology and the military, 119
  BAE recruitment, 120
  organizational relationships, 118-122
  reachback centers, 120
supportive contexts, 118-122
  team-based organizations, 118-122
Sun Tzu, 6
survey research, 53-54
Suveges, Nicole, 56, 119
Taliban, 18, 37, 66
  attacks on girls schools by, 58
  attacks on U.S. forces by, 206
Task Force Lafayette, 69
Team Lioness, 82
Tennessee, 9, 135
Terminal and Enabling Learning Objectives, 231
"The Future" Training Directorate Executive Overview, 224
The Human Terrain System: A CORDS for the 21st Century, 31
The Human Terrain Team Trip Report: "A Team of Teams", 171
The Lincoln Group, 27, 29
The New York Times, 39,
The Role of Social and Behavioral Sciences in National Security, 42
Theater Coordination Element (TCE), 14, 16, 23n42, 68, 71, 79, 227,
Theater Support Office (TSO), 14, 27, 31
TIGR, 222,
TRADOC's Office of Internal Review and Audit Compliance, 72, 75,
Training and Doctrine Command (TRA-DOC), 13, 31, 32, 34, 39, 44, 49, 50, 58, 61, 65, 69-70, 72-77, 79-80, 83, 86, 90n74, 98n283, 101n343, 102n375, 120, 159n39, 173-74, 199n93, 203, 206, 209n5, 216,
  BAE contract with; 48, 50, 79, 102n376,
  Futures Center; 27
  informal investigation of HTS (AR-15-6 investigation); 71, 101n363, 136,
    174, 199n93,
  intelligence section; 31, 34, 65, 79, 111,
  Dempsey command of; 69-70, 218
  Office of Internal Review and Audit Compliance investigation; 72, 74, 77, 102n366, 171, 174, 209n4,
TRADOC Intelligence Support Activity (TRISA); 14,
  see also JIEDDO
U.S. Army, xiv-xv, 10ff, 1, 34, 81, 216-18, 220n8, 222, 227,
  after-action reviews; 218
  counterinsurgency and; 1, 11, 20, 32, 208-209, 213, 215n5,
  irregular warfare and; 207, 209, 214, 216-17
  base budget; 76
  Chief of Staff; 3, 216
  computerized recruiting system; 70
  culture; 20, 49, 101n346, 222
  FY11 Defense Authorization Bill; 68
  historical experience with sociocultural knowledge; 8ff
  American West; 10
  investigation of Stanton allegations; 59
  leadership treatment of HTS; 66, 75-76,
  operations and maintenance funding;
  Secretary of the Army; 75, 103n392
  sexual harassment; 143-44, 224
  study on "fratricide-murders"; 208
  transition of HTT members from contractor to civilian, 60-61, 70-73, 79, 149,
  see also DOTMLPF; Philippines; U.S. Army/Marine Corps Counterinsurgency Field Manual; Vietnam
U.S. Army Special Operations Command (USASOC), 218, 220n6,
U.S. Army Command and General Staff College, 66,
U.S. Army/Marine Corps Counterinsurgency Field Manual (FM/FMFM 3-24), 12-13, 24n55,
  sociocultural knowledge in, 7, 26,
U.S. Army Research, Development and Engineering Command, 65
U.S. Forces, Korea, 55
U.S. military/forces
  American West; 10
  counterinsurgency; xiv, 1

culture; see Military Culture
HTT support to;
Iraq and Afghanistan drawdown; 85
irregular warfare during the Cold War;
    11
Operation Maiwand; 37, 39-40
organic organizations; 63, 206
post-Cold War operations; 11ff
social science and; xv, 7, 14, 16, 26, 29-
    30, 38, 42, 45, 49, 56, 110-11,
    119, 138, 142, 151, 162n209,
    165n236, 168n299, 176-77, 194,
    203, 222, 240,
sociocultural knowledge and, 2-4, 7ff,
    11-12, 26-27, 195, 203, 212, 214,
    216-17
U.S. Special Operations Command (SO-
    COM), ix, 26, 30, 57, 81-82, 106n451,
    218
U.S. Strategic Command, 26
UK Defense College, 57
United States
    allies; 64, 68, 84, 104n410, 116, 122, 246
    government; 119, 191, 203,
United States Marine Corps, 10, 35, 38, 63-
    64, 68, 151-2, 182,
    female engagement teams; 82
    HTS support of; 34, 38, 63, 68, 99n307
    Intelligence Activity, 29
    officers in HTTs; 117, 151-52,
    opinions on HTS; 63, 68, 90n85,
        99n306,
    Small Wars Manual; 7, 200, 207,
    sociocultural knowledge, 7, 10, 29, 63,
        82, 182
    Warfighting Lab, 57
        see also Small Wars Manual: U.S.

Marine Corps, 1940; U.S. Army/
    Marine Corps Counterinsurgency
    Field Manual
United States Military Academy at West
    Point, 20, 27, 36, 57, 70, 171-74
    see also Human Terrain Team Trip
        Report: A "Team of Teams"
University of California Berkeley, 57
University of Nebraska at Omaha, 139, 222,
University of Tennessee, 135,
USA Today, 57
Variables, performance, 107ff
    (see individual variables; e.g. composi-
        tion, culture, decision making,
        etc.)
Vietnam
    sociocultural knowledge, 11
    Special Forces in, 11, 151
Village Stability Program, 18, 81
Votel, Joseph
    funding CPE, 27-28
    hosting of HTT by 82nd Airborne, 34-
        35
    replacement by Meigs at JIEDDO, 30
Wardak province, 124
war on terror, 26
Warren, Mike, 71
    creation of Program Manager Forward
        position, 60
    Flynn and, 71
    Resignation, 74
Washington Post, 57
Washington, D.C, 27, 30
Wayne State University, 57
White Situational Awareness Teams, 84
World Basic Information Library, 33
Zormat district, 37

ABOUT THE AUTHORS

Dr. Christopher J. Lamb is a Distinguished Research Fellow in the Center for Strategic Research, INSS, at the National Defense University. He conducts research on national security, strategy, policy, and organizational reform, and on defense strategy, requirements, plans and programs. In 2008, Dr. Lamb led the Project for National Security Reform study of the national security system, which resulted in the 2008 report, *Forging a New Shield.* Prior to joining INSS in 2004, he served as the Deputy Assistant Secretary of Defense for Resources and Plans with oversight of war plans, requirements, and resource allocation matters for the Under Secretary of Defense (Policy). Previously he served as Deputy Director for Military Development on the State Department's Interagency Task Force for Military Stabilization in the Balkans; Director of Policy Planning in the Office of the Assistant Secretary of Defense for Special Operations and Low-Intensity Conflict; and from 1985 to 1992, as a Foreign Service Officer in Haiti and Ivory Coast. He received his doctorate in International Relations from Georgetown University in 1986. Dr. Lamb has received the Chairman of the Joint Chiefs Joint Distinguished Civilian Service Award, the Presidential Rank Award for Meritorious Senior Executive Service, and other awards from the Department of State and Department of Defense.

Dr. James Douglas Orton teaches Strategic Leadership at National Defense University. He is an expert on loosely coupled systems, organizational sensemaking processes, high reliability organizations, and national security reform. His dissertation at the University of Michigan was an interdisciplinary study of the 1976 reorganization of the U.S. intelligence community. Dr. Orton has taught graduate courses and conducted high-end organizational research at Boston College, Hautes Etudes Commerciales

Paris, MIT Sloan School of Management, University of Nevada Las Vegas, University of California-Irvine, Michigan Technological University, and The George Washington University. From 2007-2009, Dr. Orton was the Senior Organization and Management Theorist for the Project on National Security Reform. Since 2009, Dr. Orton has been a full-time member of the organizational performance team at the Center for Strategic Research at the Institute for National Strategic Studies, with a focus on using High Reliability Organizing theories to improve the efficiency, effectiveness, and reliability of the U.S. national security system.

Mr. Michael Davies is the Contributing Editor for the Center for Technology and National Security Policy, INSS, at the National Defense University. During this project he was a Research Fellow in the Center for Strategic Research, INSS, at the National Defense University. Mr. Davies recently worked as a Research Assistant in the Center for Strategic Research on issues relating to US and Chinese naval and grand strategy, and Russian strategic theory. He has previously worked for Media Monitors Australia, and The International Institute for Strategic Studies on the *Armed Conflict Database*, analyzing conflicts in Central Asia and the Caucasus. Mr. Davies received a Master of Strategic Affairs from the Strategic and Defence Studies Centre and a Bachelor of Arts in International Relations and Political Science at the Australian National University.

Mr. Theodore Pikulsky is a Research Fellow in the Center for Strategic Research, INSS, at the National Defense University. His past research has included the Middle East, development economics, and new media. Mr. Pikulsky received a Master of Arts in History from Washington College and a Bachelor of Arts in Economics and International Relations from Boston University.

Made in the USA
San Bernardino, CA
07 January 2016